R.E.M.

PERFECT CIRCLE – THE STORY OF
R.E.M.

tony fletcher

OMNIBUS PRESS

LONDON / NEW YORK / PARIS / SYDNEY / COPENHAGEN / BERLIN / MADRID / TOKYO

Exclusive Distributors:
Music Sales Limited,
14/15 Berners Street,
London, W1T 3LJ.

Music Sales Corporation
180 Madison Avenue, 24th Floor,
New York,
NY 10016,
USA.

Macmillan Distribution Services
56 Parkwest Drive,
Derrimut, Vic 3030,
Australia.

Every effort has been made to trace the copyright holders of the photographs
in this book but one or two were unreachable. We would be grateful if the
photographers concerned would contact us.

Typeset by Galleon Typesetting, Ipswich, Suffolk.
Printed in the EU.

A catalogue record for this book is available from the British Library.

Visit Omnibus Press on the web at **www.omnibuspress.com**

Contents

Acknowledgements

In the earlier editions of this book, quotes were taken or paraphrased from interviews conducted by the following writers in the bracketed publications: Bill Black (*Sounds* 4/84), Laurent Chalumeau (*Rapido* 11/88), Matt Damsker (*San Diego Union* 6/83), Anthony DeCurtis (*Record* 7/85, *Rolling Stone* 8/87, 4/89), Adrian Deevoy (*Q*, 12/88), Harold De Muir (*East Coast Rocker* 10/87, *NME* 11/88), Bill Flanagan (*Musician* 1/88), Bill Forman (*Bam* 10/87), David Fricke (*Musician* 7/84, *Rolling Stone* 3/92), Don Gilliand (*Ft Lauderdale Rag* 5/83), Robert Gordon (*Creem* 4/91), Marty Graham (*Milwaukee Express* 6/83), Robert Hilburn (*Los Angeles Times* 6/85), Bill Holdship (*Creem* 9/85), Allan Jones (*Melody Maker* 6/85), Sean O'Hagan (*NME* 12/88), Jim MacNie (*Musician* 4/91), Ian McCann (*Vox* 2/92), Hugh Morley (*Jamming* 1/85), John Morthland (*Xtra* 6/85), Jeff Nesin (*Creem* 9/84), John Platt (*Bucketful Of Brains* #11, 84), Steve Pond (*Rolling Stone* 12/87), Edwin Pouncey (*Sounds* 10/88), John Reynolds (*The Aquarian Weekly* 11/92), Karen Sclossberg (*Creem* 12/87), Mat Smith (*Melody Maker* 9/87), Jim Sullivan (*Record* 7/83), Jeff Tamarkin (*Creem* 9/84), Rob Tannenbaum (*Centrum Guide* 85), Ed Ward (*Austin American-Statesman* 6/83) and Jon Young (*Trouser Press* 8/83).

In this latest edition, from Chapter 16 onwards, I have tried to state any external sources on their first point of reference. Where no source is listed, that should usually indicate that I conducted the interview myself. My grateful thanks to everyone who agreed to be interviewed for any and every edition of this book.

To R.E.M, my initial thank-you list remains: to Bill, Mike, Michael and Peter for the music; Jefferson and Bert for being easy to deal with; Liz Hammond, Debbie Kilpatrick and Brooke Johnson for efficiency; to everyone I briefly encountered on tour who helped. For the year 2002 overhaul, I'd like to add my thanks to Kevin O'Brien, Brandy Campbell, Anthony DeCurtis, Julie Panebianco, Ethan Kaplan, Brendan Yates and to the journalists and record company employees who were very helpful in supplying background material. These names only touch on those who've offered support in one way or another.

For R.E.M. archive material in the original editions, I would like to maintain my thanks to hardened collectors Fred Mills, 'Mad' Louie, Patti Kleinke, Andy Johnson, Bryan Cook, Annie Fort at I.R.S., and everyone else who supplied me with tapes or cuttings. My stay in Athens all those years ago would not have been such a pleasure without the wonderful hospitality of Carolyn Overton, Robin Taylor and Mary Gambrell; wherever you are these days, girls, if it's half as much fun as it was in Athens, you're doing fine. Equally entertaining to be around in Athens – though not quite as easy on the eyes – were Mark Baldovski, Terry and Trent Allen. Drew Worsham, Mark Cline and Mike Richmond, along with many, many others I hoped not to fall out of touch with but have done anyway. Thanks also to Ira Robbins, Scott Schinder, Susan Myers and Melissa Manuel of The Dixie Voice, Karen Moss and Steve Fallon. I have no idea where in the world Adria might be now, but the original edition wouldn't have come about without her backing. (I know I wasn't easy for you.) Posie's been my rock ever since; if anyone deserved to attend that MTV *Unplugged* show in '91 while I waited in a hotel room across town for an unrelated interviewee not to show, it was you. Campbell, my best buddy, I hope you'll be glad in future years that we took you to see R.E.M. when you were but three years old. Believe me, it was a good show. But then they usually are.

Preface

The original edition of this book, entitled *Remarks*, was researched and written during the first six months of 1989, at a time when R.E.M. were finally breaking out of cult status and into the public domain of hit singles, platinum albums and sports arenas. At least that was the case in the USA, where *Remarks* was published in 1990. In the UK, where it came out in the autumn of 1989, R.E.M. had yet to score even a top 50 single. They were critics' darlings for sure, and their imprint was indelibly stamped on the Eighties as one of the decade's most influential groups, but they were hardly a household name.

To attract R.E.M.'s passionate but limited following, *Remarks* was kept short. It was then artfully laid out by Liz Nicholson with nearly a hundred photographs, many of them rare and/or unseen. The up side to this was a book both visually attractive and materially inexpensive, an accessible and accurate introduction to a group that had long been shrouded in mystery. The down side was that some people looked at its photo-intensive layout and took it to be frivolous and/or lightweight, as if it had been assembled from press cuttings rather than solid research.

Hardly. I had been a dedicated fan of R.E.M. from the moment I first heard *Murmur*, in 1983. I had witnessed all three of the band's début performances in the UK during November 1983. I interviewed the group on several occasions when they visited the UK; I saw the band at least once on every one of their five subsequent trips to Britain up to and including 1987. Somewhere between the release of *Document*, the band's fifth album, and *Green*, their sixth (and first for a major label), I then moved to the band's home country, the United States, which put me in an additionally good position when, shortly after the release of *Green*, the subject of an R.E.M. biography came up in conversation with Andrew King

1

and Chris Charlesworth at Omnibus Press, for whom I had written the official biography of Echo & The Bunnymen. The group was far from the kind of household name that might normally command such a work, but then Omnibus Press was far from a mainstream publisher; we all operated instead on the belief that if, as fans of the band, *we* would like to read a book about them, so too would others.

In researching *Remarks*, I spent a full week in the group's home town of Athens, Georgia, interviewing the group's friends and acquaintances, visiting first hand the locations from which they and their sound had emerged, and experiencing for myself the sometimes intangible attributes that make the town so unique. I travelled to Winston-Salem to interview Mitch Easter, to Charlotte to meet Don Dixon, and to Cincinnatti to present my case to the members of R.E.M., then on a major arena tour.

The group took the perfectly logical view that they were still a work-in-progress and therefore not yet ready to be ossified in print. At the same time, they understood that biographies were an inevitable by-product of the fame game, and so Peter Buck, their resident rock 'n' roll historian, volunteered to be interviewed on behalf of the entire group. I rejoined R.E.M. in Florida for a couple of days, interviewing Peter on the tour bus between shows. The office then helped me track down other interviewees, and confirmed my credentials to those I contacted myself. Personal lives and family backgrounds were considered firmly off limits, a rule that I respected. None of this was mentioned in the introductions to the original editions of *Remarks*: in typical R.E.M. fashion, the band's co-operation came with the strict caveat that under no circumstances could I advertise that they'd given it.

Remarks was received well by fans and band alike. In fact, R.E.M. liked it enough that when I.R.S. Records insisted on releasing a European *Best Of* in the autumn of 1991, the band asked that the sleeve notes be taken from *Remarks*; I had a call direct from management tipping me off to the request. Again, I was informed that their involvement with the project would not be announced, and the public generally assumed the band was not involved with the album.

The Best Of R.E.M. was released to cash in on the group's

sudden, enormous success in Europe after years on the fringes, for R.E.M.'s seventh album, *Out Of Time*, released in the spring of 1991, had finally connected the group to the masses. Propelled by the global hit 'Losing My Religion', *Out Of Time* spent an unprecedented two years on the UK album charts, on its way to notching up 12,000,000 worldwide sales, all without the band playing a single advertised concert.

Not surprisingly, other R.E.M. books began appearing, some much better than others. *Remarks* continued to sell well, but was in danger of becoming dated, and looking a little flimsy in comparison to rightfully weightier tomes. Omnibus Press suggested an update, and I agreed. I had interviewed the band in Athens in early 1991 on the eve of the release of *Out Of Time*, for the Rapido TV show, and aside from conducting other interviews, I sat down again with Peter Buck in New York, in the summer of 1992, as R.E.M. prepared to release *Automatic For The People*. With typical nonchalance for his rock star status, Buck suggested we meet at a long-standing, intensely popular Mexican restaurant in the heart of Manhattan's hipster Lower East Side; other than an encounter with an ex-, the interview scenario was notable only for the fact that we were allowed to conduct it entirely uninterrupted.

The revamped *Remarks* was published in 1993, and two years later, Omnibus suggested an additional chapter and a new front cover. I should have declined, for there was not much to add other than the incredible global success of *Automatic For The People* (achieved, again, without a single proper concert), but it seemed important that with so many other R.E.M. books now on the shelves, *Remarks* should remain up to date.

Shortly thereafter, I wrote, and Omnibus Press published in the UK, a massive biography on Keith Moon, which topped out at almost 600 pages. Its success proved a point I had always believed: that rock books need not be inexpensive, slight and photo-intensive (á la the original edition of *Remarks*) to succeed. So when Chris Charlesworth – still, I'm glad to say, at the Omnibus helm – suggested in the summer of 2001 that with four more globally successful albums under their belt, and with *Remarks* otherwise out of print, there might be reason to approach the subject again, he offered to raise the stakes. While the revamped *Remarks* would not be a hardback, it would be the soft-cover equivalent. Photos would be limited to two eight-page sections; my word count would be unrestricted.

I had been reticent to revisit the subject once more, but my accepted request to edit and expand the original manuscript clinched the deal. Through the years, I had held on to all my source materials – tapes, transcripts, demos, press cuttings and even early drafts – and could see that I had left many sub-topics and tangential points out first time around for the sake of brevity. Yet I could also tell that *Remarks* had become a reference for other R.E.M. books over the years, which had then added their own observations and theories to the group's legacy; I now felt a need to counter or complement some of these points in turn. The onset of the Internet also allowed me to be more precise with dates and other details, without endless visits to the vaults of the Performing Arts Library in Manhattan's Lincoln Centre. (Although, it should be noted, there is no real substitute for reading the original music papers with their cultural reference points spread throughout the pages.)

Once again, R.E.M. proved amenable to my approaches. I spent several days catching up with Peter Buck in Seattle in December 2001, including a lengthy interview on his 45th birthday. (Michael Stipe and Mike Mills have never sat down to be interviewed for the express purpose of a biography; Bill Berry, of course, is no longer part of the band.) The group's newer, semi-permanent members Scott McCaughey, Joey Waronker and Ken Stringfellow all granted interviews; likewise their producer Pat McCarthy. This time around, co-operation was *not* given on the understanding that it be kept quiet; with the publication of *Remarks Remade* in 2002, I could finally announce the band's long-term involvement with the project.

Since the publication of what I like to term that 'Director's Cut' of the book, the degree of professional respect that I hold towards R.E.M. appears to have been returned a couple of times. In 2007, I was recommended by the group's long-standing manager Bertis Downs to give the keynote speech at a symposium entitled 'R.E.M. In Perspective', held in the group's hometown of Athens; the following year, I was asked by the band to write the sleeve-notes for the 25th Anniversary Deluxe Edition re-issue of

Reckoning. In each case, I was flattered by the offer, and honoured to accept.

In the wake of the group's amicable break-up in 2011 Chris Charlesworth suggested I bring the book up to date, completing what we would now rename, after an early R.E.M. song, *Perfect Circle*. I could not accept immediately: I was in the midst of writing a major biography of the Smiths, who exhibited many musical and cultural similarities to R.E.M., and whose success could well have reached R.E.M.-like proportions too, had they only been able to stay together. While considering such comparisons, I found myself pulled again towards not just the music, but the overall story and aesthetic of R.E.M., and agreed with Charlesworth that it would be somewhat silly to leave their story unfinished. And so, after finishing the Smiths book, I took to writing up the last 10 years of R.E.M.'s 32-year career. I initially thought that with 'only' three studio albums during that time, it would be a relatively short process; by the time I factored in world tours, major compilations, intra-band disharmony and resolution, and then the fascinatingly friendly break-up, I had written almost enough to fill a 1980s era rock biography of its own. While Peter Buck declined an additional interview on the premise that it was still too soon after the band's demise for his comfort (please see this book's Endgame for elaboration), the still functioning R.E.M. organ(isation) continued to offer its support for the project, and I am grateful to Scott McCaughey and Garrett 'Jacknife' Lee for the additional interviews. With Lee's involvement, I am pleased to say that I have been able to talk to the producer of, and about, every single one of R.E.M.'s fifteen studio albums.

Perfect Circle, as we are now calling it, is somewhat unique among rock biographies in that it has been written, and then updated and expanded, over the course of four different decades. My writing has hopefully improved over these years, but in contrast to the expanded ~~Remarks~~ Remade of 2002, I have not rewritten or added to earlier material, and in this final update have tried to stay consistent to the original writing style and approach.

I believe this will be the final update of *Remarks, ~~Remarks~~ Remade*, or *Perfect Circle* – at least in as much as I can not possibly imagine R.E.M. reneging on their word and reforming (for

5

anything more than an all-star charity event). In many ways, it is sad to say a final farewell to a project that has been such a constant within my life, but as with the band itself, it's time to leave the party. It was an absolute blast, and I'm thrilled that I got to attend – if only to have stood in the corner and observed.

Introduction

ATHENS, GEORGIA, APRIL 5, 1980

All week long, the word had been passed around town. Party this Saturday. Three live bands. Free beer. Now, with hundreds of people converging upon the old Episcopal Church on Oconee Street just around the corner from the University of Georgia, the Athens grapevine was again proving unfailingly effective.

That the party location had been intended as a house of worship was verified by the steeple rising forty feet high and towering above rooftops further up the hill. But no religious service had been held here in decades, and along the way the dilapidated building had instead been converted into living quarters bizarre even by student standards.

In fact, once through the front doors, it was difficult to determine that this had ever been a church. A large open-plan living room and kitchen gave way to an insalubrious bathroom on one side and a bedroom on the other, in between which a staircase led up to four more rooms, each just big enough to throw down a mattress, some clothes, and a few books.

However, by crawling through the closet at the back of the downstairs bedroom, one came across the entire, undeveloped rear half of what undoubtedly *was* once a church. A floor space some thirty feet wide and twenty feet deep lay in front of a low-rise altar from which, by facing back inward, the thin plasterboard walls erected to create the two-tiered living quarters were clearly visible. On this April night, the altar was festooned with guitars, amplifiers and drums, ready to baptise the three latest members of Athens' already extensive musical family.

To prevent theft of their few possessions, the tenants, two of whom would be performing on stage, had locked the front doors to the church this Saturday evening. Party-goers duly walked around the back of the church and through the rear entrance once

7

used by choirboys and preachers, or simply climbed through the holes in the wall where once had stood majestic church windows. Some then chose to crawl through the closet and join selected revellers inside the apartment; others stayed outside throughout.

The first group to perform at the party was Turtle Bay, followed by the Side Effects, a trio of popular art students whose infectious, angular dance rhythms were an instant hit. By the time the final band appeared, the party was reaching a drunken climax, the police had already made a threatening appearance, and the quality of music was of only marginal importance.

This last group was so new it had not even decided on a name, and few in the audience had any real idea what to expect. But the party-goers all knew at least one of the individual members. The guitarist, Peter Buck, was a music fanatic who worked behind the counter at the town's major record store, Wuxtry. The singer, Michael Stipe, was a soft-spoken art student whose retiring nature made it all the more surprising that he should now be throwing himself about the stage with such abandon. Both Stipe and Buck lived there at the church. The rhythm section, boyish bassist Mike Mills and hirsute drummer Bill Berry, were close friends from Macon, south Georgia, whose party spirits had quickly endeared them to the locals after their move up to the college town a year earlier.

As a unit, this new band was fast, furious and sloppy, compensating with pure energy for what they lacked in expertise. People danced, drank and sang along when they recognised a Sixties' pop classic like 'Stepping Stone'. Others frowned upon the proliferation of cover songs; in a community with such a strong reputation for art, innovation was a prerequisite for performing. Such doubts were but quietly mooted, however: after all, the band were the audience's friends and the show was a shitload of fun. The group was even called back for an encore, a dilemma for a new band that had run out of songs, and one quickly solved by calling friends on stage to sing along to easily played oldies. As rotting floorboards began to crack under the pressure, Michael Stipe ended the performance by crawling among the audience on his hands and knees.

Outside, the sun was already coming up. A new day was dawning in Athens, Georgia.

One

The City of Athens lies an hour and a half's drive east of the Georgia state capital Atlanta, its tree-lined avenues of sturdy antebellum homes and glorious neoclassical mansions bearing all the trademarks of a quintessentially quaint southern American town. A place where time might appear to stand still, with sultry summer afternoons spent lazing on the front porch, and the Baptist church forever the dominant political force.

This elegant impression is accurate, but only as the freeze frame of the picture postcard; start the camera rolling and a storyline of confrontation and flux unfolds. It is a saga involving some 50,000 permanent citizens, ranging from the inheritors of old money to the perpetually poor, along with a floating population of 20,000 students. For Athens is also a college town, home to the University of Georgia and the attendant behaviour that can be found wherever teenagers – especially those suddenly freed from the shackles of family life – congregate. Athens has always enjoyed a heady reputation for partying, but for years this was shielded behind a façade of austerity, as indicated by the outwardly pristine mile of fraternity and sorority houses on Milledge Avenue. Even during the supposedly 'swinging' mid-Sixties, the University forbade such trivial activities as smoking on campus or lounging on the grass.

When at last the wind of change blew through Athens, it did so with force. Some attribute it to the provocative and liberating climate of the era, others to the growing reputation of the University's Department of Art as the best in the southeast. Either way, towards the end of the Sixties a new breed of creative student began emerging on campus: the hippy.

Among the faculty members thankful for its arrival and positive input was Jim Herbert, a painter, art instructor and film maker living in Athens since 1962 who recalls a "clash of the rednecks and the hippies" with relish. "When the hippy thing did hit here, it was extremely strong and very poignant," he says. "Kids roaming around the streets with musical instruments, parties with nude people . . ."

The hippies and their lifestyle left an indelible imprint on Athens culture, and from the late Sixties onwards, the Department of Art's status ensured that each new school year brought with it freshmen eager to immerse themselves in a thriving artistic community. Their inability to conquer the inherent conservatism of the university structure became increasingly irrelevant as they created a community of their own.

Among the new art students arriving in 1975 was Curtis Crowe, who recalls finding "a real good art school party crowd. There was a certain camaraderie just because you were in the art school; you had an instant affiliation with these people."

These new friendships extended beyond the classroom into a party scene that brought the adventurous students and progressive instructors closer together. These were theatrical parties, afternoon lawn gatherings with unique costumes and bizarre behaviour, and some of the best were thrown by the art professors themselves. Yet despite such artistic activity, Athens offered no music scene for those who weren't into the southern boogie or laid-back jazz that dominated the local clubs in the mid-Seventies.

In New York, the story was different: a new musical movement was emerging from darkened Lower East Side clubs, one which dispelled the accepted notions of musical expertise as a prerequisite for performance. It was a disparate scene, ranging from the nihilistic thrash of The Ramones at one end to the staccato art pop of Talking Heads at the other, but it carried a unanimous ethos: anyone can do it.

This dictum would soon inspire a generation of bored teenagers in Britain to seize the initiative and launch an aggressive punk rock movement that would briefly prove itself a genuine threat to society before being tamed and successfully marketed under the catch-all name 'new wave', but when word of New York's musical stirring reached the Athens art crowd, they were attracted more by the beauty of its possibilities than the anger of its defiance.

Unsurprisingly, among the first to realise these opportunities were the town's most celebrated characters. Cindy Wilson, her brother Ricky and Keith Strickland had grown up in Athens; Kate Pierson and Fred Schneider had arrived later and never left. Together, they were renowned "party terrorists", gatecrashers in garish outfits fond of starting food fights or, in Kate's case, known to soak unsuspecting guests with a commandeered garden hose. "We were just free spirits," she recalls.

Now they were all looking for a way out of dead-end jobs. Over a drunken Chinese meal one night, they decided to form a band, naming it the B-52's after local slang for the girls' bouffant wigs. Combining their effervescent personal traits with the comic book vocals of Fred, Cindy and Kate, and an irrepressible dance beat, they hit on a sensational formula.

With "no place for us to play live except for friends' living rooms," as Fred Schneider recalls, they made their public début at a St Valentine's Day party in 1977. After four or five such events, Atlanta's premier punk band The Fans invited them along for the ride to New York, where they were playing in November '77. The 'B's' left with a tape and returned with a date, at the prestigious club Max's Kansas City on December 12. The night before leaving, they played a party hosted by Curtis Crowe's roommate.

"To me, it was culture shock," recalls Curtis. "It was a kind of frightening experience for a neophyte to go and see the B-52's, and it wasn't so much the band. The entire crowd was so dramatically different from your average run-of-the-mill crowd of people; the entire crowd was the show.

"The B-52's really touched the spark to the keg of dynamite. They created what is known as the Athens music scene."

Before 1977 was out, the B-52's played a party at Emory University's Student Center in Atlanta, and a crowd of Athens socialites made the journey with them. Their host that night was a gregarious young music fan by the name of Peter Buck.

★   ★   ★

Peter Buck's life had always revolved around music. Yet he had never seriously considered making it his profession. He didn't have the talent, and he couldn't find anyone with his tastes and opinions. It was that simple.

R.E.M.

Born in Los Angeles on December 6, 1956, Buck spent his formative years in the suburbs of San Francisco. His love affair with pop music began, as for so many, with a transistor radio and the thrill of listening under the pillow to magical sounds from faraway places: Britain's fab four The Beatles, Motown goddesses The Supremes, and television stars The Monkees.

San Francisco during the Sixties was an exciting place to live, glazy-eyed beatniks roaming streets that would later become the mecca of the hippy movement. And school was progressive, his class of eight-year-olds being treated one day to a performance by an identikit Sixties pop group called The Postmen who played the latest Beatles and Byrds hits. Peter didn't have to be told the titles of the songs: every last dime he could talk out of his parents was already going towards buying records.

When the Buck family moved to Indiana, the free concerts and street culture became a thing of the past, and by the time they finally settled in Roswell, Georgia, in 1970, his parents might have expected Peter to have shaken off his infatuation with pop music. But their now teenage son's tastes had only matured and hardened; he was reading the serious rock press and buying albums by The Kinks, The Move and The Stones. By rights, he should have then followed his peers into the hard rock that dominated the early Seventies, but his love of pop led him instead to gorge on the British glam rock of T. Rex, Slade and Sweet.

Roswell was hardly the obvious place to indulge such eclectic tastes. Though a mere eighteen miles from the centre of Atlanta, Peter recalls it as "a separate town, like living way out in the country." Urban sprawl has subsequently turned it into another Atlanta suburb, but back then, "It was all old Dairy Queens and guys in overalls with hay in the back of their battered pickup trucks, poking through town and spitting tobacco juice on the sidewalk." The opening of a McDonald's in Roswell was con-sidered a major cultural advancement; the young Buck couldn't wait to get out.

Two events during the artistically bleak mid-Seventies helped him define his future. The first was discovering an old Velvet Underground record in a garage sale. Their sound was so simple and direct, so haunting and so timeless that it taught Peter Buck to value understated repetition more than overblown polyphony.

The second was witnessing The New York Dolls in concert in the mid-Seventies. The Dolls were the bastard offspring of glam rock, a provocatively vile and aggressive group commercially shunned during their short tenure as major label artists. But their rawness convinced Buck that power need not require expertise.

The seeds of making music were planted in his mind. But although Peter Buck understood the rudiments of the guitar, he was deterred from studying it properly by his only brother Kenny who, two years younger, was a classically trained prodigy whose skills made Peter's playing attempts look embarrassing. A cheap guitar of his own that he took apart to paint was left in disrepair, and on the occasions Peter and friends did get together to jam, they never ventured beyond the twelve-bar blues.

On finishing high school in 1975, Peter enrolled at Emory University in Atlanta and decided to leave home as well. His father gave him two parting shots of advice: "Don't get married before you're thirty, no matter what happens; and don't get into showbiz, it'll only break your heart." The first warning his son abided by; the second would fall by the wayside, but only over a period of time. For while playing music was becoming an increasingly attractive proposition, and Peter purchased a decent guitar, finding suitable partners was a nigh impossible task.

"By and large, almost everyone you'd meet in a band in the Seventies wanted to be rich and famous like Rod Stewart, and already had that attitude," he recalls. "You'd just think, 'What a bunch of assholes.'" This attitude didn't endear him to fellow students. "I was kind of standoffish at college. I looked down my nose at everyone. All these people were into The Grateful Dead and Hot Tuna and Little Feat."

Peter's own musical tastes by now included the new underground rock from New York. The same corner of the same big city that gave birth to The Velvet Underground and New York Dolls was beginning to spew out a whole generation of left-field talent. The first visible example was female punk-poet Patti Smith, whose 1975 début *Horses* sounded like nothing else before it. When she came to Atlanta on her first tour, Buck attended every show. The experience only further convinced him that he was wasting his time at University. After less than one full year of classes, he dropped out.

Buck had harboured ambitions of being a music critic, but this too seemed distant and unobtainable. The easiest way to earn a living off music was to work in a record store, and so he found himself behind the counter at Doo Dahs in Atlanta. There he was able to keep in step with the changing musical climate. The Ramones and Blondie released their début albums in 1976, and Talking Heads and Television quickly followed suit with stunning singles. Buck absorbed them all. He also noted that British youth was responding with its own musical explosion. The names were as uncompromising as the music – The Sex Pistols, The Clash, The Damned – and here was he, thousands of miles away from the action.

Frustrated with Atlanta, he embarked on what he calls "that whole Jack Kerouac stuff", hitchhiking around America, sleeping rough when the need arose. He was washing dishes for a living in early 1977 in San Luis Obispo, California, staying with some "real big Grateful Dead fans", when he ordered The Sex Pistols' 'Anarchy In The UK' from a local import record store. "I took it home and played it, and totally horrified everybody. They thought Kiss was punk rock."

Returning to Georgia, he found the wheels of progress moving but gradually. "Atlanta was always slow," he recalls. "I think because it's so widespread people didn't hang out together and do things." Browsing through the new releases at Wuxtry Records one day – "You had to search this stuff out; in 1977, you'd buy any record that was even vaguely punk" – his poise and knowledge attracted the eye of the store's co-owner, Mark Methe, who offered Buck a job there and then. Peter accepted. From his view back behind the record counter, he considered himself one of maybe just thirty people in the entire city who understood punk. They were the same thirty people who made up the audience at shows by The Fans.

Also included among this select crowd was Danny Beard. Proprietor of another Atlanta record store called Wax 'n' Facts, he was a close friend of The Fans and a former resident of Athens. He had seen the B-52's play at Curtis Crowe's apartment there and, captivated, travelled with them on their first trip to New York. By the time they all arrived back in Georgia, Danny had decided to launch his own 'DB Records' with a B-52's single. He had also offered to promote a party where the B's could début in Atlanta, and Peter Buck, being a musical aficionado and to Danny's knowledge, still a student at Emory, seemed an ideal person to arrange it.

Buck and a student friend were happy to oblige, hiring the Student Center's impressive Coke Room (named for the soft drink's founder, a prominent Emory donor) for $25. Danny Beard sang the B-52's praises to every customer who passed through his shop, and come the night, in late December 1977, around 100 curious onlookers turned up to the hastily arranged free event.

It was a spectacular success: not only were the B-52's so much more original than the majority of Atlanta bands, but the crowd they brought with them were far more tuned in as well. So, when during that same Christmas week in 1977 Mark Methe asked Peter whether he wanted to work in their Athens store, Buck accepted immediately. He handed over his apartment lease to Mark, swapped his Fender Stratocaster guitar for his boss's custom-built Telecaster, and moved in with his brother Kenny – who was already attending University in Athens – on the Lexington Highway, way out on the edge of town. Peter Buck celebrated a new year in a new home.

He was back in Atlanta within days for the historic American début of The Sex Pistols, opening their American tour on January 5 in what was seen as a provocative attack on the heart of the reactionary deep south. The majority of the 600-strong audience at the Great Southeast Music Hall were either media hounds, curious onlookers or threatening rednecks – but Buck was among the genuinely excited fans who had reserved tickets in advance. When he got there, however, he found that in the chaos of the event, his tickets had been given to journalists flown down from New York.

Buck was livid. "I said, 'You mean these half-assed journalists got *my* tickets?' And I was with this guy who was just so furious – he was a big guy – he knocked the doorman down, kicked the door in, and stormed through. About four of us ran in while they were playing."

For the next ten minutes, Buck kept one eye on the stage and one eye on the bouncers pursuing him. "I was moving all the time. I was just trying to lose myself, but there was no chance, they knew who I was. I got to see about a song and a half before they dragged me out and punched me out on the curb. The guy I came with got to see the whole show. I got beaten up in the parking lot – not too badly, but they definitely kicked me around." He is not too disappointed now he looks back on it, pointing out that he enjoyed "pretty much the quintessential Sex Pistols experience."

In Atlanta, Peter Buck's music tastes had been considered eccentric; in Athens they were merely *au courant*. "Of course I worked in the hip record store," he notes. "So within two weeks I had all kinds of friends." Wuxtry had one shop close to the university in the heart of town, and one a ten-minute walk west on Baxter Street. Both were constantly full of students, artists, and other young people with plenty of leisure time to soak up the newest music. Many of these customers were toying with the idea of forming bands themselves, and Peter soon joined their ranks.

"The only thing I ever remember Pete doing," recalls his boss at Wuxtry in Athens, Dan Wall, "was sitting around playing guitar along with records." By Peter's own account, he could only play a beginner's 'open' chords, but Wall recalls him as being "fairly qualified by this point." The punk explosion allowed musical novices to get up on stage if they felt they had something to say, and talent was no longer the necessity it had been during Peter's teens; he thus found himself caught between acquiring the ability to improve and the thrill of no longer needing to.

This approach applied to his education too, temporarily resumed by taking night school classes in English, at which he excelled, and maths, at which he didn't. Essentially, Peter was just making the most of his new environment. He quickly garnered a reputation around town as a good friend and a bad enemy, with a girlfriend, Allison, who was his match in every department. Walking around with both a knife and a short temper persuaded most locals not to pursue an argument with him.

Towards the end of his first year in Athens, Peter began to recognise among the new visitors to Wuxtry a quietly spoken teenager with good taste and two attractive females on his arm. "I thought, 'God! This guy's got two great looking girlfriends. He must be pretty hip.'" The girls were sisters, Lynda and Cyndy; the boy was their brother, Michael Stipe.

★   ★   ★

He was born in the Atlanta suburb of Decatur, on January 4, 1960, but John Michael Stipe felt like anything except a native Georgian once his family returned to the area in 1978. His father's military career – which included a harrowing spell flying helicopters in Vietnam – had taken him through homes in Georgia, Alabama, Texas, Germany, Texas again, Illinois and finally back to Georgia. When he later recalled that he "didn't touch base a lot during childhood," he exercised a rare poor choice of words, for his formative years revolved around the bases of the United States Armed Forces.

Army brats, as they are known, come to expect upheaval so frequently that they often consider the process of forming friendships pointless; instead, they become self-contained and introspective. Michael Stipe would appear to be a typical example, a painfully shy child who preferred to observe rather than participate. Shunning outside companionship, he turned inward to the only constants in his life, his family, forming an especially tight bond with his sisters.

"I had an unbelievably happy childhood," Stipe has insisted, though the limited details he has allowed to escape over the years are quite dramatic: catching scarlet fever at the age of two, suffering from hypothermia on a school trip at the age of fourteen. Somewhere in between he claims to have been a hyperactive child who "would just go and go until I fell down, and where I fell, I slept."

But on moving to Collinsville, Illinois, just east of St Louis, in 1973, and entering high school there, Stipe faced a real identity crisis. "It was a very outgoing, flamboyant, loud school and I hated everything about it," he later recalled. "I was very, kind of, *afraid* of a lot of things."

To provide his own entertainment and expand his knowledge, he subscribed to the New York cultural bible, the *Village Voice*, in 1975. It was an opportune choice, for New York's downtown music scene was thriving, and the writers' excitement jumped off the page as they enthused about the new denizens of the underground.

Until now, music had hardly touched the fifteen-year-old's life: his parents' tastes revolved around the likes of Gershwin and Mancini, and his own record collection was all but nonexistent. But the articles in the *Voice* were so powerful that when Patti Smith's début album *Horses* was released in 1975, he bought it immediately. As he later recounted to *New Musical Express*, he was not disappointed.

"It *killed*. It was so completely liberating. I had these head-phones, my parents' crappy headphones and I sat up all night with a huge bowl of cherries listening to Patti Smith, eating those cherries and going 'Oh My God! . . . Holy Shit! . . . Fuck!' Then I was sick."

He was also converted. New York punk, he says, "immediately put into place everything everyone else in my school was listening to." He built a record collection of select substance, snapping up essential début albums by Television and English art-punks Wire as they were released at one end, while following up on supposed influences such as The Stooges and New York Dolls at the other. When he acquired The Velvet Underground's live album *1969* for $2 in 1977, he was as astounded by their beautiful minimalism as his future partner Peter Buck had been before him.

As punk developed from an art form into a commodity, the other teenagers at his high school became attracted to it. Michael's musical knowledge accorded him popularity and, aided by the inherent con-fidence of adolescence, he became far more forceful a character, "this real loud, extreme, extroverted personality", as he later described it. Being welcomed into the hip high school crowd, he also got to experiment with the various drugs that were doing the rounds of mid-Seventies mid-America – opium, hash, Quaaludes, and even by his own brief but unextrapolated admission, "brown MDMA with heroin." His new-found confidence and public accept-ance led him to front a short-lived punk band who performed on but three occasions before his parents announced the family's next move, to Watkinsville, ten miles south of Athens.

For Michael, this was a catastrophe. Not only was he finally enjoying life as a teenager in the metropolis of St Louis after years of self-doubt, but the family trips to his grandparents in Georgia – where his grandfather was a Methodist preacher – had convinced him that the state was 'full of hippies and southern boogie music'. To some extent he was right. But then Athens was not typical of Georgia.

Preconceptions being the powerful governing force they are, however, Michael Stipe withdrew back into his shell, becoming a 'troglodyte' – his own term – on moving to Athens in 1978. That, he says, was a "particularly long and intense period" of shyness that he only came out of around 1984 – ironically, the very period that he began erecting barricades around his persona, giving a public impression of further withdrawal.

Most of his first year in Athens he spent by himself. "I just sat around reading or listening to music. That year alone, I think I really matured about five years . . . It's a long time to go without talking to people, and it really put a lot of things into perspective for me. I became much more of a quiet person after that. Much less bombastic, which is good."

His artistic instinct stronger than ever, Michael enrolled at the Department of Art in January 1979. Opinions on his ability and potential vary. Jim Herbert, who taught him on a freshman course, has no recollections of Stipe the pupil whatsoever. Michael himself, meanwhile, modestly declares that, "I was good at going to school but I wasn't good at what I was doing. I was able to convince my teachers that what I was doing was worthwhile when I was not really doing anything."

At least one of those teachers, Scott Belville, a respected artist whom Michael was under for a beginner's painting course, strongly disagrees. "He was actually one of the better students I ever had," he recalls. "You just looked at him and said, 'This person is real talented.'" Belville noted and respected both his student's reserved temperament – "When he did have something to say, it carried a little more weight, because he was generally so quiet" – and his artistic talent.

"In a couple of paintings, something else came out that made you think, 'Wait a minute, this is much more mature work, much more interesting than you generally see in a beginning class.'" Belville even rescued two of Michael's discarded paintings from destruction, believing them to be of an exceptional quality. He describes them with adjectives that would frequently be used in reviews of his pupil's future lyrics: "real brooding . . . a presence to them of another place . . . like a dream . . . abstract . . ."

During the course, Scott Belville convinced Michael Stipe to attend a show at the local Botanical Gardens by the eccentric Georgian folk artist, the Reverend Howard Finster. The student was fascinated by the old man's primitive sacred art and struck up a lasting relationship. Stipe also enrolled in a photo design course, the art form he was both most suited for and worked hardest on.

In the meantime, he would regularly stop in at Wuxtry, enquiring of Peter Buck about the best new releases. Though Michael Stipe would never again ingest contemporary music to the extent he did between 1975 and 1977, there was still plenty to excite him, and Peter began putting aside those that he thought Michael would especially like.

Buck remembers his customer as being "diffident" if not "real shy". Musically, the pair were on common ground. Both had been heavily influenced by the New York punk scene in general, and by Patti Smith in particular; and both had experienced a new emotional peak on discovering The Velvet Underground. On a personal level, however, they differed greatly: Peter was an outgoing, worldly-wise character more than three years older than the sensitive Michael. Perhaps recognising in Stipe's naïvete a refreshing antidote to his own blasé attitude, Buck nonetheless made a firm attempt to befriend his customer.

"Michael's got this great ability," says Peter. "If he doesn't know something, he'll latch on to people and learn from them. He was new to town and he was learning things and meeting people." Peter would invite Michael out for drinks after work, and as their tongues loosened and they traded musical opinions, they kept returning to the same issue: the possibility of forming a band together. Michael, still fresh from his experiences in St Louis, was determined to pursue the idea before he lost any enthusiasm; Peter had never found anyone suitable to pursue the idea with. The notion of teaming up together was not just attractive through the bottom of a glass; it felt good the next morning too.

Two

The B-52's were an overnight sensation. In the spring of 1978, they launched Danny Beard's DB Records with 'Rock Lobster', which quickly became an international cult classic and an inspiration to the region's music community. The next that anyone knew, they were living in New York and signed to a major record company.

"Of all the people I knew that played, and all the bands I'd seen in bars," recalls Pete Buck, "I never knew anyone from Georgia who had a record contract. When the B-52's put out their first single on Danny Beard's label, it blew my mind: 'These guys have made a record and I can buy it!' Then when they got signed to Warner Brothers, it was unprecedented. Literally, there hadn't been anyone from Georgia get a record contract that wasn't beer and boogie and cowboy hats, ever."

"They went to New York and became instant successes," recalls Curtis Crowe. "It looked so fun and easy, it was like, 'We can do this.' It seemed like a scream." Curtis and some fellow art students duly decided to form a band. Curtis would drum, Michael Lachowski play bass, Randy Bewley guitar and Vanessa Briscoe sing. They would call it Pylon.

"For us, it was a real art-related thing," says Michael. "We had done a lot of moving back and forth between different art disciplines. Doing art for us was an all-consuming thing. We didn't just do the work that was required at school, we did it all the time."

"Performance art" was Curtis' definition. For him, "The reason to be in a band was to go to these parties. The parties that the B-52's played at were so electric, so alive, we felt a real need to continue that excitement and energy."

But whereas the 'B's' had some degree of musical proficiency, Pylon were unschooled. From their début in March 1979 – at a party, naturally – it showed.

"I don't think they knew how to tune their instruments until they put out their first single," says Peter Buck. "I always liked in those days bands that would have one competent player and one guy who was learning, because it would push the band in different directions. Certainly with Pylon the only one who knew what he was doing was Curtis, so there was this real solid backbeat and there was all this chaotic noise and made-up words over the top."

Pylon weren't the only new band in town. There was The Tone-Tones, whose lopsided dance music saw them initially vaunted as Athens' next big thing; and The Method Actors, a more eclectic duo who débuted at a Halloween party Curtis Crowe held in '79 at his College Avenue apartment. None of them foresaw a future in music. "There was a sense of making art among these few bands," observes Jim Herbert, who socialised with them all. "I didn't see at that time any commercial possibility."

The Tone-Tones dutifully split up within a few months. The Method Actors, however, would achieve cult status in Europe (and hence be away from Athens for long periods), while Pylon found themselves in the B-52's slipstream, releasing an acclaimed single on DB and becoming the darlings of New York. Unlike the B's before them, they chose to remain living in Athens.

A decade after the initial 'clash of the rednecks and the hippies', Athens continued to struggle with its contrasting cultures. For despite its growing musical and artistic reputation, the University of Georgia remained most famous for its football team, the Georgia Bulldogs, and the macho behaviour that went with it.

Mark Cline, an art student who came to Athens in 1977, recalls he and fellow freshmen going to the wrong parties "where we'd get threatened with death – or worse! – because we were the weirdos."

Peter Buck confirms that, "All of us had those experiences. You wouldn't walk certain places at night, if you weren't with three or four people, 'cos they'd come pouring out of the frat houses and beat you up. I used to go in bars and get abused and get in fights because of the way we all looked. And it wasn't that weird: it was just very strange for some of these no-neck football players."

The female scenesters suffered equal aggravation. At Reed Hall, the only co-ed dormitory on campus, some of them were taken to student court for playing 'punk music' – like Blondie's 'Heart Of Glass' – too loudly. The culprits, Sandra Lee (aka Sandi) Phipps, Carol Levy, Cathy Russo and Linda Hopper, later joined by Kathleen O'Brien, went on to form an anti-sorority, DØU [Defy You], in spite.

This antagonism between the old and the new was not confined to the streets and dorms. Sandi and Kathleen dee-jayed at WUOG, the college radio station, where their musical tastes created a similar turmoil. So fierce was the battle between the jazz/folk crowd and the 'new wavers' that the station was taken off the air for three months to cool down.

The Athens nightclubs were equally reluctant to move away from what they perceived as majority taste. The Last Resort, for example, had a sign offering 'Folk, Jazz And Blues'. There was no mention of rock'n'roll, and perhaps with good reason: when rockabilly punks The Cramps were booked to headline the Georgia Theater in 1979, ticket sales were so poor that the show was cancelled just before show time. (The fringe music community promptly rallied together and moved the gig to a room above the downtown record store Chapter Three.)

Then in the spring of 1979 Tyrone's, a recently revamped club on Foundry Street not previously known for its adventurous booking policy, agreed to let The Tone-Tones play on an off night. (One of the band was sharing a house with one of the club's owners.) The healthy turnout suggested that these local art bands could supply their own audience; gradually, Tyrone's booked them in.

Pylon made their début on a Tuesday that July, as off peak a date as could be contemplated. "They were just floored by how many people showed up," says Michael Lachowski. "They just couldn't believe it." Though grateful for the paying customers, this young art crowd, so different from the traditional southerners who would booze the night away, weren't heavy drinkers. The owner suggested to Lachowski that they must all be on drugs. "No," he replied, explaining that, "If you're dancing, you don't drink."

Mark Cline isn't so sure. "Psychedelics have always been real big in this town," he says, from the days "in the late Seventies (when) there really were no good clubs, so people would have parties and we'd all take lots of acid and go to these parties and dance."

Peter Buck somehow raised himself out of bed every morning after these binges to work at Wuxtry, and his boss Dan Wall took advantage of the quiet summer season to sublet a semi-converted Episcopal church on Oconee Street. He was immediately intrigued by the vast unconverted space he found behind the main bedroom, and being musically minded, began cleaning it out as a possible per-formance space. Peter would frequently come around after work with a six-pack to jam on guitar while Dan played bass, and Michael Stipe too would occasionally stop by to sing along. With drummers in short supply, they used what Peter remembers as "a country Rod Stewart type" and Dan as a "redneck". His name was Tim, and he didn't last.

When Wall was called back to Atlanta to run the Wuxtry store there, he suggested Peter take over the lease, and made the same overture to Kathleen O'Brien. The pair knew each other from Atlanta, and agreed to share; with the rent a forbidding $350 a month, they scouted for other roommates too. Michael Stipe jumped at the opportunity, Peter talked his brother Kenny into relocating, and a girl called Robin Bragg made it five. They took over the church in the autumn of 1979.

Although no one expected a life of tranquillity in their new sur-roundings, they were all somewhat shocked at the reputation they inherited. "It had always been the party place," says Peter Buck. "So just because there were new tenants, didn't mean it wasn't. You'd come home at one in the morning and there'd be five people in the living room that you didn't know, drinking beer. Total strangers wandering into your house."

Sandi Phipps and the DØU girls, having moved out of Reed Hall into a house on the Lexington Highway, regularly came by after classes. "There'd always be something going on there," recalls Sandi of the church's 24-hour party status. "People were aware of it for sure." Peter's extensive record collection dominated the front room and was the subject of much attention. Peter himself, recalls Sandy, was at the time "a cynical bad ass" who enjoyed raising hell. People enjoyed his company because "he was always ready for it, and fun at parties. It's always fun to go somewhere with someone when they cause trouble."

Kathleen O'Brien might have disagreed. On New Year's Eve 1979, her attempts at civilised festivities at the church were dashed when Michael Stipe destroyed the Christmas decorations and Peter turned her elaborately prepared gastronomical spread into ammunition for a violent food fight. Furious at their behaviour, Kathleen engaged in a screaming argument with Michael's sisters, who then refused to talk to her for months to come.

For her own part, Kathleen was insistent that the church was haunted. "No doubt about it. You would hear people coming in through the back, coming up to the door, to that plywood wall, breathing. People walking around upstairs slamming doors when all the doors were shut. A window being busted from the inside, outwardly into the room, like something was between the walls. Something hitting me in the head, and I had to go to the hospital, though there was nobody in the house at the time . . ."

It was all too much for Robin Bragg. "Her parents were thinking that higher education wasn't helping her," says Peter sardonically. "I just remember this real tense day when they came to move her out, and they seemed to blame her downfall on me and Michael." Robin was replaced by a girl called Pam Reynolds, whose extensive medicine cupboard ensured more around-the-clock visits than before. In the light of it all, the mail that still arrived for a previous occupant by the name of Purple Hayes took on an acidic relevance.

Michael Stipe was having the time of his life in his new surroundings. Though still outwardly shy, with none of Peter's excitability, he pursued his performing ambitions with a vengeance. For a while, he fronted a four-piece covers band called Gangster, taking the stage in an appropriate zoot suit as he sang classic hit songs. The group was short-lived, and potentially embarrassing; he subsequently swore friends to keep their existence a secret.

In between their various day jobs, school studies and endless party-going, Peter and Michael had started writing songs that Kathleen thought were "wonderful". However, without a band, they looked unlikely to ever do anything with them. Kathleen herself performed with a group called The Wuoggerz whom no one, least of all themselves, took seriously; it was merely an extension of the friendship among the 'new wave' fans working at the radio station, whose call letters they named themselves after. Only the Wuoggerz' drummer came from outside WUOG. He was Bill Berry, whom Kathleen thought very handsome and had therefore befriended when he moved into dorms at Reed Hall on his arrival in Athens. Bill had a bass-playing friend, Mike Mills, and so, at yet another party, in January 1980, Kathleen introduced Bill to Peter. "You need a rhythm section," she told Peter; "You need a band," she said to Bill, and left them to it. Over a beer in the corner of some long-forgotten Athens front room, the pair agreed to get everyone together at the church.

★   ★   ★

Bill Berry and Mike Mills were the closest of friends when they moved to Athens in January 1979. No one thought to assume it had ever been otherwise. Yet when the pair first met as ninth graders at high school in Macon, Georgia, it was animosity at first sight. Bill was enjoying the thrills of adolescence, "just starting to experiment with drugs and stuff," whereas Mike was a self-confessed 'goody-goody' who was everything Bill despised: "great student, got along with the teachers, didn't smoke cigarettes or smoke pot . . ." Communication between the pair was almost nonexistent.

Mike Mills, though born in Orange County, California, on December 17, 1958, considered himself a local, having moved to Georgia as a baby. Bill Berry, when asked, would tell people he was born in Hibbing, Minnesota, "Bob Dylan's hometown." In fact, he was conceived in Hibbing and born, on July 31, 1958, eighty miles away in Duluth, but it was more impressive to claim the same birthplace as the nation's unofficial Poet Laureate. (Ironically, the lie was unnecessary: Dylan too was born in Duluth, only moving to Hibbing as a child.) Bill and his extensive family lived all over the Great Lakes area – in Milwaukee, Wisconsin and Ohio – before the move south in the autumn of 1972. At the time, Bill felt the same horror at relocating to Georgia as would his future partner Michael Stipe, but when the Great Lake cities took the brunt of the Seventies recession, the entire family counted their blessings.

The Berrys arrived in Macon on the first day of 'busing', the process by which formerly segregated cities attempted to racially integrate a new generation of school children. Bill was dropped off directly by his family at the school bus stop. By the time he got to see his new home that evening, he had been 'bused' from his prosperous new white neighbourhood to a predominantly black school in that part of the city and back again. One of the few other white kids of his age was the 'goody-goody', Mike Mills.

Though they little knew it at the time, Berry and Mills were drifting together through music. For Mike Mills, his father an acclaimed dramatic tenor singer and his mother a singer, pianist and guitarist, musical ability was inbred. He studied the piano from an early age, and in high school joined the marching band, at first on sousaphone and then electric bass, an instrument at which he quickly excelled.

Bill Berry also grew up around music, his elder brothers and sisters purchasing all the latest hit records, his own tastes progressing fast; by the time he was eleven, he was a big Jefferson Airplane fan. Scoring high in a music aptitude test at school one day, he was encouraged to learn an instrument and chose the drums. So it came to be that he agreed to participate in an after school southern boogie jam in Macon, showing up at the bass player's house without enquiring who that might be.

It was, of course, Mike Mills, and Berry was inclined to storm out in disgust. As it was, he grudgingly decided to see the session through, and by the end of the day Mike Mills and Bill Berry were no longer enemies.

In fact, they formed a solid friendship and a rhythm section that began working together in every likely – and unlikely – scenario. There was the school marching band with its military uniforms, playing Led Zeppelin's 'Whole Lotta Love' to spur on the football team during games. There was the lounge trio led by their music teacher, playing country clubs and weddings dressed in suits and ties and earning a hefty $60 each a show as mere 17-year-olds. And there were the rock groups, such as Shadowfax and The Back Door Band. Though they occasionally played originals, the demand was mostly for covers, be it Freddie King or Meters hits on the one hand, or the traditional southern boogie of The Doobie Brothers and Lynyrd Skynyrd on the other.

The pair would later look back and scoff at the music that dominated their teens, but at the time they knew no different. Besides, Macon was the corporate home of southern rock, the city from where the Capricorn record label and Paragon booking agency handled the careers of legends like The Allman Brothers, Charlie Daniels and The Outlaws. On the occasion that Berry and Mills played that brand of rock at the Great Southeast Music Hall in Atlanta, 100 miles to the north, they could easily have considered themselves proud musical missionaries.

However, Atlanta was as far as the young rhythm section got; it became gradually apparent that special attributes were needed to break further into the southern music scene, and Bill and Mike – or the people they played with – just didn't have them. By now they had graduated from high school and, forsaking college, were sharing an apartment together. Mike Mills took employment at the local department store Sears; Bill Berry, still entertaining notions of a career in the music business, landed a job as 'gopher' at Paragon in the autumn of 1976.

In early 1977, as one of his many duties, he drove a fast-talking man by the name of Miles Copeland to a meeting with Paragon supremo Alex Hodges. Copeland was a Beirut-born American living in Britain, where he was booking the punk tours the more conservative agents wouldn't touch because of the movement's bad name. The excitement of punk had now gripped his two London-based younger brothers as well, Stewart, an accomplished drummer who was in a new band called The Police, and Ian, a booking agent. Miles looked out for them both, managing The Police and, when Hodges expressed his desire during their meeting to employ an aggressive young agent, convincingly recommending Ian.

Paragon was aware that southern rock could not rule for ever, and wanted someone to bring in the best of the new international talent. Ian Copeland intended to do just that. He flew in to his new job, sat right down and played the company the punk music he said would change the world. The reaction from the hardened Southerners was one of horror.

"But you know how when you're obsessed with something, you want to turn others onto it?" recalls Ian. "I was determined to get other people to listen to this stuff and see what I saw in it. And the more I was determined to do so, the less they did, and the less they did, the more I was determined, and so on."

Only one person in the entire company showed the slightest bit of interest in Copeland's musical vision. "And that was this kid who worked out in the mail shack. Literally a shack that was built out the back door and across the parking lot of Paragon's offices. And in that shack was Bill Berry."

Though everyone else in Macon quickly ostracised the 27-year-old British agent, Bill Berry thought Ian Copeland was the coolest guy on earth. He introduced his roommate Mike Mills to the new guy from England, and the three of them became inseparable. Mills even sold his bass amp to Ian, only to find himself using it more than ever.

"Bill and I got to be friends with him," Mike later recalled. "We'd go over to his house and he'd start playing us The Damned, Chelsea, The Ramones, The Dead Boys, The Sex Pistols, and I would put the headphones on and play his bass along with the records, going 'Wow! This is fun!'"

"I think they had totally turned away from music," observes Copeland, "certainly as any kind of thought of it being their career. They had decided to take jobs. All the local bands were boring them stiff, it all sounded the same, it was all 'Freebird' and stuff. And when I came to town with this new stuff, it rejuvenated their interest, got their juices flowing."

Copeland even formed a part-time band with Bill and Mike at Paragon called The Frustrations, hoping to demonstrate to his agency partners the fun of playing the new basic music. The idea was to play a few Ramones songs at the end of the company picnic that year, but they were rained off. He was no more successful at converting his Paragon peers when he dragged them all along to The Sex Pistols show in Atlanta – leaving Berry behind working late on a hundred and one odd jobs. "Everyone hated it," he recalls.

The Sex Pistols split up within two weeks, torn apart by the media circus that hounded them across America, and by manager Malcolm McLaren's machiavellian business techniques. The Paragon staffers were happy to see the back of them, and hoped Ian would now bring his tastes more into line with theirs. And to an extent he did. He made plans to bring over The Police, preceded by another of brother Miles' protégés, Squeeze; both bands comprised serious musicians who would ultimately triumph on Top 40 radio. Not that the people at Paragon saw them that way, and indeed, Copeland's attempt to introduce Dire Straits floundered at the first hurdle: the band's 'punk' name. Nonetheless, Copeland deliberately routed the Squeeze tour through Macon, spreading the word in true punk style by having Bill and Mike help him graffiti the town.

Most of this graffiti was still standing when, over Mexican dinner one night, Bill and Mike decided to enrol at the University of Georgia in Athens. Macon, they knew, was a trap – "If you weren't married, you weren't welcome," is Ian Copeland's lasting memory of it – and Athens provided the nearest escape route. Bill Berry, sufficiently intrigued after his apprenticeship at Paragon, intended becoming an entertainment lawyer, but took his drums with him anyway. Mike Mills bought his bass amp back from an Ian Copeland who was delighted to have influenced just two people in all his time in Macon.

Mike Mills and Bill Berry registered for classes at the University of Georgia on January 4, 1979, the same day, coincidentally, as Michael Stipe. In May of that year, no one but its owner aware that the profits from Paragon were being used to prop up the ailing Capricorn record label, both companies collapsed. Copeland upped and left for New York to start his own new wave booking agency. The southern rock era that had dominated the Seventies was now officially over.

★　　★　　★

When Michael Stipe and Peter Buck first set eyes on Bill Berry's proposed bass player, Mike Mills, they were horrified. "He was so drunk, he was hanging on to this bar and weaving," recalls Peter. "He couldn't stand up. Michael said, 'No way am I gonna be in a band with him!'"

Stipe was more impressed by Bill Berry. "Michael said he liked my eyebrows," recalls the drummer of his dominant facial feature. "He claims to this day that's the reason he wanted us to get together!" Berry, meanwhile, considered Peter Buck "a little too cynical for his own good." Regardless of first impressions, they brought their equipment into the front room of the church – being the middle of winter, it was too cold to rehearse on the altar – and decided to give it a try.

Peter Buck, the self-confessed amateur, was immediately daunted by Mike Mills' greater talent on the guitar. He offered to learn bass instead, but Mike and Bill were already a watertight rhythm section. He suggested trying a cheap electric organ that was in the apartment, but that left them still looking for a guitarist. So guitar it was, and much to his pleasure and surprise, "Bill actually liked my style. In Macon, everyone liked to solo all the time, and I think it was maybe the first time ever he played with someone who didn't immediately start going into the Gregg or Duane Allman-isms. I think he found that refreshing."

Though he perhaps didn't realise it at the time, Buck was experimenting with the same chemistry that so impressed him about Pylon, bands with "one competent player and one guy who was learning". In this case, there were two of each, a remarkably fortunate collision of characters.

Traditionally, American bands have been bred on a diet of technique and experience, and a belief in 'paying your dues' that often entails playing other people's songs for years. This was the classic approach that Mike Mills and Bill Berry had endured, an apprenticeship of endless covers bands running the whole gamut of styles through which they had developed an enviable musical comradeship.

But the punk movement, taking a leaf out of British rock in general, tended towards the untrained approach, best exemplified by the art school student who, having formed an idea in his head, simply picks up the instrument he feels best expresses that notion. In this scenario, musical competence takes second place to originality and inspiration. Such was Peter Buck and Michael Stipe's background, one where the rules – or lack of them – were learnt as much by reading the rock press as by playing on stage, and where musical talent was never considered more important than musical intent.

Once the common ground was brought into the equation – Mills' and Berry's recent conversion to punk, Buck's love of rock 'n'roll tradition – it should have appeared obvious to any student of art or music that the newly constituted group had explosive potential.

But with his lack of experience, only time would convince Peter Buck that the successful fusion of a group's disparate ingredients were not an everyday experience – although to his credit, at age 23, he had shown extraordinary patience in waiting for the right band. "I just figured that you'd meet the right people, then you'd get in a band, then you'd make the good music, and people would come and see it," he says. "I didn't realise that most people spend their entire lives trying to find the right combination and it doesn't work. I didn't realise until about a year later that 'Gee, this is kind of special'. We never even tried anyone out. We were two separate camps. We basically walked in and said, 'Hi, how are you doing?', picked up our instruments and two days later we were a band."

Initial rehearsals at the church were in the living room. "It was winter time and it was really cold," recalls Peter. "I remember practising with overcoats and wool hats and gloves on."

Yet immediately they got together musically, the four-piece clicked. "They started rehearsing at the church," recalls Kathleen O'Brien, "and they just had this chemistry. I just knew it. I've never felt so positive about anything."

Kathleen, Sandi and the other girls would watch the practices during the afternoons, drinking and dancing and yelling encouragement. But too often the rehearsals would degenerate into drunken binges, after which Mike Mills and Bill Berry would collapse on the sofa and subsequently skip school the next day. "They were practising all the time but they still weren't doing anything," recalls Kathleen. So she again played catalyst. She was planning to hold an enormous 20th birthday party in the church on April 5, and asked the four-piece to perform at it as a birthday present.

Three weeks' frantic drunken rehearsal saw the group establish two fistfuls of originals, and a few covers to pad them out. Mike and Bill brought in a song called 'Action' from their Macon days, while Bill also had a witty ode to his childhood television hero, Jacques Cousteau, entitled 'Narrator'. As with Peter and Michael's contributions – mostly anti-'love' songs with titles like 'Baby I', 'A Different Girl' and 'I Don't Want You Anymore' – they were primitive and simple, with a heavy Sixties feel. The choice of covers was equally traditional: Johnny Kidd's 'Shakin' All Over',

The Monkees' '(I'm Not Your) Stepping Stone', and a Buck–Stipe favourite, The Velvet Underground's 'There She Goes Again'.

The daunting prospect of a public début failed to deter Michael and Peter, and two mutual friends, from taking a van to New York, where Pylon would be playing, over spring break. It would be a memorable introduction to the Big Apple for Stipe and Buck. Running out of money almost immediately, they ended up sleeping in the van (if sleep they did), eating rarely, drinking continuously, and washing only when the stench became unbearable.

But it was fun. They made friends with the performer Joe 'King' Carrasco, and thanks to Pylon, they got to attend a party of the New York élite, gorging on the free brownies and jelly beans and rejoicing in meeting the famed rock critic Lester Bangs at his most obnoxiously drunk. "You're a rotten cocksucker," were his only words to Peter Buck.

★   ★   ★

Kathleen O'Brien's birthday party would have been legendary even if none of the bands had ever played again. With her own radio show on WUOG and a job at Tyrone's, she knew as many people in town as Peter Buck, and the five kegs of beer, if not the three live bands all making their début, were bound to guarantee a strong turnout. Yet no one had seriously expected 300–500 people to show up. Through the fog of time and the haze of whatever their poison was that particular night – quaaludes were taken in abundance – those who attended best describe it as an 'event' without equal. "I was really terrified," says Peter Buck. "I'd never been on stage before. But I looked up at one point and everyone seemed to be thinking, 'Gee, this is really good.'"

More than that, many of those in attendance who knew a thing or two about live bands, saw immediately that the party headliners had something special going on. So when the three groups had finished playing and their members, all still high on the excitement of their début performances, had resumed partying, scenesters started coming forward to talk. Among them was Dennis Greenia, who lived next door to the church in a print shop with Rick 'The Printer'; they were both local catalysts who ran The Koffee Klub, a popular late night hangout centrally located on Clayton Street.

Greenia suggested that both the party's headliners and The Side Effects repeat their performances in two weeks time.

Mike Hobbs, who booked Tyrone's, was also impressed by what he saw. He had The Brains, an Atlanta band with connections to The Fans, coming into town soon and was looking for an opening act. If that last group could get a name together and would play for free, they could have the show.

Peter, Mike, Michael and Bill had been searching for a name for weeks. Now, with unexpected bookings to spur them on, they encouraged visitors to write suggestions in coloured chalk on the church walls. Among them were Twisted Kites – which some people believe was officially used at the first show – Cans Of Piss and Slut Bank. But the group wanted one that didn't mean anything, that left its connotations open to interpretation. R.E.M. ostensibly stood for Rapid Eye Movement – the condition during deep sleep when dreams are at their more prevalent – but it could also stand for anything else with those initials. R.E.M. it was.

At the Koffee Klub on April 19, the group again went on in the middle of the night. As the bars closed at midnight on Saturdays – Sundays in Athens being dry – and considering the venue's central location, it was perhaps no surprise that the police came crashing in halfway through R.E.M.'s official début. Seeing people drinking beer, they stopped the show and subsequently charged Greenia for 'improper use of a business license'. Hoping to intimidate, they also took pictures of some of the 200 fun-lovers crammed into the tiny room. The night people posed readily, with great flamboyance.

Among those in attendance was a first-year law student called Bertis Downs, who served on the Concert Committee at the University, which Bill Berry had also talked himself onto by dint of his Paragon experience. "They were incredible," was Downs' instant reaction. "Everybody at the concert committee was talking about it and saying, 'God, Bill's new band is great.'"

With word getting out, Tyrone's on Tuesday May 6 was packed to the hilt. The Brains were one of Peter's favourite local bands, but R.E.M., by all accounts, charged through their set with such gusto and abandon that the headliners were left looking remarkably average. "It was generally acknowledged," Mike Mills later recalled, with the confidence bordering on arrogance that would prove an R.E.M. trademark, "that we blew them away."

Tyrone's proprietor Oliver Diamantstein, watching the band for the first time, noted two things. One was that, "I knew they were going to be great. You just listened to them and looked at the people that were listening to them, and judged by the crowd reaction. You knew they couldn't miss if they had any breaks at all." The second was that, though "The Brains were from Atlanta and were popular, when R.E.M. went off, most of the crowd left." Diamantstein instructed Mike Hobbs to give R.E.M. their own show as soon as possible.

That gig took place on May 13, just one week later. "It was mind-boggling," says Peter Buck. "We got 350 people. Nobody got 350 people at Tyrone's. Pylon got 100. Everyone looked around and it was like 'I can't believe this'. We'd been together a month and a half and we were the biggest band in town."

For a few chaotic weeks in the late spring of 1980, as R.E.M. metamorphosed from a non-gigging garage band into the toast of Athens, all four members called the Oconee Street church home, with Bill Berry taking the place of a departing Pam Reynolds, and Mike Mills more often than not sleeping on the sofa.

But the lease was up in June, and the absentee landlord had heard enough about the incessant parties to want the band out. After nine months' depraved existence, the occupants were equally ready for a change. Their deposit forfeited for damages, they left behind a host of memories and a squadron of sand-fleas. Michael, Mike and Peter subleased an apartment on Little Oconee Street for the summer – Peter paying the impoverished, unemployed Mills' rent – and Bill and Kathleen, who had been going out together for several months already, got a place of their own around the corner. The church was duly rented out to another generation of students, who would come home late at night to a living room full of drunken strangers and ask themselves, 'Why us?'

Three

In 1980, the talents that had been bubbling away for so long in Athens boiled over in a brief, tumultuous explosion of energy. It was a period of extraordinary creativity, an outpouring from which the town never looked back.

It was the year the Athens music community created their own club, The 40 Watt, when Paul Scales, a scenester managing a sandwich shop on College Avenue, was offered use of its top floor as rehearsal space. He and Curtis Crowe instead turned the tiny room into a club, adopting the name of the Halloween party Crowe had held across the street.

"Not only was it a name," says Curtis, "it was an ethic. The ethic behind the 40 Watt Club was 'Something for Nothing'; if you can get out there and scrounge materials, you can put together something for nothing." The Side Effects opened the club on May 9, 1980, and three weeks later, R.E.M. played there for the first of many times, for a $1 admission, causing mayhem in a room Curtis describes as holding only "75 people – and you couldn't get another one in with a shoehorn." On some occasions, the floor would vibrate so drastically under the weight of pounding feet that wooden pillars were eventually erected underneath. The thermometer never showed a temperature under 100°, and Michael Stipe could often be found manning the door.

1980 was also the year that Athens' previously small population of rock bands started breeding. The party at the church was the focal occasion – giving birth to triplets, so to speak – but it was not alone. Two months later, Love Tractor sprang up, an instrumentals only group whose members Mark Cline, Mike Richmond, Kit Swartz and later Armistad Wellford were all known figures on the circuit. That Kit was also guitarist and singer with The Side Effects was not unusual in a music scene renowned for its incestuousness.

36

Socialising too reached a new zenith over this period. Michael Lachowski turned his answering machine into the "Athens Party Telephone", on which he would leave details of the night's choice of events. He and Curtis Crowe lived in a house on Barber Street above Mark Cline, with Michael Stipe across from an empty lot that became known as Pylon Park. There they held parties throughout the summer, often with live music, always with a theme.

Barber Street became more than just a magnet for the musicians and artists in Athens; it became their own private neighbourhood, its two blocks at one time housing almost every member of R.E.M., Pylon, Love Tractor, The Method Actors and The Side Effects among other bands, along with their managers and close friends, and poets and painters. Over the decade, as more musicians than ever based themselves in Athens and some of the older ones bought their own houses, the locale expanded to become known as The Boulevard, including that street and Grady as well as Barber. The members of R.E.M. would all eventually own houses in the locality.

R.E.M.'s ascension among this Athens scene was almost as fast as their on-stage tempo, and no less dramatic than Peter Buck's claim that within a month and a half of forming, they had become the biggest band in town. They again upstaged The Brains when the two bands played the University's Memorial Hall on May 15, for which they received what Buck believes to be their first fee, a hefty $200. They headlined Tyrone's again, played the 40 Watt and the Mad Hatter, and then used the occasion of their first Atlanta show, at the Warehouse on June 6, as an opportunity to allow Buck's former employer Mark Methe to film them at the Atlanta Wuxtry store. The next night they played in High Shoals with southern rock also-rans Stillwater; R.E.M. ended the month with another show at the Mad Hatter.

July proved even busier, with several relationships formed that would last for years. There was a show at the Agora in Atlanta, but more importantly, R.E.M. opened for Britain's Gang Of Four at the prestigious 688 Club in Atlanta on the 15th and 16th of the month. It's uncertain exactly how the group gained such a prestigious booking: Ian Copeland was the Gang Of Four's agent and seems a likely candidate to have booked his protégés Bill Berry and Mike Mills into the slot, but he has never made mention of it; nor have the rhythm section. In hindsight, it would have made far more sense for a band like Pylon, or the Method Actors or Side Effects, to have opened, but what matters is that R.E.M., essentially a party band from a southern college town, came up against a group of serious and politically ambitious post-punk intellectuals from the northern English city of Leeds, and proved themselves worthy of the booking. An important friendship was cemented, with the Gang Of Four becoming the first of many British bands to start spreading the word about R.E.M.

There was virtually no time to return to Athens before heading out of state for the first time, to North Carolina. Pylon had been booked to play a couple of gigs on their way to New York, but when another booking came in in the Big Apple, they cancelled what they considered were the less worthy shows.

Jefferson Holt, the young record store manager booking gigs in North Carolina as much to improve the local scene as his own pocket, called The Method Actors as a replacement, who in turn recommended R.E.M. Holt booked the band on spec into The Station in Carrboro, a stone's throw from his Chapel Hill home, on Friday and Saturday July 18 and 19, and The Pier in Raleigh the following Monday. He expected the typical Athens art band; the one he got would change him for ever.

"It was the greatest thing I had seen in my life," he recalled five years later. "They had so much fun. They didn't seem to care about anything . . . They just got up there and had a great time. To me, it was how I imagined seeing The Who before they signed a record contract. It's what I think any rock band should strive for . . . a certain sense of chaos."

During their four days and nights in North Carolina, R.E.M. hardly slept, partying with Jefferson in their one motel room and taking pride that Kathleen O'Brien and Linda Hopper had driven up to see them. Buck, Mills and Stipe ended the 'tour' at The Pier on an empty dance floor while the 25-strong audience sang 'Gloria' massed on the stage.

Only the next night the group were back at Tyrone's. It was the height of summer, and Athens was filled with freshmen in town for 'orientation', an opportunity to familiarise themselves with the University and learn about the year that lay ahead. Like most of these freshmen, Bryan Cook was more interested in finding out whether Athens' nightlife opportunities were as multifarious as he had heard and, a keen music fan, followed suggestions to check out the students' fave band R.E.M. at Tyrone's. He paid his $1 and walked in on a group such as he'd always hoped existed.

"They were wearing these cool clothes," he recalls vividly. "Pete had a long, droopy earring, and a pink silk shirt with big old collars on, and Michael was all colourful. They were doing 'Stepping Stone' and I just thought, 'This is the coolest thing in the world.' "

At these early shows, Michael Stipe in particular grabbed the audience's attention with his theatrics and extrovert behaviour. "He would get out there and shake and dance, like Little Richard or something," recalls Terry Allen, a young photographer on the Athens scene who shot the group at live shows many times during the early days. "He had hair covering up his eyes, and he'd be shaking around, pulling the microphone up like Mick Jagger."

At The Station in Carrboro that first out-of-state show, a local rock critic, Fred Mills, was told by a regional musician that Stipe was 'the most pretentious Mick Jagger rip-off' he'd ever seen. Mills thought he was too self-conscious for that, because "he would always look around. He wouldn't sing directly to you, the audience. I remember thinking he was more like Joe Cocker than Mick Jagger."

Mark Cline recalls Stipe "rocking, like Elvis, just shaking, and dancing around, and jumping", while Bryan Cook also remembers how, "He did the craziest dances. He'd go in all different directions, like a dervish, just spinning and jumping, his arms flailing . . ."

Scott Belville went to see his pupil one night at Tyrone's and was forced to do a double take. "He was hopping all over the place," he recalls. "And that was wild, because in class he generally was very quiet, very reserved." Fellow students familiar only with Stipe as an unassuming classmate "went there just to see him jump around."

It is hard to equate someone going through a self-confessed 'long and intense' period 'of extreme shyness' with the unreserved front man just described. Michael Stipe, however, would not be the first performer to appear invincible on the stage and intimidated off it: rock'n'roll has long been an acknowledged transformer of confidence for the emotionally shy. Certainly, from R.E.M.'s very first show, Stipe was bolstered by the genuine capability of the trio behind him and the obvious appreciation of the audience in front. The stage allowed Michael Stipe an opportunity to show off as he would never have the courage for on a one-to-one basis.

There was another Michael Stipe eager to be let loose in front of a crowd: the talented art student, who, taking a lead from the other Athens bands and his heroes from elsewhere, was working on the premise that art could be expressed in any form or medium, as viably on a stage as on canvas, as authentically through a microphone as through a lens.

Over a period of time he would develop this on-stage persona away from the shadows of other stars into something more mysterious and enigmatic, something closer to real art, and he would apply the same combination of inspiration, maturity and calculation to the lyrics. For now though, the words Michael Stipe sang related either to joyful quests for romance or typical teenage angst. Either way, they were embarrassingly juvenile and gave no indication of their writer's future literary credibility. Clearly enunciated choruses included the less-than-immortal lines, "Baby I don't wanna hang around with you", "I just don't want you anymore", and "I'm running with a different girl"; the most profound they got were "These are dangerous times, I don't want to grow old." The point has subsequently been made that his lyrics could be considered misogynistic, and it's true that a couple of live tapes from the era find him verbally dismissive, even to the point of threatening physical violence, to the female characters in his songs. It's hard to justify, and one imagines the modern-day Stipe would not even try.

The music of early R.E.M. was equally simplistic, both in form and substance. Largely due to Peter Buck's limited musical knowledge, the songs were all written around basic I-IV-V chord structures, with the occasional minor chord for moody variation. Buck's style of playing, however, was remarkably creative for someone so avowedly unaccomplished. Rather than strum chords, he would pick out arpeggios in the fashion immortalised by The Byrds, and throw in lots of the suspended fourths that had trademarked early Who songs. With the guitar such a dominant force in the three instrument group, the entire sound thus took on a retro Sixties feel.

Yet despite their apparent shortcomings, the songs conveyed a charm and enthusiasm that has stood the test of time. An album recorded when R.E.M. first started headlining Tyrone's – and there were certainly enough songs for it – would have been a fine manic pop record. It simply would not have been the R.E.M. that their audience has come to know.

Indeed, the eight songs that the group first committed to tape have surfaced on enough bootlegs that many R.E.M. obsessives are quite familiar with them.* And perhaps it's just that familiarity breeds a certain content, but it's hard not to be won over by their simplicity of purpose and clarity of performance. The vocal of 'Dangerous Times' rides Buck's fascination with that suspended fourth; 'I Don't Want You Anymore', though its lyric is un-inspired, would survive as 'All The Right Friends' and make it onto an album more than twenty years later. 'Different Girl' and 'Baby I' were more of the same, and nothing to write home about, but Bill Berry's 'Narrator' had a humour that played perfectly into the group's fascination with Sixties cartoon pop imagery. 'Just A Touch' had enough force of power to merit occasional inclusion in the band's set, and eventual admission onto an album. And both 'Mystery To Me' and 'Permanent Vacation' were concise, ener-getic pop songs such as many a new wave band would have con-sidered worthy of single status. "I look back on it and think that some of the songs were dumb," says Peter Buck. "But there was something there. There was a weird chemistry."

★   ★   ★

* The original editions of this book referred to them as being recorded one after-noon on the Tyrone's four-track, as that was Peter Buck's recollection to the author. The authors of *Adventures In Hi-Fi* have determined that the tape was the audio track for the video Mark Methe filmed at his Atlanta Wuxtry store on June 6; that means these songs were performed entirely live.

"That fall," says Bryan Cook of R.E.M.'s status in Athens, "was when they started owning the town. Whenever they played there'd be a traffic jam, and you couldn't park downtown. You'd see people walking, and they'd all be walking from wherever there was parking, down to Tyrone's."

R.E.M. were hometown stars. But among their musical peer group they were viewed with not a little disdain. Athens had put itself on the map by virtue of art-rock and intriguingly original dance-pop, and every time R.E.M. went into Tyrone's and struck up such familiar rock'n'roll anthems as 'Hippy Hippy Shake', 'Nervous Breakdown' and 'Rave On', they lowered the standards.

"At the time," says Terry Allen, "it was really uncool to be doing that, because it was almost like you were a bar band, just a cover band playing all the oldie hits."

"There was this kind of snobbery about bands who played covers," agrees Curtis Crowe. "The hipster scene was, 'They play covers, they're not truly hip.'"

"They were the odd band out on the scene," confirms Love Tractor's Mark Cline, "because all the other bands were art school bands, and here comes R.E.M. and they play Sixties covers. They weren't real hipsters; they were kind of these outside rockers."

Such was R.E.M.'s reputation for covers that some on the scene didn't realise that they played anything else. "We always thought that everything they were playing were covers," says Michael Lachowski of Pylon. "But then I wouldn't have known the difference. Maybe I just recognised a more formulaic approach to making music."

And Bryan Cook, who loved R.E.M., also had problems distinguishing between the group's self-composed songs and its non-originals. "I didn't know they were covers," he insists. "The way they did some of the obscure Troggs songs, and the way they'd changed the Velvets songs, I didn't really recognise them. They used to do 'God Save The Queen', which was so far different from the real trendy Athens beat. R.E.M. just stuck on their own thing; they'd take their influences, combine it with the covers and make it into their own song. I still think of 'A Girl Like You' as an R.E.M. song."

"They were real smart about that," echoes Curtis Crowe. "It

didn't occur to people until later on that what they did by playing covers was they lured in a larger segment of people who were kinda dissatisfied with the larger state of music, but at the same time weren't quite adventurous enough to go into some of the other new music camps that were all strictly original music. So they lured them in with the cover tunes that they genuinely liked, and it was kinda their way of feeling their way into what they do now. And in the meantime they were writing their original tunes."

The group were nothing if not prolific in their songwriting. Along with the eight that had made it onto tape in Atlanta, and the Berry-Mills Macon hangover 'Action', the set that fall also included songs such as 'Body Count' (with references to Vietnam), 'Lisa Says', 'Scheherazade', and 'Smalltown Girl'. They were mostly generic, lyrically juvenile, and, as Bryan Cook points out, "sounded like their covers."

There were two songs however, both written early in the summer, that stood out, and they heralded R.E.M.'s transform-ation from a group who sounded just like their influences into a group who sounded just like themselves. The first was 'Gardening At Night', written on a June afternoon on a mattress on the porch of the Oconee Street church. Michael Stipe later claimed that, "I thought it was the first real song we did," and certainly it marked a grand development in his own contribution. For one, the lyrics did not put down girls or talk crassly about war, as most of his previous efforts had; they covered some intangible subject matter that invited inspection. Such examination was then purposely compli-cated by the fact that the lyrics were not only vague but largely indiscernible. Stipe was moving away from clear enunciation towards a less guttural diction that paid only partial lip service to consonants and left the end of almost every line of verse unpronounced. With 'Gardening At Night', Stipe discovered the power of mystery, and so powerful was this discovery that his lyrical ambiguity transferred to the melody which, rather than echo the guitar chords as previous compositions had, now glided over Peter's arpeggiated guitars and Mike's roaming bass, so that the music too sounded at once both more mature and less obvious.

Mike Mills, the most musically proficient member of the band, also took an enormous step forward when he single-handedly wrote a plea to Ingrid Schorr, a new girl in Athens who had been making a big impact on all the boys, begging her not to return that summer to Maryland. 'Don't Go Back To Rockville' (named for the town she'd originally escaped from), with its deliberate country twang, singalong chorus and frantic pacing, became an instant live favourite, especially with Bertis Downs, the law student who attended almost every R.E.M. show. It was in many ways the opposite of 'Gardening At Night': it was musically traditional, lyrically clear, easy to memorise and hard to misconstrue. But it was a solid piece of songwriting all the same, and the band knew it.

Neither song made an immediate difference to the band's hometown reputation among its peer group. For while everyone stresses that R.E.M.'s members were welcome on a social level, there is no doubt that the band itself was ostracised by virtually all the local musicians. That they packed the clubs and appealed to all types only emphasised their crassness. The *real* Athens music scene, said its leaders very loudly, had never needed to commercialise itself to please mainstream elements of the local populace; the sophisticates in New York had recognised its worth without their having to stoop so low.

But R.E.M. were unruffled. They were merely having fun playing the music they liked; that it was instantly popular proved its merits. Admittedly, their traditional approach gave them appeal in the mainstream, but they still had enough of the punk and art school ethic for the more musically conservative among those who attended Tyrone's to consider R.E.M. as strange, oddballs. It was the first evidence that the group's contrasting personalities would allow them to be all things to all people.

Still, playing covers was not the only reason for R.E.M.'s 'unhipness' among their supposed colleagues. Athens was acknowledged as an oasis in a musical desert; as such, its new bands saw no point playing the musically prejudiced surrounding areas. R.E.M., however, so thoroughly *enjoyed* their first trip to North Carolina that they couldn't wait to repeat it. Rather than worry about the people who wouldn't like them, they instead focused on the few who would, and who would bring their friends next time.

It was a devotion to the work ethic that was to pay enormous dividends. By the end of their first year together, R.E.M. had opened up hitherto unknown markets in Georgia, South Carolina and Tennessee. And in North Carolina, partly thanks to their new friend Jefferson Holt, they had built a following in Raleigh, Charlotte and Chapel Hill as well as regularly playing an odd little pizza restaurant in Greensboro called Friday's. Yet they still hadn't been to New York. The other bands in Athens thought R.E.M. were mad: who, they asked themselves, would want to slum it by playing the armpit of America when New York would treat you like kings?

The new-generation of 'post-punk' bands also steered away from the rough 'n' tumble bars of rural southern America because of the preposterously long sets they were expected to play: as many as three one-hour shows in the name of entertainment. Other groups saw themselves as outside all of that.

"We had no missionary zeal in trying to change people's minds," says Michael Lachowski of Pylon. "We only wanted to go where people were going to be already receptive." R.E.M. however, "loved to be on stage and be playing this stuff, and the crowd could tell. They could play to a more conservative crowd and get away with it, out of their sheer zeal, and ability to play long sets and covers."

Not that R.E.M. ever saw themselves as mere entertainers. At many of their out-of-town bookings they would argue with promoters who'd demand three sets. "We'd say, 'No, if you hire an original band you get two forty-five minute sets and encores," recalls Buck. "They'd also say, 'Don't you play anything by The Cars? By The B-52's? We thought you were a new wave band.' 'We never said we're a new wave band; we're a rock'n'roll band, we play songs we like.'"

In the process R.E.M. were undergoing the kind of intense group apprenticeship that can be compared to The Beatles' arduous days in Hamburg. Their enthusiasm enabled them to survive shows that would have enervated their uncompromising hometown friends. "We got together in front of people who'd never seen us, who didn't really give a shit and didn't know us," says Peter Buck. "You really hone the edge, having to prove yourself every night."

Athens regulars began to notice the increased absence from local parties and bars of the four R.E.M. members. They were on the road so much already – and earning so little money – that it was both difficult and pointless to pay the rent each month. Thus when they did come back to Athens, it would often be just to stay with girlfriends or on a friend's floor for a few days before heading out again. For a period during late 1980, Peter Buck even lived out of his huge old Buick, curling up in a sleeping bag in the trunk.

"I'd park it in front of people's houses that I knew," he says. "I used to shower at the dorms – I'd sneak in every day and pretend I was a student." During this period of poverty and homelessness – his work at Wuxtry too irregular to constitute a living wage – Buck stored his clothes and records at the group's shared practice space on Jackson Street. Other bands assumed it to be junk and removed almost everything while he was on tour, including the legendary pink silk shirt and many of his prized old records.

The other members of the group were also making decisions and suffering hardships. Neither Mike Mills nor Bill Berry had seen much reason to continue taking classes almost from the moment the group had formed. For Mills, life in an active rock'n'roll band beat working at Sears in Macon, and that was enough. Berry, however, had gone to Athens with the noble intentions of becoming an entertainment attorney; if he was going to give up that ambition and quit school, it had to be for an equally viable alternative.

More than anyone else in the group it was Bill Berry who gathered the reins of the early, unruly R.E.M. "Bill has the business mind," said Sandi Phipps, looking back at the end of the decade. "He is a genius." Berry's ambition and business intuition, coupled with his experience at Paragon, had already landed him a job on the University's Concert Committee, and now he applied these attributes to R.E.M.'s cause, hustling gigs at any and every little bar in the region. For a while he attempted to start The Athens Agency, whereby he would book out-of-town shows for the other local groups, but none of R.E.M.'s peers expressed much interest in playing biker bars and pizzerias.

Berry then drew on his friendship from Macon with Ian Copeland to further R.E.M.'s cause. After the collapse of Paragon, Copeland had headed to New York to start his own F.B.I. Agency, a pun on his brother Miles' burgeoning I.R.S. Records. There he could bring in the cream of the British talent and nurture the best of young America without having to answer to superiors. Berry sent Ian R.E.M.'s 'live' demo and some press cuttings to demonstrate their popularity. Copeland promptly gave them a date with The Police in Atlanta on December 6, 1980, Peter Buck's 24th birthday. Only eight months after their first show, R.E.M. played in front of 4,000 people at The Fox Theater in Atlanta, earning an encore and incurring the promoter's wrath by inviting the audience up on stage. How was Michael Stipe to know that the rules for a major theatre were different from those for a tiny club?

By this point, the ever-enthusiastic Bill Berry had two drumming jobs, having readily agreed to fill in for Love Tractor when Kit Swartz decided that he preferred fronting The Side Effects. Berry enjoyed his new occupation so much that in the spring of '81 he told Love Tractor he was quitting R.E.M. He no doubt meant it, but in actuality he used his dilemma to establish each group's commitment to going forward. R.E.M.'s being the far greater, he left Love Tractor instead. "He had to play devil's advocate a lot, which doesn't make you real popular," says Kathleen O'Brien. She praises Bill for being "totally instrumental in keeping R.E.M. intact" in those early days.

Berry became increasingly exasperated at having to hustle every minor gig and pull every major favour. Kathleen's continual motivation and encouragement – and her willingness to pay the phone bills – helped, but she was never offered the official role of manager. "I don't think they wanted a woman doing it," Sandra Lee Phipps explains. "That's kind of their attitude."

"Back in those days I did a lot for the band but it was never acknowledged," says O'Brien. "I wasn't allowed to be an active part of the band; Bill had decreed that. They weren't going to let me manage the band and that was essentially what I was doing. I remember my mother saying, 'You are managing a band, and you've got to get it on paper now.'" Kathleen was torn. She was offering help primarily out of a genuine enthusiasm that only increased since introducing Bill to Michael and Peter. "In my heart of hearts, I knew that they could be what they are. I didn't want to manage; it just so happened that that's what I was doing by virtue of my interaction. It was just something I wanted to see happen, so

47

it wasn't like I thought about it. I just did things. However, when my mother said that, I started thinking more on that business end, that I needed to cover my ass."

It was too late. Jefferson Holt, who was so infatuated with the Athens music scene that he moved to the town in October 1980 to open a new record shop, Foreign Legion, got involved instead. "He was the roadie at first," recalls Peter. "Then he took the door, then after a while he kept the money. Bill was going insane booking, so Jefferson started booking the band. After about a year, Jefferson was fulfilling all the jobs of a manager." Perhaps as a result, Foreign Legion lasted only a few months before going out of business. The group, assured by Holt that this in no way reflected on his capabilities as a business manager, were happy to leave him to it.

Jefferson was not immediately liked by everyone in town. "He was a real smart ass," says Sandra Lee Phipps, "and he used to piss me and my girlfriends off. I used to spit beer on him at the Koffee Klub, 'cos he was a real smart ass, but kind of funny and intriguing at the same time. We'd go check him out at (his shop) and he'd be just so snide to all the ladies."

But as the store folded, and Jefferson devoted himself fully to the group, the same girls felt relieved that R.E.M. had found one of their own. "He was a godsend," says Kathleen O'Brien, "because he was the only personality that each individual in the band could relate to. So he was kind of a pivot."

And Sandra Lee Phipps understood that, for all Jefferson's eccentricity, "he knew to reserve himself and dedicate his total energy and focus to them – or decided to do that. And that's what they wanted."

As fall gave way to winter, the group itself understood that it was on a roll. "We had gone from being marginally hip to being *the* band, over the summer," recalls Peter Buck. "We were getting better, too. We had started writing songs that were good. We were actually getting to be a pretty good band, really distinctive. At that point we sounded like ourselves, we didn't sound like much of anything else that was going on in America – although I didn't know that. I guess every town had one band that was kinda like us, and we just happened to be it in Athens."

Key to the band's development was, as Buck notes, the

songwriting. 'Gardening At Night' had proven itself the watershed, and it was soon followed by two more in a similar vein, 'Sitting Still' and 'Shaking Through'. Then there were the rockers 'Pretty Persuasion' and 'Burning Down', the somewhat undeveloped 'Get On Their Way', and finally, right at the end of the year, a song called 'Radio Free Europe' – ostensibly about the American propaganda station broadcast to the eastern bloc, but in practice almost completely unintelligible – that the band immediately recognised as being both commercial and yet credible, the finest song they had yet written.

Two Tyrone's tapes from that era, one recorded on October 4, 1980, the other on January 10, 1981, catch the group in this early state of flux, somewhere between a garage band heavily influenced by the Sixties, and a rock group that would become arguably the most influential American act of the Eighties. It would be easy to sneer at R.E.M.'s choice of covers, just as some of the originals sound dumb and derivative, but what really comes across in these recordings is both how competent and confident the group sound. They are not yet a year old as a band, but there's rarely a bum note or missed beat throughout the performances; the harmonies are near perfect; and Michael Stipe's charisma comes bouncing off the tape, whether it be deliberately hamming it up on 'Narrator' and 'Baby I', name-checking the key girls in the audience (his sister Lynda Stipe and Linda Hopper join him to offer backing vocals for the cartoonish and commercial composition 'Wait'), or bastardising Aretha Franklin's 'Respect' in the middle of a cover of 'Gloria'. Allowing that the poorer material would soon be weeded out, and that the newer songs already sound well practised, there is nothing for the band to be embarrassed about. You don't need the benefit of hindsight to know that this is a band going places; if the audible audience excitement and on-stage confidence is not evidence enough, the inspired rendition of 'Radio Free Europe' on the January tape, at what may have even been its first live performance, is consummate proof.

Live recordings had their attractions, but with the songwriting so improved, it was time now to make a proper tape, and in February '81 R.E.M. headed to the eight-track Bombay Studios in Smyrna, near Atlanta. For all their live competence, however, the group were still completely naïve about studios, and they allocated only six hours for eight songs. The hurried result was "flat and dull", according to Peter: "I didn't know what I was doing," recalls the group's most studied member. "The guy who was running it (Joe Perry, no relation to the Aerosmith guitarist) was a nice guy but he didn't know what he was doing either. We mixed it in about two minutes." Only 'Sitting Still' seemed to merit the effort. Of the other songs, Jefferson Holt went so far as to say that it would do more harm than good to send the tape out, and so they buried it. Unlike the live tapes of that era, these first studio recordings have never made it into public hands.

Holt suggested they try again, elsewhere. He turned for advice to his friend Peter Holsapple of North Carolina's leading band The dB's. Holsapple recommended another local boy, Mitch Easter, who had set up a studio in his parents' garage in Winston-Salem and was looking for business. On April 13, 1981, Jefferson called Easter to sound him out: R.E.M. drove up to North Carolina the following evening.

Four

Everyone who has worked with Mitch Easter in the studio comments on his natural affinity for the recording process. Considering that Easter has been making rock'n'roll since he was 12, this is perhaps not surprising. In fact, he and Peter Buck are the same age, and a look at the two men's résumés demonstrates how late a developer Buck was musically just as it reveals how rapidly Mitch Easter took to the boards. After joining his first band in the late Sixties, Easter played in a flurry of groups through the Seventies, most notably in the decade's second half, when he was in The Sneakers with Chris Stamey, and The H-Bombs with Peter Holsapple. When Stamey and Holsapple then formed The dB's Easter set his heart on owning a studio, selling his home in Chapel Hill and investing the profits in 16-track recording equipment. Like The dB's before him, he saw no future in North Carolina, but after a stint in New York that was even more frustrating, he returned south in 1980 when his parents offered him the use of their garage. Winston-Salem was hardly on the cutting edge of music, but there were plenty of new bands in the region keen to find a studio not of the old Southern rock school.

R.E.M., though based 250 miles away, were a typical example. And when they turned up to Mitch's aptly named Drive-In Studio that April evening, they were delighted to find it located in a sizeable house in the country, with dogs running loose and Mitch's mother supplying coffee and doughnuts. On April 15 Mitch engineered as the group raced through 'Radio Free Europe', 'Sitting Still' and the surf styled instrumental 'White Tornado'. He was immediately impressed.

"I'd been recording some of the 'new wave' bands and I appreciated the spirit," he says. "However, a lot of them didn't live up to how they were live – they didn't have that many really good songs.

51

And R.E.M. struck me as a real classic singles band."

Michael Stipe, much to Easter's amusement, insisted on singing in the furthest corner of the small studio where no one could see him, facing the wall. That the words were an almost total blur worried the engineer not one bit.

"I didn't care at all," says Easter, even though Stipe had a lyric sheet with him and most producers would insist on a vocalist pronouncing his words. "Some songs that I really love and I hum in my head I've never known the words to. I like them just on the sound level. So I never worried about any kind of rule about that. I guess I had a really cavalier attitude about recording, and no concern at all for commercial stumbling blocks."

That Easter was a kindred spirit was evident not just by his comments but by the quality of the tape the group took with them the next day. Stipe may not have clearly enunciated but the vocals were up loud in the mix, and the singer was beginning to emphasise his distinct drawl. The drums on both 'Sitting Still' and 'Radio Free Europe' were clear and clinical; on 'White Tornado', they were ferocious in the best Hal Blaine/surf style, Bill Berry proving himself a far better player than he would often get credit for. Apart from his own surf twang on 'White Tornado', Peter Buck's Rickenbacker playing remained simple and almost entirely free of overdubs; instead, his arpeggiated jangle was offset by Mike Mills' extremely busy bass melodies, which ran clearly up and down octaves, neither booming at the bottom nor thinning out at the top. Where Berry, Mills and Stipe gathered in harmony, their notes were spot on, as if they'd been singing together for years, rather than just the twelve months of rough and tumble gigs. 'Sitting Still' had a keen mystery, 'Radio Free Europe' offered obvious commercial appeal, and 'White Tornado' was a deliberate riot. All bases covered in just three songs.

R.E.M. were excited to have made such a rapid recovery from the disappointment of the Bombay session, and decided to send the three song demo wherever need be to get attention. Eager to avoid appearing just another group of obsequious hopefuls landing on record company and journalists' desks, they packaged the tape with colourful hand designed insert cards and teasing instructions, 'Do Not Open'. The ploy worked: when they at last journeyed to New

York in June for a prestigious two night support slot with The Gang Of Four at The Ritz – this one an official favour by Ian Copeland – they were met with a recommendation by critic Robert Christgau in the *Village Voice* that R.E.M. were "sending out a tape with lots of impressive first time songs on it."

★   ★   ★

In Atlanta, a 27-year-old law student and musician was saying adieu to his own dreams of becoming a rock'n'roll star at the same time as he was investigating the possibility of becoming a record label entrepreneur. Johnny Hibbert had been fronting an Atlanta band called The Incredible Throbs whom he claims "were of modest renown" and had received "lots of critical acclaim". Certainly, his reputation had spread as far as Athens: R.E.M.'s second show with The Brains, in May 1980, had garnered a review in the college paper *The Red & Black*, in which Michael Stipe was said to have "a stage presence reminiscent of the Incredible Throbs' Johnny Hibbert in his best moments."

Hibbert had enjoyed his years as a front man – "from 1975 to 1983 there was a really intense new wave scene here, with places to play, a good number of club venues, and local promoters who were fairly open to local bands" – but recognised that the big time had passed him by. So when a couple of friends offered to finance a record, he suggested they all find a new band rather than waste the resources on his own flagging career. With little to get excited about in Atlanta, he turned to a student friend in Athens for ideas. Come see R.E.M., she said, and he was there the next time they played Tyrone's.

"I wasn't particularly impressed with their musicianship or their artistry, or their stage presence either," he recalls of that first encounter. "There was no one element that I thought was really superlative. But it was the only band around at the time that created the same kind of crowd response and overall experience that I had always believed in as a performer. The fervour with which they approached their performances, and their sincerity, and the crowd's response to them, told me all I needed to know."

Hibbert duly approached R.E.M. The group were attracted to the idea of a homegrown record label and, seeing that Hibbert was

53

Jefferson Holt's age and that, like Mitch Easter, he had the working musician's sympathy for their art, felt they were taking another kindred spirit on board. "They were quite responsive to me," recalls Hibbert, "because a few of them allowed that they had come to hear me play on many occasions in the past." When he offered to put them back in the studio to remix and then release a 7″ single featuring 'Radio Free Europe' and 'Sitting Still', they jumped at the chance. Hibbert offered to make the single a one-off release, on the understanding he would own the publishing for the two songs. The band didn't object.

On May 25, R.E.M. and Johnny Hibbert returned to the Drive-In to overdub and remix. As Hibbert remembers it, "the band were very co-operative, and very enthusiastic about my ideas. They liked the idea of doubling the guitar parts; they liked the idea of adding the ethereal background vocals." Hibbert's input is hard to quantify: various tapes of the Drive-In recordings do not clarify what was done before Hibbert's appearance and what was added afterwards. Either way, when they left, Hibbert says it was with "the essence of a 45 rpm single . . . A record that was just full of energy, that made people want to dance, that was kind of fun, and kind of mysterious all at once. It had an innocence, yet a slightly sardonic angle to it too, which to me is almost the quintessential American pop single."

Mitch Easter, who had created an absurd but adorable dub mix of 'Radio Free Europe' in his spare time that further endeared him to the group, wasn't so sure. "I told everybody, 'I think it's worse, I think it's murkier than the original mix.'" He now volunteered to come up with a third mix on his own time. He sent it down the following week.

When R.E.M. and Johnny Hibbert got together in Atlanta – at Bombay Studios – to make a decision, says Hibbert, "I had the attitude that if I was going to finance the manufacturing, distribution, the finished product of this single, it was to have my idea of what was airworthy." That meant his mix. The group favoured Mitch's most recent offering. Peter Buck particularly, says Hibbert, became adamant about it. "I don't know whether it was lack of sleep, or what induced this unreasonable attitude on the part, particularly, of Peter. But . . . it was my decision. I said, 'This is my favourite mix, and the way I think the record will sell is if it has this mix.'"

Further technical disagreements ensued over the mastering, and the initial test pressings were sent back as unacceptable. "I would be the first to declare the final product was not hi-fi," says Hibbert. "But it was I think as good as we could do with the budget."

Certainly the version of 'Radio Free Europe', backed with 'Sitting Still', that came out in late July 1981 on Hib-Tone Records lacked a vast amount of top end compared to Easter's mix that would eventually show up on the compilation *Eponymous*. But that was only clear to those on the inside: judged against anything else it was an astonishing début single. A feast of ringing guitar lines, melodic bass inflections and refined backing vocals set to a stomping foursquare beat with a resoundingly simple chorus, 'Radio Free Europe' was a great power pop song – but its shrouded vocal lines lent the track an indefinable edge that made it so much more. 'Sitting Still' was lighter, its guitars janglier, its vocals equally muffled. Overall, it was the definitive garage record of its era, from its release on a tiny new label run out of an Atlanta apartment, through its mid-Sixties, vaguely psychedelic sound, its almost deliberately obtuse sleeve featuring a blurred, indefinable Michael Stipe photo backed with an aerial shot of the group taken by Carol Levy, to its very recording in a suburban garage.

Before the record's release, the band understood the need to get their legal affairs in order. Less so than the contract that Hibbert had put in front of them, they had become concerned by the discovery of other R.E.M.'s and Rapid Eye Movements across America, and when they saw their friend and fan Bertis Downs on the streets one day, they stopped him and asked for advice.

Bertis, still a second year law student, reiterated what he had always been telling the band, that "Someday you're gonna sell a million records and you have to be prepared," prompting the usual strained laughter. Downs was delighted to hear that the band was putting out a single, though, and offered to look over the contract. When he did, he was horrified to see that the group was giving up ownership of the publishing on the songs. "I told them it was a bad mistake," he recalls, "but they'd already kind of agreed to it, and committed to it, and the guy had already pressed up the singles and it was ready to come out. And he had copyright notices on everything. There wasn't much we could do. My view was that from the very beginning, these guys are great great great song-writers, and it just seemed to be really short-sighted to take no advance and give someone else a piece of that. It just seemed they should always keep that themselves."

Putting his talents where his mouth was, and working for free, Bertis helped his friends set up their own publishing company, Night Garden Music, and their own corporation, R.E.M./Athens Ltd. In each case, recognising Jefferson Holt's total commitment to their cause, they cut him a piece of the action. Jefferson was now the official fifth member.

Curiously, as manager, Jefferson did not appear to have done much negotiation on behalf of his clients with Hib-Tone. Hibbert recalls Holt as "sort of like a school chum on the fringes, who was doing a really good job of bringing a fledgling band out of the woods." But he also recognised a particular trait in Holt that good managers have to be born with. "Jefferson had a terrific political acumen; he always had a good sense of which way the wind was blowing."

"Jefferson is the greatest," said Mitch Easter in 1989, "because he's got this goofy persona, but you can tell he's smart. His mum was a politician, he went to Oxford, he's this educated guy who likes to act like the world is ridiculous and he's just totally boggled by it all, he's actually really sharp."

By most accounts, Jefferson would like to have had the group entirely to himself. "He always made it a point to be the one and only as far as the management goes," says Sandra Lee Phipps, who, despite her initial view of Jefferson as an 'asshole', was by this point his steady girlfriend. But he needed Bertis Downs. "Jefferson can deal with people," observed Phipps. "But Bertis can deal with all the rest of it. He's really the brain in a lot of ways behind making it happen. Bert is also the biggest, manic R.E.M. fan that ever lived."

And so it fell to Bertis Downs to advise the group to limit their term with Hib-Tone to a shorter period of time than the whole year that Hibbert had asked for, and to ensure that the contract covered only the one single. Hibbert agreed to these eleventh-hour demands, taking the attitude that he didn't "want to be a stone around the necks of striving young musicians."

Both R.E.M. and Johnny Hibbert agreed early on to give away the entire first pressing of 1,000 if necessary to create a reaction. The band, who saw the single mainly as an opportunity to improve their live bookings, spent hours sending copies to promoters up and down the country, and for good measure, to every magazine that mattered. The record impressed the club owners: by the end of 1981, R.E.M. had expanded their circuit to include Florida to the east, Texas to the west, major eastern cities like New York and Washington D.C., and northern industrial towns like Minneapolis and Madison, Wisconsin.

Despite these successes, Johnny Hibbert slipped rapidly in R.E.M.'s favour. This was officially put down to problems unfortunately common with a new independent label: he could not afford a repress until he had the money back on those sold, and in the meantime, the stores went empty, if they stocked the record at all. But the major, unstated reason, was a personality clash. R.E.M. and Jefferson Holt had become a tight-knit unit with their own sense of vision; anyone who did not see things as they did was unwelcome. And Hibbert appears to have taken the attitude that his opinions as label owner should predominate, which only grated with a band that preferred to operate by consensus.

Hibbert thought that, considering the success of 'Radio Free Europe', which was getting college play just as it was getting rave reviews, he deserved a repeat opportunity. "Given their alleged desire to do things homegrown, keeping control and so forth, I don't see what it would have hurt to have done another record, to have done a follow-up, to have done another six months." But he could see it was not to be, and blamed Holt's increasing influence on the band as a prime reason. "A manager's authority or grasp or control of a band is tenuous at best, and I think that everything that can be brought to bear to keep potential suitors, other interests and so forth away . . . is to a manager's advantage. It's very hard of me to believe that outside of Pete, the whole band would create the ill will completely on their own."

He has a point: Kathleen O'Brien says she too felt herself being quickly brushed aside from any managerial role when Jefferson entered the picture even as she recognised that Holt was the right man for the job. Yet he was not unyielding. He understood the importance of Bertis Down's instinctive legal acumen to the group's survival and prosperity. And he was willing to entertain other possible benefactors, as long as they didn't attempt to control proceedings the way Hibbert had. In particular, Holt was willing to entertain David Healey, an art student from Princeton, New Jersey, who had been so captivated when the band played a party there in June that he too moved to Athens, almost immediately. Healey wanted to launch a record label, Dasht Hopes, with R.E.M., and unlike Hibbert, had the money to do so. Undaunted by their past experience – primarily because Healey proved himself as a friend and compatriot first – the group readily agreed and began work on an EP.

Whether it was always their intention to return to Drive-In has since been disputed. Jefferson Holt apparently began looking for other studios around Atlanta, until Mitch Easter cornered him at a gig in Greensboro in August and insisted upon another chance. The problems with 'Radio Free Europe' (such as they were) had been down to the mix and the mastering; he reminded Holt that no one had ever voiced discontent with the original recordings.

The band appeared to agree. They returned to the Drive-In for three days in October '81 on David Healey's money, "confident enough to be quietly arrogant about our talents," as Peter Buck put it. As a result, on this session more than any past or to come, they followed no rules but their own. They set the bass amp up outside, and frequently the vocals too. "We had this really almost flip attitude about recording," says Mitch Easter. "Or maybe it was me thinking, 'This isn't how you're meant to do it, so let's do it.' They appreciated that spirit as well."

Almost an entire album's worth of material was attempted, most of it brand new and following the path of mystery and intrigue introduced by 'Gardening At Night'. Apart from a re-recording of 'White Tornado' and an abandoned '9-9', the group recorded 'Ages Of You', '1,000,000', 'Gardening At Night', 'Carnival Of Sorts (Boxcars)', 'Shaking Through' and 'Stumble'. For the last of these (which included a reference to Michael Lachowski's Athens Party Phone, "We'll stumble through the A-P-T"), Mitch indulged Peter's fantasy and inserted a backward guitar among the myriad percussion effects. Easter, no mean guitar player himself, realised that in Peter Buck he was dealing with a distinctive talent.

"He played a lot of arpeggios, and he played all these kind of open chord positions with this combination of fretted strings and open strings, and I thought that was attractive. Having seen a lot of half-assed lead guitarists, it was interesting to see somebody who didn't try and be a lead guitarist, but just played this type of rhythm guitar that wasn't strumming either. It wasn't like he was playing anything that had never been heard before, but the fact that that was his sound all the time on the songs, and they were written around that, was pretty groovy."

As well as finding time to watch a firework show and see a band perform over those three days, R.E.M. even put down a marathon "beat garbage dada thing" as Mitch describes it, called 'Jazz Lips'. It was an avant-garde collage of loops, feedback and effects topped off with Michael reading a beatnik sex story from an obscure Sixties skin magazine from which they took the title.

"We probably wasted a whole night doing it," says Mitch. "But we were having a great time. When you get involved in the process, and everyone's thinking alike, you don't even think about whether anyone else wants to hear it or not. You just go for it."

R.E.M.'s decision to entrust a record to David Healey reflected not so much a readiness to repeat the Hib-Tone experience as an acceptance that there was hardly a record label in America that would consider taking them on. In 1981, the only underground movement that could have been construed as national was hard core punk, which by its very nature was avidly anti-commercial. When it came to searching out new trends to sell, the American majors were looking to the UK, from where The Police had proved themselves the first "new wave" band to have mass appeal, from where Adam Ant looked set to do likewise, and from where Soft Cell's 'Tainted Love' was on its way to becoming the big international hit of the year: what would become the so-called Second British Invasion, all synthesizers, lop-sided haircuts and androgynous clothing, was just beginning to gather speed. In this environment, R.E.M. recognised, no taste maker would pay much heed to an all American garage band from Georgia.

The only US company that seemed remotely suitable was I.R.S., whose roster included The Buzzcocks, The Cramps, The Go-Go's and the Fleshtones, and who had the power of A&M Records' distribution behind them. That the label was owned by Ian Copeland's brother Miles gave R.E.M. a possible introduction, and so Bill Berry asked Ian to help them get signed. The agent explained he would gladly shop the band around all the record labels and was immediately corrected by a group that even at this early stage, set itself extremely specific goals from which it would not be swayed. R.E.M. wasn't interested in major labels, Copeland was told. R.E.M. was only interested in being on I.R.S.

"Well, that's easily done," Copeland assured Bill, suggesting he be remunerated for arranging the deal later and giving Miles a copy of the original three-song demo. But when Ian mentioned that the band were friends of his from Macon, Miles promptly wrote them off for that very reason. Ian Copeland continued to help R.E.M. out with the occasional prestigious live show, but he couldn't deliver the record deal they wanted.

Mark Williams, a DJ in Atlanta and college radio rep for A&M (which distributed I.R.S.) now went in to bat for R.E.M. He sent a copy of 'Radio Free Europe' to the label's 23-year-old vice-president on the west coast, Jay Boberg (whom Ian Copeland also claims to have serviced). The reaction was favourable, and Williams encouraged Boberg to see the band play when they would all be in New York for a college radio conference at the end of October. R.E.M.'s show at the Mudd Club was not graced by Boberg's presence.

R.E.M. might not have meant anything to a west coast executive, but among New York's inner circle of rock critics and trend-setters, they were becoming a name to drop. The wheels set in motion by Christgau's comments in the *Voice* turned faster when their tape and single picked up favourable mentions in *New York Rocker* and *Soho News*. The latter was nothing short of ecstatic, imploring New Yorkers to see the group on their third visit to the city, at The Pilgrim Theater in the depths of the Lower East Side on September 16. When R.E.M. took the stage that night, it was to a warm welcome; when the PA broke down, and the group played instruments to fill the gap, the reaction was near hysteria.

"I remember everyone going wild," says Buck. "I guess usually

Comhairle Cathrach
Bhaile Átha Cliath
Dublin City Council

March
2019

What's On
in
Ballyfermot
Library

Enquiries to
Ballyfermot Library
Ballyfermot Road
D10 WV02
Tel. 01 6269324
Email: ballyfermotlibrary@dublincity.ie

DUBLIN
UNESCO
City of Literature

Exhibitions

- "1916 Remembering the Leaders Art
  Exhibition"   Room 4
  presented by Ballyfermot Youth Service

- Roger Casement in Peru, Exhibition in association
  with Embassy of Peru   Main Floor

- Photographic and Audio Visual Exhibition to mark
  International Women's Day. Matt Talbot Trust
  Room 1

- World Book Day Literary Showcase for local
  Primary Schools   Room 4

Displays: Adult / Children's Library

- Bibliotherapy Books - Book Display

- Healthy Ireland At Your Library - Book Display

- Teen & Young Adult Books - Book Display

- New Books - Adults & Junior

- Work Matters - Book Display

Events

Ballyfermot Heritage Group Meeting — every 2nd
   Thurs in month @ 7.00pm: 7th & 21st March

Traditional Music performance with local musicians to
mark Seachtain na Gaeilge. Tues 5th March @
                         Tues 5th March @ 12.30pm

Events cont.

Chair Yoga & Meditation, all levels, ages and abilities
Every Thursday at 11.30am

Irish Language Class for adults. Elementary/Lower
Intermediate Level. A 5 week course each Tuesday.
Starts Tues 12th March @ 6.15pm

Traditional Music performance with BCFE students and
local music group from De La Salle school to mark
Seachtain na Gaeilge.
Thurs 14th March @ 12.00pm

Getting Citizens Online, basic computer skills using a
tablet or laptop. Course takes place over 4 consecutive
days. Tues 19th - Fri 22nd March from 2.00-4.30pm

Children's Events

"Baby Bounce" Toddler Storytelling each Tuesday at
11.00am.
"New" Irish/English Bi-Lingual Toddler Storytelling
each Fri. 11.30am - 12.15pm

Book Clubs

"Monday Afternoon" Book Club - meets **2nd Mon of the
month @ 2.30pm (next meeting 11th Mar)**
New members always welcome

Facilitated Groups

**Ballyfermot Creative Writing Group (adults)
meets Weds 6th and 20th Mar 2019 @
6.30pm
New Members Always Welcome**

"Ballyer Traditional Hub" - Come and try out a
musical instrument, maybe join in with other
musicians.   Saturdays from 11.00am - 1.00pm

"Smashing Barriers", it does what it says on the tin
- it smashes barriers for adults with a disability
through the medium of drama.
Thursdays 10.00am - 1.00pm
Contact Maureen at 085/2277033

Getting Citizens Online - Beginners Course on Computer use. Leave your name at the desk for possible
future courses

<u>**Library Opening Hours:**</u>
**Monday -Thursday: 10.00am - 8.00pm
Friday & Saturday: 10.00am - 5.00pm**

when PAs break, everyone says. 'Well, we'll come back later.' We were used to playing bars, where fuck! You get paid, you gotta play."

One New York promoter particularly intrigued by the Athens scene was Jim Fouratt, who along with writer Tom Carson, visited the Georgia town for a week that fall. Both men had received and admired 'Radio Free Europe' and were surprised to find R.E.M. so unpopular among the other Athens bands; Fouratt recalls being made to feel "really embarrassed" for liking the single. And when taken to see Linda Hopper and Lynda Stipe's band Oh OK support R.E.M. in Atlanta, their hosts even suggested leaving before the headliners. Fouratt insisted on staying and he and Carson were subsequently blown away by the band that night. But at a price: on the drive back to Athens, Fouratt recalls, "It was clear that I was not hip."

Fouratt was setting up a production company with New York producer Kurt Monkacsi, and R.E.M. seemed an ideal first act to take on in the hope of signing them to a major record label. With their contacts at RCA – specifically, Kurt was engaged to the label's A&R manager Nancy Jeffries – they commandeered free studio time for the new year. Fouratt arranged it around the reopening of his club Danceteria on February 3 and 4, which he asked R.E.M. to play. "I wanted them to open up because I thought it was very hip," he says. "I knew I would get critics."

By the time the group played the shows, that hip quota was even higher. 'Radio Free Europe' had featured in Robert Palmer's prestigious roundup of the Top 10 Singles Of The Year in the *New York Times*, and Tom Carson, still stunned by the show in Atlanta, had told the *Village Voice* readers that 'Radio Free Europe' was, "plain and simple, one of the few great American punk singles".

Why R.E.M. should have appeared so credible to trendsetters among New York's artistic community and yet not to those in their Athens hometown possibly had something to do with the 900 miles between them. Jim Herbert says that, "Up north, they thought 'This is exotic', whereas down here, it may not have seemed quite so strange. Some people argue that we didn't quite get it because it didn't seem so unusual."

Neil McArthur, another member of the Athens art crowd who admits to viewing R.E.M. as "a traditional pop band" when they formed, verifies this. After moving to New York in the summer of '80, he returned south on a visit and, seeing R.E.M. live, "was just really struck by the southern glow they projected." New York enthusiasts saw R.E.M. as maybe the first post-punk band to emerge unapologetically from the south and imbue their sound with the region's intangible aura; the more cynical among the Athens intellectuals saw such efforts as pandering to Yankee pre-conceptions of southern obfuscation, especially allowing that only one of R.E.M. had been born in the south. Peter Buck and Michael Stipe came in for especial criticism (at least Berry and Mills had attended school together in Macon), as if they were trying a little too hard to live up to the cliché of writers like Flannery O'Connor. And yet, it should be emphasised, R.E.M.'s guitarist and singer did as much to champion the south from a post-punk's perspective as any other musicians from the era. Sometimes it takes an outsider to offer a fresh and slightly distanced perspective on a scene or a region that locals take for granted.

In New York on February 1 and 2, recording seven songs at RCA's studio, R.E.M. surprised producer Kurt Monkacsi with their professionalism. He wasn't to know they had come north straight from another two-day session at Drive-In, where they had put down a furiously paced take of a song 'Wolves'.

The recordings in New York proved equally speedy. And though rarely discussed by R.E.M. obsessives, there's an accessibility to these tapes that indicates why Fouratt and Monkacsi were wise to gamble on the Athens group. R.E.M. had never been afraid of pop music and, assuming that Michael Stipe made himself heard, as he did on these recordings; that the snare drum accented the off beats, as it did; and that the group didn't complicate proceedings with overly smart or deliberately obtuse arrangements (which, probably for reasons of limited time, they didn't), then the group's commercial appeal could be laid bare for all to see.

The group committed three songs to tape for the first time at RCA ('Romance', 'Laughing', 'Catapult'), re-recorded three from the October sessions at Drive-In ('Stumble', 'Carnival Of Sorts' and 'Shaking Through') and added the new song they'd just recorded with Mitch Easter on the way to New York ('Wolves'). All seven reveal R.E.M. as a power-pop band *par excellence*, the kind of group that with a little moulding from the record label and with a few compromises by the band, could be considered as contenders for the mainstream.

There weren't that many groups occupying territory similar to R.E.M., however, and those that did exist – like The dB's and The Bongos – were having problems getting released in the States. This meant that, pop accessibility notwithstanding, RCA would be taking a risk in signing R.E.M., and that was one thing the label was not known for.

"RCA is notorious for not being timely in their decisions," says Monkacsi. "They've missed a lot of good chances because they're so big and it takes them so long to make up their own mind." Recognising as much, R.E.M. proved its talent for astute career moves by staying committed to the David Healey/Dasht Hopes EP despite the major label interest. As RCA's A&R department hummed and hawed, R.E.M. gave the major label indecisiveness not a second thought and went back to the Drive-In yet again in mid-February for mixing. On March 9 they sent Mitch Easter to Sterling Sound in New York to master a five-song EP; they were not going to skimp with the sound quality this time. 'Ages Of You' they dropped from the running order.

★ ★ ★

R.E.M. thought they had played enough no-hope little bars in their two-year existence to last a lifetime in hell. But The Beat Exchange just off Bourbon Street in New Orleans, where they were booked on March 12, 1982, outdid them all, a junkie's haven with only a handful of patrons. In the middle of the show, the sound man simply disappeared, leaving the PA system to hiccup its way through the rest of the night. Afterwards, Michael Stipe sat in the tiny dressing room trying to laugh off their latest disaster when a smartly dressed young man walked up and introduced himself.

"Hi, I'm Jay from I.R.S.," he announced.

"I was afraid of that," the singer replied.

At Mark Williams' suggestion, Jefferson Holt had mailed Jay Boberg an early tape of the proposed EP. The young label Vice-

President who had enjoyed the commercially apparent 'Radio Free Europe' but not acted upon it, was immediately won over by the new, less obvious material. Despite some scepticism from colleagues (*Where were the tunes? What was the band singing?*) Boberg asked Holt to keep him informed of upcoming live dates. Fortunately for the band, Boberg's girlfriend was attending university in New Orleans, which when he saw R.E.M.'s limited itinerary gave him a great opportunity to go and see her at his employer's expense. Despite the junkies, despite the bad sound, he recalls turning to his girlfriend three numbers in and telling her, "I'm going to sign this band." Over lunch the next day, the two sides talked. Less than three years out of university – hell, he was younger than Peter Buck – Jay Boberg seemed to understand what the band did, and as importantly, *didn't* want to do. He was particularly intrigued by R.E.M.'s subtlety on tape.

"The thing that made me play the cassette again and again was that it kept getting better," he recalls. "It was not the kind of thing you listened to once or twice, casually, and said, 'Oh my God! This is tremendous!' It had a depth to it."

Boberg subsequently offered R.E.M. a deal. I.R.S. would release the EP R.E.M. had been working on, and then sign the band for five albums. The group would get good royalties against modest advances. "We agreed with that philosophy wholeheartedly," says Peter Buck, "because we figured the more we owed a record company, the more control they had over us."

Unknown to Holt and Downs, who assumed that Boberg carried the clout to make his own decisions, Boberg still required Miles Copeland's consent to sign the band, which he had not yet acquired. It was proof of Boberg's belief in R.E.M. that he wanted to present a *fait accompli* to his superior, yet had he confided in Miles earlier, he might have found out how hard Ian Copeland was already pushing on the band's behalf. As it was, says Jay, Miles told him, "If Ian will book them, you can sign them."

Ian Copeland at this point was already in the unprecedented process of signing R.E.M. to F.B.I., with or without a record deal. The following that R.E.M. were building in every little town they played, not to mention the acclaim the New York élite was pouring down on them, was ample justification for such an honour. It is nonetheless unthinkable that any band would have enjoyed the same good fortune without the relationship that existed between Copeland and R.E.M.'s rhythm section. Ever since Mills and Berry had befriended him in Macon, Copeland had promised himself, 'If they were going to be in a band, I was going to be their agent.'

Egos being as they are in the music business, there is continual dispute over who really got R.E.M. signed to I.R.S. Jay Boberg is right when he says that, "The deal had been done before I ever talked to Miles about it," just as Ian Copeland is correct when he insists that, "There's no question I was on to I.R.S. to please sign this band six months before Jay went to see them." Miles Copeland claims, incorrectly, that he agreed to sign the band as soon as he realised how serious his brother was, and correctly, that "the initiating factor was F.B.I." So adamant was Ian Copeland that he had got R.E.M. the deal they wanted, he claimed his "point" (a 1% royalty) as he had previously, if perhaps vaguely, discussed. Boberg, taking the attitude that he had discovered the band through the usual channels, and that the relationship between I.R.S. and F.B.I. was incestuous enough already, bravely refused to pay it, and Ian doesn't appear to have pushed his brother Miles on the issue. Indeed, it's worth considering that, as R.E.M.'s unchallenged agent, and given that he could now book the band with the support of a well-known independent label, Ian Copeland was already a beneficiary of the group's record deal and didn't need further compensation. In the end, Bertis Downs, whose ability to deliver accurate legal advice found him placed on a salary by the band after the deal was signed (though it was negotiated on R.E.M.'s behalf by experienced New York City lawyers), agreed Ian should get a single point on the first album alone, to be paid directly by the band.

Jim Fouratt and any proposed deal with RCA were left behind. The more Fouratt pressured Holt to consider a major label, the more he came to the conclusion that Bill Berry's loyalty to the Copelands prevailed. Perhaps so, but it seems more likely that it was the band's eagerness to get on with the job here and now – and their understanding that major labels were slow-moving behemoths – that swung them away from RCA.

"We were in kind of a hurry at that point," admits Peter Buck. "We were writing songs like mad. We wanted to tour the country, we wanted to go overseas, we kind of realised this was possible. We were in a real creative space, and we just didn't want to sit around for two years waiting."

Fouratt and Monkacsi lost nothing financially and stood only to gain credibility should R.E.M. succeed; they were hardened New York professionals and accepted the decision accordingly. David Healey, however, who had put up the money for the EP's recording on the understanding he would be releasing it, was devastated at being cast aside. He felt betrayed, and with no role to play in the R.E.M. organisation, left Athens almost immediately in dejection. Only in time would he come to understand the group's decision and resume his friendship with them.

Johnny Hibbert had harboured no such illusions that the group would stay loyal to him, despite the 7,000 single sales that pointed to 'Radio Free Europe' as a bona fide success. But he did still own the publishing rights to the single. I.R.S. wanted to re-release the songs, and when R.E.M. explained their short-sightedness at having signed them away – and their insistence that they would never again allow anyone else to own a piece of their publishing – Jay Boberg encouraged the group to buy themselves out of their relationship with Hibbert, making allowances for such among the advances.

Fortunately for the band, Hibbert needed the cash. "I was real hurting for money," he admits. "And had certain pressures and crises in my life at the time. I didn't have anyone really close to me who understood the music business enough or had the discretionary income to help me through the problems." All he had were two songs by a group undoubtedly going places. He considered that I.R.S. might be interested in co-publishing, but couldn't get anyone to talk to him about it on the phone. Jay Boberg's understanding is that it would be entirely impolitic for the label to get immersed in the group's previous relationship, especially allowing that the group had made it clear its publishing was not for sale.

Johnny Hibbert's memory is that R.E.M. then called him asking to buy back their songs. Prices were discussed. Peter Buck's memory is that Hibbert said, "'I've got this publisher who publishes disco songs who will remain anonymous. I'm going to sell the rights to those two songs for $10,000. And he's not going to let you record them. So you have to buy the rights back from me for $10,000.'"

Neither party disputes what happened next. R.E.M. decided to call Hibbert's bluff. They offered him $2,000 not just for the publishing, but for the parts, the artwork, the rights to repress, everything to do with the single.

Hibbert could have called the group's bluff in return, whether or not he had another publisher in the wings. His ownership of the songs was legally watertight, and as long as he paid the writers their royalties on time, no one could force him to let them go. In the long run, they may have made him a wealthy man. In the short run, he could have continued pressing the single, demand for which was only likely to increase as the band became more popular. But he didn't have the cash flow to carry him through. Besides, the group raised the stakes when they offered him just $2,000. "The band swore they would never ever release 'Radio Free Europe' and 'Sitting Still' on vinyl again if I didn't sell it to them," says Hibbert; it's a threat Buck has confirmed.

Keen to continue Hib-Tone Records, Hibbert says he was encouraged by R.E.M. to believe that if he sold up, "it would present me to the music world, and artists in particular, as a fair player." In the meantime, he took on work as a roadie. Backstage at the Atlanta Omni one afternoon, Andy Slater, a former school friend of Peter Buck's and now a hip young writer with *Rolling Stone*, approached him.

"He said, 'Give the band what they want'," recalls Hibbert. "'Give them a good deal, and get out of their hair. If you don't, your name's gonna be mud.'" Concerned at "the threat of a black-balling" and desperate for money, he sold up for $2,000. He never heard from the group again.

It was the first example of R.E.M.'s tendency to close ranks when they see themselves challenged by outsiders. While the group's individual reputations as inherently good people has rarely been questioned, neither has their ability to play hardball if needs be. The way R.E.M. saw it, Johnny Hibbert took a recording they'd already made on their own dime, messed with it, exploited their naïvete to get the publishing free, released a poorly mastered single that they never saw a penny in royalties from, and when the group tried to buy back what they believed to be rightly theirs to begin with, then in Buck's words, "he did try to blackmail us."

Hibbert saw himself as having stepped in to promote a young band that didn't realise its own potential, as having put his own money on the line, as having legally and honestly acquired the publishing, as having given the group an otherwise hassle-free recording contract, as having done everything possible to make the single as successful as possible, only to believe that, when attempting to regain some of his outlay at the point that the group were clearly leaving him behind, he was threatened by the group's acquaintances with a local "black-balling".

Both parties considered it a harsh lesson. "If I were to wish for an alternative course," Johnny Hibbert said seven years later, "then I really wish I'd just played hardball with them, period. I wish I'd given them what they have come to expect, what their preconception of a record label is. The difference was, I wasn't really a record label. I considered myself a fellow musician."

"An experience like that is good to learn in the negative," says Pete Buck. "We learned a lot of things: never ever again, we will never give up rights to our songs."

R.E.M. signed to I.R.S. Records on May 31, 1982. The very next day, they were back at the Drive-In recording a slower version of 'Wolves' and touching up the mixes. Their début EP, *Chronic Town* was released on August 24, 1982.

★   ★   ★

The period of intense activity leading up to their record deal with I.R.S. may have kept R.E.M. away from Athens for long periods at a time, but it also ensured they made the most of the town while they were there.

Just after Bill Berry had left Love Tractor because of R.E.M.'s supposed single-minded determination, Michael Stipe sat down with Lee Self, guitarist with the band Vietnam, and formed another group. Stipe had already experimented with all-out noise with a short-lived outfit called Gaggle O. Sound, and now he went the whole way. Tanzplagen was the German word for dance torture, and Michael's choice of name was an apt one. The music was harsh and experimental, built around Lee Self's distorted guitar motifs, the untrained Neil McArthur's bass melodies, and the tumultuous drumming of Oh OK's Dave Pierce. Michael Stipe, in Lee Self's words, "had an old, gigantic, lumbering super-deluxe extra-big Farfisa organ with two keyboards and a big reverb unit which was kicked and shaken and dropped continuously during any given performance"; Stipe and Self both sang. The result was a glorious mess – what one onlooker recalls as "heavy metal dance disco before there was such a thing" – and the Athens art crowd loved it.

"One of the reasons we became friends and started working together," says Lee Self of his relationship with Stipe, "was that I was one of the few local musicians at the time to really respect and appreciate R.E.M." Certainly, Michael Stipe's standing among the art crowd was severely damaged by his continued participation in the much derided R.E.M., and his role in Tanzplagen allowed him to regain some of that respect while indulging his artistic pretensions at the same time. Understanding this, R.E.M. encouraged his participation; in fact Tanzplagen had been due to support R.E.M. at Tyrone's a few days after the club mysteriously burnt down in January 1982.

Tanzplagen was a serious enough venture to undertake a tour of nearby states, and record a single – far less turbulent than the unlistenable live tape Michael Stipe would hand furtively to visiting New York critics – that included a duet between Michael and his sister Lynda. Its planned release on Dasht Hopes became exactly that when R.E.M. signed to I.R.S. and David Healey left town. Lee Self promptly moved to the natural habitat for his musical ambitions, Germany.

Seemingly at odds with its musical eclecticism and intellect, Athens during this era also experienced the formation of a private society for the male party animals in town. 'Men's Club' was a loose organisation that included virtually all of Athens' male musical entourage, among them Bill Berry and Mike Mills, the men in Pylon, and most of Love Tractor, Side Effects, and The Method Actors. Men's Club met at a maximum of 48 hours notice so as to enforce the spirit of spontaneity; in an attempt at formality, members were to dress in tuxedos, and to increase the air of sophistication, everyone would smoke cigars and drink spirits. These grand intentions rapidly degenerated, however, into feasts of beer and boiled peanuts.

"Everyone would intentionally be rude, and fart and burp, and tell stories," recalls Michael Lachowski. "Most of that was just posturing on a cartoonish level – telling a dirty joke and laughing super loud. We all knew as we did it that it was a joke. It was a reference to the concept of the Men's Club."

Attempts were nonetheless made to take this masculinity to extremes. "We always tried to get one girl there," recalls Mark Cline, "and she had to be topless and wait on everybody, and be in a really demeaning position." Curtis Crowe's future wife Diana volunteered – fully clothed – but "that didn't work out too well," says Curtis. "The trouble with her was we all knew her, and so we couldn't really be demeaning to her."

Men's Club therefore became exactly that, an exclusive male organisation. "There were some true social exchanges that could never have happened in mixed company," recalls Lachowski. "And that's where that specialness came in: there was this kind of *esprit de corps* that evolved. It evolved its own charge."

When Neil McArthur returned to Athens in October 1981 and heard of these gatherings, he considered it an appropriate welcome back gesture on his part to host the next one. He had no idea what he had let himself in for. The Athens women (led as usual by Sandi Phipps and Kathleen O'Brien) decided it was time to put an end to the men's chauvinism and gatecrashed the party.

"I guess they didn't understand that to tamper with our moods at that point was a real uncool thing to do," says Michael Lachowski. As soon as the girls walked in, they were seized upon and fiercely ejected. Kathleen in particular needed five men to control her as she twisted like a wildcat. It was an ugly scene.

"We thought they were going to regroup," recalls Neil, "and so, in our drunken stupor, we thought we had to barricade the doors. People started picking up every piece of furniture I had in my living room and throwing it against my front door – which included sofas and telephones and lamps and one glass table which got shattered."

The destruction at Neil McArthur's apartment convinced Bill Berry and Mike Mills, who were now living together on Barber

Street, that they would be the perfect hosts for the next Men's Club. They were. The night started with the building of a 'Moon Pyramid' of male buttocks – of which photos were taken – and ended with a paralytic Bill Berry standing on the living room table with his favourite golf club, crying 'Fore!' and launching every single piece of glass in the house into the fireplace while his companions ducked for cover in hysterics. Legend has it that it took days to remove all the splinters of glass from his face.

Five

The group that released *Chronic Town* was essentially still a garage band. R.E.M.'s live show had sacrificed none of its gritty core in accommodating the new material, and as individuals, they remained down to earth rock'n'roll fans on a constant quest for the next good time. But on record, they had turned into something else entirely. With *Chronic Town*, R.E.M. learned how to isolate themselves from the pack by becoming an enigma.

The first integral factor in the public's perception of R.E.M. was Mitch Easter's production, his carefully layered tracks and array of effects staving off an otherwise overt Sixties obsession without bringing the result too closely into line with its contemporaries.

Another key element was Michael Stipe's vocals. Swathed in blankets of fog, their haunted quality was like nothing heard in years. Unable to pick out more than a few key phrases, observers assumed they were hearing a vocal buried in reverb or drowned in the mix, something Easter vehemently denies.

"A lot of people literally ask me what the box was. But there's nothing like that going on. It was absolutely standard vocal processing you do on anybody. I've read so many people talking about Michael's vocals being buried, but they're not. You go back and listen to 'Wolves' and it's as loud as a Tom Jones record. He's out front, but he just sounds like that."

The third ingredient in R.E.M.'s recipe for intrigue was packaging. Neither the glum gargoyle on the front sleeve, the band's bemused expressions on the back, or the 'Chronic Town'/'Poster Torn' subtitles for sides one and two (whose track listing was reversed on the cover) gave the EP as much mystery as the song titles themselves. They were, without doubt, wilfully obscure: adding the word 'Lower' to the title of 'Wolves', for example, was a master stroke of perversity, giving an ostensibly clear title a completely indirect meaning. 'Wolves, *Lower*'?, people asked. '1,000,000' *what*? 'Stumble' *where*? How *many* 'Carnival Of Sorts'? And as for 'Gardening At Night' . . .

"Some people think it's about my father; some people think it's about drugs; and some people think it's about gardening at night," said Michael Stipe to this last, frequently asked question. "It's all of them." Or none, as the case may have been. He readily admitted that after the 'simple pictures' of his early song words, he had "started experimenting with lyrics that didn't make exact linear sense." He was also trying to avoid using the first, second or even third person in his lyrics.

"Part of it," explained Peter Buck on Michael's behalf, "is that as we went along we realised that we didn't want to be a straight narrative band that has stories in our songs that began and ended. You can put meaning in there – you can write a song about something without ever really referring to what you're writing about – by using evocative phrases, by association of words that you wouldn't normally associate, by repetition, by the power of the music itself and the melodies. You can get the feeling from that experience without ever actually referring to the experience itself."

Bill Berry too caught the mystery bug. A Chronic Town, he said when asked, "is a city in the state of mind". It was also a line from the song, 'Carnival Of Sorts (Box Cars)', which along with '1,000,000' most typified a newly developed R.E.M. sound built on chiming guitars and wistful refrains. 'Gardening At Night' suggested a similar yearning though its meaning was emphatically masked by Stipe's deliberate mumbling of the vocals. However, for all Mitch Easter's insistence to the contrary, it's well worth noting that the group in fact had another vocal take of 'Gardening At Night' from the Drive-In sessions, on which Stipe clearly enunciated the lyrics; that it was rejected in favour of a version on which words were barely discernible says much about the group's intent to mystify itself.

Of the EP's other songs, 'Stumble' was the most deliberately experimental, toying with rhythms and overdubs in a manner that suggested the group had been listening to some of the home-grown releases that were coming out of the British post-punk independent scene. And 'Wolves, Lower', the late replacement for

'Ages Of You', was arguably the highlight, building from spoken verses through perfectly constructed bridges into a heavenly chorus, on which Mills and Berry intoned the apparently irrelevant "House in order" as Stipe cried wordlessly beneath them. Throughout, Buck picked rapidly away at his Rickenbacker, which Easter had the sense to stereo-separate. The backward guitars after the instrumental break elevated the arrangement a step further, though the *coup de grâce* was the sampling of crickets outdoors, which were then placed, in tune, on the first beat of every other bar of the last chorus. All in all, it was the profound example of R.E.M.'s inherent instinct at work, not just for returning to Drive-In to record the song in the first place, but for going back once again when they realised the original version was too fast. It's hard to imagine *Chronic Town* sounding quite so impressive without the inclusion of 'Wolves, Lower'.

'Radio Free Europe' had sold a not unimpressive 7,000 copies or so (there were no royalty statements to provide exact figures) and picked up glowing reviews as far afield as New York's *Trouser Press* and Britain's esteemed *New Musical Express*. As a result, *Chronic Town* had something of a ready-made audience. But the EP was less obviously commercial than the single; the more that R.E.M. employed subtleties and riddles on record, the harder it was going to be to break the band. And the music business was in the doldrums.

"1980, '81, '82, the record industry was not doing well at all," recalls Jay Boberg. "A&M fired their entire college department. A lot of them were losing money, the economy was in the toilet. That was great, because we learned how to survive in a very, very difficult economic environment."

I.R.S. therefore decided to promote R.E.M. in exactly the manner R.E.M. wanted to be promoted, on a grass roots level, market by market. Given that the group had already built a following in Georgia, in New York, and in many points in between, but that I.R.S. was based in California, where the group had never stepped foot, Jay Boberg brought the group out to their biggest untapped market, the west coast, to put the personal approach into practice.

R.E.M. spent an entire month in California, gradually turning a lukewarm reception into another firm fan base. Their LA début at the Music Machine was ill attended, but they succeeded in winning over the team at I.R.S., whom Boberg had felt were somewhat dubious about his signing up to that point, and even made a video for 'Wolves, Lower' at Club Lingerie in Los Angeles, an inexpensive, single camera shot that they hated but that nevertheless got some exposure. They spent a few days in San Francisco, opened for The (English) Beat and played some dates on their way back east with their heroes The Gang Of Four. And in Los Angeles, they found other groups like Dream Syndicate and The Three O'Clock sharing their love for psychedelia and The Velvet Underground. College radio was playing them, and the press wanted to write about them. Maybe they would just stay on the road for ever.

★   ★   ★

At the beginning of 1989, talking to *Rolling Stone*, Michael Stipe reflected on the R.E.M. that was once permanently on tour. "If there's an extension of *On The Road* and that whole Kerouacian . . ." – laughing at the word and continuing – "If there's an extension of that, probably forming a rock band and touring is the closest you could get."

There was a time, from 1980 through 1982, when R.E.M. really did live on the road: four young men and a devoted manager, in the prime of life, travelling from town to town across America in a 1975 green Dodge van bought with the profits from a couple of well attended home town shows, playing a backwoods circuit no rock band had yet discovered. Permanently broke, often without a home to return to – legend has it that when they were unable to meet the rent, they simply padlocked their doors and went out on the road to earn it – frequently playing to a handful of disinterested drunkards, testing each other's nerves . . . such circumstances should split even the most determined of rock'n'roll bands. And when they don't, when that band keeps coming back for more of the same arduous lifestyle, when they actually look forward to the next gruelling trip with the anticipation of a five-year-old on an outing to the country, then it's obvious they have a fire burning of such intensity that nothing can stop them.

There were occasions when someone wanted to quit, certainly. When personality clashes reached a head, or a particular show was such a complete waste of time that someone would say, That's it, I've had enough. But each time, the injured party came to realise that they had come too far to turn back now, and that the magic of R.E.M. was the product of the four individuals combined; if one of them bailed out, the ship would probably sink as a result.

The other Athens bands could only look on with a mixture of befuddlement and admiration. "It's the standard business formula for success," observed Curtis Crowe enviously in 1989. "Have an idea and go for it morning, noon and night. Just do it with absolutely relentless desire." Pylon never had that sense of drive, and unwilling to confront the business side of the music business, ground to a halt in 1983.

Love Tractor, too, were not prepared to endure the hardships. Despite R.E.M.'s entreaties to join them on their new found circuit, they had college to attend and jobs to keep. Weekends in Georgia and the occasional trip to New York would suffice for their live schedule.

Similarly, Johnny Hibbert, for all his disappointment with the group's treatment of him, recognises what made them ever have anything to fight over. "The biggest reason that record ['Radio Free Europe'] and this band was a big success was because of the band getting in this drafty old green Dodge van that leaked exhaust up into the cab, and travelling from here to Timbuktu and back, and living like a young starving band on the road. Which meant sleeping on floors, sleeping in the truck, night after night, mile after mile. They would be gone for two and three weeks at a time. They get the credit."

"I had that kind of romantic view of going on the road with a rock'n'roll band," says Peter Buck, who has always enjoyed a reputation as the R.E.M. insomniac. "What does a band do on tour? You drink all the time and meet girls, and don't sleep. I could go a week without sleep in those days, just about. I don't think I touched a bed in two months sometimes; I'd sleep sitting up in the van on the way to the show. Or usually, we'd play, go to a party, drink, steal food from the fridge and then at around four in the morning, we'd go, 'OK, time to go on to the next town.' We'd drive into the next town, and arrive there at noon, park behind the club and sleep until five."

In 1981 Hüsker Dü burst onto the scene with an album called *Land Speed Record*, a direct reference to their ingestion of amphetamines as they criss-crossed the country, and nobody who knows R.E.M. has ever denied that the Athens band's own impressive displays of adrenalin were aided by the use of illicit substances. Indeed, Athens developed quite a reputation as speed capital of the south in the Seventies, and there are those who have only semi-joked that bands chose to play the town as much for its amphetamine connections as for its college audience. The fact that R.E.M. never made a public statement about drug use, especially as members of a scene that mostly celebrated it, says as much about the group as if they had bragged wildly of their experimentation. Such reticence was partly a certain southern professional civility at play ('Oh, let's not talk about such matters'); partly a built-in protective instinct ('We won't say anything now that may later come back to haunt us'); and partly a further and very clear example of R.E.M.'s ability to close ranks ('What we do privately is no business of anyone else's').

These traits have dictated the band's professional conduct and public announcements throughout their career, and they have come into play in other areas too – especially regarding rumours of Michael Stipe's sexuality. Away from the macho frat houses and the football team, Athens was well known as a hotbed of sexual freedom, but that didn't mean the group were ever going to comment on their individual preferences, nor did they expect anyone else from their home town to do so on their behalf. Besides which, the gaggle of home-town girls that was still following R.E.M. throughout much of its touring, the reputation of the Men's Club, and the three playing members' active libidos ensured that questions about the fourth member were rarely raised.

Besides, there was little private space to be had in those days. As Buck has told it, many nights the band slept on the road, and even when there were hotels to be had, the group was adamant it would not spend more than it could afford. "They always stayed at the Iroquois," says then-promoter Jim Fouratt of the group's New York visits. "I remember going up there and they were all sleeping in the same roll-out couch. They had a real good attitude about work and about playing. Even though they were getting all this press, they were still sleeping in one room at the Iroquois – and I paid people reasonably well."

The band were young enough, strong enough, content enough and confident enough to put up with the hardships. Despite the heavy partying – and on that personalised circuit of small clubs, someone would always offer up their apartment for a post-gig soirée – and despite the lack of sleep or comfort, they were consistently capable of putting in energetic shows night after night.

From the outset, R.E.M. saw a circuit opening among the increasing number of 'new wave nights' being promoted by the assorted bars and nightclubs around the south central area. Such nights were usually held on weekdays, the weekend reserved for the southern rock acts and their hard drinking audience or for the disco crowd, depending on location. But the inane catch-all term paid off for clubs like The Pier in Raleigh, North Carolina, whose 'New Wave Mondays' were able to attract prestigious names looking for a date on their way through to bigger towns. Local audiences slowly turned on to the fact that it just might be worth going out to these events.

As R.E.M. progressed on that circuit of backroom bars, night clubs and college parties, they noticed the same names crisscrossing paths with them: Black Flag and The Minutemen from California, The Replacements and Hüsker Dü from Minneapolis, The Neats and The Lyres from Boston . . . As they got to know these bands, and many more, by turning out for each other's shows, even sharing the same stage on occasions, they got to form friendships and a loose affiliation of kindred spirits. The major labels and FM rock stations were operating on another stratosphere, intractable and unreachable; but down here at ground zero, audiences were building, college-aged crowds desperate for something new, something alternative, something operating purposefully outside of and unaffected by the mainstream.

R.E.M.'s following grew steadily, but there was always a badly advertised or ill-arranged show to bring them back down to earth. In May 1982, living on the road to make the most of 'Radio Free Europe's surprising success, they followed up a couple of prestigious

New York dates with a midweek trip to Detroit on a night that the venue rarely even opened.

"There were five people there who happened to be driving by who were all on mescaline," recalls Peter Buck. "They enjoyed the hell out of it, they all had a great time. They asked us for an encore, and we came back out and said, 'Listen, this is ridiculous, there's as many of us as there are of you. We'll just take you to dinner.' We made $300 that night, so we took them to this Greek restaurant."

Such occasions did nothing to dampen R.E.M.'s collective spirit. "I remember playing at The Antenna Club in Memphis," says Buck, "and we were playing really well. But there were only about eight people there, and two of them were this old wino man and woman, and they were dancing in front of us, like waltzing, and slobbering on each other, and groping. Some people would think that's humiliating, but I thought, 'We're playing really well; I don't care if there's old winos having a good time and six people at the bar.' Even if you only had three people, those three people would be saying, 'God, they're pretty good.'"

On signing to I.R.S., and with the backing of F.B.I., R.E.M. might have assumed those days were over. Their two most sublime shows were yet to occur.

Driving out to the west coast in August 1982 for that first month in California involved a 1,400-mile, week-long void between Austin and San Diego. With no 'new wave Mondays' or progressive pizza restaurants in this neck of the woods, F.B.I. could come up with just one date, in Albuquerque, New Mexico. The band drove into town only to find they were opening for a Hot Legs contest.

"These professional strippers were coming and doing obscene dances," says Peter Buck, whose memory of the club is a drunken audience a thousand strong chanting for 'tits and ass'. The promoter looked at the oddly dressed bunch of Athens ex-college boys, at his raucous crowd of cowboys, and back again.

If you go on before these naked women, he told the group, I'm worried that these guys are going to kill you. Better I pay you your $500 and you go on your way. A flabbergasted R.E.M. took the cash and hurried off on the next 700 miles of their journey before the promoter could change his mind.

More than a year later, with their début album causing a noticeable stir and a considerable following in much of America, F.B.I. booked R.E.M. and Mitch Easter's new group Let's Active into an Air Force Base in Wichita Falls, Texas. Michael Stipe's sense of déjà vu as they drove up to a compound all too familiar from his childhood was enforced when they took the stage to face a sea of rednecks with crewcuts. The music that was winning them critical acclaim across America did not score points with the men of the USAF.

"There were oranges flying out of the audience," recalls Peter Buck. "They were passing notes: 'If you play one more song like this, you DIE, faggots!'"

"These guys would not get really violent, because they'd be arrested by the MPs," said Michael Stipe a year later. "But they had this mock violence and mock threatening and that was more frustrating to me than just having them come up and smash our heads in."

Not even the group's repertoire of Rolling Stones songs could appease a crowd hungry for ZZ Top and Van Halen. Finally, Bill Berry stormed offstage, leaving Sara Romweber from Let's Active to take his place and finish the show to thunderous booing.

"I remember Peter demanding the band break up over that, (because) it was so unprofessional," recalls Mitch Easter of Bill's abrupt departure. "It was actually sort of funny. Everybody got mad with everybody, and everybody was gonna quit, and so and so wasn't ever going to play in a band with so and so again. There were varying degrees of temper within the band. It takes a long time for it to sink in just why you have to put all of that aside."

A night straight out of the celebrated rock'n'roll satire documentary *This Is Spinal Tap*, the events of Wichita Falls were matched only by the drive from New Jersey to Michigan for the aforementioned ill attended Detroit show.

High up in the mountains of Pennsylvania in the still of night, Bill and Peter pull the van over at the Howard Johnsons to get coffee and relieve themselves. They ask if anyone needs anything, but are greeted by silence. Everyone is asleep.

Almost a full hour after resuming the long journey north, Mike Mills wakes up. He asks what happened to Jefferson. Peter tells him he's asleep in the back. Mike insists he's not. Michael Stipe wakes up and confirms it: Jefferson is not there. Realisation sinks in. Their manager had got out at the service stop without telling anyone, and the group had driven off without him.

With Jefferson carrying the tour float, they must turn around. But on this winding mountain road with a fence running along the central reservation, there is nowhere to do so. It's a further twenty miles before they find an exit, another hour and a half before they return to the Howard Johnsons. There, a despondent Jefferson Holt sits by the kerbside, waiting patiently. No one says a word as he gets back in and the group resume their journey, almost 200 miles and two and a half hours behind schedule.

Years later, travelling in luxury coaches equipped with bunk beds, VCRs and stereos, to towns where their equipment would already be set up and five-star hotel bookings under individual pseudonyms had been pre-paid, where the shows were already sold out and the strippers were confined to the local go-go bars, they would look back on those days in the faithful Dodge van, on the sleepless nights, the endless drinking, the disasters, the triumphs and the pocket-sized crowds they knew by name, and think, We wouldn't have missed it for the world.

★   ★   ★

Chronic Town exceeded expectations, staying on the Top five of the college radio charts for three months, and notching up 20,000 sales by the end of the year. The press buzz was considerable: in October the group received their first *Rolling Stone* story – enthusiastically penned by Buck's ex-college associate, Andy Slater – and in February, *Chronic Town* was voted second best EP of 1982 by the nation's music critics in the *Village Voice*'s Pazz & Jop Poll, T-Bone Burnett taking top place and fellow newcomers The Dream Syndicate coming third.

R.E.M. had performed live relentlessly through the second half of 1982, building their fan base town by town, and almost every month found them introducing yet another brand new song as good as, if not better than, anything they had written before. Clearly, given R.E.M.'s considerable following, critical acclaim, and palpable confidence, then the opportunity was there to make a

début album not just of merit but also of importance and popularity. Both band and label were itching to get to work on it. Jay
Boberg, who would have heard the RCA demos that had presented
the mainstream appeal lying just beneath the band's opaque surface,
and who would have known that an entire album as opaque as
Chronic Town might well see the group squander their golden
opportunity, therefore asked R.E.M. to try recording with one
Stephen Hague.

"It was a total left-field idea," says Boberg, noting that Hague's
only production credit was for the band he had played keyboards
in, Jules and The Polar Bears, fronted by singer-songwriter Jules
Shear. (The result was so unsuccessful that the band's major label,
Columbia, shelved a third album and the group disbanded.) "He
had called me up and said he was trying to get into production, and
I had a lot of respect for what he had done."

Peter Buck says the group's attitude at the time was "We'll try
anything," and so the two sides went into a 24-track studio in
Atlanta that December to work on one of the band's most overtly
accessible songs, 'Catapult'.

Once in the studio, however, R.E.M. were subjected to the
rigidity of performance and lack of artistic control so familiar for
newly signed acts; it's hard to imagine that the first recording
experience for a major label like RCA would have been any more
dispiriting. Recording to a metronomic 'click track', they played
'Catapult' so often that they lost the feel for its emotion, after
which Hague took the tapes to a Boston studio and added synthesizer overdubs that would probably have aligned the group's sound
to that of the 'Second British Invasion'.* The band was mortified,
though with customary civility it was reluctant to say so. "Steve has
done great production work . . ." says Peter Buck of the man who
would go on to make his fortune producing New Order, Pet Shop
Boys and Erasure. ". . . for bands that are not like us. It was just not
a very pleasant experience."

Mitch Easter, who watched the proceedings from the wings,
proved less afraid to speak his mind. "I just thought, 'This is exactly

* Though it's impossible to vouch for certain: this particular tape has been successfully buried, or even burned, in R.E.M.'s private vaults.

what I would expect,'" he said in 1989. "Because no doubt I.R.S. thought I was some Southern good buddy sound man friend of theirs who's not qualified to make a real record for a real record company. They'd never heard of me before, so understandably they'd go for somebody they had heard of." In fact, Easter was angry enough to consider it an example of the Yankee superiority complex at work. "I do think there's still an almighty ingrained view of what the south is, that it's populated with idiots. I just don't think that the idea of making a record down here sounded very wise to them."

Jay Boberg totally refutes this opinion – "By that point we'd already talked about signing Mitch Easter" (and indeed, Let's Active joined the I.R.S. roster in '83) – and stresses that it was just "an idea . . . I thought that even though (Hague's) musical inclination was different than R.E.M.'s, they would get along on a personal level. But they didn't."

Either way, it had already been agreed that Mitch Easter would have an equal shot at producing a new song before a decision was made; determined not to waste the opportunity, Easter opted to move up from his own 16-track Drive-In to the 24-track Reflection Studios in nearby Charlotte. But, he says, "I didn't really have the confidence in those days to walk into a studio like Mr Big Producer." He therefore asked Don Dixon to help him out.

Dixon and Easter had attended high school together, and though the former was five years older, they had similar characteristics. Dixon was a proven musician, whose band Arrogance laid claim to being North Carolina's most popular homegrown act of the era (Peter Buck had seen them, of course) and who was proving highly able behind the mixing desk too. He had helped Easter out on a mix for 'Wolves, Lower' (Easter says it "wasn't used", which suggests that it was the original, uptempo version), had been stunned by R.E.M.'s potential when taken to see the band perform live by Easter and had a particular disdain for the often dictatorial music industry.

"I think we understood things about the band the record company didn't," says Dixon. "We understood that the combination of their limitations as musicians was a big part of the sound, so you don't just throw those out, and go in and put a Curtis Mayfield arrangement on it. It was important for them to understand that we very much liked what they were doing, and we wanted to preserve that over the record company's dead body."

Although the group were, according to Dixon, undergoing "a real crisis of confidence" after their experience with Hague, they calmed down once they realised that Dixon, like Easter, had their best interests at heart, and after just two days at Reflection in January 1983, emerged with a big, bold and beautiful rendition of a new song 'Pilgrimage', enhanced by layer upon layer of Gothic background vocals.

History has sometimes had it that I.R.S. balked at 'Pilgrimage', and pushed either for the band to work with Hague or attempt a fresh recording session with a third party. That appears to be Mitch Easter's memory of events. But both band and label recall differently. "We did a really bad version of 'Catapult' with Stephen," recalls Peter Buck, "and we did the finished version of 'Pilgrimage' with Mitch and Don. And we said (to I.R.S.), 'Obviously, this is the good one and this is the bad one,' and they said, 'Well okay.'"

"They came to me (with 'Catapult') and said they didn't like it, and to be honest, I agreed with them," says Jay Boberg. "When they came back (with 'Pilgrimage') and said, 'We think we should do this thing with Mitch and Don,' I said, 'You're right, let's go do it.'"

Any A&R person walks a perpetually dangerous thin line between being his artist's confidant and his corporation's spokesperson. When the artist is interested only in credibility and the label only in commerciality, that relationship is destined to fail. As a young VP at I.R.S., Boberg was in a particularly precarious position. He was responsible for ensuring that his artists made money, and he reported directly to an outspoken, hit-minded label boss whose main job at that point was managing the biggest band in the world (The Police); as such he could not give R.E.M. *carte blanche* to be completely anti-commercial. At the same time, his record label was supposedly independent and theoretically free-thinking, which meant he could not be seen to assail the band's credibility. Ultimately, Boberg allowed his instincts as a fan to influence his decisions as a businessman: he had, after all, been won over to the group for all the right reasons (the *Chronic Town* demos, a live show under appalling circumstances) and in allowing R.E.M.'s first album to be overseen by Easter and Dixon, he astutely recognised that the group's happiness was a necessity for hipness.

This didn't stop Boberg showing up at the start of the recording sessions to freak Easter and Dixon out with a hefty pep talk about the need for a commercial record. But unlike at a studio in New York or LA, the label couldn't stop by every day to pass judgement, and once they were left alone, the team quickly relished Reflection's semi-rural isolation. But there was another bonus to the location. The studio received most of its bookings from religious organisations – from Jim and Tammy Faye Bakker's notorious PTL television ministry to less materialistic black gospel groups – and there is no question that R.E.M. inherited some of the spirituality that hung in the studio air. *Chronic Town* had opened up myriad possibilities the group now wanted to explore further, and, having begun to describe themselves to the media as 'folk rock', it was obvious they wanted to capture an entirely different R.E.M. on record from the one that performed such energetic and emotional, but ultimately traditional live shows. As a career move, it may have been the smartest decision they ever made.

To this end, acoustic guitars became the rule rather than the exception – backing tracks often featuring Buck, Mills, Berry and either Easter or Dixon all strumming the same chords together – and ideas sprang from all sides. For the new version of 'Radio Free Europe', they re-routed the studio's inherent hum through Mike Mills' bass for a futuristic intro; on 'We Walk', they amplified and altered the sound of Bill Berry playing pool underneath them; with 'Perfect Circle' they incorporated backward guitars and a childlike pattern played on both a grand and an out of tune upright piano; on 'Talk About The Passion' they brought in a cellist. 'Sitting Still', meanwhile, was left almost intact from the B-side of the Hib-Tone single.

Michael Stipe again recorded out of view, in a stairway off the control room leading downstairs, "with his match book covers that had words written on them, and slips of toilet tissue," says Dixon. The elder studio man was no more worried about Stipe's singing technique than Easter before him. "Michael had a delivery whereby you could solo the vocal and still have no idea what he was saying," says Dixon. "It's because he liked the way things sounded as much as he cared about what he was trying to say. And I think that's a big part of pop music." Dixon was equally fascinated by Mike Mills' backing vocals that eschewed traditional harmonies, interjecting to the extent of becoming secondary melodies.

So thorough were the group's arrangements, so instinctive their studio knowledge, that Dixon is hesitant to take much credit as a 'producer'. "We were interested in trying to simply supplement what they already had. For the most part we would end up with the things they had already worked out themselves in the practice room, and just sonically supplement those things and then slip some weird ambience, a sort of undercurrent, in."

"We were really strong with what we wanted to do with the record," says Peter Buck. "They wouldn't know the name of a song, say, and we'd do the basic track and I'd say, 'Okay, I want to put on this guitar, this guitar, this guitar.' Of course they were responsible for getting the good sounds."

There were still occasions when Easter and Dixon's suggestions would provoke confrontations from a group paranoid about sacrificing their soulful essence to hi-tech production values. The most memorable was when Easter recorded some backward guitars for the end of 'Perfect Circle' while the band was absent. "They came in and heard it and hated it. I thought it was great, and I was determined to defend it. So me and Dixon sort of yelled at them about that and sure enough they came back a few hours later and said, Yeah, it's okay. They were just worried about what had happened to them with 'Catapult'." The backward guitars stayed.

Such occasional disagreement aside, the month long session is remembered by all as an untroubled collaboration. "Every time the tape would roll, it was pleasurable to hear it," says Mitch Easter. "We were ignoring everyone totally and just making this record that completely out of nowhere sounded good to us."

"Mitch and Don," says Peter Buck, "thought their job was to make us make a good record, and not worry about selling records for record companies. So they were like partners in crime with us; they were protecting us from outside influences or financial influences that might come into it. So they were gambling in their own way too. For both of them, it was their first major label record. It was like. 'What if everyone hates it?' But they were willing to go that distance for us."

So smooth were the sessions that a night was dedicated to recording other material live onto two-track. Some were originals already in the group's set – 'That Beat', 'Pretty Persuasion' and 'All The Right Friends', a less blatant title than its previous 'I Don't Want You Anymore' – but the band also recorded some covers at Peter's behest, the group's archivist already thinking ahead to future B-sides. Two of these recordings would eventually end up on vinyl: Archie Bell & The Drells' 'Tighten Up', on which Easter played xylophone, and The Velvet Underground's 'There She Goes Again', on which the propulsion of Buck and Easter's dual acoustic guitars and the superb vocal harmonies made for an honourable rendition.

"When you've just got through something, you don't really know what you've got there," says Mitch Easter. When R.E.M. finished *Murmur* – an apt title indicative of tentative first steps, whispered suggestions and also, as the group were wont to say, 'one of the seven easiest words to say in the English Language' – they were excited but nervous.

"I remember thinking, 'God, I can't wait until everyone hears this,'" says Peter Buck. "Because it was different: it didn't sound like our other records, it didn't sound like us live, and it didn't sound like anything else that was coming out. It was the first time I thought all the songs were really strong; some of them were so on the money I was real happy. I didn't know if anyone else was gonna like it or not. In fact, we played it for our friends and they were all saying 'God, that's weird, it doesn't sound like you at all.'"

"I felt like we'd done a real cool thing," says Dixon of his and Easter's efforts. "But we figured it would be like a lot of other good records we'd made: it would sell a few thousand, cool people would like it and most people would never get to hear it."

They were wrong.

Six

Rarely does a début album succeed in perfectly capturing a thrill-ing new group that has already honed its craft into a distinct sound, that has the ability to capture that identity in the studio, and the purpose of mind to retain control while doing so. *Murmur* is such an album.

But it was far from an obvious classic. On first exposure, the uninitiated would be likely only to agree that there was promise lurking inside. Only over repeated playing did a web of intrigue weave its way inside the listener's conscience, subtle melodies and barely discernible phrases gradually permeating the pleasuredome until they took up residence - at which *Murmur*'s beauty became apparent.

And what beauty. *Murmur* ran a gamut of styles, from the power pop of 'Radio Free Europe' and 'Catapult' to the melancholy ballads 'Talk About The Passion' and 'Perfect Circle'. It featured deliberately deconstructed arrangements on songs like 'Moral Kiosk' and '9-9', but it also exhibited a love of convention, even of folk traditions, on 'Pilgrimage' and 'Laughing'. And it was unafraid to touch on child-like naïvete, as with 'We Walk' and its 6/8 time signature.

Yet all these styles congealed in a distinctive sound which, as per the group's intent, presented them as so much more than another energetic new wave band. There was a subtlety and intellect to R.E.M.'s compositions and arrangements that suggested a maturity far beyond their years and which endeared them to critics and older listeners; yet there was a simplicity of purpose that communicated directly to young rock'n'roll fans. In time, *Murmur* would become recognised as one of the great début albums – ever – and twenty years of repetition and competition have done nothing to dampen this impression. *Murmur* was, is and will always be a masterpiece.

Fortunately, it was recognised as such almost immediately upon its April 12 release. *Murmur* showed up on the May 14 *Billboard* chart at 190, was Top 100 a fortnight later and Top 50 six weeks after that. At the beginning of August, with the revamped recording of 'Radio Free Europe' at number 78 in the singles charts (though they little knew it, their biggest hit for the next four years), *Murmur* reached a chart peak of number 26. It was a phenomenal start.

The question begs: Why such relatively instant success? The first answer lay with college radio. With 'Radio Free Europe' and then with *Chronic Town*, the band had accrued a solid fan base on the left of the dial, aided by their willingness to visit every 100-watt station that wanted to meet them; thankful in turn to have received such personal attention and gratified that a group from their own scene had made a record of such majesty, the college radio programmers nationwide immediately propelled *Murmur* to the top of their airplay charts by the dozens and boosted the band's core following of students tenfold.

Similarly, the music critics, who were starting to see the emergence of an alternative rock movement and were keen to appoint it some spiritual leaders with a chance of living up to the role, were equally ready to be receptive. Had *Murmur* been a disappointment they would surely have stated as much, but given the album's obvious quality, they were almost unanimous in their praise. *Rolling Stone* gave *Murmur* an uncommonly high four stars ('intelligent, enigmatic, deeply involving . . . it reveals a depth and cohesiveness to R.E.M.'); *Musician* ('R.E.M. has the most hypnotising sound of any group playing rock today'), *Record* ('music of movement and portent, driven with vague obsession') and the *New York Times* ('. . . will sound as fresh ten years from now as it does today') all followed suit.

And of course, R.E.M.'s loyalty to the live circuit did not go unrewarded. They'd capitalised on *Chronic Town*'s warm reception by touring relentlessly through the second half of 1982. As soon as *Murmur* was finished, they were out for a month opening for The (English) Beat. From May through July, they toured continuously as club-level headliners. Given their energy on stage, it was inevitable that they'd sell albums on the back of their live work.

R.E.M.'s success with the three Cs – college radio, the critics, and concerts – cemented the band's cult following, and may have even been responsible for *Murmur*'s first 50,000 sales. But R.E.M.'s achievement with *Murmur*, selling 170,000 in just a few months, far outstripped what the usual alternative channels were capable of delivering. Somewhere along the line, R.E.M. transcended the scene they'd emerged from, and it's worth examining why.

Much of it was simply to do with being in the right place at the right time. The American music industry found itself in an all-time trough at the beginning of the Eighties: disco had died overnight, southern rock was mortally wounded, and punk had not success-fully translated from working-class Britain to suburban America. Punk's meltdown movement, however, the amorphous 'new wave', looked like it could make that perilous transition to the heartland and America duly reached out to Britain's pop explosion of the early Eighties like a drowning man to driftwood. By the time *Murmur* was released, the American chart was aflow with the likes of Soft Cell, Duran Duran, Culture Club, Haircut 100 and ABC: the fabled Second British Invasion.

R.E.M. benefited twice over from this pendulum swing. Firstly, the American industry was obliged to unearth indigenous bands as well as accepting those handed them on a plate by the UK. Yet the majority of left-field American music – from the complex psychedelia of The Dream Syndicate to the speed-ridden anthems of Hüsker Dü – was too awkward for mainstream ears. R.E.M.'s wistful, subtle pop was pleasant enough to be played alongside the proliferation of pretty-boy English music while simultaneously making radio look adventurous.

In reviewing the two-year old 'Radio Free Europe' in July '83 *Billboard*, the American industry Bible, admitted as much: "Even a few months ago, the dense, bass-heavy, thumping sound of this Athens, Georgia quartet would have been considered too abrasive for pop radio; but the airwaves are gradually opening up to what used to be underground music . . ."

R.E.M. readily acknowledged that the winds of change were blowing in their favour. Talking to Britain's *Jamming!* magazine at the end of that year, Peter Buck explained how because of dwind-ling listening figures, radio had been "going through a real panic situation because they don't know what to play. Then they've been hiring all these guys – who also don't know what they're doing – to tell them what to do, and they say, 'Play new music.' So what's new music? They don't know! We sneaked in the back door – 'Oh, they've got guitars, they're a little different, let's put them on . . .!' We got a foot in the door through all the confusion."

Yet while riding the new wave airwaves as American counter-parts to the 'British Invasion', R.E.M. themselves had nothing but disdain for such vacuous pop. "You'd see some little twee synth pop band that had one hit for thirty seconds and they'd get 3,000 people in America," lamented Peter Buck after the fact, "and yet a local band that made really good records and worked their butt off would play to 200 people. It was frustrating." Perhaps so, but it was the localised American bands that were building audiences for the long run, as college-aged kids across America sought out a music they could call their own, and R.E.M. conveniently found them-selves at this movement's vanguard.

They tried to downplay their good fortune – "Every city had several bands that would do it themselves, put out their own records, tour," explained Buck, "but in America, you can be a great band for five years and no one will look at you" – yet R.E.M. soon came to recognise that fate had dealt them the ace card. A year or two earlier, a year or two later, it may not have happened for them. (Indeed, it may not have happened for anyone in the States; it's impossible to claim that R.E.M. succeeded at a band of equal quality's expense.) They therefore decided that they would share some of their spoils. So while they continued to open for visiting UK acts on the F.B.I. stable, they insisted that their own support groups be drawn from an increasingly fertile pool of alternative-minded countrymen: Jason & The Scorchers, Peter Holsapple, The Replacements, Let's Active and The Dream Syndicate all benefited from this attention in 1983, and R.E.M.'s credibility on the nascent anti-new wave scene multiplied accordingly. The group was becoming a veritable Rorschach test for music fans; its blurred intent allowed people to take the four-piece for whatever purpose they wanted.

The band's self-packaging therefore played a vital part in selling R.E.M. as something more than a Sixties garage group with art-

folk pretensions. For a record brimming over with southern exoti-
cism, using a photograph of kudzu, the all-pervasive creeping vine
of Georgia, for the front cover was an inspired touch. (Buck later
admitted that the band was "looking for something real Flannery
O-Connorish," thereby adding fuel to the Athens-based argument
that they were merely playing up to southern stereotypes.) The
back cover picture of a trestle bridge outside Athens was equally
appropriate, given the vague references to travel on songs such as
'Pilgrimage', 'We Walk' and 'Catapult'. There were some at A&M
(I.R.S.'s parent company) who panicked at the proposition of
placing such obscure imagery in record stores and on posters, but
on this issue Jay Boberg sided firmly with the group. "At the time
we were really focusing on this regional concept," he says of the
label's determination to break bands market by market. "I thought
the kudzu was a regional thing that had to do with their roots and
where they came from. I really liked the fact that they had a unique
sleeve. My concern was that from a marketing standpoint, you
could walk in to a store and see it and know it's an R.E.M.
record." That was debatable in the case of *Murmur*, but in its understated manner, it said as much about the music inside as any album
cover of its era.

Yet *Murmur*'s meticulous attention to detail, believe those close
to its over-seeing, was often misinterpreted as one glorious error.

"The sophisticated aspects of the record were not appreciated
right off the bat," says Don Dixon. "It was viewed as this naïve
accidental thing, because nobody really knew who Mitch and I
were in the industry. So since they didn't know us and we were
southern, obviously we were really stupid, and we just stumbled
across this stuff. And we were so dumb we didn't know how to
make it into a real big record."

"It sounds like someone who's never mixed a record mixed the
record," admits Peter Buck, but stresses that, "We worked with
two real pro mixers, we knew what we were doing . . . We didn't
just find this thing. We had the songs written, we had them
arranged, we knew what we were doing with the overdubs, we
fought over mixes, we remixed stuff, we worked really hard to get
it just like that. That was the record we wanted to make, and
people tended to, at least in those days, just go, 'Oh well, that must

have been an accident.' No it wasn't. Mitch and Don went out on a limb to make a strange sounding record."

Murmur's strangest facet of all was, no doubt, its hide and seek vocals. The beauty of their tone aside, it was hard to decide which presented a greater challenge: interpreting the words where they were audible, or deciphering them where they weren't.

Over a period of time, the group were willing to give clues. 'Moral Kiosk' was "more or less a reaction to all those Jerry Falwell-ish TV ministries", and 'Talk About The Passion' was saying "that passion is just something you experience, not talk about". 'We Walk' Michael admitted was an example of simply repeating other people's phrases, as naïve a lyric as its tune was childlike, yet 'Laughing' drew on Laöcoon, a freak mythological figure, for inspiration. '9-9', meanwhile, had an element of the wind-up about it. "It was purposely recorded," said Stipe, "so you could never be able to decipher any of the words except the very last phrase, which was 'conversation fear', which is what the song was about."

Occasionally the group's own interpretations differed, as with 'Perfect Circle'. Peter Buck recalled how in October '82, his emotions frayed through constant touring and lack of sleep, "I was standing in the City Gardens in Trenton, New Jersey at the back door and it was just getting dark. These kids were playing touch football, the last game before dark came, and for some reason I was so moved I cried for twenty minutes . . . I told Michael to try and capture that feeling. There's no football in there, no kids, no twilight. But it's all there."

Michael Stipe countered by saying, "That song concerns my old girlfriend, and it was an intensely personal song to me. I really like that it can mean two different things. But the feeling is exactly the same as what I think about the song and what Peter thinks about the song. It's the exact same feeling but the details are different."

In the midst of such confusion, R.E.M.'s following worked with what they thought they could hear. During one interview, Stipe admitted that, "There's a line in 'Sitting Still' that apparently sounds like 'We could gather, throw up beer'. And what it really says is 'We could gather, throw a fit'." To which a nearby fan exclaimed, "You're kidding! I thought it said, 'We could gather through our fear'."

"No, but that sounds great," replied Stipe. "I might use that. It's probably far superior to what I wrote, actually."

*   *   *

The music industry repeatedly held out its arms to R.E.M. in 1983, enticing them into its protective clutch with promises of fame and fortune. The group tentatively stepped forward, found themselves crushed by the giant's bearhug, and recoiled.

The first attempt at abduction was with the video for 'Radio Free Europe'. Michael Stipe proposed as a location the rural Paradise Gardens of the Rev. Howard Finster, to whom Scott Belville had introduced him. There was no connection with the song, but the words themselves were so indirect that a non-linear video almost made sense. They were thus filmed wandering aimlessly around the Gardens for hours on end.

I.R.S. were disappointed. Video was still a new medium, but the British pop bands who were dominating, and being broken by, the new cable television station MTV, all favoured fast moving, colourful storylines. I.R.S. added footage of R.E.M. playing live, much to the group's chagrin. The group were even more dismayed that the final cost of the exercise was around half the $28,000 spent recording the album. "You hire two people to make the record, and eight people to make the video," notes Peter Buck. "I've never understood that." He had nothing but disdain for the medium. Michael Stipe merely longed for the opportunity to take full control of it.

Then on October 6, R.E.M. made their first major live television appearance, on *Late Night With David Letterman*. The producers asked that the group's leader come up to the host's desk for an interview. R.E.M., having no leader, instead suggested Letterman come down to their level to talk. They won, the nervous host chatting briefly with Buck and Mills on the stage in between a rendition of 'Radio Free Europe' and an as-yet untitled new song (to become 'So. Central Rain'). Television working on the principle of stars among stars, the garrulous Peter Buck was nonetheless paid twice that of the other members.

But the group's biggest dispute with the industry was over their greatest opportunity yet, opening for the now multi-platinum

Police on the east coast. R.E.M. had spent much of the past year on the road supporting The Gang Of Four and The (English) Beat, groups they shared an affinity and an audience with, and were at last enjoying the prestige of selling out clubs as headliners. Opening for The Police in major Coliseums went beyond what they felt was the call of duty.

"We weren't ready to play 45 minutes in a place that big," says Buck. "We didn't have the right equipment, didn't have a sound man really, didn't have a light man. Then we were going to play to people who'd never heard of us, never gave a shit."

Ian Copeland had already found in failing to convince R.E.M. to tour with The B-52's and The Clash that he himself had put forward the reasons for the group – or at least Bill Berry and Mike Mills – to say no.

"These guys had been listening to all my punk dogma. Part of what I was preaching all along was how a band should play to ten people that came to see them, rather than playing to 1,000 people who came to see someone else. And every single date The Police did in America, they never supported anyone. But that was mainly because there was no one to support. Well, R.E.M. remembered that and suddenly I was offering them all these tours and they were saying, 'Nah, we'd rather do a club tour.' And I'd say, 'But you're going to play to all these people,' and they'd say, 'Well, Ian, don't you remember when you said . . .' It was funny. I'd say, 'Guys, forget what I said!'"

The pressure to play with The Police, however, was overwhelming. The Police's agent, Ian Copeland at F.B.I., was R.E.M.'s agent; The Police's manager, Miles Copeland, owned R.E.M.'s record label, I.R.S.; and The Police's drummer, Stewart Copeland, was brother to both. The Police's new album, *Synchronicity*, was about to start a four-month run at the top of the American charts, vindication to the Copeland brothers that their instincts had been correct in bringing The Police over for relentless touring back when nobody wanted to know them. For R.E.M. to refuse the opening slot would appear not just professionally rude to the Copelands; given the familial circumstances, it would be taken as a personal insult.

So R.E.M. acquiesced, agreeing to open for The Police over five shows at three indoor arenas, then at Shea Stadium in New

95

York on August 18 and JFK Stadium in Philadelphia two days later. The money – $10,000 for 20 minutes at each of the outdoor shows – was no doubt a convincing factor.

In subsequent interviews over the years, R.E.M. gained great kudos from their pronounced distaste for the events, once calling them "the most wretched, abysmal experience of our lives". It's a viewpoint they still cling to.

"We knew it was gonna be horrible, but we got talked into it," says Buck. "It just taught us that we're pretty much right on these things. Everyone said that, 'Oh, this will make you have a hit record,' but we did the seven dates and we didn't sell one record out of that. It was a waste of fucking time."

"Very much a self-fulfilling prophecy," argues Jay Boberg on that point. "I'm not trying to say that those audiences were great, but R.E.M. could have blown them away, and I think they probably did. Those shows were probably a lot more successful in their career than they will ever acknowledge. But they hated the experience."

"I would guess they were probably miserable," says Ian Copeland. "First of all because of the fear of it all, plus they were the third act on [at the stadiums, they appeared before Joan Jett]. And they went out (at Shea) and played in the rain and probably thought they were terrible. But they didn't hear what I heard, from out in the audience. When they played 'Radio Free Europe' the whole crowd went fucking berserk. I looked up on the stage and there was these two kids I used to hang out with. My heart was going crazy. That was the moment I finally realised, 'Shit! This isn't just my buddies out there. This band is going to make me rich! And I'm going to make them rich!'"

"I don't think anyone liked us," contests Buck. "I really don't think anyone did. I'm glad I got to play Shea Stadium, it was cool. But the other dates were just boring."

Arguably, Buck was right in saying that The Police shows didn't sell R.E.M. records: *Murmur* began a rapid downward chart slide that very week. But five years later, above the stairs at the R.E.M. offices in Athens, the last photo one saw before departing was one taken from Shea Stadium's stage, R.E.M.'s backs silhouetted against a never-ending sea of umbrellas. Its central placement in

their headquarters possibly says something about its central placement in their hearts.

★　　★　　★

British rock'n'roll fans were not proud that their country was
dominating the American charts in 1983; they were actually deeply
ashamed that the 'Second British Invasion' should be so shallow
compared to the original, that which conquered the States in
the mid-Sixties and changed rock music's complexion for ever.
But, they insisted, America could only blame itself. It was apparent
to even the most enlightened British musicologist – or so he
thought – that the rock scene there had dried up after London
wrestled the title of 'punk capital' away from New York. America's
idea of "new wave" had proved laughable, The Cars and The
Knack with their skinny ties and insipid songs, and the hard core
scene of which the British had some knowledge was obviously
leading up a blind alley. There seemed to be no American band of
worth walking a middle path.

Launched into this void at the end of August, boosted by its
American success, *Murmur* was an instant critics' delight. The three
major UK music papers, *NME*, *Melody Maker* and *Sounds* were all
hustled into running stories on R.E.M. by their American corres-
pondents, eager to spread the word. The readers of these papers,
used to being bombarded with critical hype, prepared to be
disappointed.

But I.R.S. Records, strong in Britain given that Miles Copeland
had built his business there, were determined to prove otherwise,
and when the influential Friday night television programme *The
Tube* offered R.E.M. a chance to play live on the show, I.R.S. will-
ingly fronted the money to bring the band over, arranging live
dates at London's Dingwalls on November 19, The Marquee three
days later and a visit to France after that. Appearing on *The Tube* on
November 18, R.E.M. introduced themselves to British audiences
by performing 'Radio Free Europe', 'So. Central Rain' and 'Talk
About The Passion' (which was released as lead track of an EP that
week) with typical élan. The two London shows were packed to
the rafters.

The memory of that night at The Marquee remains vividly

etched on the author's memory. Compared to the perfection of the image that typified Britain's new pop culture, R.E.M. plumbed the depths of fashion, Michael Stipe wearing an ugly sweater in a club where temperatures frequently hit the 100° mark and Mike Mills looking, as ever, like the all-American high-school graduate. While Bill Berry pounded out the beat at the back, Peter Buck, shirt flapping wildly, chased his Rickenbacker around the stage with the same enthusiasm as Pete Townshend in the days of 'The Who before they signed a record contract' – as Jefferson Holt had described the experience – at the same club almost twenty years before.

English audiences familiar with casual 45-minute sets even from headliners at major concerts were amazed when R.E.M. almost doubled that in the heated club. Stipe, who had started the night motionless, clinging protectively to his microphone, ended the show tumbling all over the stage with the same disregard for personal safety as Buck. When they finally left the stage, The Marquee's walls were soaking wet.

Walking back out into the Soho night air, wrote a reviewer in the *NME*, 'I found myself dazed and reborn. This is the most vital American group of today.'

R.E.M. weren't so sure. "We like to think of ourselves as the tip of the iceberg," Peter Buck told *Jamming!* magazine. "We're not the most commercial band in the world, but we're one of the more accessible of the new American bands. It's one of our duties while we're over here to say, 'It's not a wasteland over there.' There are great bands in the midwest that you'll never hear unless you go to their town."

That was liable to change.

Seven

Every group relishes good press, and R.E.M. were never an exception. But even the four young men whose moderate success thus far owed a lot to the hyperbole of America's print taste makers must have felt overwhelmed – and not a little over-burdened – when the various critics' polls for the year 1983 hit the news stands.

The writers at *Rolling Stone* named *Murmur* nothing less than their Album of the Year – above Michael Jackson's *Thriller,* The Police's *Synchronicity* and U2's *War.* These same critics also rated R.E.M. Best New Artist and even third Top Band. The *Village Voice,* whose Pazz and Jop Poll is perhaps America's most prestigious, was almost as generous, placing *Murmur* second only to *Thriller* in the year's best albums, while *Record, Trouser Press* and the *LA Times* all pitched in with similarly high ratings.

Such bestowals of praise – saying much more for *Murmur*'s likely lasting influence than its modest sales of around 170,000 – could easily have rendered the group uncomfortable in recording its follow-up. But by the time these unanimous jury verdicts were announced, America's great white hope already had their second album in the can and were keeping busy by playing cover songs in local bars.

Aware that their two I.R.S. releases to date had presented a more nebulous, folksy, and experimental side of the band, R.E.M. determined that their second album should be harder rocking and more overtly song-orientated, a closer approximation of their live set. As a result of the continual touring and the confidence that accompanied their growing status, they were writing new material at what would prove to be a peak rate, and a week before going to Europe in November 1983, they put down a staggering 22 songs in one day in San Francisco with Elliot Mazer, Neil Young's producer.

"We were going through this streak where we were writing two good songs a week," recalls Peter Buck. "We just threw hundreds away. I don't even know where they are. We just wanted to do it; whenever we had a new batch of songs, it was time to record."

The session was as shambolic as one would expect (despite Mazer's reputation, it's hard to consider it as 'produced') and some of the recordings were off-the-cuff covers or parodies that were as much for the band's amusement as they were serious suggestions for an album. Still, the group knew to get back into the studio proper while they were on a roll. Although Mazer's name was briefly mooted as a possible album producer, there was never much doubt that the group would return to the production partnership and recording environment that had served them so well on their first vinyl outing. Over two stretches of eight consecutive days either side of Christmas, they recorded *Reckoning* – a title acknowledging and, by its very context, digging at the seriousness with which a second album is viewed – with almost effortless ease.

"They were on a roll," recalls Mitch Easter, who says he felt an unspoken understanding to ignore *Murmur*'s surprise success, rather than get bogged down trying to emulate it. "We knew that was the worst thing we could do. The minute you start to get into deliberate music you screw up, I think. And the thing that they had that was so attractive was this sort of ease of writing these nice songs. We didn't want to lose that by overanalysing them. They came in and they had a bunch of songs they wanted to record. It was that simple."

These songs were a disparate collection, reflecting the group's refusal to pigeonhole themselves, and Easter recognised the problems of collating such varied material on to one record. "When I heard the songs they had, I kept saying at the time – tongue in cheek, but not totally – that this record would be like their *Led Zeppelin II*, (which) was supposedly made in different studios all over the place because they were touring. R.E.M. were in the same position in a way: they'd had some success with the first record, they were on their way up, and they weren't making as much of a unified record. But maybe those songs would express that band-on-the-move feel. That live sound always appealed to them back in those days, and so I thought, maybe we can get that on this record."

They did, largely by refusing to labour over the process, as Mike Mills made clear a few months later in describing the group's recording techniques. "We go in there and we just knock out the basic tracks on first or second take. The vocals are pretty much the same way. We even use the reference vocals sometimes, because the more you do it, the less spontaneous it becomes. It sounds like you're trying real hard to get it perfect. But if you just go ahead and knock out the tracks and vocals, you can spend most of your time getting whatever overdubs you want and doing the mixdown. That's where we spent ten out of our fourteen days in the studio, remixing."

The speed of recording was of great pride to R.E.M. On the sleeve to *Reckoning* they listed fourteen days' work, and Peter Buck quickly chopped three of those off in interviews. To Dixon and Easter, this seemed like so much good copy.

"We were here at least 25 days," insists Dixon. "And I was here eighteen hours a day every day of that period." Mitch Easter concurs: "When I read 'eleven days', I thought, what the fuck! It was twenty days, which was still short, but it's not eleven."

Still, the Reflection diaries list only sixteen days, and confirm the group's proud claim that they even cancelled studio time, much to I.R.S.'s amazement. And, points out Peter Buck, "We took a day off to play at Friday's (the pizza restaurant in Greensboro, which was closing), and we took a night off to see a movie. We took a day off to shoot the video too, in the studio." He does, however, allow for the intensity of recording. "We would work until three or four in the morning, then Don and Mitch would get there at 10.00 . . . So by midnight those guys would be exhausted."

Don Dixon, who recalls "just being completely burned out" at the end of recording, nonetheless stresses his enthusiasm for the speedy process. "We were making the records very quickly by the period's standards. You can make records that are better thematically by making them quicker, where you don't have the luxury of second guessing yourself."

The result with *Reckoning* was a roughly hewn celebration of spontaneity, emboldened by a clarity of production and maturity of songwriting that would once more outshine its contemporaries.

At its loudest extreme was 'Pretty Persuasion', which came to be viewed as the 'archetypal' R.E.M. anthem, a rapid descending arpeggiated lead guitar motif paving the way for a verse built on emotive if inscrutable choral harmonies, underlined by ringing guitars and thrusting drums; as with most R.E.M. songs, rather than the series of catchphrases that become a traditional chorus, the focus is on a concise, repetitive refrain. And at all times, the song bristles with a wanton energy.

'Pretty Persuasion' had been in the set since 1981, when, according to Peter, "Michael had a dream three nights in a row that he was a photographer taking the last Rolling Stones picture sleeve. They were all sitting in a dock with their feet in the water and the cover was 'Pretty Persuasion'."

A Rolling Stones reference could also apply to the equally abrasive 'Second Guessing', the arrogant challenge, "Why are you trying to second guess me . . . Who will be your book this season?" met with the joyous refrain of "Here we are" that many saw as reminiscent of an equally young and confident Jagger and Co.

But *Reckoning*'s central theme was not so much the bravado apparent on the record's louder cuts as the watery metaphors elsewhere, beginning with the working title printed on the spine, *File Under Water* (which also doubled as a joke at the group's lack of easy categorisation), and evolving over the three opening songs.

'Harborcoat', the first of these, is one of the least fathomable of all R.E.M. numbers, Stipe's own band mates admitting little comprehension. Likewise, 'Seven Chinese Brothers' appears at first to be little more than a play on the proverb of the five Chinese brothers, one of whom could hold the ocean in his mouth, and 'So. Central Rain (I'm Sorry)' is ostensibly a straight narrative about severe flooding in Athens, with the phone lines down and R.E.M. unable to contact their hometown from on tour. But these two songs, along with 'Camera', are also a hymn to a departed friend: Carol Levy died in a car accident in the spring of '83, as did two passengers. Her memory lived on in the promise "She will return" from 'Seven Chinese Brothers', the helpless cry "I'm Sorry" from 'So. Central Rain', and the forlorn question "Will she be remembered?" from 'Camera'.

Perhaps it's no coincidence that on two of these songs, the producers had trouble coaxing Michael Stipe to emote sufficiently. "I remember on 'Camera' that we were having a hard time getting a vocal take that was really accurate enough," says Mitch Easter. "And Michael sort of got to where he wouldn't do it enough, and that's the one you hear. And I think it's the best one too. We had to push him to a lot of takes on that one. I still hate to make somebody sing to where they don't feel it anymore and they don't care, but I do think sometimes it takes some plain old hard work. He didn't like to do it a lot, but fortunately most times he didn't have to."

When Stipe proved reluctant to lend 'Seven Chinese Brothers' the energy the producers were looking for, Dixon found an old gospel album and threw it to the singer who, enthralled by the liner notes, began reciting them, with gusto, to tape.* 'Seven Chinese Brothers' was taped, with the requisite emotion, immediately thereafter.

It may be that on those particular songs, two of the most personal of the album, Stipe did not want to be accused by cynics of trying too hard – a criticism frequently lobbed at the singers with major new rock acts Big Country and The Alarm, as well as their mentors U2. With the success of *Murmur*, Stipe had found himself in the spotlight for the first time, and he was not necessarily comfortable with it. "Michael began being self-conscious during *Reckoning*," says Don Dixon. "During that period when they went on tour with The Police, I think it was very hard on his psyche. Michael was kind of naïve about pop music, and when he started to get compared to people, he withdrew some because of that."

But for all Stipe's restraint, *Reckoning* was hardly lacking in character. 'Time After Time' emulated the haunted spirit of the most possessed of Velvet Underground songs, while 'Camera' came good as an equally moving, if more traditionally structured ballad, replete with ghostly effects and a gentle guitar solo. On 'So. Central Rain', the sense of grief finally overcame Michael Stipe. As he emitted a hollow, wordless cry at the song's finale, he fell off balance and down the stairs that he sang from, breaking a microphone in the process; hence his voice's sudden fade before the end of the song. It may also be no coincidence that the song on which

* That recording became known as 'Voice Of Harold'.

he finally let go, literally and metaphorically, became the single.

The theme of departure was further continued with '(Don't Go Back To) Rockville', reluctantly recorded in one take to humour its number one fan, Bertis Downs and, as a joke, slowed down from its original thrash into an easy-going country song in the process. The result was almost eerily beautiful, its emotive performance carrying an appeal that crossed musical continents. Though the lyrics had a specific subject matter (Ingrid Schorr and the town of Rockville in Maryland), they were vaguely stated enough so as to apply to anyone returning to anytown, and on release the song would immediately become a standard of the new American underground, as well as lasting testament to Mike Mills' songwriting ability.

Reckoning's finale was 'Little America', a "perverse view of us driving around the country seeing things that are really nice and really horrible," said Peter Buck. Michael Stipe seemed unsure which was which. "Another Greenville, another Magic Mart," he shouted at the generic mid-America R.E.M. had just spent three years driving through, before delivering an in-joke jibe at their manager and hapless navigator, "Jefferson, I think we're lost". R.E.M. were anything but lost and they knew it. They were merely exploring a possible vocation as storytellers of small-time America.

The plethora of available songs and the speed at which the band were recording encouraged them to toy with the idea of a double album. At various points during the session, they recorded 'Ages Of You' again (as fine a song as they would ever discard, and a track that Jay Boberg had been trying to secure as a possible single for two albums in a row), 'Burning Down', a heavy metal stomp 'Burning Hell', two versions of 'Windout' (the better one with Jefferson singing), 'Mystery To Me', 'Just A Touch', and acoustic versions of 'Gardening At Night' and the Velvets' 'Pale Blue Eyes' and 'Femme Fatale'. As if this was not enough, a night of live recordings for B-sides was set aside as had worked so well during *Murmur*. Easter encouraged the band to take "a little while off so everybody could come back in and be in the mood to do it like a show," which the group took as an invitation to get uproariously drunk, recording only a proposed commercial for Walter's Bar-B-Q in Athens, and a tuneless rendition of 'King Of The Road'. Given the hurried, incomplete nature of the additional songs, the band settled for a single album – but I.R.S. would still get an array of B-sides and half a future compilation album out of the three-week session.

The only apparent disagreement of the recording process occurred over the running order. "I think the biggest single problem with *Reckoning* is the sequencing," says Don Dixon. "Sequences are probably the second most important thing for an album. You can take the same batch of songs and put them in different orders and really, really change the mood a lot. And with *Reckoning*, I finally threw my hands up. They just came back from supper one night and made up the sequence and that's what we stuck with. And I just don't think it's the strongest it could be. If a record is really sequenced well then songs are allowed to unfold; if you do it exactly right, you have allowed every song to have its ability to capture somebody's attention."

It was a sign of the group's impatience that they were willing to cancel allocated days in the studio but not allow their producers sufficient time to experiment with a running order. It was also a mark of their own self-confidence, a determination to make their own decisions – and mistakes.

The same attitude applied to the video process. R.E.M. brought in Atlanta film-maker Howard Libov to shoot 'So. Central Rain' in the studio at Reflection, succumbing to the demand to be seen performing only to the extent of playing behind screens. The compromise worked for both industry and band: although the group were evidently there in front of the camera, they were still playing hide and seek with the public. Michael Stipe, refusing to lip synch, made the unusual but welcome step of singing live to tape, thereby providing an entirely new mix of the song available only on video.

Stipe was keen to experiment further with the video medium and secured the backing for an art piece that would accompany the entire first side of *Reckoning*. His idea, similar to that of the 'Radio Free Europe' video, was to spend a day at primitive sculptor Bill Miller's whirligig gardens in Gainesville, Georgia. He recruited the Athens painter and film-maker Jim Herbert to make it.

"The idea was that I would be more sympathetic, and the band respected me as an artist," says Herbert, who saw a connection between Stipe's lyrical approach and the choice of location. "A lot of his lyrics seem to be built on collecting art phrases and just putting them together, and there's a kind of letting things happen, letting things fall into place, that some of the primitives have."

As a result, Herbert produced something every bit as unspecific as the group's music. After shooting them walking and running among the whirligigs, he then used the 'rephotography' method to edit, a process that involves taking photographs of finished frames at random, closing in or pulling back from them with no preconception of what is coming next. "It's really a new film occasion," he explains. "With *Reckoning*, there was no attempt to edit the music, and as it happens, the way the songs came up on the album, and the images that were done, were uncannily related . . . I think the band understands that layered process, especially back with their early music where things were so layered and diffused. Michael knows about muddling through – he knows about the grey areas out of which clarity comes."

Left Of Reckoning, as the project was called, had limited outlets, but I.R.S. did use Herbert's film for the promotion of 'Pretty Persuasion'. "It was a very unorthodox video for that time," says Herbert. "But it just seemed like within weeks that there were lots of those kind of videos out."

Michael Stipe also took control of the album sleeve, bringing a drawing of a two-headed snake to Howard Finster and suggesting he turn it into a fully fledged painting. Stipe later described it as an attempt to define the elements: "Part of it is rocks and part of it is the sun and part of it the sky." However, his attempts at a long-distance painting partnership – let alone the problems of reproducing a Finster artwork on an album sleeve – led to disappointment with the final product.

But the purposely askew snapshots on the back and the handwritten notes on the inside, particularly coming after the cultured finesse of *Murmur*, served to indicate that *Reckoning* was a deliberate step back into the garage, that R.E.M. had decided they did not yet wish to meet the masses head on.

★   ★   ★

Having been on the road almost continually since first discovering the joys of the lifestyle back in July 1980, R.E.M. used a long overdue break between finishing *Reckoning* in January 1984 and its release in April to reacquaint themselves with their hometown.

Athens had changed considerably over the last five years, from a conservative college town with a fringe artistic community into one of the most talked-about musical hotspots in the country. The varying success of The B-52's, Pylon and now R.E.M. – along with R.E.M.'s proclamation in interviews that the University of Georgia "is known all through the south as a place where if you couldn't hack it anywhere else you'd go there and fuck and drink your way through school" – proved an irresistible magnet for the region's would-be bohemians. Students moved to Athens and formed bands not because there was nothing else to do, as R.E.M.'s generation insisted was the case, but because it seemed the right thing to do, thus helping the town to enter a continual self-perpetuating period of activity – and to lose its innocence.

The club scene had recovered after Tyrone's burnt down in 1982 with no insurance policy, and gone on to cater for an increasingly larger live audience. The 40 Watt Club expanded from its College Avenue loft to the site of the old Koffee Klub on Clayton Street and then up to Broad Street, where it flourished as the hub of activity for local music. The spacious Uptown Lounge, formerly just a drinking bar, then also started booking local and touring bands in late 1983.

R.E.M. themselves had long outgrown these venues, playing the 1,000 capacity I&I Club as early as 1981, and the University's free outdoor shows at Legion Field in June '82 and October '83. By March '84, when they played two nights at the 1,200-capacity Madhatter, they recognised the danger of becoming godlike in their home town, and opted to make Atlanta the location for home shows on future national tours.

But Athens was still their residence and nothing was going to change that. The myth that groups had to move to the music biz capitals of New York and Los Angeles to make it was proving only slightly less transparent than the one dictating that all good management should also be based there. Jefferson Holt, finding that he could far better represent his clients' desires by being close to them than by being close to the industry, had rented a small office on College Square, employed Sandi Phipps as secretary the same month he split with her as lover, and continued to handle the group with the same laid-back confidence he had always displayed.

Bertis Downs, though available for advice at all times, was off teaching now. With Jefferson usually by the band's side, this meant constant work for Phipps, who was credited on the albums but still felt underacknowledged. "I worked for them for minimal wage," she says. "I was in from the beginning and I think I was taken for granted. You let yourself do that if you work for nothing." More than being underpaid, she felt there was a delineation of responsibility according to sex. "They were always adamant that I was a secretary, and then eventually they called me an office manager. But I did a lot of everything. I hired Liz (Hammond, credited from the *Fables* sleeve onwards). I started the fan club; I did all that as well as the office stuff. When there became an organisation to the point that there needed to be policies about things, it was definitely that we were the girls in the office. I didn't like that because I'd never been that before. I'd been part of the management team. I would do the books and be financially responsible, yet I was still just the secretary."

Coming off the creative burst of the *Reckoning* sessions, R.E.M. found they could not stop working just because the calendar had some empty spaces in it. Michael Stipe gave an indication of his professional future by, firstly, immersing himself in the visual presentation of the group, then travelling to New York to record with Anton Fier and Bill Laswell's ensemble group Golden Palominos, adding three vocals for its second album *Visions Of Excess*. (Other guests would include John Lydon, Chris Stamey and Syd Straw.) Choosing an entirely opposite path, his three full-time partners stayed home in Athens, and decided to return to their roots as a sloppy bar band playing silly pop songs.

The notion of an alter ego was not unfamiliar to them, having spent Halloween '83, with Michael, opening for The Cramps at New York's Peppermint Lounge as the suitably horrific It Crawled From The South; now they decided to become The Hindu Love Gods, a long-cherished would-be band name of Peter's. They asked Bryan Cook, who had been establishing an extrovert's reputation of his own with his band Is Ought Gap, to sing.

Cook – who says "I never figured out why they asked me" – joined the others in Bill Berry's front room, singing through a practice amp, working up a set close to that with which R.E.M. had first started out, "songs that Michael was tired of doing and wouldn't sing anymore, or that somebody else was tired of doing." These included 'Permanent Vacation' and 'Narrator', "All these songs that I remembered from three years before, that were just killer . . . And I got to sing them!"

The Hindu Love Gods made their live début at the 40 Watt Club in January 1984, hiring a limousine to drive them all of three blocks to the club and play up their supposed stardom. Nobody turned up early enough to get the joke. The 40 Watt was nonetheless packed by the time they took the stage that night, as was Bourbon Street, a former strip bar in the basement of the Georgia Hotel, when The Hindu Love Gods performed with new bands Kilkenny Cats and Dreams So Real.

The three playing members of R.E.M. also kept busy recording demos with 'Werewolves Of London' legend Warren Zevon, who was searching for a new record deal after years out of the music scene. R.E.M. invited him to Athens to record at John Keane's studio there in the spring, and enjoyed the learning process of being someone else's session band. And when they found themselves with a couple of free hours, the opportunity to record a Hindu Love Gods single seemed too good to miss.

The live versions recorded that day of 'Narrator' and 'The Easybeats' 'Gonna Have A Good Time Tonight', with Bryan Cook singing and Warren Zevon on piano, were typically exuberant, and would eventually see the light of day on I.R.S. in 1986. The five-piece even made a brief Love Gods appearance that same week at the 40 Watt as part of the encores of Love Tractor's own covers band, Wheel O'Cheese.

The Hindu Love Gods lived on in spirit – years later, when glam rock songwriter and producer Mike Chapman heard that his 'Little Willy' and 'Tiger Feet' were part of the makeshift group's live set, he volunteered his production services to Peter Buck – but spirit alone.

★   ★   ★

Unlike *Murmur*, which qualified itself as a masterpiece to almost everyone who gave it a second listen, *Reckoning* was not a conspicuously classic album. Whereas the group's début presented an unusual and carefully crafted sound that carried twelve extraordinary songs along in its wake, the follow-up was a less cohesive collection of material rejoicing in variety and spontaneity. As Mitch Easter puts it, "*Murmur* is this thing called *Murmur* whereas *Reckoning* is just album number two."

But in presenting such an honest self-portrait, R.E.M. showed themselves to be a rock'n'roll group in every sense of the word, a decisive – and smart – move. For however successfully musicians can come together in the studio incognisant of each other and produce excellent – or at least popular – results, it is the groups that go down in history.

And as much as it may be about bringing together a number of talented musicians, a group is essentially a boys' club for eternal adolescents whose collective adventures become an ongoing public saga. The Beatles were the first and most successful group to sell the world this notion of eternal friendships: the public fell for the four Liverpool lads' camaraderie as much as for their music until ultimately the two became inseparable.

From then on, the myth of the great band as an impenetrable gang has proven impossible to shake. It mattered not that members of The Who were known to punch each other out both on and off stage but that they did so out of love. Led Zeppelin maintained the same line-up for over a decade, and when their drummer died, broke up immediately. The Clash liked to style themselves as 'The Last Gang In Town'. What united all these groups was their own sense of unity – and a palpable division of talents and character traits. By 1984, as their cult following expanded in numbers and intensity, it became apparent that R.E.M. had a similarly unique unity.

There was Michael Stipe, the artist. A lyricist who gave little of himself away, sang in riddles and metaphors and was at his most content working with visual imagery; whose love of his partners was total, but who preferred isolation.

There was Peter Buck, the rocker. A music obsessive of unusual sincerity who longed for nothing more than the next opportunity to get on stage and play; whose reputation for partying preceded him and whose opinions he could not keep to himself.

There was Mike Mills, the musician. A classically trained performer accomplished on several instruments and responsible for the intriguing nuances that so distinguished his group's music; whose studied expression belied his sense of adventure.

And there was Bill Berry, the businessman. An intelligent, hard-working professional who put paid to the myth that drummers were followers, not leaders; whose determination saw the group through many an early obstacle and whose songwriting contribution was not to be ignored.

R.E.M. were not alone in having four distinct characters. But they were the first potentially successful American group to have emerged in many years in which such disparate ingredients came together with perfect symmetry to produce such an intoxicating single-minded whole.

All this was obvious to the press, who fell over each other in the rush to acclaim the band in the loudest tones possible. 'How much better can they possibly get?' asked *Musician*; 'There is no richer pop music being made today,' opined *Record*; 'These guys seem to know exactly where they're going,' observed *Rolling Stone*. In Britain, where reviews are rarely pedestrian, the *NME*'s Mat Snow successfully wrote himself into R.E.M. history with his talk of 'vinyl cathedrals' from 'one of the most beautifully exciting groups on the planet', and his belief that, 'When I get to heaven, the angels will be playing not harps but Rickenbackers. And they will be playing songs by R.E.M. . . .'

Record buyers promptly propelled *Reckoning* into the *Billboard* Top 30 only a month after its April 16 release, keeping it at No. 27 throughout June, and in the 200 for almost a full year (even if 'So. Central Rain' made but a small dent on the Hot 100 and 'Rockville' not even that).

While it would have been very easy for the group to ride in to mass acceptance on this wave of adulation and leave other contenders behind, R.E.M. had no intentions of severing any ties with their peer group. As they came to grasp the extent of their possible influence in America, the confidence that had always marked them turned into a perceptible arrogance.

111

R.E.M.

R.E.M.'s knowledge of the media's workings had been apparent to fellow students of the culture from the beginning. Peter Buck and Michael Stipe had spent their teenage years reading the rock press and had long learned the importance of image and the need to deliver good copy. Therefore, their early interviews were festooned with embellishments and white lies. Indeed, Peter's willingness not to let facts get in the way of a good story had long ago led friends to place such anecdotes in 'Buckland'.

There was nothing particularly dishonest or even original about this approach; in fact, R.E.M. seemed to adopt it almost out of respect to the tradition of rock'n'roll. But there was certainly planning behind it. It only escaped into the press once that Mike Mills had been arrested for "cavorting nude with a young lady on a water tower"; like Buck's early assertion that "We're not much of a drinking band", it was important they did not appear as decadent as the pre-punk dinosaurs. That honesty was not always encouraged was proven when Jefferson publicly admonished Peter Buck for admitting in an early *Rolling Stone* article to earning only $350 a month. "Some day," said Holt, "you guys just might be making money, and then some reporter can say, 'Well Mr Bigshot rock star, how much are you making now?'" Buck admitted to earning $24,000 before songwriting royalties in 1985, after which, as band income spiralled into the six-figure bracket, such honesty duly clammed up.

Sometimes the quotes were so perverse that it was hard to believe journalists were not merely playing along, as when the group collectively denied an affinity with The Byrds while at the same time introducing the band's 'So You Want To Be A Rock'n'Roll Star' into their set, or when they gained credibility for turning down support tours with The Clash and The Go-Go's while supporting Bow Wow Wow, Squeeze, The (English) Beat and The Police.

Yet there was a genuine integrity beneath many of their fibs. R.E.M. honestly did prefer headlining the small clubs to opening at the big stadiums, they really did record chart albums faster than anyone else of their stature, and they truly did disdain the old fashioned spoils of rock'n'roll. Michael Stipe's most common quote during 1983 – "On the ladder of important things in this world, being in a rock band is probably on a lower rung, but then again, being Secretary of State is probably way down there too" – was well rehearsed but it was sincere.

Throughout 1984, R.E.M. made it clear that if they were going to climb that ladder, they wanted to bring the new underground up with them. They took The Dream Syndicate and The dB's on their 'Little America' tour with them. They enthused about harder edged bands than themselves at every turn. Peter Buck not only played on The Replacements' album *Let It Be* but reviewed it for a leading rock magazine. They toured Britain – twice – and not only chastised the pompous attitudes they encountered there, but included songs by The Replacements and Jason & The Scorchers in their set to prove their point. And on the I.R.S. production *The Cutting Edge*, which was broadcast on MTV in July of that year, they truly went to town.

"Pop music for most people is really bland," said Peter Buck. "You don't have to understand it, it's just this boring little nothing. It's just cheeze whiz for the airwaves. That's what people buy now: they don't buy something because it's exciting, they buy it because it's bland enough that they can put it on at home and it won't bother them. Most of the bands that I like are a little bit more threatening. R.E.M. is the wimpiest band that I like, and I'm not even sure that I like us yet."

"Me neither," said Mike Mills, who elaborated, "most of the people that we think are great you'll never hear about unless you're into music enough to go and find this stuff at local record stores. You won't find it at the big chains, and you'll never hear it on the radio. It's a real shame that radio is so locked into a format that very few good things ever get played."

"Fanzines are great, college radio is great," continued Buck. "Everything else about the music business just stinks at this point. And it's really a shame too, because I think right now America is having the best music ever . . . And I think it's your duty as Americans to go out and buy Black Flag. Buy our records: what the hell, it doesn't hurt me any!"

Looking back at this candidness, Buck comments that, "I just didn't want to be one of those showbiz careerists: 'Oh yes, all the little people that made me the man that I am.' Fuck that. We were playing every city and there'd be great bands and no one would go see 'em, and then some guy with a funny haircut from a foreign country would come over with one record that was unplayably bad and get 800 people, and that was the hippest thing in the world. It was infuriating. We wanted to reiterate that we hadn't completely sprung out of nowhere. We came from a post-punk perspective where a lot of people were doing the same things, and maybe we were a little bit more commercial, but there was no difference between us and Pylon, or Black Flag."

In April '84, an angry Buck told the British weekly *Sounds* that at home, "American bands don't get signed, American bands don't get promoted, American bands don't get played on the radio. The only thing the industry is interested in is leasing the latest British album to get a piece of the supposed 'invasion' action. There's no money left for new American outfits."

In the October issue of American magazine *Record*, he put pen to paper in an essay entitled 'The True Spirit Of American Rock', inspired by "the complacency of the music business" in England where "shocked laughter greeted my assertions that there are plenty of good bands making exciting music in America."

By the end of the year, he had obviously seen an improvement, telling *Jamming!* that, "Suddenly an audience has sprung up who don't listen to the British invasion bullshit and are slowly returning to American groups. Three years ago there wasn't anyone making interesting records in America, but in the last year a lot of bands have come up from nowhere."

Despite R.E.M.'s animosity, the British were welcoming them, on a cult level at least, with open arms. A six-date British tour in the spring and a 14-date excursion in the autumn – during which they played to 1,500 people in London and performed live on another prestigious TV show, *The Whistle Test* – proved that there was an audience eager to hear new American music.

But only those acts with the support of major labels could afford to follow them over. This included Jason & The Scorchers and Violent Femmes, but it didn't allow for Hüsker Dü or The Replacements. And although I.R.S. sank large sums of money into breaking R.E.M. in Britain, the chances of an all-important hit single there remained remote. On continental Europe, progress was even slower, the group's dates in Germany bombing so badly that other American bands had their tours cancelled as a direct consequence.

R.E.M.'s limited fondness for the UK was hardly helped by comparisons to The Smiths, Britain's finest new rock group in years. Just like R.E.M. in America, The Smiths were walking a tantalising tightrope, trying to remain staunchly underground even as they became massively successful. They too juggled a Rickenbacker jangle with an eccentric singer: Morrissey's avowed celibacy was as removed from the hardened partying of the other Smiths as Stipe's artistry was from the pure rock'n'roll spirit of *his* band fellows. The two groups should have been keen friends and allies, but R.E.M. were put out to find themselves accused of being influenced by a band they'd preceded on stage and record by several years, and introductions were never made.

In America there was less confusion about R.E.M.'s musical inspirations, as proven when MTV selected them to exemplify the 'folk rock' segment of a series called *Rock Influences*. The band could hardly have been happier than to have the country's major TV music outlet – which, by airing this show and *The Cutting Edge* before it, was clearly aware of R.E.M.'s growing appeal with its young audience – play matchmaker with some of their icons.

Given that Peter Buck had grown up infatuated by The Lovin' Spoonful, the opportunity to play with that band's singer and songwriter John Sebastian on a rendition of the hit 'Do You Believe In Magic?' was a dream come true. And the distinct jangle of Buck's Rickenbacker guitar was obviously reminiscent of The Byrds (as, indeed, was the sound of The Smiths' Johnny Marr) so MTV had the band share the stage with former Byrd Roger McGuinn to perform 'So You Want To Be A Rock'n'Roll Star'. It turned out R.E.M. had been playing a bridge section with the wrong chords, but McGuinn decided after twenty years, he preferred the Athens' band's arrangement, and so that was the one played on stage. (All the same, Peter Buck continued to insist that the influence was second generation, that he was more inspired by Big Star or The Soft Boys, a maligned British neo-pyschedelic group. As if to prove the point, he and former Soft Boy Robyn Hitchcock, who was now recording and performing solo, began teaming up regularly.)

By the end of 1984, it was R.E.M. who were considered

influential. Club owners nationwide noticed that new groups were showing up with the same haircuts (or lack thereof) as R.E.M., the same Sixties-style thrift store clothes, the same instrumentation, the same combination of studious lead singer and traditional playing members, and, to hammer the point home, the same choice of contemporary cover: 'Radio Free Europe'.

The press raves, the college airplay, the rawly passionate live shows, the American audience's desperate desire to find alternatives to the British new wave, and the band's eagerness to do the same and to tout its peer group in the process all played a part in making R.E.M. the standard-bearers for an entire burgeoning generation that year. The decisive factor, however, was the group's almost accidental appeal: they were by far the most populist band of what claimed to be a non-commercial movement. As such they formed a bridge between the groups that couldn't make a mainstream record even if they wanted to, and an industry that was ready to embrace any group from the underground that would meet them halfway. In addition, by their ability to deliver sharp-witted yet honestly delivered soundbites, they became favourites of both a media that needed a band like them, and a public that craved a band like them. In short, 1984 was the year that R.E.M. became the superstars of their own cult. And they thrived on that status. They performed over 100 shows on three continents, recorded and played under pseudonyms, promoted their peer group, guested on other people's records, joined their icons on stage, and improved upon their popularity and credibility by delivering a superbly rambunctious and heartfelt second album. They had no reason to imagine that being in R.E.M. wouldn't continue to be the most fun career in the world.

Eight

O n the return leg of a business swing through Europe in the spring of 1985, Jay Boberg took the opportunity to visit R.E.M. while they were recording their new album in London. He expected the familiarly happy scenario he had always encountered at Reflection in North Carolina. Instead, he walked in on an atmosphere that could be cut with a knife.

"There were a lot of problems," he recounts. "There was a real strain. It was the first time I was in the studio where I didn't feel like everyone was having a good time."

Everyone wasn't having a good time. In fact, everyone was having the most miserable time of their lives.

The problems had started with R.E.M.'s determination to get straight back into the studio for a third album. *Reckoning* had come together easily, proven successful and besides, the group's placement on an independent label, with small annual advances, meant that they could not afford to stay off the road for too long. A lucrative tour of colleges looming during the peak season of spring parties necessitated that they finish the new album by then or hold its release until the autumn. This would not have been a disastrous option for a band with money in the bank but, determined to maintain a furious work rate and full of youthful zeal, they opted for the former path.

Recognising the many options in the recording world and the limited time in which to try them all, they had already decided to end the successful partnership with Mitch Easter and Don Dixon. With Easter's group Let's Active now full-time I.R.S. recording artists, Dixon pursuing a solo career, and *Murmur* and *Reckoning*'s success ensuring that lucrative production opportunities awaited their every spare day, the North Carolina duo were not perturbed.

But R.E.M. hadn't decided on a replacement. And suggestions

from the record company were not greeted warmly. "We were speaking to this one guy who said, 'I always spend six weeks doing basic tracks,' " recalls Peter Buck. "We were like, 'We do the record in a month.' " Buck had suggested the English-based American Joe Boyd, whose work with Fairport Convention, Richard Thompson and Nick Drake made him an ideal candidate with whom to further explore R.E.M.'s folk-rock leanings. Boyd, however, was booked for several months. Meantime, the band finished off their victorious 1984 with a New Year's Eve concert at the Civic Center in Atlanta, at which they performed six new songs: 'Old Man Kensey', 'Hyena', 'Good Advices', 'Auctioneer', 'Driver 8' and 'Wendell Gee'.

Throughout January, they worked on the arrangements for these songs and a handful more. Names of potential producers came and went. Then Joe Boyd called R.E.M. from Canada, where the project he was meant to be working on with singer-songwriter Mary Margaret O'Hara had just fallen through. Did R.E.M. still need a producer? he asked. The answer being affirmative, Boyd jumped on a plane south, and on February 17, he and R.E.M. spent a day in a local studio together recording demos. The following night he saw the band perform a benefit show at the Moonshadow Saloon in Atlanta. In addition to the new songs played on December 31, the night's set included 'Kahoutek', 'Maps And Legends', 'Feeling Gravitys Pull', 'Life And How To Live It', 'Green Grow The Rushes' and 'Bandwagon'. That made twelve new songs, a full album's worth.

During those two days together, R.E.M. and Boyd spent little time talking about *whether* they should work together, which appeared to be a foregone conclusion, but rather, *how* they should work together. Joe Boyd suggested they record at his preferred Livingston Studios in north London, and given how he now had time on his hands, that they start immediately. The band, possibly against its better instincts, agreed. "We were totally burned out, we'd been on the road too long," acknowledged Buck several years later. All the same, "The work ethic thing was really there, we wanted to make a record, we were ready to make a record. And so we just pushed ourselves really hard." Within ten days of the two parties meeting, they were working together in London.

As Joe Boyd prepared for their arrival, he began to grasp the seriousness of the job he had taken on. "I was very aware that there was pressure on this record, that everybody had very high expectations, that they'd done two very cheap records, sold more than anybody else had ever expected, and now everyone, the record company in particular, had high expectations that this was going to be a much bigger sound, a much different type of production and was going to be better."

This assessment was reached without actually meeting the record company. R.E.M. suspected that Boyd might not be I.R.S.'s prime candidate for the all-important third album, and averted a potential veto by pretending they were going all the way to London just to record demos. (Jay Boberg was not easily fooled and timed his visit to the studio not long after the sessions started.) But by preventing the record company and producer from cementing a relationship, R.E.M. put Boyd in an awkward position. "The record company was working for them, and I was working for them," Boyd says of the group's attitude, "and that was a slightly unusual experience for me. That was probably one of the most difficult things for me to adjust to." He is unsure that he ever did.

Boyd had not been overly familiar with R.E.M.'s music before the first enquiring phone call, only aware that, "Sometimes you hear about a record and you just know from the kind of confidence with which it's released that it's good." Buying the albums proved his instinct correct, but also confirmed Easter and Dixon's worst suspicions by giving them the impression that they were "a little raw and unsophisticated from a sound point of view." Only when back in London awaiting the group did he realise that, "Those two records were actually great, and the sound is perfectly suited to the band." At which "I got a bit more nervous about it, because I realised they wouldn't be quite so easy to improve upon."

One other element that neither group nor producer had fully taken into consideration was the change of environment. R.E.M. came from a hot, wet climate. London in March was cold, damp, foggy and, if Buck is to be believed, snowy too. The TV offered just a handful of channels – none of them showing the college basketball tournament that was in full swing back home and to which Mike and Bill were perennially addicted. And whereas in Charlotte they were used to being just minutes from the studio, Livingston was on the outskirts of London, yet the band were housed in the centre of town. This meant either a long, arduous journey through constant traffic if they decided to use the driver they'd been provided with, or an even more tiresome voyage by public transport if they came in on their own.

The result was a lack of direction. "It's the only time we've walked in and didn't have a clue," says Buck. "We had this batch of songs that we'd written really fast, with not even the beginning of an idea on how to make them. We couldn't agree on tempos, we'd argue about things like keys . . . We forgot some of the things you have to remember, like you have to know what you're doing."

Homesick, fatigued and, for the first time in five years, unsure of themselves, R.E.M. began to wonder if this was all worth it. As a group, they had achieved more than their wildest dreams, playing every venue from biker bars to baseball stadiums, becoming cult stars and leaving a mark on Eighties' American rock that would remain through the rest of the decade even if they were to break up tomorrow. But they could see how along the way they had become a business, paying taxes, employing staff, dealing with corporations, under constant pressure to deliver 'crossover' records and 'commercial' videos. Even worse, there was no clear break visible in their schedule for the rest of the year.

"We were all looking at each other," recalls Buck, "going, 'We're probably going back to the nicest weather in the nicest town to have spring in the entire world, and we're only going to be there for four days, and then we're going to be gone until Christmas.' We started thinking, 'Maybe we should just cancel this and enjoy the springtime, and then who cares whether the record sells or not?'"

Jefferson Holt, aware that this year, with so much goodwill predisposed toward them, they could at last capitalise on the five years' hard work that had come before, rallied them together. They could 'do it like hippies' and become a part-time band, playing at weekends, selling maybe 100,000 albums a time, or they could seize on the opportunities at hand, work one more year flat out, start banking the royalties and hefty concert fees that would be coming their way, and then buy some time off the following year. The group were swayed; they would finish what they'd started. But still, it was a close call.

Partly because he'd barely met them before, Joe Boyd claims he was unaware of these internal problems – "They seemed to be a very well balanced, well adjusted group of rock'n'rollers, and have a very healthy and positive approach to what they did" – but he was concerned about having the freedom to produce.

"There were certain tracks where I felt more involved because there were outside musicians," he says. "The fact that there was this outside element injected into it meant that it was less producing a group, and more like producing a record. And for that reason, I felt much more in control of those three tracks, and ultimately was the happiest with those. And I guess my main disappointment with the record was not achieving on the other tracks the same impact."

Still, the sessions were not completely soul destroying. For outtakes and B-sides, the group recorded their mock metal anthem 'Burning Hell', a cover of Pylon's 'Crazy' and the easily appreciated 'Bandwagon'. 'Hyena' was recorded but omitted for being too fast. There was also a brooding song entitled 'Theme From Two Steps Onwards', for which saxophones were added and a final mix completed. Though not intended for the album itself, it seemed a likely candidate for a B-side – except that when it came time to assemble masters, nobody could find the tape. Nor an acoustic version of 'Driver 8' recorded with it. The band soon forgot how to play 'Theme', and it disappeared entirely from their legacy, an appropriate anecdote for an album of fables.

The final stages of the album proved particularly painful for all concerned. Boyd's continual search for the ideal mix came as a shock to a group used to reeling them off like so many demos; conversely, the producer found their musical modesty of no assistance. "With most bands," he recalls, "everyone's saying, 'I can't hear my guitar, or my voice. Turn it up, push it up louder.' With R.E.M. everyone was saying, 'No, there's too much of me in there, pull it down.'"

★　★　★

Looking back on the internal crisis, homesickness and loss of vision that was R.E.M.'s time in London, Michael Stipe concluded that,

"The result of that overriding environment is the record, which is dark, dank and paranoid."

"It's the most tense record we've ever made," says Peter Buck. "And if you take the stance that a record's supposed to show where a band is at, that does it perfectly."

Fables Of The Reconstruction Of The Fables, to give the album its full cyclical title, did indeed capture the mood of the band that made it. The tension and misery were obvious from the opening song 'Feeling Gravitys Pull', wherein Boyd's string arrangement tugged at the melody from enough different directions to produce a discordant effect that thrilled some and horrified others – Bill Berry among them.

Fables, as it is most commonly referred to, was full of surprises and extremes. 'Can't Get There From Here', with its stomping Stax-styled brass accompaniment, 'Driver 8' and 'Life And How To Live It' were all possible single material; 'Wendell Gee' – on which Buck played banjo – and 'Green Grow The Rushes' demonstrated again the group's penchant for tenderness. Yet the album frequently meandered. Occasionally, as with 'Old Man Kensey', this could be interpreted as subtlety; 'Kahoutek' (spelled 'Kohoutek' on the label) could only be described as ponderous.

Lyrically, the album was another progression for Michael Stipe, as the *Fables* half of the title clearly indicated. 'Old Man Kensey' was written about a real-life dog kidnapper who used his ransom rewards to get drunk; 'Wendell Gee' was inspired by a family of Gees that owned small businesses in Athens; and 'Life And How To Live It' by a radical book of that name found in the house of a local eccentric called Brivs Mekis after his death.

"That's Michael's storytelling record," says Peter Buck. "There's a whole other side to the south: it's the last place where the old tradition really exists. People pass stories down. Being a good story-teller is something that people are known for." On tour that year, Michael would frequently introduce these songs with long and entertaining monologues – or fables.

But what then was the 'reconstruction'? While the title *Recon-struction Of The Fables* could apply to the group's storytelling ability, or to an examination of their myth, its reverse title *Fables Of The Reconstruction* seemed a pointed reference to the Reconstruction of the defeated South by the North after the American Civil War. Though R.E.M. wanted to redress the image of Southern rock, they felt no need to apologise for their roots.

"The Southerner," said Buck, "is the terminal outsider. In movies and on TV, the Southerners are always hicks. They're idiots. Everyone always tends to look at you as if it's a miracle that you're a normal person from the South."

"It's a very wistful, nostalgic thing," said Mike Mills when asked to draw the correlation between the South and R.E.M.'s new album. "Like trains – when you think of trains in the night, that tugs at your heart a bit . . . The songs remind me of sitting in my room, fixing to go to bed, and hearing a train a few miles off."

"There's more of a feeling of place on this record," said Buck, "a sense of home and a sense that we're not there."

These emotions were best expressed on the delightful 'Driver 8', with its line "We can reach our destination, but it's still a ways away." Stipe described this 'destination' as "something that's almost unobtainable, it's almost an idea, almost this fantasy or this dream, and you're fooling yourself into believing that it's almost obtainable, when in fact it really isn't." In other words, 'Can't Get There From Here'.

Admitting to their lack of musical direction and personal unhappiness in London led to an understandably restrained reaction by the American press. 'The band sound predictable, stalled,' said *Record*; 'R.E.M. don't aim for much more than enigma,' complained the *Village Voice*; 'murk' and 'boredom' were two of *Creem*'s less enthusiastic adjectives.

But this mooted response mattered little now that the group had secured so large a cult following, and even less so when American rock radio jumped on 'Can't Get There From Here' with long overdue but nonetheless welcome enthusiasm. (Proving the traditional record company theory that any album can succeed, no matter how dark, provided it has one obvious single.) The video for the song – based in the small town of Philomath, Georgia as referenced in the song – was a giant leap by the band towards MTV accessibility. Filmed for the first time in the lurid colours of the video format, it featured a crazed trip to the drive-in movie starring Mills' and Berry's recently purchased old cars, plenty of self-effacing comic acting from the group and Jefferson Holt, and even the occasional sighting of the song's lyrics. There was still no discernible plot, but it was far from obtuse. Not surprisingly, it too received more play than its predecessors. And although 'Can't Get There From Here' showed absolutely no signs of becoming a bona fide hit, the album roared into the Top 30, its sales quickly overtaking *Reckoning*'s 250,000 mark. R.E.M. were still travelling inexorably forward.

Yet *Fables* is rarely viewed with great fondness. Joe Boyd expresses relief "that from the professional point of view it fulfilled its function in terms of sales, so everybody can say it's a success, but I know the group doesn't like it. And that's obviously a source of disappointment to me. We got along very well while making the record, but I think they couldn't wait to get out of England, and basically look on it as a sort of aberration. I was trying to enjoy the role of employee, and ended up disappointed that I didn't satisfy my employers."

★　★　★

In 1984, R.E.M. had proclaimed from the rooftops the existence of a vibrant alternative American music scene. In 1985, the music industry, having learned the hard way that the British pop they had been so avidly pushing had but a limited lifespan, finally acknowledged the depth of homegrown talent. The Replacements, Hüsker Dü, 10,000 Maniacs, Guadalcanal Diary, and Green On Red were all signed to big record companies, the first four to divisions of Warner Brothers; the independent label Slash, home to Violent Femmes among others, itself got a major licensing deal. The British were equally enthusiastic: in April of '85, Peter Buck adorned *Melody Maker*'s front cover in front of a giant U.S. flag to promote a four-part 'State Of The Union' American rock special, and Island Records even signed California's The Long Ryders direct to their London based label.

Although it was commonly referred to as one, R.E.M. were anxious to avoid the term 'movement'. "It is really just a bunch of musicians who worked out their own philosophies all across the country," said Michael Stipe. "It was only after we started travelling and met each other that we began to see we had all these things in common."

A loose affiliation of groups or a movement, the underlying philosophy was to follow one's own instincts and refuse to accept the myth that the industry knew better. "One of the most gratifying things we could do," said Peter Buck in '85, "would be to prove that you can become successful on your own terms. You don't have to submit to all the business crap. They tell you you have to dress real flashy and be real showy and open for the big bands and take the usual routes to success. And that's just not true – just because it works for some people doesn't mean it works for everybody."

It rarely worked at all for those aforementioned acts who embraced the major label chequebook. Though no one could blame a poor hardworking band on a penniless independent for signing on the dotted line, the gradual dilution of ideals and music by corporate America proved sufficient to take the sting out of whatever movement may have existed during the prime underground period of 1983 and '84. It was only those bands whose record labels gave them creative leeway, such as R.E.M. enjoyed with I.R.S. (who had now switched their manufacturing and distribution from A&M to MCA), that could really carry the ethos through.

Not that one would know it from R.E.M.'s comments. Referring to the 'debacle' of The Police support slots, Bill Berry pronounced that, "Our intuition has been more valuable to us than any of the great words of wisdom passed on to us by the damned record company."

A record company is indeed damned to be the bane of a group's existence: every suggestion made to increase the band's profile is viewed as an attempt at coercion, every box of unsold albums as a failure. R.E.M. may have viewed I.R.S. as interfering but, as the experiences of their peer group would prove, almost no other label of any serious size would in fact have been so accommodating.

"I think a major label would have dropped them," says Miles Copeland of R.E.M. "Because they weren't prepared to make the normal concessions that people would expect, i.e. coming up with a single. Major labels just don't have the time to bother with an act that takes a long time to build."

Not that the I.R.S. supremo didn't try the major label approach himself. Early on, he sat them down and, as Bill Berry recalled, told them that, "We didn't have the image, we should be going on all these monstrous tours opening for people all over the world, we should do this, we should do that, we should have a big-name producer, we should make high-tech videos . . ."

The band replied that they wanted to do it their own way. "I said, 'Well then you have to pay the price of those decisions,'" recounts Copeland. "'You can't expect us to give you a number one single if we don't think that there's one there,' and they said 'Well, we're prepared to pay that price.' And the surprising thing – and the thing that I will always respect them greatly for – is that when the albums didn't have a number one single, they didn't come back and say, 'Well where is our number one single?' They lived by the rules that they set."

"I want to make my own mistakes," comments Peter Buck. "We just figured we knew what we were doing more than anyone else in the world. I took advice from Jay, I took advice from my girlfriend, I took advice from my dad . . . I listened to it anyway. Didn't always do it. We'd never do anything against our will. We almost felt we had to be in creative control, because if you make a record and someone butchers it or forces you to do something you don't wanna do, there's no reason to make it. You might as well go back and work in the garage for someone else, taking orders."

Fortunately Jay Boberg, who Miles Copeland appointed President of I.R.S. in March 1985, understood R.E.M.'s philosophy, even if he didn't always agree with it.

"My relationship with them was never to *tell* them what to do, in the classic A&R-record company-band relationship," says Boberg. "It was always this pot-pourri of ideas. The band were the ultimate arbitrator. They would never come back and say, 'Yeah, what a great idea, we're going to do it,' it would just be that they would slowly grasp the concept, and then implement it at their own pace."

His daily conversations would be with the band's management, which increasingly meant legal advisor (and part-time university teacher) Bertis Downs, as well as the long-standing Jefferson Holt. "It's interesting how they played off each other: Jefferson would be really mad about something, and then Bert would call me up the next day and be buddy-buddy. I'm not saying it was good cop–bad cop, but it definitely was a tandem."

Interestingly, Peter Buck saw the roles in reverse. "Jefferson was the front guy who was genial and would schmooze people, this southern guy who was mellow and everyone liked. Then Bertis would put the boot in! It was good because we got what we needed."

Mitch Easter recalls the management's intransigence when negotiating the producers' fees (which would ultimately come off the band's royalties). "Dixon and I fought to get more money out of them. We couldn't get it. I had to admire Jefferson. He's just like a rock. And we didn't dislike him at the end of it either. That's what a manager has to do."

For their own part, Holt and Downs presented themselves as "hands-off" managers. Their job, claimed Downs, was "relatively easy, because the band manage themselves. They're involved in business decisions, delegating very little of their career to other people. They really don't count on us for all that much judgement."

This is true. R.E.M. may have been college dropouts, but they were blessed with high IQs and an intrinsic business sense. "They always paid the corporate dues before anyone else got any money," says the group's first secretary Sandi Phipps of their fiscal responsibilities. The band had banked on making money in the long run, by holding on to their publishing, touring within budget, and recording inexpensively. Most importantly for the sake of a settled professional future, they had agreed to share all proceeds equally among the four of them, including songwriting.

"My feeling is always that money and ego break up the band," explained Peter Buck, the most prolific songwriter in the group, many years later. "And so everyone (in R.E.M.) is going to have his name on the songs, and everyone is going to have the same amount of money, so it's not a matter of some lead guitarist or singer saying, 'We're not going to tour this year,' and another member saying, 'Well what am I gonna do? I live in an apartment.'"

The first rewards of this long-term planning were seen in 1985, even before *Fables* was released, as royalties came in from *Murmur*'s surprise success. A group on a major label, recording in big city studios with costly producers, taking tour support and making expensive videos – all of which get charged back to a band's account – might not have seen a penny from an album that sold 200,000 copies, but R.E.M. had big enough pay-days that spring for Peter Buck to buy a house, and for Mike Mills and Bill Berry to purchase their dream antique cars. Michael Stipe spent his money on art.

Perhaps the most important of all the group's original policy decisions was that all such policy decisions be agreed by unanimous vote. "They understood the ramifications of democracy pretty well," says Don Dixon. "They less followed the rules of parliamentary procedure than some bands do, but it was still very much a democracy with veto power employed by everyone." He saw the occasional argument and resulting sulking match but considered such confrontation healthy. "They got along well enough while still retaining enough tension to be worth a shit."

★　★　★

After successfully hoodwinking The Uptown Lounge in Athens into booking them as a promising out-of-town band called Hornets Attack Victor Mature, R.E.M. then made the tour of colleges during the peak spring party season of late April and early May '85 that they had scheduled their album's recording around. *Fables* would not be out until June 10, but the group's enormous popularity on campus gave them the opportunity to break in new material on enthusiastic audiences, and the fee of around $12,000 a night put money in the bank for the rest of the year.

June found them back in Europe. While the American press had cut back their praise when it came to judging *Fables*, their British counterparts were proving uncharacteristically faithful. But the front covers and general ballyhoo counted little when R.E.M. accepted U2's personal invitation to support them at huge outdoor shows – their first since The Police dates. Like that day at Shea Stadium two years before, it was raining furiously when R.E.M. took the stage at Milton Keynes Bowl on June 22, coming on just before the headliners. The 50,000-strong crowd was in no mood for a band opening a set with as downbeat a song as 'Feeling Gravitys Pull', and the group spent the entire set dodging missiles, the most common of which were plastic bottles full of urine. R.E.M. went on to play other major European festivals in Ireland and Belgium to friendlier responses, filling the time in between with club dates.

Back in the States, their popularity proved to vary region by region. In Milwaukee on August 5, they played to 1,100 people in a hall built for almost four times that many; the next night in Chicago, they played to a phenomenal 6,000 avid fans. Their increased success was bringing with it a dubious new audience, however.

In Ottawa on August 17, playing a 500-capacity club after weeks in halls up to ten times that size, they were greeted like conquering heroes, despite the fact that they were drunk, tired, and as far as they were concerned, playing by rote. As a result, Michael Stipe broke into his beloved a cappella version of 'Moon River' halfway through the set.

A lone, harsh cry of 'Fuck Off!' bellowed forth from the crowd. The group reacted angrily, and once Mike Mills was restrained from attacking the heckler ("You come up here and fuck off!") Stipe began the song again, was again heckled and at the end of it was met with calls for 'Catapult' and 'So. Central Rain'.

Frustrated with themselves and disappointed in their audience, the group played only three more of their own numbers all night. Instead they covered songs as perverse as The Sex Pistols' 'God Save The Queen' and Lynyrd Skynyrd's 'Sweet Home Alabama', as old as 'Paint It Black' and 'Secret Agent Man', and as ridiculous as 'The Lion Sleeps Tonight' and 'Smokin' In The Boys Room'. It ended as one of the most enjoyable nights of the tour, a triumph of the band's convictions, and a bold statement that no degree of commercial success would dictate that they perform a set-by-numbers.

Similarly volatile emotions were displayed when the group played New York that year. On August 31, the first American leg of the tour ended with a sold-out show to nearly 6,000 people at Radio City Music Hall, one that was enjoyable if uneventful until, during an encore of 'Windout', Peter Buck suddenly, inexplicably threw his new Rickenbacker across the stage and stormed off.

Then on November 9, they performed at The Beacon Theater for the New Music Awards as promoted by the College Music Journal. *Fables Of The Reconstruction* had become the most reported (i.e. air-played) album in the history of college radio, a medium whose influence had grown to the extent that CMJ was able to attract guests like U2 and Andy Warhol for their awards show, and even sell the live broadcast to MTV. R.E.M. were happy to display their gratitude to college radio and to collect their award for Album Of The Year; they didn't, however, wish to be seen performing across the nation's living rooms. It was agreed they would go on stage after the awards – and TV broadcast – were over.

R.E.M. duly played an inspired acoustic set, including The Everly Brothers' '(All I Have To Do Is) Dream', a new song that would become known as 'Swan Swan Hummingbird', 'Angel' by The Neats, and a finale of 'Rockville' on which Mike played piano, Peter Holsapple guitar, and two of the Bangles sang backing vocals.

An electric set followed. But during the third song, 'Can't Get There From Here', Peter Buck's Rickenbacker was seen flying through the air to exit stage left while its owner disappeared stage right. The show was evidently over. An apologetic Michael Stipe returned to sing 'Moon River' before the entire group congregated backstage for a fully fledged row.

It transpired that the sound crew, hired for the television broadcast, felt that their job was done when the broadcast finished. "Nobody could hear anything," recalls Buck of the electric set. "I went over to the guy and said, 'The monitors aren't working.' He said, 'Hey! I'm off work,' so I said 'Fuck you!', took my guitar and threw it at him. It was like, 'If we're supposed to be such big guests at this thing, and they're not going to bother to even turn the monitors on, I'm not going to play.'"

The incident was duly blown up by the music media to significant proportions. Certainly it was an unprofessional outburst at such a prestigious event, but that was the last of Buck's concerns. It was not merely ironic that he considered it more important to finish a show at an air force base in Texas – where he had berated Bill Berry for the same actions – than at an awards event in New York. It was a clear statement that the music industry disgusted him as much as ever.

It was also probably the act of someone who had used the time spent waiting to play to get uproariously drunk. R.E.M. have never been slouches when it comes to boozing, and Peter Buck has readily admitted he spent much of 1985 in an alcoholic haze.

Michael Stipe spent it confounding people's expectations with an ever-changing array of increasingly bizarre images. The golden curls that had grown over 1983 and '84 were shorn at the beginning of '85 for a monk's tonsure and an Abraham Lincoln-styled beard. That was followed by his shaving his entire head, eyebrows included, and then by dyeing the new growth with peroxide. In late October he took to a Glasgow stage wearing watches all over his body and with the word 'DOG' written in felt tip across his forehead. As he began sweating in the heat of the show, and the ink dripped down his face, the audience was inclined to believe his sanity was slipping away with it.

He was sick, he admitted later, but not mentally. "I couldn't stand up. I hadn't eaten anything but potatoes for a whole week 'cos the food is so bad in England. I was vomiting and shitting. I felt like a dog so I took a felt tip and wrote it across my face."

That British tour ended with two nights at London's 3,500-capacity Hammersmith Palais. The British capital was not far behind New York in terms of the band's live appeal, but national acceptance seemed as far off in the UK as it seemed within reach in the US. I.R.S. had released 'Wendell Gee' as a single with incentive bonus tracks – including, at last, the vastly underrated 'Ages Of You' – and the group again appeared live on *The Tube*, but album sales were not justifying the expense of touring the UK, money that was coming out of R.E.M.'s pockets.

"We couldn't get arrested," says Jay Boberg bluntly of the label's attempts at airplay in the UK. "We tried: we tried 'Talk About The Passion', we tried 'Wendell Gee', we tried fucking everything. They had this hard core following, but it just stopped there. You hit a wall. (R.E.M.) felt frustrated by it. In Europe, with CBS International (which licensed I.R.S. product there), I don't think they felt the kind of energy, so they just said, 'Fuck it'."

It would be two years before R.E.M. would venture back to Europe. The renewed interest in American rock subsequently ground to a halt in fad-conscious Britain. But enthusiasm for R.E.M. remained. And the group that finally returned would be a much happier one than that which decided that three months a year spent away from their American homeland was three months too long.

Nine

Athens at the beginning of 1986 was an even greater centre of activity than usual, with a film crew in town documenting what had become a legendary scene. *Athens, Ga – Inside/Out* should have been a cause for celebration – national recognition that their city was like no other – but it brought out a competitiveness unimaginable five years previous. Jim Herbert, who was hired as Director of Photography, recalls how it "caused so much antagonism: bands that didn't get in, bands that feel they didn't get shown the way they thought they were going to get shown . . ."

R.E.M. were above having to worry about such matters. After initially declining to take part, they contributed two songs to the film and soundtrack, a cover of The Everly Brothers' '(All I Have To Do Is) Dream' and the new song 'Swan Swan H'. And although, as a documentary, it was not supposed to have any 'stars', Michael Stipe's influence over the film was apparent in the inclusion of so many of his favoured primitive artists; his charisma outshone that of any other front man or woman among the bands featured; and his ever-changing visage – his painted eyebrows and dyed hair – threatened to steal the show. As a film, *Inside/Out* was an excellent portrayal of a unique community, and was warmly received wherever an audience could find it; the soundtrack album, released on I.R.S. a year later (with The Everly Brothers' song 'Dream' mistitled), was a more patchy souvenir. When the Los Angeles film-makers departed, Athens attempted to revert to business as usual, but it would never be quite the same again.

* * *

Rather than rush into a decision on producers as had proven a mistake with *Fables*, R.E.M. began contemplating the possibilities for their next album while still on tour during 1985; the name that elicited the most positive response was that of Don Gehman. The man responsible for John Cougar Mellencamp's hit records, Gehman was renowned for a direct approach but a 'big' sound; this sat well with a group who, after the detached pessimism of *Fables*, now wanted to make an upfront rock album. They invited him to meet them as they wrapped up their 'Reconstruction' tour.

Like Boyd before him, Gehman was familiar with R.E.M. only by reputation; when he got hold of *Fables*, he was disappointed. "I couldn't listen to it," he says. "I thought it was just a dirge." Watching them live at the Washington and Lee University in Virginia in December '85, with a bad sound and yet to a crowd so frenzied that the band ended up performing acoustically to ease the crush, failed to clarify his thoughts. "I was intrigued," he says of the experience. "I wouldn't say impressed."

That night, as he met with the band, Michael Stipe avoided him. On the tour bus the next day, for an official meeting about their record-making methods, the same again. Gehman admits to feeling "some resentment to that: I like to know what I'm dealing with." Assured by the playing members that it was nothing personal, he laid out his intentions: "I wanted to make records that were more clearly focused," he says. "That were really what I call records, and not just things that go from one end to the other and you don't know what happened . . . To be able to introduce some production styles that maybe they had never used before on their instruments . . . The idea of being able to hear and understand the words that Michael was saying. I was aware that even if I did that you may still not understand what he meant, but at least you'd have a sense of its presence."

The playing members emphasised that they didn't want to be Bryan Adams, or to "run down the middle", which Gehman assured them he had no interest in either. However, he did emphasise his determination "to make a commercially viable record."

The group must have felt it was time to take that step, for in the new year they flew him down to Athens to spend several days at John Keane's now 16-track studio working on new songs – and given that there weren't many of them, on some older songs too. The most promising appeared to be one called 'Fall On Me'. The result, with Michael Stipe's voice to the fore, was convincing:

Gehman was hired. I.R.S. in turn were happy to underwrite an increased budget in the knowledge that they would receive a more mainstream record.

R.E.M. and Gehman reunited at The Belmont Mall studio in Bloomington, Indiana in a springtime environment that was the opposite in every way to that which the band had endured the previous year in London. Bloomington was a college town not dissimilar to Athens, though the group was housed half an hour away in lakeside apartments for their three week stay. (The record was subsequently mixed in LA.) Michael Stipe, when not in the studio, spent all his time either out on the lake or in the surrounding countryside, with pen and notebook permanently to hand.

Signalling their intentions to have fun this year, R.E.M. decided to name the album after a phrase in the Peter Sellers film *A Shot In The Dark*. Whenever problems befell the band, as they frequently did to Sellers' hapless character Inspector Clouseau, they would brush them off with his expression that they were all part of "life's rich pageant". (As with 'Feeling Gravitys Pull', apostrophes had no place in R.E.M. titles.) But there were no such misfortunes during recording. Despite Gehman's attention to detail and his insistence on confining the working day to eight hours, the backing tracks were recorded within a week. They had an energy and enthusiasm missing from all the group's recordings bar the most raucous elements of *Reckoning*.

"Making that record was a blast," recalls Gehman. "There was a tremendous amount of creative energy, it just came flying out. Also, between me and them, there was that chemistry you hear about. I was enough of a disciplinarian to make sure everybody got the job done. Other than that, I was willing to accept their ideas and they were willing to accept mine." On 'The Flowers Of Guatemala' for example, Bill Berry suggested using glasses for added ambience, "and it all happened in one take, three minutes." When R.E.M. asked for a pump organ, the studio immediately found one in the vicinity that had been gathering dust for decades; "things just kind of came to us," says Don Gehman, sounding somewhat amazed. The organ's underlying grandeur is present on every song except 'Swan Swan H', contributing enormously to the album's expanded sound.

Gehman built songs through time-honoured techniques. "We had a collection of songs, and we were working on them, letting them be what they are. I look on everything as a single, and that in order to make something communicate there's a set of tricks that you use to bring the core ideas forward, and let the listener have the opportunity to be carried through."

"In the past we always tried to stay away from big, booming, stupid-sounding drums," said Bill Berry on the album's completion. "But as a result, they ended up sounding wimpy and lacklustre. Don gave us a big drum sound, but it's natural."

"Don helped me question why I play at certain places," observed Peter Buck. "If he had done this on the last album, I would have said forget it. But this time we wanted it to be more dynamic."

This newfound dynamism – the 'colouring' technique – was most evident on the crescendo leading up to the simple but carefully pronounced guitar solo that carried 'The Flowers Of Guatemala' into another musical realm; the overall energy was nowhere more apparent than on the resurrected 'Just A Touch', its first take vocals ending with Stipe spouting a Patti Smith line – from the album *Easter* that so enthralled him and Peter Buck a decade earlier: "I'm so young, I'm so god-damned·young."

'Just A Touch' was not the only song from the band's pre-*Chronic Town* set to be dusted off; 'What If We Give It Away' was a resurrection of the long forgotten number 'Get On Their Way', and 'Hyena' had originally been intended for *Fables* but considered too fast. (They *increased* the pace this time round, which says much about the difference in spirit between the two albums.)

There was in fact a real dearth of new material that might have endangered a record not recorded in such uplifting circumstances. Along with the three older songs, the album was further padded out with a spaghetti western instrumental to which Stipe added muffled vocals, 'Underneath The Bunker', and a cover of a 1969 song by Texas group The Clique, 'Superman', which had been the B-side of the band's lone hit, 'Sugar On Sunday'. Mike Mills and Bill Berry had played the song at a makeshift 40 Watt Club gig with some other Athens friends just two months back; Peter Buck had given them the single to begin with. Michael Stipe left the three of them to it, and so impressive was the rendition that it became the first non-original song to appear on an R.E.M. long-player, the first to be issued as a single, and the first R.E.M. song to feature Mike Mills on lead vocal. In its exuberance and obscurity, it was the perfect R.E.M. cover, the kind of power pop anthem they might have written themselves in '81 had Michael Stipe continued to pen boy-girl lyrics.

But he hadn't. And if *Lifes Rich Pageant* is to be remembered for its significance in R.E.M.'s ongoing history, it should be primarily for the blossoming of Michael Stipe's talents.

Certainly, as already noted, the 1980 edition of Michael Stipe offered little clue as to his future role in society. Painfully shy and insecure, he could temporarily rid himself of these drawbacks by climbing on stage and singing old rock'n'roll songs while catapulting across the boards in homage to every great musical performer rolled into one unrestrained 20-year-old. On the basis of this, there are plenty of people in Athens who believe that he then consciously *contrived* a mystique around him, that he *created* an enigma; that his persona resembled more the cold calculation of a pre-fabricated new David Bowie image than the unrestrained outpourings of, say, a Jim Morrison. This argument would explain his move away from the simplistic lyrics and extrovert showmanship of earliest R.E.M. into the less linear songs and more restrained performance that separated the group from the pack in '82–'83. It would explain, perhaps, why Stipe swore the few people who knew of his brief existence in a covers band to secrecy, afraid that such a pastime would detract from his image as an outsider and a musical novice.

These detractors claim Stipe's every artistic move to be stolen from those around him: that singing through a megaphone was a trick first employed by The Butthole Surfers, the riotous squalor merchants who spent much time in Athens in the mid-Eighties; that de-robing down to another layer of clothes was taken from Mimi Goese of Hugo Largo, with whom he recorded in 1987; that banging a drumstick on a chair was a popular trait of R.E.M.'s old touring partners The Gang Of Four; even the splendid 1986 group promo picture in which Stipe appeared shirtless seemed identical to one taken by a local band only weeks before. Imitation may be the most sincere form of flattery, but at what point, these people say, does it become plagiarism?

This view is then contrasted by those who have always seen in Michael Stipe a rare originality: his painting instructor Scott Belville, or Jim Herbert, who says of the early frenzied performances that many felt derivative, "Even then it looked different. It was an invention. His thing looked like it was coming from some inner place."

Stipe's 'inventions' were tried out not only on the stage, but on a personal level as well. As an art student, there were days when he and his friends would refuse to talk; those who knew him would have to elicit a nod of the head as confirmation that he was undergoing such an exercise. And at Athens parties, if conversation bored him, he would feign a faint, a signal for Peter Buck to drag him home.

His confidant and guitarist evidently enjoyed the process. "People think he's always serious and yet he makes all these weird jokes," Buck said of Stipe in 1986. "He has one of the weirdest senses of humour I've ever seen. It's so weird people don't know it's funny. They think this guy's out to lunch, when in fact I'm giggling up my sleeve."

That humour had been most apparent in R.E.M.'s very earliest days, when Stipe had exerted a playful control over an audience that could have them all crouching down on the dance floor if he so desired. The humour remains, most noticeably in a continued on-stage narrative confidence. But so does the intrigue. As he explained in 1988, "Any wife or husband, any lover, can tell you the importance of mystery, what a large part it plays in life, and how important it is to leave a little bit for people to work out for themselves." Working out the mystery of Michael Stipe became a popular hobby among critics and audiences alike as R.E.M.'s popularity grew, and the singer would not always enjoy his placement in the goldfish bowl. While Peter Buck handled growing success by becoming increasingly nonchalant about it, Stipe attempted to avoid scrutiny by becoming more inscrutable.

When Stipe did crack open the door to his psyche, it was only to admit – perhaps with an element of false modesty, perhaps genuinely – that he himself did not always understand what he was doing.

"A lot of the time I'm grabbing around and bumping into things," he said in '86, "and I'll throw them together and something will come out . . . a combination of conscious and subconscious. So a lot of times I figure something out after it's happened: a song, for instance, exactly what was intended. I'm not about to start trying to figure things out beforehand.

"I guess I really focus on detail more than the grand picture, and that detail becomes the words to the song. And given that detail, I guess it's left up to the listener to spot it in and put a frame around it."

It was on *Lifes Rich Pageant* that Michael Stipe began to erect the frame as well as paint the picture. He was helped by the dramatic improvement of his voice over the years, both on R.E.M.'s records and through side projects like The Golden Palominos. Coming into *Lifes Rich Pageant*, he finally felt comfortable at making his voice more prominent within R.E.M.'s often blurred sound. Don Gehman then worked to make its content more tangible.

"Don was the first person that hauled me aside and questioned what I was doing," said Stipe after finishing the record. "That can be really good to have some objective voice saying, 'Why are you choosing to say this?' 'Why are you singing what you are?' A lot of the time it was rhetorical, it wasn't the kind of thing I had to answer to, but he would just place the seed for me to think about or change."

"I would sit down with Michael and say, 'Well, what are you trying to really say here?'" confirms Gehman. "We'd run around the subject four or five times and come up at the same place we started! There's no way to manipulate Michael."

Perhaps it was this battle of wills that inspired Stipe to write a song of intent entitled 'I Believe', only to pronounce that belief to be in 'coyotes', and 'time as an abstract'. If so, it was a rare case of deliberate obscurity, for on the whole *Lifes Rich Pageant* was Stipe's hour of assertion: "We are young despite the years, we are concern, we are hope despite the times," he assured listeners on 'These Days', and that confidence resonated from start to finish.

So did a political edge, one which often pitted mankind against nature, and, as ever, featured two or more subjects running concurrently within each song. 'Fall On Me', for example, focused first on Galileo's experiments on gravity ("feathers hit the ground before the weight can leave the air") and then on acid rain and the corporations that "buy the sky and sell the sky". 'The Flowers Of Guatemala' ostensibly concerned that country's indigenous flora but also alluded to the United States' military involvement in central America; and 'Hyena', much of which was typically vague, suddenly took on clarity with a middle eight whose lines – "The only thing to fear is fearlessness, the bigger the weapon, the greater the fear" – evidently referred to the threat of nuclear war.

The lyrical peak was surely 'Cuyahoga', in which springtime swimming in a mud-red Apalachee river was juxtaposed with the rivers of blood of slaughtered American Indians that runs shamefully through the country's history, and an Ohio river contaminated with poison. On top of this, the opening lines "Let's put our heads together, and start a new country up" sounded like nothing less than a call to arms.

All of which was a long way removed from the singer who announced in 1983 that "if you want to talk about politics . . . then you should do it somewhere other than the stage," and in 1984 that "I have no idea what I'm talking about . . . My ideas about how the world fits together are not clearly defined yet."

But like countless bands before them, R.E.M.'s youthful naïvete had turned into a political savvy as touring the world opened their eyes. Michael Stipe's own politicisation was not surprising given his long-term interest in conservation and health foods. He now began acting upon his policy to 'Think Global, Act Local', campaigning during the elections for Congress and turning up at City Council meetings to voice his opinions.

This, noted Peter Buck, was "always fairly strange . . . The things he says in City Council meetings are fairly amusing to say the least, totally befuddling to these old Baptist guys that run the Council."

But they could also be effective. The Congressman he rooted for was elected, and with Bertis Downs' legal expertise, some of the Council's attempts to tear down or put up buildings purely for profit were stalled.

As much as 1986 was the year that Michael Stipe came to the fore as a lyricist, singer and spokesman, it was also the year that his role as visual co-ordinator for the group reached new heights. As a photographer, he had had exhibitions in Athens and Greenville, South Carolina. As sleeve designer, he had made an impact with the colourful chaos of *Fables*. As lighting adviser, he helped shape R.E.M.'s unusually dark stage presentation. And in the world of videos, he had already taken co-production credits on those for 'Can't Get There From Here' and 'Driver 8'. Now, for 'Fall On Me', he took full control, handing in a promo focused on the ground from above and then turned upside down, resembling the imminent collapse of the sky. As a pointed reference to the crass-ness of video – and as further evidence of his confidence in them – the words appeared on cue throughout.

In 1987, taking his interest in the medium even further, Michael Stipe provided a video interview for use by the broadcast media. "If you were to say that videos are not commercials," he told the camera, "you would be lying to people. The other band members and myself didn't like that aspect of videos, but I've always looked at it as a way of being able to get across the more visual part of R.E.M. And if you can make a video without compromising your-self, without giving in to the look they want, they may never play it on TV, but you've made it, it's there."

The very day that Stipe was working on the 'Fall On Me' promo, Peter Buck was engaging in one of his own favourite pastimes, handling interviews. And videos came in for his familiar drubbing. "The whole idea is despicable," he told *Creem*. "I've never seen a video that made me like a song . . . They all suck. I think it's just a horrible thing that I'm forced to do that shit. Ours, I think, are half-dumb and half-intelligent. I give so little thought to it that I don't really care."

Once again, R.E.M. had cornered both sides of an argument.

★　　★　　★

"We finally got to the point where we could take a little bit of time and relax," says Peter Buck of R.E.M.'s low profile during the first eight months of 1986. Yet relaxation seemed to be the last thing on their minds. Along its uncharted course, the band members had given each other the individual freedom to pursue private or col-laborative projects as long as they did not interfere with R.E.M.

itself. With less time spent on the road in 1986 and '87, its members seized that opportunity with zeal.

Michael Stipe toured with The Golden Palominos and produced a mini-album *Drum* for New York's Hugo Largo. Mike Mills also moved behind the mixing desk alongside Mitch Easter, for the album *Hermitage* by a Virginian group Waxing Poetics, and helped Jefferson Holt record a single to launch the manager's own independent label, Dog-Gone, under the rather dubious name Vibrating Egg.

Peter Buck, meanwhile, somehow found time to produce two notable albums for Coyote Records, the label for which he had already recorded an EP with one of The Fleshtones as The Full Time Men. In January 1986, he headed up to New Jersey to produce the long-awaited, and highly acclaimed, second album by the recently reconvened Feelies, called *The Good Earth*; in June, he and fellow Athenians Dreams So Real travelled to Minneapolis where they recorded *Father's House*.

Making three complete albums in one year was a feat that even Buck would have a problem repeating. The urge to keep moving was part of his spirit, but the need to stay occupied through '86 may also have been down to the death of his father and a break-up with his girlfriend of five years' standing, Ann. During the summer, so as to avoid getting depressed over these personal losses, he returned to working behind the counter at Wuxtry, taking his pay in vinyl. It was a nice idea, but it exemplified R.E.M.'s changing home-town status that, rather than talking about and selling other bands' music, as was his intent, he was continually besieged by the new generation of R.E.M. fans, those who had moved to the town to get close to the band.

Though Buck endured a break-up, Bill Berry went the opposite route: his private project that year was to get married in March to his girlfriend Mari, whom he had been seeing for over two years since breaking up with Kathleen O'Brien. He was the first to take final leave of the Men's Club.

* * *

'Fall On Me' seemed destined to be a hit single. Warm, melodic, insistent, produced to airplay standards and under three minutes long, it was the most commercial offering yet by a cult group who were poised to explode. On the week ending October 4, 1986, the song reached the Top five of the AOR playlists – a notable achievement for a group that had spent years railing against the musical format – and the single entered the Hot 100 at number 96. The next week it rose only two places, the highest it would go.

Though Top 40 radio was proving resistant until the end, R.E.M. weren't complaining. The same week the single peaked, *Lifes Rich Pageant* reached its own zenith of number 21 – a fair placing considering the plethora of major albums released in the autumn – and the group played the 10,000-seater Coliseum in California. In January, the album was certified gold, the group's first 500,000-seller. Hit singles? Who needed them?

Good press, however, remained important if the band was to maintain its all-important grass roots credibility. Just as *Reckoning* had been a direct response to *Murmur*'s subtleties, so was *Lifes Rich Pageant* a hard-rocking reply to *Fables Of The Reconstruction*'s dense confusion. But *Lifes Rich Pageant* was so obviously a bigger, more commercial and avowedly *rock* record than anything before it, that the group were ready to feel the stabbing of critics' knives in their backs.

The most they suffered was a slight grazing. Reviews were generally good-to-excellent, especially in the UK, and R.E.M. would again find themselves in the Top 10 of the national US Critics poll for the *Village Voice*. There was a certain amount of discontent that the group was heading directly into the mainstream, and yet the political content, the still befuddled artwork, the 'Fall On Me' video and the inclusion of 'Superman' and 'Underneath The Bunker' all advertised the group's continued opposition to convention.

This last aspect brought a criticism from Anthony de Curtis, who wrote in an otherwise glowing four-star *Rolling Stone* review how "signing off both sides of an LP as rousing and raucous as *Lifes Rich Pageant* with self-consciously hip jokes is an unfortunate waste. Two more top-flight songs might have made *Lifes Rich Pageant* a masterpiece – ranking with *Remain In Light* and *Born In The U.S.A.* as seminal American records of the Eighties." He was absolutely right. But the group would have been absolutely wrong to have gone that route: they would have had little defence against the argument that they had finally, inexorably, 'sold out'. Instead, *Lifes Rich Pageant* was at once the band's most exuberant, boisterous and coherent record and yet, because of – not despite – the dearth of new material and two deliberately throwaway sign-offs, it was a total garage album. As such, it remains unique in the band's catalogue, and the favourite of many a hard-core fan.

R.E.M. spent the months of September through November that year touring North America, consolidating their home country success, and saving loss-making foreign ventures for another year. Support slots again went to American bands R.E.M. believed in, specifically Fetchin' Bones, Guadalcanal Diary and Camper van Beethoven. Those who came along envisioning R.E.M. as re-constructors of the fabled term folk-rock were in for a surprise: the shows those three months were a powerhouse express, a step closer to arena rock territory that found the group totally prepared to take on the challenge.

As ever, the group's set varied night by night, but it usually started with their new anthem 'These Days' and ended with a melancholy acoustic rendition of 'So. Central Rain'. In between were a smattering of favourites, a handful of surprises, the odd cover and the occasional try-out of a new song. One of them was a jerking number built around the refrain 'firehouse'; the other was a smoother, more repetitive song with a blatantly mainstream guitar hook and a recurring scream of the word 'fire'. It would become 'The One I Love', and as R.E.M.'s year of optimism drew to a close, it was poised to become a lot more than just another album track.

Ten

"Mitch and I viewed R.E.M. more as The Grateful Dead of their college generation than as a hit record machine," asserts Don Dixon of the group he and Easter worked with from 1982 through '84. Perturbing though the comparison might have seemed to some, there were similarities – and not just because R.E.M. were often labelled as hippies. By 1987, like The Grateful Dead more than a decade before them, R.E.M. had become the biggest American cult band of their era, filling concert halls and arenas nationwide, and selling over half a million albums a time without a hint of a hit single. The by-product of such a devoted following is always the same: bootlegs.

From the outset, R.E.M. were a collector's dream. Their steadfast refusal to play the same songs night after night, rarely using a set list, frequently introducing covers and previewing new material as soon as it was written, meant that anyone who brought a cassette recorder to a show was bound to document a unique experience. The disparity in singles' releases between America and Britain – especially over B-sides – kept the avid fan constantly scouring import shops. And the vast amount of unreleased but circulating material, such as early discarded songs or album out-takes, ensured that attaining the complete R.E.M. catalogue was a full-time occupation.

As a result, ardent fans formed an unofficial network by which to swap and collect. Two fanzines – *Radio Free Europe* and *Perfect Circle* – sprang up, devoting whole pages to details of a tour's differing set lists or the complete catalogue of available videos. And rare items, such as the Hib-Tone single or the 'Tighten Up' flexidisc given away with the British fanzine *Bucketful Of Brains*, soared into the three figure price range.

Seizing on this devoted following, illegal records began flooding the market. Some of these bootlegs were of genuine historical interest: those first ever demos recorded in 1980; the live tape from Tyrone's in January 1981, widely revered as the 'definitive' early show; the RCA tapes. Some bootlegs were live recordings worthy for their excellent sound quality or unusual material. And some were atrocious, poor quality audience recordings of mediocre performances.

Acknowledging them as a supreme form of flattery, R.E.M. at first actively endorsed bootlegs; Peter Buck in particular discussed their contents with a collector's enthusiasm. In time, the group became frustrated with the bootlegs' increasingly poor quality, but still refused to campaign against them, allowing even the shops around the corner from their Athens office to remain well stocked with unofficial releases by the hometown heroes.

R.E.M. could have helped quell the demand for bootlegs by releasing a live album of their own, but they considered such records a poor substitute for the real event. They did, however, assemble the aptly titled *Dead Letter Office* album of B-sides and other gems in the spring of '87.* Not surprisingly, Peter Buck took control of this assignment, suggesting in the sleeve notes that "listening to this album should be like browsing through a junk-shop." And so it was, with all the delights of unearthing rusty old trinkets that such a rummage entails. Who else, for example, would place three songs by their biggest influence – The Velvet Underground in this case – on one album alongside heavy metal pastiches like 'Burning Hell' and the Aerosmith song 'Toys In The Attic'?

Dead Letter Office was the final proof – if any were still required – of the playfulness that so endeared R.E.M. to their fans. Its drawback, a serious one in retrospect, was that every recording on there had already seen the light of day, however limited its original pressing. The early out-takes, demos and live tapes have still not surfaced on a legitimate recording; one can only assume that the band itself assumes that hard-core fans can track them down.

Spring cleaning time that it was, R.E.M. complemented the vinyl B-sides compilation with a home video of A-sides. As well as

---

* The compact disc added the whole of *Chronic Town*, which had yet to be released in that format.

the group's original choice for the 'Radio Free Europe' promo, there was 'So. Central Rain', 'Can't Get There From Here', 'Driver 8' and 'Fall On Me', along with a half hour of Jim Herbert's rephotography, in the shape of *Left Of Reckoning* and live videos for 'Feeling Gravitys Pull' and 'Life And How To Live It'. As a collection of some of the era's most uncommercial promos, one might have expected Michael Stipe to use the opportunity to justify his fascination with the medium. Instead, it was Buck and Holt who introduced the mockingly titled *R.E.M. Succumbs* with the equally derisive promise that, "What you are about to see is a representative sample of an outmoded art form."

R.E.M. laughed all the way to the bank when *Succumbs* replaced Bon Jovi at the top of the best selling home music videos chart.

★   ★   ★

"The biggest mistake of my life," is how Don Gehman looks back on his inability to free up studio time to continue working with R.E.M. Penned in by album projects, he could not offer his services when they came straight off the 'Pageantry' tour and into the studio over Thanksgiving weekend '86 to record an old song 'Romance' for a film soundtrack. Gehman suggested they use Scott Litt instead, with whom he shared management.

A New York-born producer then in his early thirties, the convivial Litt came recommended to R.E.M. not just from Gehman but from The dB's, whom he had produced while R.E.M. were still playing pizza parlours, and from I.R.S., who surely noted his credits on hits such as Katrina And The Waves' 'Walking On Sunshine'.

Not that these credentials shone through on the result of their hurried two day session together. The group were physically exhausted from touring, and 'Romance' sounded livelier back in 1982 when demoed for RCA. But the two camps hit it off splendidly, and R.E.M. jettisoned their original plans to continue working with Don Gehman in the new year. In their minds, his meticulously high standards meant that he viewed *Lifes Rich Pageant* as less than a total success.

"We were talking to Don, but he was getting kinda cold feet," recalls Peter Buck. "He was saying, 'I really want to make a record that's a huge commercial success and much as I like you all as people, and I like the band, the way you work I can't hear that you're going to have a huge hit.' "

Gehman might have lost out by expressing these opinions; in truth, the band's typical impatience worked against a big-name producer who was used to booking his projects several months ahead. But there seems little doubt that R.E.M.'s first gold album was a useful education: Mike Mills in particular, says Gehman, learned "how to arrange and colour" songs from him.

"I felt that I was responsible for giving them a set of tools that worked for them," says Gehman. "I showed them a methodology of approaching a song, and production and sound, and they just took the next step. Scott has got a history of knowing exactly the same sort of stuff, and if anything, has got a more commercial background than I have."

Litt and R.E.M. worked on demos in Athens in January. They then set a date to start recording in Nashville at the end of March. In between, Buck, Mills and Berry used the downtime to reconvene with Warren Zevon, backing him on most of the singer's comeback album *Sentimental Hygiene*. It was indicative either of the three playing members' own musical progression or the record's sterility that at no point did they sound like R.E.M. Michael Stipe joined in with backing vocals on one cut of a record that was an enjoyable experience but ultimately a commercial disappointment.

The R.E.M. sessions in Nashville were a different proposition entirely. The band, confirming the extent to which they had learned from Don Gehman – and Joe Boyd, Don Dixon and Mitch Easter before him – had insisted to Scott Litt that they be credited as co-producers. Litt, who thought R.E.M.'s early music was that of a band "a little unsure about being out there", nonetheless had his own agenda. "I like having a big sound, I like having bold sounds, and I like having a singer that grabs you. I wouldn't accept anything less." The results of the month spent recording the fifth R.E.M. album suggest that he got his way, Michael Stipe's clearly enunciated vocals riding a booming radio friendly texture on each song.

Critics and fans alike subsequently questioned whether the group's continued move towards the mainstream signified capitulation to outside influence, a calculated decision on their own part, or was merely the result of a natural, unspoken progression that could be observed almost record by record since *Chronic Town*.

Scott Litt's comment that, "We talked about pop songs when we were cutting the record; they wanted to hear their stuff on the radio too," points to a determination by the group to gain a commercial coating, yet the one issue both parties insist was never raised was the most noticeable: the vocal levels.

"We didn't set out to mix the vocals louder, it just seemed natural," said Mike Mills after the record's completion. "There was a point where we sat back and listened to it and realised that the vocals were clearer and more out front, but nobody had really noticed it or worried about it up to that point."

It was "certainly not a thing Michael would discuss," confirms Litt. "They would like the sound and they would just go with it. There weren't band meetings about how loud the vocals should be, I'm sure of that. I really think a lot of it has to do with Michael being sure of what he was doing."

Here was something else with which to credit Don Gehman. Having been goaded, pressured and all but physically forced into becoming more audible and focused on *Lifes Rich Pageant*, Stipe must no doubt have been encouraged by the response – commercially, in the hefty increase in record sales, and aesthetically, in the favourable reaction of fans to lyrics that closer attended to the troubles of the world. For the new album, Stipe took this social awareness a step further.

"The whole album is about chaos," he explained. "I've become very interested in chaos and the hypothesis that there is order within chaos, so I guess that kind of carried over into the recording."

It certainly did on the apocalyptic 'It's The End Of The World As We Know It (And I Feel Fine)'. This was Michael Stipe's own 'Subterranean Homesick Blues', a cataclysmic vision of doom with its tongue firmly planted in its cheek. Among its litany of seemingly unrelated catchphrases and rhymes was a reference to the New York hipsters party Stipe and Buck attended back in 1980 – with jellybeans, cheesecake and a drunken Lester Bangs – throwing Leonid Brezhnev, Leonard Bernstein and Lenny Bruce's names in for effect. Stipe's voice was that of a planet going happily insane.

"I wanted it to be the most bombastic vocal that I could possibly muster," he said later in '87. "Something that would completely overwhelm you and drip off your shoulders and stick in your hair like bubblegum."

He succeeded, even to the extent of shocking his partners. "It was so quick it caught Peter by surprise," says Scott Litt of the vocal delivery, recalling that the guitarist's first reaction "was that he didn't like it. He was worried that it was such a departure." Only when placed alongside a familiarly stomping R.E.M. chorus – during which Mike Mills played up the song's essentially positive outlook, singing "Time I had some time alone" over Stipe's refrain of the title as if he had not a care in (the end of) the world – was Buck convinced.

Trouble and confusion were themes evident in almost all the songs. 'Welcome To The Occupation' was a continuation – or clarification, considering how vague its predecessors were – of the theme first explored in 'Green Grow The Rushes' and 'The Flowers Of Guatemala', Stipe referring to a politically imperialist United States prepared to "fire on the hemisphere below". The increasing power of America's right wing and the lure of the dollar were also the subject of 'Exhuming McCarthy', with the line "By jingo! Buy America!" attacking the renewed nationalism of the Reagan years and the group's antagonism toward it. Although Ronald Reagan had been elected President before R.E.M. released its first record, the national shift rightward had become more pronounced during the Republican's second administration, which would not expire until the start of 1989, and R.E.M., for all their down-home-Southern roots, wanted nothing to do with it.

"(America) would be a nice piece of land if you could wipe out most of the people," said Peter Buck to Mat Smith of *Melody Maker* that summer of '87. Two years earlier, he had posed for magazine covers in front of the national flag.

"In America, if you can't make money, they think it's because you're a failure," Stipe said in the same interview. "The work ethic is really intrinsic to American thought and that has a lot to do with the LP."

Ironically, no one better exemplified the American work ethic than the singer himself. He set up a desk behind the mixing console at which he would be constantly working, either on his lyrics or writing letters to friends. "It made you feel like you wanted to be working too," says Scott Litt. "He was great at just being motivated, and challenging his energies."

When he needed solace, or wished to type without disturbing his partners, Stipe would retire to his vocal booth where the tapping of the keys bled through the microphone with a delightful vibrancy. Their sound was placed at the beginning of 'McCarthy' with little prethought, but they came to serve as a reminder of the omnipotent Big Brother, keeping files on one's every move, that symbolised the McCarthy era.

Stipe's work ethic showed up in the reveille 'Finest Worksong', and in the decision to name the upcoming shows 'The Work Tour'. It was Stipe, too, who came up with the album's title. As the group mixed the album while watching various historical films – the 1936 Berlin Olympics, the televised transmission of the McCarthy hearings – he suggested *Document*. That, says Litt, is when "everything came together".

The record defined itself both as a document of the latest year in R.E.M.'s life, and as a documentary of the world around them. As such it was able to draw on a wide range of subject matters to make its point. An old Wire song, 'Strange', brought into the live set the previous year, was originally intended as a B-side, but with lines like "There's something strange going on tonight . . . Michael's nervous and the lights are bright," it made more sense amidst the chaos of the first side. A stirring speech by Mother Ann Lee, 17th century founder of the Shakers, an American religious sect who practised celibacy and communal living, formed the lyrics for 'Fireplace'. Athens winos became the subject matter for 'Oddfellows Local 151', and a ramble about 'Lightnin' Hopkins' gave birth to a song of that name.

The lilting sensitivity of 'King Of Birds' opened up the possibility that Stipe was following the well trodden path of a star examining his own psyche with the lines "I am the King of all I see, my kingdom for a voice" and "standing on the shoulders of giants leaves me cold". Yet Stipe, as usual, would never let on.

The lyricist also retained some of his cherished ambiguity with 'Disturbance At The Heron House'. Scott Litt, sensing that it read "like a short story", chose to discuss its content with Stipe – something he otherwise shied away from during the album's recording. "I remember sitting down with him and saying, 'This is what it means,' going into this long spiel, and he looked me in the eye and said: 'You're right, that's exactly right.' Now that I know Michael, I realise that he could have been bullshitting me – which he probably was!" When, in subsequent interviews, Stipe expressed his (supposed) exasperation at the fact that "not one single person understood what that song was about", that only appeared to confirm Litt's final assumption.

But the biggest misunderstanding was reserved for *Document*'s centrepiece, 'The One I Love'. The first R.E.M. song to feature pop music's most overused word in its title, it was frequently taken at face value, the opening line, "This one goes out to the one I love", suggesting that Stipe was indeed relating a genuine passion. If so, the second line, "This one goes out to the one I left behind", was probably a reference to a faraway partner from a touring musician, and the third, "a simple prop to occupy my time", merely acknowledged how uncomplicated these emotions were.

In fact, it was a song of betrayal. "The one I left behind" was someone who had been rejected, cast off. He or she was no more than a "simple prop to occupy" the singer's time, useful only for brief moments of passion. If love had ever been expressed, it had never been meant. Final proof of deception came in the third verse, with the only new line of the entire song stating that "another prop has occupied my time". The singer had moved on to the next object, evidently with no more intention of longevity than with the previous one.

Michael Stipe, as well as insisting it was not autobiographical, has claimed that the lyric was so brutal he felt reluctant to commit it to vinyl. Even were this true, the sheer emotion of the performance ensured that it would always be a key track. The group recorded an acoustic version to cover all options – in future live shows, they would play the first verse that way – but agreed on the more powerful treatment for the album. On this, each of the three verses began with the same explosively direct guitar motif, each ended with the anguished cry 'Fire!' The result was both succinct and draining. Visitors to the studio would encounter an excited

R.E.M. ready to blast the finished track to them from the loudest speakers. "We were so proud of it," says Litt.

★　　★　　★

It had been two full years since R.E.M.'s last European performances, two years of intense longing by a hard-core fan base whose thirst had previously been sated every few months. When it was announced that the group were performing a mere four shows on the entire continent in September '87, stopping off only in London, Utrecht, Paris and Düsseldorf before rushing back to the sanctity of their homeland, tickets sold out instantly.

At London's Hammersmith Odeon on September 12, R.E.M. opened the 'Work' tour with their first concert in almost ten months, the longest such absence of their career. Suspicions that they would be rusty were dispelled by the opening chords of 'Finest Worksong'; doubts that their UK following might have lost some enthusiasm were proven equally without foundation when the audience sang along to its every word – even though the album was still two days away from official release.

Absent from the stage was the Michael Stipe who had appeared so physically sick during 1985, replaced by a healthier extrovert who engaged in amusing banter with the front rows and spun across the stage with an enthusiasm not known since the group's earliest days. Gone, too, were the doubtful songs from that fateful album recorded in London, replaced by the energetic anthems of the last two records. Performing under a purposely askew lighting gantry, they turned the usually comfortable seated confines of the Odeon into a club atmosphere, and responded to the audience's fervour in kind, deciding on the spur of the moment to perform 'Wolves, Lower' "for the first time since 1983". It was a beautiful mess, guitar riffs going astray and quizzical looks being passed among the performers. They subsequently asked the audience: How many times *should* the chorus of 'house in order' be played? Three times, as the group had just done, or four, as Mike Mills asserted? *Chronic Town* had never been released in the UK, but almost 4,000 voices roared back the correct response: four. They knew the songs better than the band.

At the end of three encores, the house lights went up and the

The very first public performance of R.E.M. at the Church on Oconee Street, Saturday, April 5, 1980. (*Sandra-Lee Phipps*)

Michael Stipe at the University of Georgia Art Department in Athens, 1979, before the formation of R.E.M. (*Terry Allen*)

R.E.M. photographed by their friend Carol Levy during the same session which produced the shot on the back of the 'Radio Free Europe' single. Carol later died in a car crash; the song 'Camera' was largely inspired by her. (*Carol Levy*)

R.E.M. go through their paces at Tyrone's during 1981. The Athens club was their favourite haunt in these formative days. Michael Stipe was so quiet and reserved at art school that fellow students went to Tyrone's "just to see him jump around."
(*Terry Allen/Jay Thomas*)

Among Bill Miller's whirlygigs, Gainesville, Georgia, filming *Left Of Reckoning*.
(*Laura Levine*)

Bertis Downs IV,
the loyal fan and lawyer
who became R.E.M.'s
co-manager with
Jefferson Holt.
(*Sandra-Lee Phipps*)

R.E.M. unload at Leeds, England, during their 1984 tour. At far
right is co-manager Jefferson Holt. (*Cheshire*)

The group in Paris, 1984. (*Cheshire*)

Performing 'So You Wanna Be A Rock'n'Roll Star' at New Jersey's Capitol Theatre for MTV's Rock Influences show on folk rock with the song's composer, Roger McGuinn. (*Sandra-Lee Phipps*)

Clockwise, from top left: Michael, Peter, Mike and Bill. (James Herbert)

Peter Buck outside his Athens home during the filming of 'Athens, Ga. – Inside/ Out'.
For the best part of a year he walked around town in Pyjamas and smoking jacket.
(*Sandra-Lee Phipps*)

Michael Stipe and Bill Berry, discussing *Out Of Time*, in Athens, February 1991. (*LFI*)

R.E.M. on stage at Hammersmith Odeon, London, May 28, 1989,
during a soundcheck on the *Green* tour. (*Steve Double/SIN*)

audience were duly expected to leave. But they didn't. After two years' waiting, many simply couldn't bear the thought of another such absence, stomping their feet, hollering and applauding until, several minutes later, a bemused and exhilarated R.E.M. returned to satisfy the hunger, pulling 'Radio Free Europe' out of the mists of time to conclude an unforgettable night. Four shows over an entire continent were not going to win R.E.M. too many new fans, but they did serve to rekindle old flames.

★　　★　　★

Peter Buck was talking about *Document*'s commercial potential just before its American release on August 31, 1987. "With virtually every record we turn in to the record company we hear outside opinion that 'this is the one that's going to break you guys'. I think at this late date it would be really delusional to even think that's going to happen. Then again I don't care."

The apparently unambitious hero of the underground had been saying pretty much the same thing every year – that R.E.M. and mainstream success were ill suited to each other. Sooner or later, he was bound to be proved wrong.

Document was received with near unanimous acclaim by both fans and critics alike, all of whom recognised that for the first time on album, R.E.M. were not deliberately swimming against their own tide; rather than reacting against *Lifes Rich Pageant*, *Document* was instead a convergence of that album's accessibility and the complexities of *Fables*. The subtleties of *Murmur* and the rawness of *Reckoning* were in there somewhere too. It was the sound of a band entirely at ease with itself – and whatever fortunes such confidence might bring.

Document duly charged into the American charts, and within three weeks became the group's first Top 20 album. That was to be expected, however much Buck hated to admit it. It was even to be anticipated that 'The One I Love' would become an enormous hit on rock radio – although its authors must have found it somewhat perverse to be challenging Yes, Pink Floyd and Rush for the honour of the biggest AOR song.

What no one had hoped or imagined was that 'The One I Love' would cross over into that last bastion of resistance – Top 40 radio –

to become a genuine hit single. During October, it did exactly that, a combination of the song's tailor-made radio sound and the surface appeal of its lyrics helping render it one of the most familiar hits of the autumn. Its climb up the singles chart was steady and deliberate until, in the first week of December, it peaked at number nine. By then, *Document* had also – just – made the Top 10 and been certified gold, and the group had finished an eight week American tour, with guitar tech Buren Fowler playing a second guitar on stage on several songs, as he had done the year before. It was a short stint, true, but it involved playing to 250,000 people, more than a year's arduous touring would have achieved four years before.

That same week, clearly the zenith of the group's career thus far, R.E.M. received a notable accolade when *Rolling Stone* put them on the front cover under the headline 'America's Best Rock & Roll Band'. The magazine which had been born of the first alternative rock movement, in San Francisco in 1967, had dominated the American music media throughout the Eighties as the 'hip' voice of mainstream and, as such, its support for R.E.M. was vital to the group's credibility, both within and outside the music industry. Understandably, the cover story caught the group at a pivotal moment, desperately trying to adapt to its new-found fame. Peter Buck, for one, seemed to have concluded that the band was as big as he was willing to let it become. "I will never, ever, *ever* play a place that's bigger than the place we played tonight, ever," he said the day after playing a general admission show to 12,000 people in Williamsburg, where there was yet another audience crush. "If we ever did a stadium tour, I would imagine it would be about the last thing we'd ever do together."

Then again, it was no real surprise that when R.E.M. finally broke through, they did so with such a vengeance. For years, their cult success had been threatening to overflow like floodwater against a crumbling dam, merely waiting for the right song to burst the banks.

"'The One I Love' I always heard as a hit record," says Scott Litt, claiming that he even bet Bill Berry it would make the Top 10. "People would laugh, but I never had a problem hearing that record on Top 40 radio between a Whitney Houston song and something else, the beauty of it being that it's so simple and stark."

Don Dixon says he always believed it would take time – and the right song – to break down radio resistance. "Regardless of what 'The One I Love' sounded like when it came out in 1987, had that come out in 1983 on *Murmur*, it wouldn't have got radio play. They built a reputation for not selling out, not trying to jump on any bandwagon and creating their own thing. So even though not all radio programmers are going to be sitting on the edge of their chair waiting for the new R.E.M. record, all will have enough interest and respect for the band to see what it is they have proffered for their use this time. So many records just don't ever get listened to, where there's not this respected background."

F.B.I. President and R.E.M. agent Ian Copeland agrees that this respect – which he accurately refers to as 'credibility' – is of supreme importance. "It's so fucking hard to get it. Once you've got it, you can go for a lot longer without having a hit record than if you had a hit record and had no credibility – then you're dead the minute it zips out of the charts."

With a hit single and a Top 10 album, R.E.M. found plenty of challenges to their credibility – and their peace of mind – at every turn: the bigger, impersonal venues they had often vowed not to play; the money that they had never expected to earn, and were almost embarrassed to possess; the cameras that clicked without asking; the local clubs that publicised their appearance when they dropped in after a performance for a quiet drink or to watch a local band . . . all these they handled with the same familiar nonchalance. Only one issue arose to suggest that the star machine was having an effect on its newest members.

New York State's whimsical 10,000 Maniacs were also beginning to taste commercial success during late '87, and their support slot with R.E.M. lent the 'Work' tour the air of a graduation party for the college radio generation. Each night, Michael Stipe would join Maniacs' singer Natalie Merchant on stage to sing 'The Campfire Song' (as he had done on their album), and soon Natalie was appearing on stage with R.E.M. to sing 'Swan Swan H'.

This mutual appreciation society started fuelling rumours of romance, encouraged with a wink and a nudge by the British music press. No one actually dared to confirm the rumour in print but wasn't it enough that the pair were travelling alone to each show on Michael's private tour bus?

Michael's private tour bus? The notion was as far removed from that of an entire band sleeping together night after night in a rusty old van or one seedy motel room as it was painfully true: Michael Stipe was indeed travelling separately from his companions.

It was not that R.E.M. had grown to hate each other. Far from it. But the differences in lifestyles between the three playing members and their singer had grown ever wider, so that with the money now available, they decided to take two buses on the road: one, at Stipe's request, would be quiet, with open windows; the other would cater for the more raucous beer swilling elements. Similarly, while Buck, Mills and Berry were happy to mill around with friends in one joint dressing room, calming each other's pre-gig nerves with furtive jokes and the odd drink, Stipe sat in isolation in a room of his own, carefully psyching himself up for what was becoming an increasingly theatrical performance. "I'm the odd man out," he explained. "They're all football fans and I'm not."

★   ★   ★

'It's The End Of The World As We Know It (And I Feel Fine)', released as a single at the beginning of 1988, failed to emulate the crossover appeal of 'The One I Love', perhaps not surprisingly given its unmitigated chaos. But it did produce one of the group's more enduring videos. Michael Stipe had initially suggested that the entire promo should consist of watching a river go by; fortunately, his proposed director Jim Herbert flatly refused to collaborate on such a non-event and instead suggested capturing the song's mayhem by taking a whirlwind journey through a young boy's room. He found a perfect youthful specimen among the skateboard team Michael Lachowski now managed in his spare time, and the result – shot in a country barn – captured the crazed media assault of the lyrics without trying to allude to their every detail.

Stipe himself took control for the album's third video 'Finest Worksong' (as with Herbert's production and New York artist Robert Longo's near-sculptural interpretation of 'The One I Love', it was shot the preceding summer). Released as a single in March, 'Finest Worksong' broke the three-singles-off-an-album barrier, and was R.E.M.'s introduction to the extended 12″ mix (arranged by Litt and Stipe, with the addition of the Uptown

Horns brass section), but even the inclusion of a beautiful live medley ('Time After Time'/'So. Central Rain') failed to entice more than the most devoted of fans. A 7″ version was never even released in America.

Perhaps, for a group within which some elements treasured cult appeal, this was just as well. Even with just the one hit single, *Document* almost doubled the sales of *Lifes Rich Pageant* – just as that album had its predecessor – and stayed in the Top 40 of the album charts for five months. By January '88, R.E.M. had their first million-selling album.

Eleven

In the Los Angeles headquarters of I.R.S. Records, the platinum sales of *Document* and the group's long overdue singles breakthrough was a cause for both celebration and trepidation. For while such success justified the label's faith in the group and its ability to turn a hip college band into one of the country's major acts, *Document* was the last album of R.E.M.'s five record deal. The group were now free to sign with any record label in the world – and could name their price.

I.R.S. had frequently tried to stave off this eventuality over the years by offering to 'renegotiate' the band's deal, increasing their royalties and upfront advances in return for more records from the group. Most artists, always eager for as much money in the hand as possible, respond to – or even initiate – such a tactic; R.E.M., much to Miles Copeland's chagrin, preferred to sit it out and wait.

Not that I.R.S. expected the group simply to desert them. The group may have frequently put its foot down in regard to a finished mix, video or sleeve design, and occasionally the label had insisted it knew better what song should be a single, but these were nothing compared to the daily tug of war that exists between most artists and their labels.

"I really think there was a level of communication there," says Jay Boberg of his 'special relationship' with R.E.M. "They were dealing with the head guy in the company. They didn't need to explain many things to me. I knew. They would say, 'We wanna do this,' and I would just know why they wanted to do it, how they wanted to do it, and how I could go make it happen for them."

Because R.E.M.'s fan base was so large, the group was sure to be guaranteed complete artistic control by every competitor. Boberg therefore had to hope that loyalty, friendship and experience – the fact that I.R.S. had actually *given* the band complete control rather

158

than just promise them it – would win the day. At the back of his mind, he knew that any doubts R.E.M. had about re-signing stemmed from the size and youth of I.R.S. – qualities that, ironically, had endeared the band to the label in the first place.

"A bigger company is more powerful; a bigger company has more leverage in the market," says Boberg. "I.R.S. is a closely held company. Miles and I are the owners. What happens if I get run over by a truck one day? Then where are they? It was just less stable."

R.E.M., believed Boberg, "felt that great as I.R.S. was, I.R.S. was best at doing exactly what we'd done for R.E.M. Which was: take a baby band, develop them, feed them like a little seedling, give them the space to grow, create that family, and break them. I felt that their analysis was that when it came to take that act from one million to three million units, there were probably companies that did it better than I.R.S."

The group, while confirming the above suppositions, were most concerned about their almost complete lack of success overseas. This applied partially to the UK, where they found it hard to understand how such a supposedly progressive musical country still excluded them from the mainstream; it applied in particular to continental Europe and other territories where I.R.S. were licensed through CBS International, a company that the group believed neither understood nor cared about them.

"I'll be the first to admit that CBS did not necessarily get the plot in those early days," says Jay Boberg of the years when R.E.M. consistently toured Europe. "But from that point forward R.E.M. only did one four date tour. So for them to complain . . ."

"I can see his point, but we did five tours of Europe," counters Peter Buck. In the end, he says, the group started asking themselves, "Why are we going to Europe if basically American servicemen come to our shows? If the records aren't promoted? It just doesn't make a lot of sense."

It was this attitude Boberg had to contend with when he attempted to talk R.E.M. into planning, well in advance, a major world tour for *Document*. It was his best and last chance to prove I.R.S.'s capabilities abroad and, "They came back and said they just didn't want to do it."

"I wasn't sure I wanted to be on the road all that year," says Peter Buck, "when we'd been over there a lot, and spent weeks and weeks and weeks beating our heads against the walls, playing to nobody, and we didn't have that much fun anyway."

The sour experiences of recording *Fables* in London in 1985 and the limited live successes in Europe that year had tainted their view of the continent, to the extent that the band appeared willing to engage in a self-fulfilling prophecy: the less they toured, the less they would sell records in Europe, and therefore the more excuse they would have for seeking out a bigger record label.

With this and other factors in mind, Jefferson Holt and Bertis Downs duly made the rounds of American majors, narrowing I.R.S.'s competitors down to Columbia, Arista, A&M and Warner Brothers.

All these companies would give the group almost anything they wanted. But Lenny Waronker, President at Warner Brothers, believed he had three ace cards in pursuing the group. The first was that, "We could offer them very strong distribution. Warner Brothers has built itself up over the years to be a very powerful record company," particularly in the international sphere that was so important to the group.

Secondly, "You had this company that aligned itself with acts that they all liked – most of their favourite records came out of this company." Warner Brothers was still home to the commercially unpredictable Van Dyke Parks and Randy Newman and had recently taken on Neil Young; if the label could keep these often difficult musicians content, it could presumably do the same for R.E.M. Besides, during the Eighties, Warner Brothers or its subsidiaries had taken the lead on the alternative post-punk scene, having signed The B-52's, The Replacements, and Hüsker Dü, none of whom seemed particularly unhappy with their experience.

Finally, there was "the fact that we understood the mentality of the band, and wouldn't pressure them to do certain things they couldn't do, aesthetically. We absolutely understood their aesthetic concerns. And at the same time wanted to get them as far as we possibly could get them without interfering with that." In other words, the all-important ability to sell a band without the band selling out: an ability that could only be proven by practice.

Eleven

R.E.M.'s decision to go with Warner Brothers was not financial. "The last thing we wanted to do was to make it an auction," says Bertis Downs, and Lenny Waronker confirms that, "We never talked about a deal until they made a commitment. They wanted to make a choice based on the qualities of a record company and how they felt the relationship would be, rather than on money. They took a risk in a way, because they made their choice and then negotiated, but I thought that was an incredibly fair way of doing it."

That means it was almost a done deal when the group acquiesced to I.R.S.'s request to know the figures being discussed. Miles Copeland understandably went into shock when he was informed, as he recalls, that the advances over five albums would break the $10 million barrier, ranging from $2m–$3m a record, that royalties would break 20 points, and that R.E.M. would maintain ownership of their master tapes, merely 'leasing' them to a label for an agreed period of time. Copeland believes this period to be ten years; Downs insists "he wouldn't know", but that it would be long enough for any label to "make a lot of money off them." Either way, it was a near-enough unprecedented demand. By convention, record companies always owned the masters of the recordings they financed; as these recordings moved into back catalogue, they became the label's long-term assets. (The fortunes of RCA without Elvis Presley's annual sales, or EMI without The Beatles', would have made for very different reading.) But R.E.M.'s business acumen was second to none. Like many acts, they owned their own publishing; like many acts, they couldn't see why they shouldn't own their recordings too. Unlike other acts, however, they were in a perfect bargaining position. Still, most labels would have balked at any band insisting on such a condition in 1988, and I.R.S. was among them.

"The deal was a deal that it was impossible for I.R.S. to make," says Miles Copeland, who as manager of The Police, and now its solo former front man Sting, knew a thing or two about driving a hard bargain with a record label. Unlike a major corporation with its own pressing facilities and distribution, I.R.S. was tied to the constraints of its own manufacturing and distribution contract with MCA. Copeland was prepared to match the points and advances, admitting that he needed R.E.M. "just for the credibility; even if we made no money from the act, just to have it for our volume was important," but he could not offer reversion of the masters when his own deal with MCA did not allow for such. Neither could he offer the full royalty on compact discs as Warner Brothers was willing to do; MCA was among the major labels still deplorably deducting royalties from artists (and distributed labels such as I.R.S.) under the guise that CDs were a "new technology" – despite the fact that they had been a profitable venture for years and were costing less to manufacture than vinyl, while retailing for nearly 50 per cent more.

Jay Boberg, determined not to lose the band, says he "worked out a way" to "deal with" the problem of CD royalties, and threw down his own ace card, "the ability to offer them higher royalties on their back catalogue." I.R.S. put in the biggest bid of its life.

But it was not enough. R.E.M.'s minds were made up. Besides, they must have been aware that such a deal could have bankrupted I.R.S. Where, for example, would the money come from to market the band if I.R.S. had risked the bank merely re-signing them? For a company of Warner Brothers' size, the group's financial demands – which, while the group never talks specifics, were certainly close to those discussed by Copeland – were easily met. "I don't think that any record company that was involved would have shied away from it," says Waronker who, along with Warner Brothers chairman Mo Ostin, was prescient enough to recognise that the 'leasing' issue should not hinder a potentially momentous deal. Peter Buck blithely observes, "We could have gotten more money elsewhere," and he is probably right, were money the only aspect of the deal that mattered. But it wasn't.

Negotiating with Warner Brothers was therefore the easy part. Letting I.R.S. down was, says everyone concerned with R.E.M., the hardest group decision of their lives. Jay Boberg was invited to Athens to be told in person.

"It was a terrible, terrible day," says Downs, "because Jay to this day is a very good friend of the band's. The thing I finally explained was their having only one career, they had to make the right decision. If they knew they were going to be doing this until they were 60, maybe we would have re-signed with I.R.S. for a few more years and seen what was going to happen. We felt it was the critical turning point, it was going to be the next significant chunk of the band's output, and they had to maximise what they were going to do, not only with the money, but their career."

"It was a real hard move," acknowledges Peter Buck. "There's no label in the world that could have done for us what they did. What other label would have been able to get us to where we were, trusted us to give us the artistic control? Sometimes you just feel it's time to move on."

None of which comforts Jay Boberg. "I think injustice occurred, in that the little guy got beaten out for no apparent, no obvious reason," he said almost a year after the dust had settled. "I can't begin to tell you that I'm not still bitterly disappointed."

★　★　★

Financially secure thanks to the Warner Brothers deal, R.E.M. might have been expected to take time off. But their determination to release an album every calendar year got the better of them, and they were already back at John Keane's studio in Athens, recording demos, by February of '88.

The intent was to emerge with a new sound. For although *Document* contained more dark, forbidding moments – particularly on its second side – than *Lifes Rich Pageant*, R.E.M. were concerned that their platinum breakthrough had sounded too much like its predecessor(s). In their view, by opening successive albums with ready-made anthems like 'Begin The Begin' and 'Finest Worksong' they were falling foul of their own myth; in embracing what they feared was an arena rock sound, that they were becoming too formulaic.

The three playing members decided to get around this problem by picking up each other's instruments. The process was partly an education, forcing themselves to learn to play equipment they'd often taken for granted, and partly an attempt to explore the inherent chemistry of the group, to see whether R.E.M. remained R.E.M. even when its characters changed their roles.

"We wanted to do something a little different," explained Peter Buck the following year, "and also to get away from the whole idea that you had to have bass, drums and guitar to be in a rock'n'roll band." Michael Stipe had felt hemmed in by the group's rock instrumentation, and "wanted to start painting some of the landscape himself," according to Scott Litt, who was re-hired as co-producer and worked on the demos. Whereas previously Stipe had allowed the band to write all the instrumental parts before he began on lyrics, now he joined in at the initial stages.

When these new lyrical and musical approaches collided, as they did on the song 'You Are The Everything', the result was the remarkable stylistic change the group had been hoping for. Despite a certain fear expressed in Stipe's lyrics, the effect was more wistful than melancholic, a love song as he had never sung before. Behind his yearning voice lay a ballad as emotive as the group had attempted, with simple instrumentation that found Mills on accordion, Buck on mandolin and Berry taking to the bass.

"'Everything' opened it all up for Michael," says Scott Litt. "Because he didn't have to fight against the drumbeat, he didn't have to fight against instrumentation that he might not accept." A song 'Hairshirt' came together in a similar manner, starting out "as just a couple of chords on a mandolin or a piano," as Litt recalls. "Michael would take that tape and come up with the whole verse and chorus, and then we would add the instrumentation after the vocals were done. This was a marked departure from their previous writing. Instead of doing the vocals last, they started doing the vocals first."

Seven songs were demoed to vocal stage, another five left instrumental; the group deemed this sufficient and, while the ink was still drying on their new recording contract, entered Ardent Studios in Memphis, where Big Star had frequently recorded, in May. *Document* had been recorded and mixed in only seven or so weeks; for the new album, a whole three months was put aside for recording alone.

The group could well afford the increased expense. Ever since the surprise success of *Murmur*, R.E.M. had recouped recording costs the day of an album's release, and now that they were in the platinum sales bracket, such a lengthy stay was sure to be financially viable. They were also admitting that they were no longer the biggest fish in a small pond of cult popularity, but a medium sized fish in an enormous river of mass acceptance, and as such, had to comply to certain production standards that necessitated time and money. As much as anything though, they simply wanted time to experiment, to break with tradition, to try things out without watching the clock.

"We had a great budget, we had the time to do it, and there was a group of people that were very close, that really trusted each other, and it was really time to shoot for the stars," says Scott Litt. Not that he found the process easy. "*Document*, which was really effortless, turned into *Green*, which was the hardest effort I've put forth."

"It wasn't hard, it just took longer," counters Peter Buck. "And it took longer because we allowed ourselves a lot of time to do it."

With the exception of its reference to the colour of American money, of which R.E.M. were now known to have plenty, the title *Green* was chosen early in the day for its many positive connotations: the group's 'Green' politics, for naïvete and enthusiasm. It was, says Michael Stipe, a slap in the face to the 'shop-bought cynicism' of the era. Lyrically, he made a conscious decision to turn the political anger expressed over the last two records into optimism. Cynics might suggest that he wanted to avoid controversy with a major label, but any ulterior motives were probably born more out of a desire to avoid the microscopic attention the 'social' lyrics had brought upon him. Stipe was still under thirty, and yet was getting ordained with the 'spokesman of a generation' mantle. Time, perhaps, to erect some distance from that public perception.

The only political number that made it to *Green* therefore was 'Orange Crush'. Ostensibly about the effects of Agent Orange and the Vietnam War, it was a hangover, both musically and lyrically, from the apocalyptic mood of *Document*. Yet while it gave the new album a much needed anthem, it was also close in style to the bombastic stadium rock of U2; for these reasons, Michael Stipe sang what might have been construed as the song's chorus through a bullhorn.

It was also to avert claims of repetition and to push themselves forward that the group rejected many of the demos recorded back in Athens: a song 'Title' that had appeared throughout the 'Work' tour and three other instrumentals that bore all the hallmarks of familiar R.E.M.; in addition a samba called 'Carnival', complete with overdubs and melody, "just didn't fit the tenor of the album," says Peter Buck.

In between the extremes of anthems and ballads, the group found an upbeat, commercial middle ground that would dominate the first side of the record. The opening number was titled 'Pop Song 89', and on it Stipe alternated between calling 'Hi!' while wondering aloud about the songwriter's perceived motivations: "Should we talk about the weather/should we talk about the government?" Its successor, 'Get Up', was a similarly sanguine rallying call that at least allowed for some confusion, Stipe singing "Dreams they complicate my life" while behind him Bill Berry echoed "Dreams they *complement* my life".

The most overtly commercial track was left for later. Early in the demo proceedings, the group had come up with a chord structure so inane and simplistic they decided to follow it to its logical con-clusion. Peter Buck even went out and bought a wah-wah pedal specifically for a cheesy guitar solo in the middle. By the time it was done, they had pulled out the old pop producer's trick of raising the final chorus a key – and then ridiculed themselves by doing the same again. Michael Stipe decided to rise to the challenge by dumbing down lyrically. His words seemed straightforward to the extreme: "stand in the place where you live, think about direction, wonder why you haven't before." They were in fact a reference to his friend Georgina Falzarano, whose sense of direction was so bad that in a strange town, she would "make a real conscious effort to know where north is," and then "visualise I'm standing in front of my house."*

Musically, these three songs at once both celebrated pop music and commented on it. They could therefore be taken at face value, with a smile, or with a large pinch of salt – and still with a smile. But they didn't exactly challenge, as had been the band's original intent. That was left to other material, some of which came together but slowly. The caustic 'Turn You Inside-Out' was written and recorded during the mixing stages in Woodstock, NY. It concerned the power of the performer, a threatening refrain, "I

---

* In Denise Sullivan's oral history of R.E.M., *Talk About The Passion,* Falzarano also claimed to be the object of 'You Are The Everything'.

could turn you inside out, but I choose not to do", being met by the object of the singer's charisma promising, "I believe in what you do, I believe in watching you". But, as Stipe pointed out, he could as easily be referring to the power of Hitler or Martin Luther King as that of Michael Stipe.

'World Leader Pretend' was less ambiguous – and intentionally so, allowing that its lyrics were printed on the album sleeve, a first for the band. Stipe appeared to be admitting to colouring his presentation with elements of charade and pretence over the years: "I've a rich understanding of my finest defenses" and "I recognise the weapons, I've practiced them well, I fitted them myself". Then, teasing his audience like any good rock chameleon – or was it a promise to come clean and be honest from here on in? – he announced that "it's high time I razed the walls that I've constructed . . . This is my mistake, let me make it good."

The lyric was less an attempt by Michael Stipe to debunk his own myth as much as a confession that he had created one, something he elaborated upon during interviews at the time. To the *NME*'s Sean O'Hagan in late '88, he described his image as "an accurate representation of what I put out, which is not of course an accurate representation of me, but those are two different things. I'm aware of the power of it and I'm aware of the ways to manipulate it, the word manipulate being both good and bad. I think I'm aware of how people perceive me."

And to Q magazine's Adrian Deevoy, he commented that, "I know what I'm doing. I recognise when that caricature is getting out of hand and I pull back and I recognise when it needs to go further and I push it."

None of this new found honesty served to quell the fanaticism with which Stipe was treated by his followers – or Distiples, as they were cynically referred to, a term of derision which applied as much to the small coterie of followers always around him as it did to the audience that roared approval at his every word.

In Athens it therefore caused some consternation among those who remembered Stipe as a regular, fun-loving person, when he would deny to the press that he still lived in the town (although he did purchase a sizeable country retreat as well as maintain an Athens residence) or would turn around upon entering bars and restaurants when confronted by a sea of awestruck collegiate faces.

"I think he just suffers from anything that a person would have with success," says Jim Herbert in his defence. "Egotistically I think he likes it very, very much, and in terms of esteem, one of the things artists enjoy is the success, the fame. But I think like most artists, he would like to have the work be better than he is; I think artists secretly would almost sign somebody else's name if they could. They watch through a keyhole as people are in awe. The ego is the awe of the audience. But they really don't want the self-aggrandizement, they don't want to actually have the compliment delivered to them. They're shy of that bit. And they probably don't always receive that bit well."

Ultimately, the inconsistencies within Michael Stipe's character – the early denial of purposeful mystique countered by the later confession of a performer's persona, the supposed approachability confounded by the apparent reclusiveness – were testimony to the inconsistencies within human nature. People were all too keen to note Michael Stipe's talent and intrigue; they sometimes seemed to forget he was mere flesh and blood.

The other members of R.E.M. suffered no such dilemmas with their egos or concerns with fan worship. When Peter Buck attempted to show Bill Berry the drum pattern he intended for *Green*'s closing song – with typical perversity, it remained untitled – the drummer was amazed. It was so bad, he said, that it was impossible to repeat for three whole minutes. Buck duly held on to the drumsticks and played the jerky, "undrummerish" rhythm himself. Despite its hesitant beat, it rounded *Green* off in soothing style. "This song is here to keep you warm," sang Stipe. "This song is here to keep you strong."

Twelve

R.E.M. stayed off the live circuit completely during 1988. For a group that seemed to so enjoy playing, the respite was unprecedented. But away from the stage the band was as active as ever. There was the intense period of business meetings which culminated in the move to Warner Brothers; the four months spent rehearsing, recording and mixing *Green*; and further time taken up by video and press chores. Outside all this, the individuals indulged in personal projects with relentless enthusiasm.

Mike Mills produced an album, *Sixes And Sevens*, for Athens group Billy James. Bill Berry worked with Atlanta singer-songwriter Michelle Malone on her album *New Experience*, and recorded a pseudo country single 'My Bible Is The Latest TV Guide'/ 'Things I'd Like To Say', for release on Jefferson Holt's independent label Dog Gone Records under the name 13111.

Michael Stipe teamed up with Natalie Merchant and The Roches to record a delightful rendition of 'Little April Showers' for inclusion on the tribute album of Walt Disney songs, *Stay Awake*. He also established a close friendship with Michael Meister, for whose West Coast independent label Texas Hotel he produced the début record by his sister Lynda's new band Hetch Hetchy, recommended other eclectic Athens musicians Chickasaw Mudpuppies and Vic Chesnutt, and began work on a much vaunted solo album, *Field Recordings*.

Stipe also headlined the summer's Athens Music Festival, performing alongside Atlanta duo The Indigo Girls. Both he and the playing members of R.E.M. then separately contributed to The Indigo Girls' acclaimed eponymous début album produced by Scott Litt, Stipe providing a vocal on the song 'Kid Fears', and the band a backing track on 'Closer To Fine'. Proving that they had not yet settled into adult sobriety, the trio turned up at the studio too inebriated to record; they returned the next day to do the job properly.

But all this activity combined could not match the irrepressible Peter Buck. He became an eager sidekick for his former hero Robyn Hitchcock: having played on the former Soft Boys' *Globe Of Frogs* album in '87, Buck toured with him during '88 and then brought his distinctive 12-string guitar lines back into the studio for Hitchcock's early '89 album, *Queen Elvis*. He recorded an un-released album with exiles from the Georgia Satellites and Swimming Pool Qs as The Nasty Bucks (named not after him but another member's previous band); played on the album *Mystery Road* by Atlanta rockers Drivin'n'Cryin', the band R.E.M.'s former onstage second guitarist Buren Fowler had just joined; co-produced the album *Hardly Not Even* for Minneapolis group Run Westy Run; and kept an ancient promise by financing the release of a live album by Atlanta's once-finest, The Fans, on DB Records.

Buck's extracurricular activities, as producer or guitarist in the studio, and 'special guest' at almost any show he attended, was all the more remarkable for having come to the guitar so late in life. This proof that it was never too late to choose a vocation and become a leader in it, along with his modest demeanour and genuine enthusiasm for live music, had long made him a role model among the underground, and he was further deified when he became the star of his own comic strip, drawn and published by a local Athens music fan. In it, the caricature super hero Peter Buck engaged in a quest to preserve the future of rock'n'roll while knocking back six-packs and stopping off to jam with any creaking door that he passed by – remarkably like the real life character. Buck feigned embarrassment at the strip; his credibility continued to soar.

On April 29, however, he appeared to wave a permanent fare-well to his restless past by marrying girlfriend Barrie Greene, co-manager of the 40 Watt Club, in Mexico. What better bride for a man who spent his every night in bars and clubs than a woman who ran the best live joint in his home town?

I.R.S. Records was also busy during 1988. Stung by R.E.M.'s departure from the label at the peak of the group's popularity, Jay

Boberg decided to capitalise on his assets and release a 'best of' compilation. "There was no vindictiveness," says Boberg, but "from a business standpoint, I certainly wasn't going to let that opportunity go away." R.E.M. could (and in retrospect maybe should) have distanced themselves from such a project and urged fans to boycott it, but it was a mark of their respect for the label's hard work thus far, and its right to reap further rewards, that R.E.M. instead collaborated on the project, ensuring their satisfaction with its outcome in the process.

Eponymous was released in early October with minor incentives for R.E.M. collectors – 'Romance', from the soundtrack of *Made In Heaven*, and alternate mixes of 'Radio Free Europe', 'Gardening At Night' and 'Finest Worksong' – along with seven previously released singles and 'Talk About The Passion', for which a new, politically uncompromising video was shot by Stipe's friend Jem Cohen. The back sleeve was dominated by a teenage Michael Stipe gazing absentmindedly from above his mid-Seventies open collar shirt. On one level, this appeared as a further thrust by the singer to the forefront of the group's visibility. On another, it was merely a joke at his image's expense: across the top of the photograph was printed, 'They Airbrushed My Face'.

★　　★　　★

November 8, 1988. Across the United States, millions of voters go to the polls and elect Republican George Bush as President of the United States, in a landslide over Democrat rival Mike Dukakis. Across Athens, Georgia, a flurry of music media professionals go to assorted locations in town to interview R.E.M. And across the world, *Green* is released.

The timing was no coincidence. *Green* may have lacked the direct political tones of its predecessors, but the group that recorded it were becoming increasingly disgusted with the American way of life. Rather than merely pass comment from the safe distance of a music press interview, both Michael Stipe and Peter Buck gave money to the Dukakis campaign, Stipe extending his involvement to the point of placing pro-Dukakis adverts in local newspapers. They read: 'Stipe Says – Don't Get Bushwacked – Get Out And Vote Smart – Dukakis.'

There's a not-so-thin line between rock musicians writing songs about political affairs, or talking about their personal beliefs in interviews, and those same rock musicians standing on a soapbox dictating to the public how they should behave. With these ads, Stipe stepped boldly, bravely, and not a little foolishly, right through that line. Given that Dukakis never had a real hope of getting elected, Stipe's views could be passed off as the continued championing of the underdog, but they also represented the first occasion that R.E.M.'s popularity had been used in what could be considered a patronising manner.

The singer seemed aware of this almost immediately thereafter, telling *NME*'s Sean O'Hagan that, "We're a pop band . . . You do what you can. I was aware of pushing the limits of my job. . . . I mean, there are subtler ways in which you can endorse things."

Clearly there was a level of defensiveness about the band at this point. They knew all too well that their commercial breakthrough the previous year and the size of their new record deal would lead to murmurs of the dreaded term 'sell out'. Inviting the music media for its annual pilgrimage to Athens upon the release of their new R.E.M. album placed the town heroes under closer scrutiny than usual. Could R.E.M. remain the same humble people now that they were recognised on the streets everywhere they went? Could they remain politically active when a mayor they didn't even vote for wanted to give them the keys to the city? Could they still associate with other, struggling bands now that they were one of the biggest industries in the city with a turnover in the millions of dollars?

R.E.M. believed so. Their humility was preserved, they said, by the fact that here they were hardly noticed, let alone harassed. Outsiders indeed observed an almost wilful refusal by locals to acknowledge the rock stars in favoured hangouts such as the Georgia Bar or Rocky's Pizzeria. The group explained, in interviews conducted on the porch of Peter Buck's enviable new mansion, that once each year's new intake of students realised they could see their heroes any night of the week, they simply left them alone. (Michael Stipe, by virtue of his increased public visibility and image-mongering, suffered the harassment on behalf of everyone.) And if Peter Buck's personal humility was endangered by the size of his house, it was reinforced by his inviting the world to his door to laugh at the perversity of it all.

As for their politics, Stipe decided to walk it like he talked it, going beyond his endorsement of Dukakis to get more involved in grass roots politics. Where possible, R.E.M./Athens Ltd. used its clout as a major local business to block conservative council proposals, and where necessary, used its finance: when the city would not back a $5,000 study to find ways of preserving historic buildings in a new civic centre design, the group donated the money themselves.

And if their musical contemporaries were jealous or bitter, they didn't show it. R.E.M.'s constant championing of Pylon as a major influence even caused that band's members to consider re-forming, at which R.E.M. promptly offered up their rehearsal space as an incentive. It worked: Pylon became a group once more.

★   ★   ★

It had been widely assumed by the music industry that with its first major label album, R.E.M. would make a comfortable transition from arena appeal to stadium stardom. "So many people were expecting *The Joshua Tree*," says Scott Litt, referring to the U2 album that, to put things in perspective, had spent nine weeks at number one and yielded two chart-topping singles the same year R.E.M. barely grazed the American top ten with *Document*. "And early on I said (to Warner Brothers), 'Listen, I'd like to deliver you a record that's gonna sell five million copies, but *Green* is not that record.' "

It certainly wasn't. Warner Brothers hardly even got the same band, allowing for the number of songs on which the band switched instruments. And while *Green* certainly started as strong as any R.E.M. album, with the swift one-two punch of 'Pop Song 89' and 'Get Up', and the ludicrously cheerful 'Stand' sandwiched between the ballad 'You Are The Everything' and the introspective 'World Leader Pretend', the trio of obvious singles hardly represented the artistic reinvention the group had promised. On side two, only 'Turn You Inside-Out' really found the band pushing their musical envelope; the rest sounded stylistically discordant and individually unspectacular.

The American critics recognised as much. Those who could not spare *Green* repeated listens to unravel potential complexities opted to maul it, just as they would if R.E.M. *had* delivered a *Joshua Tree*. *Green* rocketed into the American top 20 but as the new year came round it was at number 15 and slipping, having fallen short of the top ten. I.R.S. was heard to complain that it could have done as good a job – if not better. Observers who had calculated that R.E.M. plus Warner Brothers added up to a chart topping certainty deduced that *Green* was a disaster.

In fact, *Green*'s slow start was part of a carefully planned strategy by R.E.M., its management, and their new record company. *Green* was, after all, the fourth R.E.M. album released in only 18 months, and even if two of those were compilations, both had been endorsed by the band. *Eponymous* in particular, despite Jay Boberg's denials of intent, had almost scuttled anticipation for *Green*, reaching number 44 on the US album charts the same month as the new studio album's release; the re-release of 'Talk About The Passion' only further confused radio and video programmers.

Perhaps as a result, no single was released from *Green* before Christmas (although 'Orange Crush' scored a direct hit on rock radio); after fulfilling their media obligations in November – at which time Michael Stipe even flew to Europe to conduct interviews solo, an unthinkable proposition only two years before – R.E.M. and their management preferred to let the album sink in with fans and took the rest of the year off.

They were merely catching breath before commencing the busiest year of their lives. In 1989, R.E.M. would work with the dedication of a band that had something to prove – which, for the first time since 1983, it did. At the end of January, the group travelled to Japan for the first time since 1984 and from there to New Zealand and Australia for the first time ever. During March and April they would tour America and Canada, playing almost without exception the arenas that had been successfully introduced on the 'Work' tour; in May and June they would attack Europe with uncharacteristic vengeance, and after a month or so off, they would make another complete circuit of North America. The entire year had been planned out as far in advance, and on the scale, that Jay Boberg had begged for on *Document*. But the band had been conserving its energy until such time as a major conglomerate could wield its global power. That time was now.

Australia greeted R.E.M. as heroes. The audience there knew the group's repertoire by heart and yet were prepared to listen – rather than shout – through Michael's a cappella songs. The Australians were relieved to discover in R.E.M. so humble a group and, in a country which takes its beer seriously, one that could drink with the best of them. *Green* promptly turned gold there.

R.E.M. then began their nine-week circuit of America with almost impeccable timing. 'Stand' had been released as a single at the beginning of January and, commercial airplay unsurprisingly forthcoming, broke into the top 30 just as the tour kicked off. For three weeks in the middle of it – during which R.E.M. played to 27,000 people over two nights in Atlanta and sold out the 16,500 tickets at New York's Madison Square Garden in an hour – 'Stand' resided at number six in the pop charts. Its playful video, primarily featuring Stipe and three friends dancing on a giant compass, topped the MTV playlist. *Green* entered a fifth month in the top twenty, overtaking *Document*'s million-plus sales in the process. *Murmur* was now past the 500,000 sales mark, with *Reckoning* and *Fables* close behind. *Rolling Stone* put the group on the cover again, this time calling R.E.M. 'America's *Hippest* Band', an important endorsement of credibility for a group charting with their most blatant pop single to date and performing in venues designed for ice hockey and basketball.

The audience at these shows was almost exclusively adolescent, a natural by-product of hit singles and MTV exposure. At Madison Square Garden that June, the author of this book endured his most dispiriting R.E.M. live experience, not down to any lack of effort by the band, but from a teenage girl right behind him screaming "I love you Michael" at the top of her voice at the most inappropriate moments, and for the hit single 'Stand', which wasn't delivered until the first encore. All around the hall, similarly young fans were screaming their own desires with equal disregard for the group's musical nuances, let alone the singer's sexual leaning. Many of R.E.M.'s first-generation fans opted simply to stay away from the tour, cherishing their memories of the band playing half empty clubs or at the most, packed out small theatres, back when mistakes were routine, impromptu covers a ritual and screaming teenage girls non-existent. "That's fine," Peter Buck told *Rolling Stone*. "A lot of people like bands when they're smaller – and I'm one of them." After many a show, he would run off stage, jump straight into a rented minivan and head for a decrepit local bar to see rock'n'roll played in the atmosphere he himself craved.

Yet R.E.M.'s concessions to the impersonal venues and younger fans were far from predictable. A screen at the back mocked arena rock's routine empty gestures with the message 'Are you ready to rock'n'roll?' and the assertion that 'It's really great to be in (your city here)'. The dB's having finally split, Peter Holsapple became an honorary on-stage member, flushing out the sound on guitar and keyboards, allowing 'World Leader Pretend' to reach its potential and 'Perfect Circle' to become part of the set after almost six years' absence. Bill Berry came off the drums to play bass during 'You Are The Everything'.

But it was Michael Stipe who dominated proceedings. The combination of critical praise, commercial success and increasing personal self-confidence had served to turn him into rock's most commanding performer. Whether singing with his back to the audience, prone on the floor, standing on a chair or through a bullhorn; whether imitating the childish dance of the 'Stand' video, furiously shadow-boxing, or stripping down to his bicycle shorts and T-shirt; whether singing Hugo Largo's 'Harpers' a cappella or dangling the audience on tenterhooks at the finale of The Velvet Underground's nightclub reverie 'After Hours'; whether sarcastically introducing 'Stand' as a work of high culture or urging his audience to boycott the Exxon Corporation, Michael Stipe transfixed all-comers. Even the fact that his phrases and actions were almost identical every night only slightly lessened their effect, and those who had seen R.E.M. in their earliest days were heard to remark on the similarity between the uninhibited Michael Stipe of yore and the charismatic frontman of now. It was another Perfect Circle.

In continental Europe, Warner Brothers' international arm WEA appeared to be helping ferment the all-important difference in sales, which rendered it something of a catastrophe when Bill Berry came down with Rocky Mountain Spotted Fever in Germany. (He'd contracted the potentially devastating illness from a tick bite in his garden in Georgia the week before.) Fortunately, only four shows were cancelled – and subsequently rearranged – before the group moved on to Britain, where there were no such disappointments.

Whether R.E.M.'s absence from the UK over the last three years had served to fuel the fires of fanaticism, or whether continued attention to the area would have resulted in an even quicker eruption of acceptance is an ultimately hypothetical proposition. Certainly by 1988 – The Smiths having split up, U2 having moved into another stratosphere and nothing of equal potential having emerged from a fragile British club scene – R.E.M. were the number one choice of rock fans all over the country. *Green* had been received by the British rock press with an enthusiasm remarkable even by their own hyperbolic standards. "The best band in the world? I think so," wrote *Q*; "the world's smartest, most mysterious group in motion," said *NME*; and Allan Jones, exercising the editor's prerogative to write about his favourite group, wound up a review of ecstatic intensity in *Melody Maker* with the assertion that "they could bow out now with *Green* and we would remember them with nothing but awe."

Green had entered the British charts upon release at an impressive number 27 – quickly to disappear, of course – and R.E.M. had featured high in the music papers' annual readers' polls. 'Stand' had been a near hit in February and their two-week tour – including two nights at Hammersmith Odeon – had sold out immediately. Now they found themselves adding a date at Wembley Arena to cope with demand; once more they would be playing to as many people in London as New York.

The week R.E.M. arrived in the UK, the *Sunday Observer* magazine put them on the cover with the caption 'The best band in the world' as if it were beyond question. *Green* re-entered the album charts on its way to becoming the group's first gold album in the UK. More visibly, 'Orange Crush' finally gave the band a top 30 single, the reward being the curious sight of R.E.M., cult group of the decade, lip-synching on the notoriously superficial television show *Top Of The Pops*. Like America before it, the British Isles had succumbed. Like American fans before them, the British would have to adapt to sharing their most prized secret with the masses.

Thirteen

On an international level, R.E.M. may have jumped the previously insurmountable barrier between cult popularity and star status with *Green*, but in the States, it was not quite a watershed release. For the second album in a row, R.E.M. found themselves with a one-hit album. 'Pop Song 89' only dented the lower regions of the Hot 100. The three-month arena tour in the autumn, planned long in advance to consolidate the album's anticipated long-term success and to provide an opportunity for fans who had missed out on the sold out shows in the spring, instead coincided with *Green* the album falling off the charts and 'Get Up' the single failing to chart. For the first time in years empty seats became a common sight at an R.E.M. show.

In New York for example, where the group had so easily sold out Madison Square Garden in the spring, they now played the area's two other main arenas – Meadowlands and Nassau Coliseum – back to back and did little more than half fill either. In their enthusiasm to play the touring game for their new label and to capitalise on years of hard work for their own benefit, R.E.M. had finally overreached themselves.

By the tour's end, the group realised as much. Spending 1989 on the road had seemed a worthy enough idea at the time, and in public, no one regretted the move. But as Bill Berry later noted, "Halfway through the tour we were so burned out by it we were just on stage going through the motions. We really felt we were robbing the audience of what they deserve. We were playing in arenas a little larger than we were comfortable with and the whole thing was pretty depressing."

So, as the home stretch came into sight with a series of southern shows in November, culminating at the Fox Theater, Atlanta, they breathed a collective sigh of relief. R.E.M. loved playing live, and they had proved they could bring a sound that had originated in backwoods bars into sports arenas and still make it work. But this was not how they wanted to continue. If their touring routine was to reflect their popularity, and they stayed at this level of success throughout the Nineties, they would be spending the rest of their lives inside these sports halls; if they became bigger, it would mean the even more impersonal stadiums; and if they had in fact peaked, it would be a trip back through the halls and concert theatres and the inevitable bitterness that would probably attach itself to the downward spiral.

No one was quite certain what the future would therefore hold for live work, except that it wouldn't be this. So for the last five shows of '89, in Virginia, North Carolina and Georgia, R.E.M. brought in the film crews and recorded themselves on camera for posterity.

Or rather, Michael Stipe brought in the film crews. Many successful rock musicians spend their new-found wealth starting record companies to finance other exponents of their art; Michael Stipe, his interest in visual imagery on a par with his musical enthusiasm, instead formed C-00 Film Corps (pronounced C-Hundred) with film-maker Jim McKay. The two had been friends since McKay was a DJ in Boston and R.E.M. were unknowns, but only when McKay moved to Athens at the end of the Eighties did their plans for an independent film company become reality. Their first productions were music videos, for the Henry Rollins Band, Chickasaw Mudd Puppies and Flat Duo Jets, along with Jem Cohen's 'Talk About The Passion' clip for *Eponymous*. McKay and Jem Cohen also used C-00 as an outlet for, respectively, a documentary and a collection of short films.

Michael Stipe had kept himself busy with the video medium by directing the clip for R.E.M.'s 'Pop Song 89'. In a direct response to MTV's steady diet of "gratuitous tits and ass", as he called it, he presented a video of himself and three female friends dancing, all wearing the same jester's trousers, all bare-chested. A version was handed to MTV with deliberately provocative 'censored' bars covering their nipples, including Michael's. Jim Herbert, who had directed a semi-live video for 'Turn You Inside-Out' on the dance floor of the 40 Watt Club, warned Stipe that he still didn't think

179

the cable channel would show it.

"Oh they'll show it," Stipe replied. "They'll show it 'cos it's R.E.M."

Herbert notes that this is the first time he had heard Stipe so confident with R.E.M.'s standing and his own video directing ability, but in the final analysis, they were both right. MTV showed the video, largely for the reason Stipe stated, but they never got fully behind it as they had with 'Stand'. Unperturbed, Stipe saw C-00 as an opportunity to throw himself fully into the visual medium. "There's really no market for independent film," he commented in late '89. "In a way, we're creating a supply and we're hoping the demand comes."

The company's first major project was Direct Impact, a series of Public Service Announcements. Once an essential part of television broadcasting, President Reagan had made PSAs a 'voluntary' responsibility of the networks, who immediately discarded them in favour of more paid commercials. C-00's involvement in resurrecting the form came about, as Stipe recalls, because, "We asked ourselves, what would be the most effective way, using film, to get complex ideas across with simplicity?" and also, "We wanted to provide a forum for all types of people who are involved in different mediums and sometimes not even the arts at all, to get a gripe out."

As such, C-00 gave time and facilities to such apparently disparate people as *Sassy* magazine editor Jane Pratt (who chose the theme 'Pro-Choice Is Pro-Life') and rapper KRS-One ('World Peace'); Stipe himself made a particularly humorous attack on chemical farming. Direct Impact was unveiled at a press conference in New York in February 1990 to a warm reaction but confusion about exactly how the items would get shown on mainstream TV. Stipe and McKay admitted that beyond submitting the tapes to networks and appealing to their consciences, they lacked the resources to fully monitor the response. MTV and several smaller music video cable shows picked up on the PSAs as well constructed comments on issues that affected their viewers, and cost nothing to broadcast, but Direct Impact was predictably ignored by the major networks.

Michael Stipe the film-maker was better able to indulge with the

Green tour concert film. He and McKay had the shows shot almost exclusively in Super 8 and 16-millimetre film rather than the usual 35 mm film or video and farmed the editing process out among five people – Stipe, McKay, Cohen, Ernie Fritz and Chris Lovett – for greater variety. The results ranged from nearly conventional colour live footage, through to out-of-synch black and white Super 8 shots that were combined with outside photography to create a more diffused impression. R.E.M. had always promised to steer clear of a live album and this artefact was as close as they would come to it, but *Tourfilm*, as the inventive and wonderfully visceral 85-minute home video was called when it was released towards the end of 1990, was also a farewell present of sorts. It closed with the statement: "In the first week of November 1989, we rolled tape and shot film at a number of shows . . . with a wild and unforgettable decade of touring behind us." The message was subtle, as ever, but it was there.

★　　★　　★

Still, if 1990 was meant to be the year that R.E.M. took time off, their fans could afford to feel a little confused. The holiday season saw a cover version of Syd Barrett's 'Dark Globe' appearing as a flexi-disc free with *Sassy* magazine, while spring brought the release of *Pop Screen* – a collection of videos from *Document* and *Green*, including an uncensored 'Pop Song 89' – and autumn the release of *Tourfilm*. 'Stand', meanwhile, became the theme song for the short-lived American television show *Get A Life* – something which might have jarred with the philosophy of a younger R.E.M. but one that they strongly defended as they entered their thirties. "There's a whole world out there that's never heard our music," said an uncharacteristically eager Peter Buck. "I want them to hear it."

By February, Buck was back in the clubs, touring with Drivin'n'Cryin's Kevn [sic] Kinney to promote the album *MacDougal Blues* he had produced and played on. Buck also roped Mike Mills and Bill Berry into playing on an album for British cult musician Nikki Sudden, recorded at John Keane's studio in Athens during April (though not finished until the following year).

And the end of the year saw the eventual release of an eponymous

Hindu Love Gods album, culled from the sessions Buck, Mills and Berry undertook with Warren Zevon for *Sentimental Hygiene* back in '86, at the end of which everyone had gotten drunk and ploughed through a set of live cover versions, ranging from Robert Johnson's 'Walkin' Blues' to Woodie Guthrie's 'Vigilante Man' and Prince's 'Raspberry Beret'.

"We spent four hours on that," said Peter Buck of the session in early 1991. "I've had longer lunches. It was a nice little thing we did for fun. Warren was between contracts and labels and he decided to put it out. Which is fine with me, as long as people know it's not a serious career move."

It could hardly be misinterpreted as such. Loose to the point of falling apart, and packaged much like a bootleg, reactions ranged from those who saw the exercise as a spirited example of musical purity to those who wrote it off as drunken tomfoolery unfit for commercial release. It's safe to say the album would not have enjoyed a brief stint in the American charts had it not featured the musicians from one of America's top bands.

Michael Stipe, meanwhile, toured eastern Europe with Billy Bragg and Natalie Merchant in June, a trip he later referred to as "perhaps the most educational overseas trip I've ever taken". He also co-produced, along with blues legend Willie Dixon, an album by the rootsy, almost comically down-home Chickasaw Mudd Puppies, who switched from Texas Hotel to PolyGram Records as interest in them surged; recorded a song with the Indigo Girls called 'I'll Give You My Skin' for an animal rights benefit album; and furthered his friendship with KRS-One by working on a hip-hop track about the environment. His *Field Recordings* solo project he abandoned amidst all the other activity.

"There's no question in any of our minds," Stipe explained the following February, "that R.E.M., for every reason I can think of, is the Motherlode. We always come back. Because this is what we know, and what we know the best."

It's the speed at which R.E.M. return to the Motherlode that surprises outsiders. Most groups who reach pop music's platinum sphere find themselves taking an increasing amount of time between albums. A major release might take a whole year to write, rehearse and record. There may be three months of promotion before the release, three months pausing while the opus sinks in. Then starts the touring, which increasingly takes up a year and a half if one is to cover the whole globe and fully satisfy the paying public. At the end of all this, it's no surprise that band members crave time away from each other to recharge their batteries and pursue personal lives, a process that of itself can last for a year before anyone's ready to start all over again.

It's a potentially four-year cycle that got the better not only of U2 and Def Leppard, Bruce Springsteen and Michael Jackson in the Eighties, but R.E.M.'s own contemporaries too − 10,000 Maniacs, having also broken into the platinum sphere in 1989, wouldn't release another album until late in 1992. If the members of R.E.M. were ever to take a sabbatical, this would have been the time.

Which makes it all the more surprising that the members found themselves back in the rehearsal studio in January, two months ahead of even their own ambitious schedule. "It was like, 'This is what we do,'" Peter Buck explained in his usual flip manner, but whether or not he wanted to examine the reasons, it went a lot deeper than that. These four musicians knew they had something special between them, a chemistry, a bonding and a friendship that few other bands can rival, and they had long ago grasped that they would be foolish not to capitalise on it for as long as those relationships thrived.

"There's something about them that you want to get to know, that you want to be friends with," says Scott Litt, not a man easily star struck. "I've never experienced quite that feeling. I don't want to compare it to The Beatles, but each personality being separate, and something loveable about each of them, I get that feeling. Four-piece bands are wonderful that way.

"R.E.M. have this amazing ability that when you're with them you're really happy, and when they leave it's a little sad. It's the best of what America has to offer − any country really − of friends, of a good group of people that are respectful, and that's basically the bottom line. Everyone that's lucky enough to come into contact with them has a good feeling about it."

Scratch the surface and it's not hard to find people who express antagonism towards the band's behaviour, individually or collectively, especially among those in Athens who never worked hard enough for similar success. And Michael Stipe, by dint of his self-created enigma coupled with a strong but defensive personality, left more than a few former friends wounded or slighted as he made his journey to global stardom. But, perhaps because R.E.M.'s rise was so gradual (it's generally agreed that it's the pop stars who've just 'made it' that have the worst egos), their reputation for doing the right thing seemed only to gain with their increased fame.

And it applied to everyone working around them. The stress that would have been a daily part of life for management in New York or LA seemed to dissipate as it travelled down to collegiate Athens, where the group's office staff operated on a level of politeness unrivalled among major rock bands. As often as not, it was the band's management that sent out thank you notes after radio appearances, interviews and business meetings, not the other way round. On the *Green* tour, for all that R.E.M. was playing to arena-sized crowds, the band doled out tour passes like they were promotional stickers. Naturally, there was always an inner sanctum that was held private, but so were there meet-and-greets with radio winners and fan club members that went beyond the call of duty for a band of R.E.M.'s stature.

At Warner Brothers, the excitement among the staff, many of whom had come of age as R.E.M. fans during the Eighties, was palpable: here was a band that had every reason to act aloof, but instead seemed to treat the employees of a major international conglomerate as if they were team members. The staff pulled out the extra stops for the band in response. Similarly, among the world's press corps, who endure ego eruptions from yesterday's (and tomorrow's) nobodies on a daily basis, R.E.M.'s ongoing engagement, the group's willingness to trust journalists as potential friends rather than treat them as open enemies, played an enormous role in offsetting any potential backlash.

At the end of 1988, the group took the personal touch a step further, sending out a 7″ single in special packaging to the members of its (surprisingly small) fan club. A 3,000 pressing of 'Parade Of The Wooden Soldiers' coupled with Television's 'See No Evil' was followed in 1989 by a 4,500 pressing of 'Good King Wenceslas' and

Mission Of Burma's 'Academy Fight Song'. Fan club membership increased as people learned of the future collectibles (which would have paid for membership ten times over, if anyone was selling). Regular updates – printed, but of course, on recycled paper – alerted fans as much to other bands' tour dates and to political causes as they did to R.E.M.'s own, sparse activity.

The group were not staying quiet, but they were toning down the volume. Throughout the spring of 1990, the three playing members of R.E.M. got together sporadically at the rehearsal studios under the band's Clayton Street office and worked their way through new songs. After a year on the road together, they still weren't sick of each other. But they were sick of playing their own instruments which, despite attempts to abandon them on *Green*, they had found themselves saddled with for all those months on the road.

But at least they had a reference point. With 'You Are The Everything', the decision to switch instruments had not only radically changed the group's sound but produced one of the album's finest moments. While it had seemed an odd track out on *Green*, it would now form the basis of the new album.

Peter Buck, having tired of his self-confessed "competency" on electric guitar, focused instead on the acoustic mandolin; it offered as equally bright a chime as his 12-string, but with a noticeably different timbre. Bill Berry decided to persevere further with the bass. And Mike Mills wanted to play more keyboards, at which he had always been highly proficient. The three members thus began rehearsals for the new album playing these instruments; the result gave them a fresh sound and the encouragement to experiment and expand.

"I stayed away for a month and a half and let them get to it," recalls Michael Stipe. "And when I came in, they had this group of songs that were unlike anything I'd heard from R.E.M. It was classic R.E.M., but the instrumentation was skewered, completely different from what we'd done in the past."

"In a lot of ways it was almost my idea," says Peter Buck. On the arena tour the previous year, he'd told the author of his desire to record "a real chamber record, with 'cellos and oboes and harpsichords and tambourines and stuff." He was determined that the new songs should be written with that possibility in mind.

"I'd been dropping a bug in everyone's ear that it would be interesting to use more strings when we were recording," he recalled in '91, "and have the strings be an integral part of the process, rather than added at the very end."

"Strings and keyboards are very similar," says Bill Berry. Having Mike Mills playing keyboards during the writing process for the first time therefore meant that, "Early on it was pretty evident that the songs were lush enough that they would lend themselves to that kind of treatment."

There being no question about keeping Scott Litt as co-producer, R.E.M. finally entered Bearsville studios in Woodstock to record backing tracks in September, moving back down to John Keane's now 24-track studio in Athens for overdubs and winding up in December at Prince's Paisley Park in Minneapolis for mixing.

By many groups' standards – particularly those in the platinum sphere – this would be seen as a quick schedule indeed, but for R.E.M. it again represented a new length for recording. *Green* had been difficult to make, but the fact that it had eventually outsold *Document* had eased the unspoken pressure.

"The success of *Green*," reflects Bill Berry, "literally afforded us the time to not have to hurry through it, to take our time. If things didn't work, we'd start again."

Mostly, however, things did work, and easily. Bringing in Peter Holsapple to participate in the recording process enabled R.E.M. to record live more than usual. On three occasions, Mike Mills didn't even play bass on the finished song, sticking to the organ and letting Peter Holsapple or Bill Berry record the bass line as they'd rehearsed.

"There's a certain synergy that goes on when people are playing live and it's not easy to capture when you're overdubbing," notes Mike Mills. "You don't get the feel, the ebb and the flow of the songs that you do when you're actually playing it all in one room at one time."

"I like having another guitar player," was Peter Buck's comment on playing alongside Peter Holsapple. "It frees me up so I don't feel quite as busy. We've always played live in the studio, but this time we made a concentrated effort. So most of the songs have a really good performance feel. Songs like 'Belong' and 'Low' sound almost exactly the same as right the second we played them." Then again, 'Belong' and 'Low' were the only two songs to have been previewed on the *Green* tour.

"The record took a while to make," comments Michael, "because of all the extra instrumentation and the recording process itself, but probably half the songs are first take or second take. I think Peter had this idea that he should only have to put his guitar part on one time on each song with no overdubs, and I think he really came close to doing that."

With the backing tracks laid down so smoothly, prospects for unusual instrumentation loomed large. R.E.M. had by now made a collective decision not to tour with the next album, to free themselves of the ever lengthening rehearse-record-tour-rest-rehearse syndrome. For the first time, they wouldn't need to worry about replicating the songs live; that, in turn, gave them the freedom to do what they wanted in the studio.

For string arrangements, they recruited Mark Bingham, whom Michael Stipe had worked with on his contribution to the Disney tribute album. Bingham in turn brought in members of the Atlanta Symphony Orchestra for eight of the album's eleven songs, a series of arrangements that Mike Mills, who had previously handled the group's strings (and still arranged those for what would become the album's best-known song), gushingly referred to as "brilliant".

Also brought into the fold were legendary New Orleans horn player Kidd Jordan, who supplied saxophones and clarinets to four of the songs, and The B-52's vocalist Kate Pierson, who sang on two songs, the first time a female voice had been heard on an R.E.M. record. John Keane supplied some pedal steel guitar, and Michael Stipe brought his friend KRS-One in to rap through one number.

As the songs themselves took shape, Stipe was determined to take them a step beyond what was expected of him lyrically. "In order to challenge myself, I decided to write an album of love songs," he explained upon the album's release.

"When I say love songs, I don't mean 'love you baby, love you baby'," he elaborated, "but maybe the French definition of a love pop song, a pop song that deals with love. I've never written an outright love song, and I'm not sure that of the eleven songs on this record I've written an outright love song, but I'm trying!"

And so Stipe's slightly askew stance on the world continued. He took a one-chord riff written by Mike Mills and turned it into the folksy 'Me In Honey', "about pregnancy from a male point of view". He took another of the group's more gentle compositions, this one revolving around Peter Buck's distinct mandolin line, and wrote 'Losing My Religion', which he boldly described as "the classic obsession song, a song of unrequited love". True to form, it didn't mention "love" once, although the line "That's me in the spotlight" did raise queries about the song's autobiographical nature.* While 'Losing My Religion' is a southern phrase for being "at your wit's end", Stipe placed just enough religious imagery ("Every hour I'm choosing my confessions") to give the song a possible hidden meaning.

"You've got every kind of love on this record," Stipe elaborated. "The record is about love and it's about memory·and it's about time. Those are three things that for me as a songwriter are pretty new territory."

To *Musician* magazine, Stipe put forward the theory that "the real and the fantastic became one when channelled through memory, and that your past is kind of what you make it. I love that blurred area."

He maintained that famous Stipe blur across most of the new songs, even suggesting the album title *The Return Of Mumbles* for the fact that his voice was now back down in the mix. And indeed, many of the songs were as open to interpretation as anything he had written. With 'Country Feedback' for example, Peter Buck and Bill Berry recorded most of the original music in a matter of hours. "Michael came in the next day and scatted the words," recalls Buck. "Usually, he has pretty concise words. We get to look them over. With 'Country Feedback', he just had two little drawings on a piece of paper – an Indian head and an arrow, I think – and he just kind of shouted."

And 'Half A World Away', which owed much to 'You Are The

---

* Stipe was later heard wishing he'd written "That's me in the kitchen" to avoid the perceived notion of the rock star lamenting his woes.

Everything' in instrumentation and sound, Stipe later admitted "doesn't make sense to anybody but me. It's a complete fabrication, but there's something there."

Mike Mills found himself taking lead vocals on 'Near Wild Heaven' and sharing them on 'Texarkana'. He too fell into the new mood. "'Near Wild Heaven' sounds like the happiest song in the world but it's not. 'Texarkana' is an unhappy song as well. They're pop songs, but they aren't pop lyrics. They're just not lyrics about the state of the world – they're more lyrics about the state of our minds or our lives. It's a more inward looking record."

Perhaps so, but one track was notably outward looking. "It's a relentless mindless upbeat happy song," says Peter Buck fondly of 'Shiny Happy People'. "There's not much you can do with something like that. It's inherently a jolly little song. Michael would try and undercut that on past albums, make it a little darker, but I don't think you could make that song a very dark song. It makes you happy to play it, and he came up with the jolliest little melody and lyrics he possibly could."

"I laughed for two weeks when I heard the guitar line," recalls Stipe. "I thought it was the happiest guitar line I'd ever heard in my life. And the challenge for me was to write a song that was as happy as the music. It's so much harder to write a happy song than it is to write a sad song. It's so easy to think sad thoughts. Emotionally speaking, to put that across in an intelligent way is very simple, compared to intelligently commenting on happiness. Because happiness is not something you can really define."

Stipe did his best to change that – "Throw your love around . . . Take it into town . . . Put it in the ground where the flowers grow," he sang clearly and joyously – and turned the chorus into a three part round with the additional, wistful vocals of Kate Pierson and Mike Mills. The song was earmarked as the obvious single, the new album's equivalent of – or sequel to – 'Stand', but the group could not help but throw a spanner into its merry dance, cutting suddenly from a 4/4 rock beat to a 3/4 orchestral waltz after the second chorus, before returning with a "Whoop!" from Michael and several refrains of the chorus to close.

'Endgame', everyone decided, didn't need any vocals at all. The group added strings, clarinet, saxophone and flugelhorn to a riff they already had, and the result, a baroque instrumental, sounded perfect as it was. Had Mills and Stipe not decided to add some "la-la's" over the refrain, nobody would have known it was R.E.M. That was how far they had come.

The whole process seemed an unstrained delight. "Every record you make you get lost somewhere," commented Peter Buck. "This felt really strong right to the end."

In fact, the group's only dilemma was in choosing a title. Four pages of ideas pinned to the studio wall didn't help. The group were deep into mixing when Warner Brothers told them that the release would be delayed unless they came up with a title that day. Mike Mills exclaimed, "Well, we're out of time," and everyone agreed with him.

Fourteen

"When I say that this record is going to alter the course of pop history, I say it with my tongue pretty firmly in my cheek and a little snicker on my lips, but I think it really is, for 1991, a pretty peculiar record."

Michael Stipe was sitting alongside Bill Berry atop an old freight train in a disused Athens railway yard. It was a bright and crisp February morning, and the pair was discussing *Out Of Time* for a visiting TV crew on the eve of its mid-March release. All the promotional parts were in place – the group had recently returned from Los Angeles shooting a video for 'Losing My Religion' and had spent the last two days at the Georgia Theater in Athens making another for 'Shiny Happy People' – and now Stipe was presenting his revised public persona, one totally at ease with his celebrity status and deliriously happy with the group's seventh album.

"In the context of pop music right now, I don't think a lot of people are doing what we've done with this record," he continued. "So in a sense, it's out of time, out of place – it's not really fitting in with what's going on in music right now. I like that. It's not something we rigged, it's not something we were necessarily striving for, but that's the way it happened. It seems typical of R.E.M."

Exactly. The title *Out Of Time* had been chosen in a moment of desperation, only for the group to discover that it made sense, as so often, on many different levels. The most apparent of these was the manner in which it stood alone from its contemporaries. From the opening few seconds – KRS-One muttering about the choice of radio, an archetypal Peter Buck guitar arpeggio, Michael Stipe's cry that "the world is collapsing around our ears" and then the unexpected funk groove of 'Radio Song' – through to the gentle one-chord folk-rock finale of 'Me In Honey', there was nothing around musically to compare it to.

R.E.M.'s peer group felt similarly displaced. The college rock movement that R.E.M. had unwittingly spearheaded had gradually disintegrated.* Instead of Hüsker Dü, The Dream Syndicate and Black Flag, now there was Bob Mould, Steve Wynn and Henry Rollins, former front men dealing with adulthood by striking out on their own, angling for a corner of the market where their music and ideas could still be heard.

The young band down the street no longer sounded like R.E.M. Rather than structuring minor chord sequences on jangling guitars, they were likely to be churning out the raw funk metal popularised by the likes of Los Angeles' Red Hot Chili Peppers. R.E.M. were survivors, but the release of *Out Of Time*, two and a half years after *Green*, also marked them as loners.

"We've never really been in synch," said Stipe. "I don't think we've ever really followed a straight path as a band. But I do think this record particularly is much stranger in this time and place than maybe anything we've ever done before."

He was right. And R.E.M.'s separation from the pack was further accentuated by the decision not to tour behind it. Although everyone assumed R.E.M. would take some kind of step back from arenas, still it came as a shock to the fan club members who received their Christmas 1990 package to find a 7″ single pairing 'Ghost Reindeer In the Sky' with George Gershwin's 'Summertime', a card, and a note that made it official: 'We are not planning any live dates for 1991.'

"We've lived on the road for ten years and it's time to take a break, shake things up a little bit," explained Bill Berry that February morning. "We will miss playing live, but the only alternative is to go out and beat our heads against the wall for another year, and we're just not prepared to do that."

"It's amazing," he continued. "When we started out we were a live band that just pulled off the road now and again to make a record. Now it unfortunately can't be that way. If there was some way we would go out for two or three weeks and play theatres,

---

* Even The Replacements, considered for so long by so many as likely to follow R.E.M. into the mainstream, were about to give up battling against all the compromises and frustrations and call it a day.

we'd do it. But when we do play small places, the old fans say, 'I had to buy a $200 scalped ticket.' We play big places and the fans who followed us at first say we've sold out."

"It's like being shackled by fame," observed Stipe, before avowing, "Our next record is going to come out much sooner than two and a half years from now, because we're not touring."

Over a pint of Guinness with Mike Mills in an Athens bar that afternoon, Buck echoed Stipe's assertion. "We toured, we did it really well. The last tour seemed a really good peak, and a good place to stop for a little while. I think we're going to concentrate on making records for now."

Here was the silver lining. *Out Of Time* represented something of a return to *Murmur* in its frequent use of acoustics; it also marked the group's determination to issue albums annually. "We're in our prime as far as writing songs goes," said Bill Berry. "And that's what we feel like right now – a studio band."

Amidst all the confidence in *Out Of Time* and the noted intent to become prolific again, still R.E.M. recognised the possibility that, having made less of a rock record and deciding not to tour behind it, there was every chance they would have to live with decreased record sales.

"We've always been very lucky that every record we put out sold more than the one before it," acknowledged Mike Mills. "But that has to stop at some point, and this may be it. It's a very distinct possibility that our not touring means we don't sell as many records."

Yet however apt a title *Out Of Time* had seemed, there was one sense in which the group could not have predicted its appropriateness. For R.E.M.'s avowedly apolitical album was released at a time of intense international upheaval: the Gulf War started just as R.E.M. began advance promotion for *Out Of Time*, and even the notoriously left-wing activists from Athens postponed a promotional trip to Europe. Singing 'Shiny Happy People' while a foreign country was being bombed "back into the Stone Age" seemed more out-of-time than anything else about the new album, but Stipe readily defended his new-found optimism.

"With everything that's going on on a global level right now, a song that will make people happy, and lift them out of the general mêlée of the world, is not a bad thing," he said. "Maybe we can help turn the tide a little bit with a really good, really positive, really happy song.

"I don't think it's ever easy to be happy. I think it's much easier to slide into cynicism and say, 'The world sucks and I'm going to be miserable about it.' You can't ignore the problems that are around you, but you don't have to dwell on them 24 hours a day, and you don't have to let them overwhelm and overpower every action that you've been taking."

Elaborating on what appeared to be a personality shift – Michael Stipe projecting unrelenting optimism – he explained how, "Basically, over the last eleven years, people have watched an extremely introverted person become extroverted by their career. And you've pretty much seen me grow up in public. I'm 31, I'm one-fourth of an incredibly successful pop band, I sit around, people come to me, talk to me, photograph me . . ."

He paused to consider his good fortune and then returned to the matter in hand. "It didn't always look like this record was going to be really great, and it turned out that it's incredible. It's probably the best thing that we've done."

★   ★   ★

The public reaction was one of unanimous agreement.

Out Of Time was the beneficiary of glowing reviews amidst a mass of press coverage upon its release. Any doubts expressed as to R.E.M.'s direction on *Green* was forgotten; the critics knew a masterpiece when they heard it. Such continued good ink helped preserve the band's profile, certainly, but two new factors came in to play an enormous role in crossing R.E.M. over to the masses.

The first, and it's hard to overstate its importance, was the video for 'Losing My Religion'. Michael Stipe had decided, as part of his new pop persona, to ditch his previous refusal to lip-synch and initially proposed a straight performance piece, singing direct to camera. But the director hired for the clip, the enigmatically named Tarsem, planned instead to "film it in the style of a particular kind of Indian movie in which everything is melodramatic and very dreamlike." The result was a beautiful combination of the two: shot in an empty room with a window looking out to the countryside, the musical members of R.E.M. made but fleeting, almost ghostlike appearances, leaving Stipe free to dance, sing and act out the 'obsession' of his lyrics.

Michael Stipe's claim that the song itself was not about religion did not deter Tarsem from building up a visually stunning subplot that toyed blatantly with the crucifix and homoerotica – a combination that subsequently got the video banned in staunchly Catholic Ireland. The legend of Icarus was also alluded to with an ageing angel in heaven who loses his wings when industrious workers on Earth turn their spotlight on him; the workers subsequently rebuild his wings through toil and inspiration.

But what truly distinguished the 'Losing My Religion' video was its cinematic quality. People immediately started talking of it as high art – especially the TV programmers who put it into the heaviest of heavy rotations. Radio quickly followed suit. 'Losing My Religion' even crossed over to portions of the dance market, something the group had barely ever thought about. R.E.M. had themselves a genuine, quality, crossover hit.

The second factor that helped R.E.M. was, ironically, their decision not to tour. To compensate, the group made a number of well timed 'live' appearances around the release of *Out Of Time* and found that these generated as much, if not more, publicity and acclaim than perhaps a whole year spent in arenas. All acoustic and ostensibly for promotional purposes only, the rarity of these performances helped turn each one into a major event.

Once it became apparent that the Gulf War was no longer a threat, if indeed it ever had been, to Americans travelling in Europe, R.E.M. packed their bags for a hectic promotional trip, which seemed to include as many acoustic shows for television and radio as mere interviews. While the group felt reasonably secure that their popularity in the States would not decline dramatically by taking a year off the road, they could not guarantee the same of Europe, where they had finally seen some real progress with *Green*. They duly smiled for the cameras, performed in TV studios, shook hands with the record company and answered journalists' questions without complaint.

In London, however, they couldn't help but get the desire to engage a real audience out of their system. They lined up two secret shows at the Borderline, a tiny club under a Mexican restaurant in the heart of the West End, for March 14 and 15, under the *nom de plume* Bingo Hand Job. The secret lasted all of five minutes. 'Losing My Religion' had just become the group's first ever top 20 hit in the UK, *Out Of Time* had been in the shops for less than a week, and R.E.M.'s last show had been at the 8,000-seater Wembley Arena almost two years earlier. Tickets were seen exchanging hands outside for £250.

The shows were not the tightest performances in rock'n'roll lore, but they were to be treasured all the same. R.E.M. had re-arranged several old songs for the acoustic format – 'World Leader Pretend', 'Disturbance At The Heron House', 'The One I Love', 'Pop Song 89', 'Fall On Me' and The Troggs' 'Love Is All Around' (sung by Mike Mills) – as well, of course, as playing much of the new album. There was also a sad, sparse song called 'Fretless' that had been left off *Out Of Time* and given to the soundtrack for Wim Wenders' film *Until The End Of The World* instead. Billy Bragg came up for solo songs, and Stipe joined him for numbers they had played in eastern Europe with Natalie Merchant – John Prine's 'Hello In There' and an old country song 'Dallas'. Robyn Hitchcock and The Egyptians performed brief sets. The second night ended with Hitchcock and Bragg joining R.E.M. for a bizarre encore of 'Tom's Diner' by Suzanne Vega, 'Baggy Trousers' by Madness and 'Unbelievable' by EMF. Those who were there would be talking about it for years.

The next week, *Out Of Time* rocketed into the UK charts at number one. For a group whose previous album had peaked at 27, it was both a major shock and a notable achievement. Still, the British charts are notorious for high entries and quick demises; of greater significance was the fact that almost four months later *Out Of Time* had not left the top 10, indeed was back at number two. Released in May, 'Shiny Happy People' reached number six in the British singles charts, another peak for the group.

Back in the States, R.E.M. chose just two television appearances, each for maximum effect. *Saturday Night Live* was American TV's best opportunity to reach a vast record-buying public in a live format. Yet more high-profile was their appearance on MTV's *Unplugged*. Recorded on April 10 in New York and broadcast two weeks later, the 60-minute show featured Stipe, Buck, Mills, Berry and Holsapple sitting throughout, looking for all the world like a bunch of comfortable old folkies rather than leaders of the post-punk movement. As well as songs played at the Borderline, they featured, at MTV's request, the once-cataclysmic 'It's The End Of The World As We Know It' (for which Berry played just a tambourine and Stipe gazed anxiously at his lyric sheet) and went all the way back to 'Perfect Circle'. Stripped to the core – to the manner in which most new songs had been written – the group seemed as comfortable as they'd ever been performing electrically, and certainly emitted the same emotion. It was a dream performance. Blatantly billed as "R.E.M.'s only concert this year", the event proved that R.E.M., the former outsiders, were now MTV's prodigal sons.

R.E.M. played just one more "show" in 1991, in Charleston, West Virginia, for American Public Radio's roots music show *Mountain Stage*. Again they were joined by old friends Billy Bragg and Robyn Hitchcock and again the performance could have been written off as mere 'promotion' had not the group played a further ninety minutes on their own initiative. "Western Virginia is totally broke," noted Peter Buck. "Personally, I like it, and I liked the idea that all the city and culture snobs had to come there and see us play."

The video, the press, the select television appearances – and that unmanageable intangible, word-of-mouth – all conspired to monumental success. *Out Of Time* was a top five album – by far and away the group's highest position – within three weeks. From there it kept moving. In the middle of May, it finally happened. R.E.M. had the number one album in America.

The irony was not lost on the band: almost every year for the past decade, they had travelled America, and often the world, to play to loyal fans and find new converts, to enjoy themselves and to promote their music. The one time they opted off the treadmill, America embraced them wholesale.

Of greater significance was what R.E.M.'s success said to the music world at large. Though the band rarely paid attention to such events, there were plenty others eager to note that *Out Of Time* was the first rock album to top the charts since Sinéad O'Connor's

I Do Not Want What I Haven't Got over a year earlier (and that had sold primarily on the back of a Prince cover song); in the twelve months since, the number one spot had been held exclusively by MC Hammer, New Kids On The Block, Mariah Carey and Vanilla Ice, a nadir in American pop culture. The cultural significance of R.E.M.'s chart-topping was therefore celebrated across the vast swathes of America that were more musically attuned: it felt like the humble, small town, unconventional, rule-busting former road band had conquered the mainstream on behalf of an entire generation – albeit one that no longer really existed.

Out Of Time dropped five places the week after it hit the top spot, due to the introduction of the new SoundScan method of researching the *Billboard* chart by pure sales, without airplay influence; any suggestion that R.E.M. had not in fact been the best-selling band in the country was refuted the following week when *Out Of Time* bounced back to the top. In June, 'Losing My Religion' peaked at number four, the group's biggest hit to date and now being talked about as the song of the year. *Out Of Time* topped the charts in Canada and Germany; it came close in Australia, Italy, Spain, Austria and even France. It took up residency at the top of the Israeli charts, where 'Losing My Religion' was known simply by its opening line, "Oh, life". In July, *Out Of Time* was certified double platinum in the States. By the time 'Shiny Happy People' had broken the group's stigma of the one-hit album and made the American Top Ten in September, *Out Of Time* was well on its way to three million sales in the US, and another three million abroad (almost one million of those in the UK). R.E.M. had made, by all appearances, the album of the year.

★   ★   ★

Had the world at large finally grasped the beauties of R.E.M.'s idiosyncrasies, or had R.E.M. simply matured into a mainstream musical group? Could the band still be considered "alternative" when their new album was popular with housewives and office clerks, or were they the perennial outsiders who had finally gained mass acceptance through sheer persistence?

These questions were answered at the annual MTV Video

Awards in Los Angeles on September 5, 1991. Neither as prestigious as the Grammys, nor as conservative, the awards recognise videos only and in a country of TV addicts more accurately reflect the mood of youthful American pop culture – especially MTV's influence over it.

That 'Losing My Religion' had nine nominations was a phenomenal achievement given R.E.M.'s often frustrating long-term battle to make videos that were marketable without being blatantly commercial. That the group actually won in six categories was even more extraordinary.

But if their domination of the Video Awards reflected the group's new-found popularity with the masses (and the medium), the ceremony itself better revealed R.E.M.'s politics. Peter Buck, a vocal foe of public backslapping and industry shoulder-rubbing – and an avowed enemy of the video format to begin with – went out for a Mexican meal while the awards took place, turning up for the post-show party only. While Bill Berry and Mike Mills looked as delighted to make repeated trips to the podium as would be expected from a couple of former high school marching band musicians (though Berry prominently and importantly gave "thanks to college radio"), Michael Stipe seized on the opportunity for some mass-culture communication.

Receiving an award early on for Best Group Video, the vocalist appeared in a T-shirt with the word "Rainforest" emblazoned across it; receiving the Breakthrough Video Award, he then wore one stating "Love Knows No Color". When at the evening's conclusion, R.E.M. were awarded the night's star prize, Best Video of the Year, he came to the stage with a T-shirt reading "Wear A Condom"; in front of a worldwide television audience he then stripped to reveal another with the word "Choice", yet another reading "Alternative Energy Now", and on down to "The Right to Vote" and finally "Handgun Control". Allowing his clothing to talk for him, he limited his vocal pronouncements to simple thanks.

While the much talked-about body language brought a few protests from those who thought he simplified the issues, Stipe had few regrets. "If it was misunderstood or if people thought it trivialised any of the causes, then I'm very sorry," he said in a cover story for *Rolling Stone* the following spring that marked the group's (first) landslide victory in the magazine's readers and critics poll. "The feedback I've gotten from that alone was more than anything else I've ever done. I was getting mail from countries that I couldn't even find on the map."

The action was indicative of Stipe's continued self-confidence in his role as eccentric rock star. Asked whether his forays into videos, films, production and activism might not get him portrayed as a pretentious "Renaissance Man", he seemed remarkably unconcerned, stating that, "I'm not going to let that get in the way of things I want to do." While acknowledging that the rock star's ego can be blown up to "the size of a major planet", he concluded that "as a normal person, it's not a bad thing to feel that nothing is impossible."

Stipe spent much of 1991 immersed, predictably perhaps now, in videos and film. Apart from 'Losing My Religion', three more songs from *Out Of Time* were slated for singles, and therefore videos. The first of these was 'Shiny Happy People', in which director Katherine Dieckmann revived the format that had worked for 'Stand': lots of dancing and laughter. This shoot featured children from an Athens elementary school as additional dancers, but it was most memorable for Michael Stipe and Kate Pierson's contagious good vibes as vocalists. Watching the clip a decade on it's clear that Stipe meant it when he said, the day after the shoot, "I wrote that completely from the heart . . . The last thing I want is for anyone to be critical of that song, and say it's clever or there's cynicism involved." The group had astutely avoided those potential charges by going to the public with 'Losing My Religion' first; such was that song's evident artistic quality that 'Shiny Happy People' was welcomed in turn. And, compared to 'Stand' it was better-constructed, more clearly defined, and yet with its time change in the bridge, more challenging too. It really was a pop classic.

The clip for 'Near Wild Heaven' was shot in New York in sepia and blue tones, with the group seated in bohemian cafés surrounded by beautiful people; while it took the pressure off Mike Mills as the song's vocalist, the result looked remarkably like the kind of "commercial" that Buck had always hated about mainstream videos. 'Radio Song', shot in a warehouse and featuring KRS-One offered more originality, projecting images of the group onto blank cue cards held up by its members.

Perhaps aware that the hi-tech, classy approach to these promos suggested a visual "sell-out", Stipe turned to his own C-00 company to produce four more clips. The directors were obvious local choices: Jem Cohen for 'Belong' and 'Country Feedback', Jim McKay for 'Half A World Away' and James Herbert for 'Low'. The latter was a stellar effort, taking a trio of paintings from the Georgia Museum of Art and then, by combining Herbert's rephotography method with some painstaking human modelling, making the figures come alive – literally. These four independent clips joined the four "professional" ones, along with acoustic renditions of 'Losing My Religion' and 'Love Is All Around' from R.E.M.'s television appearances, on yet another video compilation, *This Film Is On*, released in September. Stipe then began publicly discussing C-00's first full-length feature film, a bleak road movie about America's decay to be directed by Jim McKay, entitled *Desperation Angels*. His energy seemed boundless.

Just as staying in Athens for the year allowed Michael Stipe the opportunity to indulge his visual obsessions, so it gave all the band members a chance to continue their penchant for collaborative recording, but this time on home turf. Peter Buck had been gradually building a studio at Buck Manor, as his impressive home came to be known, and invited Billy Bragg to stay during the spring of '91. From demos there came Bragg's excellent single 'You Woke Up My Neighbourhood' (recorded at John Keane's studio in Athens), with Stipe on backing vocals and Buck on guitars. The subsequent video featured the two R.E.M. members outside Buck Manor, trying in vain to gain admittance to a cheerful hoedown inside (and with good reason: the interior scenes were shot in London). Another fun session at John Keane's led to 'Tighten Up Your Wig', credited to Billy Bragg and the Athenians with DJ Woody Dee; it closed KRS-One's *H.E.A.L.* album, one track after the 'Civilisation Vs Technology' collaboration between Stipe and KRS-One and his wife Harmony.

John Keane's studio was also used by R.E.M. to record songs by Roky Erickson (the light-hearted 'I Walked With A Zombie') and Leonard Cohen (the sombre 'First We Take Manhattan') for tribute albums; and it played host to the most unusual side venture

R.E.M.'s three musical members had found themselves contributing to since the Hindu Love Gods.

Early in their career, R.E.M. had often covered 'I Can't Control Myself' and 'With A Girl Like You' by The Troggs, the British beat-punk group of the Sixties from Andover in Hampshire whose West Country accents and all round lack of sophistication had endeared them to both fans and fellow musicians alike.* After adding 'Love Is All Around' to their 1991 acoustic shows, R.E.M. joked publicly about recording an EP of Troggs' songs.

For the remaining founding members of this ageing band, still treading the golden oldies circuit in England, such high patronage initially went ignored. "Someone came up to us and said that R.E.M. had covered some of our material," recalls lead singer and songwriter Reg Presley. "I thought R.E.M. must be a company; I didn't know who they were." The Troggs' manager, Sixties entrepreneur Larry Page, was more astute, contacting R.E.M. (who were indeed a "company", and a big one at that), and asking if they'd like to work on The Troggs' next album. "We have a sense of humour about this stuff," was Peter Buck's explanation for himself, Berry, Mills and Peter Holsapple agreeing. "We went into it thinking either it's going to be one of the most fun, or most awful, things we'd ever done."

Titled *Athens Andover* after the two groups' hometowns, the album was both: fun *and* awful. The Troggs' own songwriting had not progressed much from the untamed innocence of the mid-Sixties, while contributions from the R.E.M. musicians – 'Nowhere Road' and 'I'm In Control' – were hardly imaginative. The album nonetheless captured the same kind of simplistic good-time feel as the Hindu Love Gods before it; like that record, it attracted much press for R.E.M.'s involvement, then died a quick death. It is well worth noting that a collaboration with R.E.M. does not guarantee a revived career.

While R.E.M.'s members were bouncing in and out of John Keane's recording studio (stopping off again for a fan club Christmas single coupling The Vibrators' punk classic 'Baby Baby' with a

---

* An in-studio argument, recorded in the Seventies by a mischievous engineer, was infamous among musicians worldwide.

self penned 'Christmas Griping'), the band's former label I.R.S. was proving equally industrious. The 1988 compilation *Eponymous* had sold well to R.E.M.'s new American fans after the break-through of *Document*, but had achieved little in Europe where the group were still then a mere cult act. Now that *Out Of Time* was one of the best-selling albums of 1991 across the European con-tinent, I.R.S. decided on another compilation. *The Best Of R.E.M.* assembled sixteen of the group's finest songs up to *Document*, without the alternative versions or rarities offered on *Eponymous*. While somewhat frustrated at being repackaged once more, R.E.M. again realised they had no choice in the matter, and it was their idea to incorporate quotes from the first edition of this book as the sleeve notes. The extent of R.E.M.'s new-found European fan base was clearly proven when the album rocketed into the British Top Ten on its release in October.

By the new year, with *Out Of Time* still riding high in the British and American album charts – sales would soon top a daunting 10 million worldwide – only a few people were clinging to the concept of R.E.M. as an alternative band. Evidently, most of them must have been the music business 'old guard' that vote in the Grammys, the industry's most esteemed but restrained annual awards ceremony. In a year that saw Natalie Cole sweep the board for an album of duets recorded with her long-dead father, perhaps it was only just and proper after all that the 'Best Alternative Album' accolade went to R.E.M. at the very point the band had finally, irrefutably escaped that pigeonhole. (They also received awards for Best Video and Best Pop Performance By A Group, both for 'Losing My Religion'.) Michael Stipe swapped the T-shirt controversy for a hat that read "White House – Stop AIDS" and Peter Buck showed up in pyjamas as a protest to the whole affair. In other words, business as usual.

But in the real world, everything had changed in that half-year between the MTV Video Awards and the Grammys. Most notably, *Out Of Time*'s claim to the left-field hit album of 1991 had been well and truly usurped by a trio from Seattle called Nirvana. Right at the time that 'Losing My Religion' was sweeping the MTV awards in September '91, Nirvana released a single, 'Smells Like Teen Spirit', and an accompanying video, shot in a high school gym, that could not have been more diametrically removed from R.E.M.'s artful breakthrough had it been scientifically planned. On film and on tape, 'Smells Like Teen Spirit' was the sound of barely restrained suburban fury and it touched a raw nerve with millions of socially disenfranchised American kids. The accompanying album, *Nevermind* featured more of the same and proved similarly popular. It had taken R.E.M. until three months into their fifth album to go gold in the States; *Nevermind* was only Nirvana's second release and it passed that barrier in three weeks. It had taken R.E.M. twelve years to make something with the critical and commercial impact of *Out Of Time;* it took Nirvana five years. It took *Out Of Time* a year to sell three million copies; it took *Nevermind* less than six months. In January 1992, *Nevermind* went to number one on the *Billboard* charts on its way to outselling *Out Of Time*. A musical revolution was at hand; it was labelled grunge.

In Nirvana's wake, other Seattle groups like Soundgarden, Pearl Jam and Alice In Chains all became million sellers; The Red Hot Chili Peppers surged to mega-platinum stardom; and the Lollapalooza festival tour, launched by Jane's Addiction front man Perry Farrell in 1991, quickly became the must-attend touring rock festival. Jangly 12-string guitars and murmured vocals had never sounded less fashionable; the new American alternative was into all-out noise.

R.E.M. couldn't have been happier at the arrival of a new musical movement. Finally, they could step down from their position as reluctant leaders of the underground and hand over the baton to groups ten years younger. Musically, the fact that they no longer represented a generation would allow them even greater freedom. Philosophically, however, they couldn't help but note the role they had played in laying the groundwork for a band as vitriolic as Nirvana to achieve overnight what had taken R.E.M. ten years.

"The received wisdom is that punk was a failure, because it didn't have success," reflected Peter Buck in the summer of '92. "But it was successful in that it influenced a whole generation. All those bands that are reaching fruition right now, that's great. The only fear I have is that of our peer group, we're the only ones that made it."

Fifteen

Money – it was not the reason R.E.M. had entered the music business. It had barely ever influenced their decision-making, and never their music. Frequently over the years R.E.M. had pulled career moves guaranteed to lessen their short-term income, and at times (quietly, without fanfare) given the green stuff away. But once you sell 10 million albums, money can't but help rear its ugly head.

R.E.M.'s decision early on to divide their songwriting income four equal ways had served well to avoid the minefield that splits up so many pop groups – and which usually explodes when the one songwriting member is discovered to be earning three or more times that of his non-songwriting partners. Being keen students of rock'n'roll history, R.E.M. understood that if a band was a gang, then that gang had to cover each other's backs.

"The songwriting money we share isn't necessarily for writing the songs," Peter Buck would explain a full decade after *Out Of Time*'s multi-platinum breakthrough. "It's for sleeping on the floor for ten years while we toured, it's for the eight hours of rehearsal we used to do, when we were making forty dollars a month."

Only two other people were given a share in those proceeds: the management partnership of Jefferson Holt (who had a contract to that effect), and Bertis Downs (who after years of insisting that his role as legal advisor would conflict with a job as co-manager, finally accepted the latter position but insisted on a handshake agreement). Both men were considered to have been integral to the group's success since 1980 and to have earned their percentage. New additions to the camp were not granted the same benefit. Talking just prior to the release of *Out Of Time*, Peter Buck agreed with the suggestion that his friend Peter Holsapple had pretty much become R.E.M.'s fifth member – "except for the salary part", he noted with a chuckle. As it turned out, he was being deadly serious.

Peter Holsapple was in a difficult situation by 1992. R.E.M. had looked up to Holsapple's best-known band, The dB's, before the two parties met. Holsapple had recommended Mitch Easter as a possible R.E.M. producer to Jefferson Holt back in 1981, without which tie-up who knows what might have happened. The dB's had opened for R.E.M. in 1985 and gotten on so well that each band frequently joined the other on stage. And so, after The dB's broke up in 1988, Holsapple was R.E.M.'s immediate choice as extra musician on the *Green* tour. A generally easy-going southerner from a similar musical background, he came across less as a session musician or a hired hand than a kindred spirit. After all those years of friendship he felt at home in R.E.M. He began talking a little in group interviews and no one seemed put out; he was even part of the line-up that introduced the songs 'Low' and 'Belong' on that tour.

Holsapple was not invited into the demoing process for *Out Of Time,* during which period most of the other songs were written, but his involvement in the recording process was crucial: the presence of a fourth, all-rounder musician allowed more instruments – especially keyboards – to be played live on the first take, adding to the "ebb and flow" of which Mike Mills referred. He then performed with the group on their acoustic shows, and was seen on television screens around the world huddled in with the other members of R.E.M. as though there were no barrier between them.

Peter Holsapple may have looked at the 10 million album sales, conducted some mental arithmetic on the sums of money coming R.E.M.'s way, and thought it not unreasonable given his apparently key role to ask at what point he could expect a percentage as opposed to a wage. In particular, he might have thought he had a claim to his share of future songwriting royalties.

All parties remain tight-lipped about exactly what happened between them, but it seems safe to say that someone on Holsapple's side pushed the idea a little too far and that the matter was not resolved amicably.

"Things happen – you sell a lot of records and things get weird,"

Peter Buck said after making the next album – without Holsapple. "It just isn't easy being the fifth member of our band. No one else is going to write songs with us. It's a closed shop and it's tough to deal with. I wouldn't want to be in a band where I didn't have input in the songwriting or arrangements and stuff.

"I wish money would have nothing to do with this. We played for free together for so long that it's a shame to have business things get in between us. But on the other hand, we write the songs, we're the band. It's fucked in a way, but we're not going to open it up. It's not a monetary thing; it's just that's the way we are."

Asserting that the arguments about business were "more on his manager's side than ours", Buck tried to stay optimistic about the relationship. "I'm assuming we'll work again some time as friends, and whatever the misunderstandings, they have nothing to do with him and us as people. There's going to be business misunderstandings: business sucks and business can make people get pissed off and that's why I'm not a businessman. But it enters into what we do sometimes."

Contacted in 1992 for his thoughts, not just on his break-up with R.E.M. but his period with them too, Peter Holsapple was terse, and evidently still upset, stating that he had determined not to talk about his situation with R.E.M. and that he was instead concentrating on the future.

His own career remained sadly stuck in perpetual second gear. At the peak of *Out Of Time*'s success, the independent label Rhino Records released an excellent new album by Holsapple and his former dB's partner Chris Stamey; *Mavericks* received a predictably warm critical response followed by the kind of inconsequential sales that had been the sad story of Holsapple's (and indeed Chris Stamey's) life.

*   *   *

"If we'd done a year-long tour (for *Out Of Time*), it would have been three years between records," observed Peter Buck in the summer of '92. "You get to that and it's your twice-decade statement." Equally to the point, conducting a year-long tour after the gruelling experience with *Green* would have pitched band members against each other with potentially ruinous results. Instead, hanging out in Athens for much of 1991, recording with visiting musicians, playing the very occasional secret gig at the 40 Watt, otherwise joining friends on stage at various local venues – and occasionally leaving town to pick up awards at high-profile cere-monies, such as in February to the UK, where they received their first Brit for Best International Group – the four members of R.E.M. found themselves as close together as ever. Here they were, having sold more records than ever contemplated, having reached the very pinnacle of the industry without knowingly com-promising, having made more money than was wise to count, and the best thing about it was they were still friends.

So it was no surprise that as the promotional activities died down and the daily sales-and-awards updates lost their sheen, R.E.M. simply got back to work. Several times a week, the playing members would meet in the rehearsal studio. One week a month they would take a break.

"We find the great way to work is to write together but not with drums," said Peter Buck the following summer, explaining why the songwriting process would often find Bill Berry playing bass guitar, Mike Mills the organ or piano, and himself the mandolin. When it then came to making demos at John Keane's, the group would resort to the more conventional band line-up with Berry on drums, Buck on guitar and Mills on bass and keyboards; by then, the subtleties of a song were already ingrained. "We'd write them as we did on *Out Of Time* but then go record them as a band. It was a nice combination."

Much has been written about various band members' personal unhappiness influencing the mood of the subsequent album. Most of it is exaggerated. While it's true that Peter Buck's marriage was not working out quite as planned, that he was drinking heavily and putting on weight accordingly, he was making perfectly good records with the likes of Billy Bragg and Nikki Sudden (and depending on taste, with The Troggs); the argument could easily be made that had R.E.M. toured that year as usual, the drinking would have been offset by the on-stage gigging, he wouldn't have got any bigger, and no one would have been any the wiser. Simply by staying put in Athens for two years, the thirty-somethings in R.E.M. were forced to grapple with growing up and settling down; they had time to reflect on their good fortune and consider their future. Some of that reflection may have made its way into the new songs, but it was never the band's deliberate intent to slow the pace down further from *Out Of Time*. Mike Mills subsequently told David Fricke of *Rolling Stone* simply how, "We wrote fast songs. But it's funny: fast songs are easier to write, but it seems like it's harder to write *good* ones. This time, the slow ones sounded better."

Similarly, Buck recalls "a wide variety of material; without lyrics there were 30 songs. We had one that could have turned into 'Shiny Happy People', it was obnoxiously bouncy . . . We had this one that was called 'The Fruity Organ Song' and I wrote it on this funky bouncy bass, and Mike on Farfisa organ and it was real cheesy. We decided we didn't want to go that way. The stuff we ended up working on was the stuff that was more discordant, almost morose."

Michael Stipe was again excluded from this writing process, given how well his absence had benefited the material for *Out Of Time*; he was instead presented with instrumental demos in the new year, which he immediately described to *Rolling Stone* as "pretty fucking weird". Fortunately, he was up to a challenge that might have flummoxed lesser front men; confronted with such brooding material, he would write his most inspired (and inspiring) lyrics to date, set to some of his most memorable melodies.

R.E.M. had no idea they were about to make the album of their career; in fact, they seemed so certain that they could not possibly match *Out Of Time* either for cultural relevance or crossover appeal that they decided to ignore all pressure and be as steadfastly uncommercial as their hearts told them they could get away with. Such is the manner in which great art is born.

But if they were keen to avoid the familiar rock star trap of second-guessing their own success, still they found a way to enjoy the trappings of fame. No longer touring the country to perform concerts, they decided to traverse the nation instead while recording, stopping off in various cities for a few weeks at a time. All kinds of excuses were subsequently offered – that each city had a particular soundboard (or control room, or vocal booth) that the group had long desired to use – but the reality was shiningly simple:

R.E.M. wanted to indulge themselves in the recording process, and have some tourist fun along the way.

With Scott Litt once more on board as co-producer, the band cut some demos at John Keane's in Athens during February. Later that month they made their first pit stop, at Daniel Lanois' studio in New Orleans, a city that had long impressed Peter Buck, who bought a house there as he finally looked beyond Athens as home. In New Orleans the group afforded themselves a carefree "see what happens" vibe – which could be interpreted as meaning they still had songs to write – out of which came a couple of instrumentals and what would be the album's opening cut, an almost one-take performance of a dirge-like guitar cruncher called 'Drive'.

'Drive' would end up layered with guitar overdubs, but it proved to be the exception. From New Orleans the group moved up to the familiar territory of Bearsville to record backing tracks; without Peter Holsapple in the studio to bolster the line-up, and given that for the first time ever none of the songs had been tested on stage, these tracks remained remarkably simple. "It's a record cut live with three players," said Buck on completion. "We realised as we were going that the songs were smaller, they were spare, there wasn't a lot going on in them, what was there was real concise. This one is really conscious of leaving as little on as possible. It definitely has less instruments on it than any other record we've made."

That sparseness might also have something to do with the fact that for overdubs the group moved down to Criteria Studios in Miami, where they all rented beach houses and the more sporty members of the band promptly shirked the studio for the sun, sand and surf, leaving Michael Stipe to develop his lyrics further and record his vocals. That said, it was Stipe who was depicted in the ocean on the album's inner sleeve; curiously for a band that had always swum against the tide, R.E.M. invited Anton Corbijn – photographer and video director for all the major post-punk stars, most notably U2 and Depeche Mode – to Miami to photograph them for promotional purposes. As is Corbijn's style, his shots showed the band members looking cool, calm and collected – an ineffably arty portrayal and yet entirely accurate too.

Following the sunny sojourn in Miami, the group moved to

Atlanta, to record the string parts that would prove vital to the final texture of four songs – each of which, not so coincidentally, would be a single. For this role, Scott Litt hired none other than John Paul Jones, whose role as Led Zeppelin's bassist, keyboard player and string arranger mirrored that of Mike Mills in R.E.M. The influence of punk rock had never shaken Mills' and Berry's high regard for hard rock's greatest exponents, and it's fair to say that Jones' presence in the studio was the first time any of R.E.M. had been seriously star-struck since playing on stage with Roger McGuinn and John Sebastian for MTV back in 1984.

Finally, R.E.M. then flew on to Seattle – the Athens of the Nineties, home of Nirvana, Soundgarden, Pearl Jam, Alice In Chains, Mudhoney, the Sub Pop label and coffee bars galore – to mix the album. The grunge sound of the Pacific Northwest was never likely to rub off on R.E.M. given that they had by now grasped that this was to be their most understated record to date. If anything, their presence in the new capital of alternative America confirmed their own obsolescence within that scene, and it worried R.E.M. not at all.

"I like the idea of rock'n'roll, but there are so many people doing it now with the whole Seattle thing," Peter Buck commented shortly after returning from that city. "Right this second making a big guitar record doesn't make a lot of sense. The Nirvana record can't be beat in that sense. So for us it was just the way we wanted to go. No one else is really trying to make records like this right now, for better or worse."

★   ★   ★

It turned out to be for the better. Greatly for the better. A collection of songs that Peter called "spooky" and "morose", that Stipe had reacted to as "fucking weird" and Mills announced upon release as "screwball" hardly suggested a major artistic, let alone commercial triumph. But just as The Beatles' decision to quit touring in 1966 promptly resulted in the inimitable *Sgt. Pepper's Lonely Hearts Club Band* and then the ambitious yet initially impenetrable White Album, so R.E.M.'s conscious withdrawal from the touring treadmill delivered first, the incomparable *Out Of Time*, and now, the brilliant yet initially opaque *Automatic For The People*.

211

In time, R.E.M.'s audience would become familiar with all the whys and wherefores of this album, would readily acknowledge its lyrical inspirations and applaud its musical direction, but the initial reaction was startled confusion at its musical sobriety and lyrical morbidity. That the band advertised its release with the news that they would not be touring behind this one either, that Michael Stipe's only public statement was to confirm that he would not be talking on its behalf, that Bill Berry decided to follow suit, and that R.E.M. lined up not a single acoustic show in support, all served to present *Automatic* as an enigma.

It was left to the garrulous Peter Buck and Mike Mills to unravel some of the mystery. With the album only just finished, and while the group was visiting New York in August to record with 10,000 Maniacs on a song entitled 'Photograph' for a benefit album, Peter Buck sat down with the author of this book for margharitas at a lower east side Mexican restaurant. There he talked with his familiar enthusiasm about an album he had wanted to call *Unforgettable* after the Natalie Cole "duets" record that had swept the Grammys that year. "I thought it was funny," he said, acknowledging that everyone else thought it would be seen as "sour grapes".

The group finally settled on *Automatic For The People,* the catch-phrase from a soul food restaurant in Athens, Weaver D's, where each order would be greeted with the friendly response "Automatic". Mike Mills saw R.E.M.'s job as similar to Weaver D's. "It's like, here's some songs and we hope you like them." Similarly, and subconsciously, the title was also a continued mark of involvement and respect for the group's home, a metaphorical return to the kudzu that defined *Murmur.*

But if *Murmur* was a distinctly southern album in substance as well as appearance, *Automatic For The People* was patently universal, especially in regard to Stipe's lyrics. The first example was the distinctly down-tempo and discordant opening track 'Drive', a couple of quietly competing acoustic guitar lines giving space for Stipe to enter with a heavily reverbed couplet that was one of his more strident opening gambits. "Smack, crack, bushwhacked/Tie another one to the racks, baby/Hey kids, rock and roll/Nobody tells you where to go, baby."

"It can be read a couple of different ways lyrically," Buck

offered, allowing that Stipe was not going to be around to elabor-
ate. "It's about, Oh there's an election coming up, no one tells you
what to do, and he mentions bushwhacked – you don't necessarily
have to think about George Bush although I know Michael was –
and then on the other hand it could be a dumb 'raise your fists in
the air' rock'n'roll song: Hey kids rock'n'roll – 'Come on Cleveland.'" Though there was hardly an R.E.M. fan who didn't spot
the reference to the US President ('Bushwhacked' was the term
Stipe had used in his advert for Dukakis in '88), neither were there
many of a certain age who didn't spot the lift from the David Essex
song 'Rock On', which Stipe later admitted was one of his first
musical memories. Fans of Pylon also saw a lyrical similarity to that
group's 'Stop It'. A video made that August featured the very
Nineties concert-goers trend of body surfing, except that on (black
and white) film, it was Michael Stipe passing over the heads of a
young rock crowd, the star as audience member being treated as a
star, purposefully blurring the issue.

By this point, R.E.M. had already decided that the opening
song, which could most positively be described as "brooding" (and
one that, for all its eventual use of bone-crunching electric guitars
was notably devoid of a chorus), would also be the album's first
single. "We don't want to be known as this band who make singles
that are bouncy ditties and then make these weird depressing
albums," said Peter Buck, as if to suggest that at this point in time,
the band wanted to be known for "weird depressing" albums *and*
singles.

After all, much of *Automatic* seemed desperately downhearted on
initial impact. This was apparent not just in the restrained musical
mood, but by the subject matter. Three of the album's first six
songs concerned death. The first of these, directly on the heels of
'Drive', was 'Try Not To Breathe', the initial inspiration for which
had been perfectly life-affirming: recording a mandolin track for a
demo, John Keane told Peter Buck he could hear the guitarist's
breath over the track. Buck responded, "Okay, I'll try not to
breathe," and Stipe heard a song title. He came back with a lyric
written from the perspective of an old person at death's door
talking to a younger listener. Years later he confessed to the subject
as being his grandmother; he must have not told the others, who

initially talked of the narrator as being male. Either way it was possibly his most poetic lyric to date, a song of great empathy for the elderly. The narrator notes (s)he has "seen things that you will never see", and concludes, with the graceful acceptance that comes at the end of a full life, "Leave it to memory me". If it was rare for a rock star in his commercial prime to consider death from old age as subject matter, well then, that said all the more for Stipe as a songwriter.

'Sweetness Follows', which closed side one for those still buying vinyl albums rather than the now dominant compact disc, covered similar territory. "Readying to bury your father and your mother, what did you think when you lost another?" asked Stipe on one of rock's more funereal opening lines – though later, as a cello scraped, an organ reverberated, and a lone electric guitar wailed, the apparent gravity was countered by the line, "Live your life filled with joy and wonder."

Evenly spaced between these two songs was the album's first indisputable triumph, 'Everybody Hurts', the ballad R.E.M. had always had in them but had never dared attempt. "I always feel if we approach some black music styles, we're stealing," said Buck of a song he considered "a mutated Stax thing", noting how Stipe in particular "feels if he's doing something real soulish he's afraid that he's approaching that Michael Bolton territory." Perhaps that explains why it was Bill Berry who primarily composed the song on acoustic guitar; the down-to-earth drummer, raised on covering The Meters and southern rock, rarely worried himself with issues of imitation.

A slow-burner in 6/8 time, 'Everybody Hurts' opened with a gentle acoustic guitar arpeggio and softly stated electric piano chords; underneath clicked a drum box.* Stipe's voice, when it entered, was as far forward in the mix as it had ever been, as keenly enunciated and as emotionally empowered, and his lyric left no hint of ambiguity. "When you're sure you've had enough of this life, well hang on/don't let yourself go, everybody cries and everybody hurts sometimes."

---

* Ironically, despite being the primary composer, Berry would barely appear on the recorded version.

Fifteen

It was a song of sympathy and a show of solidarity for anyone weighed down by life, for anyone who might be considering ending it all. And as a mark of how far R.E.M. had come since those days of purposefully shunning the commercial polish, it used almost every trick in the arrangement book to pull at the heart strings. The first verse (like 'Drive', 'Everybody Hurts' lacked a chorus) was sparsely accompanied; it rolled effortlessly into the second, whereby Stipe's vocals began overlapping each other.* For the middle eight, the electric guitar entered at the same moment as tear-jerking violins and a lyrical insistence to "Take comfort in your friends . . . Don't throw your hand . . . you are not alone" before stopping in mid-air and returning to the simplicity of the song's introduction. A final verse built in drama as it extended and then headed into a coda – only now accompanied by a proper drum beat – that by the nature of Stipe's overlapping vocals and crescendoing strings needed sufficient repetition to hit home. It was only R.E.M.'s second song to clock in over five minutes ('Camera' had been the first) and yet it seemed totally succinct – and of incredible clarity. "There's a time for obfuscation," Mike Mills told the *East Coast Rocker*, referring to Stipe's long-standing lyrical trait. "But that wasn't it."

Two other songs also advertised themselves as singles, though for more traditionally upbeat reasons. The apparent subject of 'The Sidewinder Sleeps Tonite' was an American desert snake that moves laterally; as per its titular reference, the opening vocal blatantly recalled 'The Lion Sleeps Tonight', an American number one for The Tokens in 1961, and a British number one for Tight Fit in 1982. R.E.M. contacted the song's composers up front, agreeing to record the original song as a B-side for when they in-evitably released 'Sidewinder' as a single (ensuring a significant publishing royalty to the composers). Considering that R.E.M. had included 'The Lion Sleeps Tonight' in its live set at various points since 1980, this settlement seemed more pleasure than penance. Certainly, 'The Sidewinder Sleeps Tonite' was pure entertainment musically; its near frivolous nature allowed Stipe to rant so much

---

* The singer had wanted to duet with his idol Patti Smith for that second verse, but as Buck remembers, "her husband wasn't into it."

apparent nonsense that in the middle eight his reference to childrens' author Dr. Seuss caused him to break down in laughter. Being R.E.M., that was the vocal take that made it onto tape – and served to embody the song's sense of mischief. The initially un-fathomable chorus line, "call me when you try to wake her up", was presumably a reference to the sleeping sidewinder snake – unless, of course, Stipe was laying claim to that role himself. "I don't know what that snake imagery is about," Buck told *Melody Maker*. "I'm just a fan."

Stipe's fondness for pop culture peaked with *Automatic*'s other upbeat standout, 'Man On The Moon'. All manner of apparently random proper names got referenced – Mott The Hoople, Moses, Darwin, Fred Blassie, Monopoly, 21, checkers and chess. And most frequently, Andy Kaufman, the iconoclastic comedian whom non-American R.E.M. fans could reference only by his appearance on the sitcom *Taxi*, knowing nothing of his penchant for pro wrestling, situationist chaos, and Elvis impersonations. In fact, such was Kaufman's reputation for prime time stunts that there were those who refused to accept his death (of cancer), just as there remain many who believe Elvis is still alive. By taking the con-spiracy theory that man never went to the moon but concocted the space landing in a TV studio, dovetailing that with the suggestion that Kaufman and Elvis had faked their own deaths (and/or that the former was "goofing" on the latter in heaven), by throwing Darwin and Newton's proven theories up against Moses' supposed miracles – and by imitating-Kaufman-imitating-Elvis with a hefty 'Hey baby!' – Stipe left us questioning what was real and what was memorex. That the song had a country twang, a sing-along chorus and an indisputable *joie de vivre* hardly harmed its cause.

The pop culture obsession continued in a similar, albeit less immediately impacting mid-tempo vein on 'Monty Got A Raw Deal', about actor Montgomery Clift. Stipe's perspective was not – initially – too clear, though both the title and lyrics like "just let go" suggested that Stipe was addressing Clift's repressed homo-sexuality; Monty was of an era when all major movie stars were required to live up to their media image as objects of female fantasy.

There was no such ambiguity about the cultural implications of

'Ignoreland', "the most specific political song we've ever written", as Buck volunteered before its release, and also the album's lone rock-out. Though the lyrics were buried in a mix that the band came to detest, those that could be heard were angry to the point of revolt. Two albums and four years on from *Green*, *Automatic For The People* was to be released just before the next Presidential election: R.E.M. wanted a song that would stand as a testament to the Reagan revolution whether George Bush was re-elected or his new opponent, the baby boomer Bill Clinton, took his place instead. Stipe's fury at the last twelve years of American politics was apparent in occasionally deciphered vituperatives like "bastards . . . duplicitous . . . heartless" and a crude reference to George Bush's vomiting at a Japanese state dinner in the line, "throw-up on your shoes".

Buck readily supported Stipe's attack. "They turned this country into a dictatorship," he said of the Reaganites, though of course in real dictatorships outspoken musicians are censored and/or imprisoned rather than being afforded such a populist position of influence as R.E.M. Perhaps recognising how his support of Dukakis four years earlier had made so little difference, Stipe's most discernible line was as follows: "I know this is vitriol, no solution, spleen-venting, but I feel better for having screamed, don't you?"

It was all a far cry from the romantic mood behind *Out Of Time*. The lone love song on *Automatic* was purposefully "weird and obsessive", with Mike Mills sampling his backing vocal onto a keyboard line, in tribute to an effect first employed by 10cc on 'I'm Not In Love'. Stipe whispered his way toward a concluding line, "I'm in your possession, so fuck me kitten." These last three words were originally intended to be the song title; it was subsequently changed to 'Star Me Kitten' to avoid a possible 'Parental Advisory' label, offering a nod in the process to The Rolling Stones, who had employed the same trick with 'Star Star', which was originally titled 'Starfucker'.

Sexual tension was also evident on the album's penultimate number, the gorgeous 'Nightswimming'. That this was the first R.E.M. song to be composed on piano since 'Perfect Circle' was more than coincidence, given that both songs yearned for the innocence of youth. "We used to go swimming naked," says Buck, who didn't even play on the final recording. "It would be summertime, it would be 100 degrees, we were all younger, it was pre-AIDS, so no one had this fear of sex. We'd go to this swimming hole, two in the morning, twenty to thirty naked teenagers. You'd assume what would happen would happen and it did. Is it also about performing? I tend to read it a little bit that way, although Michael would probably tell you no, definitely not. I don't think Michael has any inhibition about writing about anything, it's just that none of our songs have ever been real manifestoes. It tends to be filtered through his vision."

Automatic's finale, 'Find The River', was an apt example of Stipe's filter at its most hazy. Following in the wistful vein of 'Nightswimming', this visual poetry, written in Miami, was reflective of the album's uncertain mood. After bemoaning how "life can pass before my eyes, and nothing is going my way", the focus shifted at the song, and the album's, very conclusion, where Stipe announced, "The river drifts to the tide, all of this is coming your way"; the song then ended in mid-air as quietly picked acoustic guitars wound down the volume towards an understated finale.

Ending as tentatively as it began, *Automatic For The People* hardly sounded like music for the masses. Yet for anyone willing to give it time, it was difficult to dispute that R.E.M. had made an album that represented a triumph on every level. In pure songwriting terms, with the possible exception of 'New Orleans Instrumental No. 1' tucked away on side one, each track stood on its own merits; half-a-dozen numbers sounded like nothing less than the best songs R.E.M. had ever recorded. On the arrangements front, R.E.M.'s continued experimentation was paying increasing dividends: the use of organ, strings, mandolins, cellos, bouzoukis, even drum boxes spoke of a group that knew no bounds and yet also knew not to clutter. Michael Stipe's voice had never been stronger – or more fragile, when that was called upon. And his lyrics . . . well for all that they seemed focused on the darker side of life (and death), they maintained an optimism throughout, an insistence that the cup of life was half full; they were certainly his most eloquent and poetic to date. Was there any reason to doubt that R.E.M.'s hiatus from touring had paid stupendous dividends in the studio?

Sixteen

Curious though it seems with the benefit of hindsight, the members of R.E.M. were genuinely, seriously concerned that *Automatic For The People* would not be recognised for its artistic merits. Ever since *Murmur*'s surprise success, R.E.M. had been in the habit of predicting their imminent demise, but this time, there was real sincerity in the nervous pronouncements of limited expectations.

Talking to David Fricke for a major *Melody Maker* feature, Mike Mills announced how, "This is not the same record that *Out Of Time* was. I think it may be a better record, but I don't think it's going to sell like *Out Of Time*. It's smaller, personal, more intimate. It's not gonna have the splash like the last one did."

Likewise, in a series of statements dotted throughout his conversation with this author in August '92, Buck allowed for commercial disappointment even as he affirmed his own artistic self-belief. "I think if we'd waited a long time, we might have worried that this album isn't commercial enough," he said almost the moment he started talking about *Automatic*. "But this was a quick record. If this one sells a mere two million – which is one fifth of what the last one sold – that's cool. Two million is still two million and we'll make another one. I like putting out a lot of records. We're pretty much at a creative peak."

The latter sentence was self-evident. But still he felt the need to defend his band. "I have a feeling this one won't do as well as the last one," he insisted. "I think nine million records is a fluke. I'd rather make a record that's a little bit difficult and have it successful on our terms, than make a great record five years down the line that fails because it's not like the last four. If we do a million in America and a million outside America, I'll still be happy."

And later on, a serious introspective: "Everyone's career in the music business has its ups and downs, and ours has been straight up. We've never had a record that's sold less than the previous record. Maybe a little bit of adversity would be good for us. Even for U2, *Rattle And Hum* didn't sell that well. We're going to be in it for a long time, we don't have to worry about ending on a high note. (With this album) we're not going to tour, and we're not going to do the promo tours. We're just going to do the videos. There's a feeling that it's a real strong record but it's not single oriented. It's just a matter of, can we bring our fans along with us, to get something that's a little bit less than what they expect?"

The answer would soon become apparent. For with *Automatic For The People* R.E.M. made an album that transcended genres, traversed musical continents; they released a record so deeply and permanently beautiful that it reached beyond R.E.M.'s fan base, beyond the 'alternative' market, beyond, even, the mainstream the group thought they had already conquered. In many countries it became one of those rare albums that sell to people who don't normally buy albums. Buck's assertions that *Automatic* was not "single-oriented", and that two million sales worldwide was a respectable goal were proven so much pessimistic thinking. In the US, it spawned three top 30 hits and was certified double-platinum within two months. And in the UK *Automatic* spawned no less than six singles, four of them top 20 hits, on its way to the two million domestic sales Buck thought was the album's global potential.

Indeed, with *Automatic For The People* R.E.M.'s primary market switched – from the USA to the UK. During their first decade – the Eighties – R.E.M. had been the all-American alternative, rising steadily in sales and stature with every release in their home country, until with *Document* the group finally broke the platinum sales bracket, and with 'The One I Love', the top 10 too. The rest of the world had been, until then, if not entirely uninterested, limited to pockets of cult appeal. The UK was always the largest of these pockets, thanks to the rapturous press coverage, but such appeal didn't translate into serious sales until the new record deal, the album *Green*, and the substantial touring of 1989. R.E.M. ended the Eighties as a major act in the UK *and* the USA.

They entered the Nineties with *Out Of Time*, which not only propelled the group to the superstar stratosphere in its US homeland

– but did the same in many other countries too, the UK especially. *Automatic For The People* kept them there, but with a subtle shift: in the USA *Automatic* sold a little bit less than did *Out Of Time*, and in the UK it sold a little bit more. By 1992, R.E.M., an American group if ever there was one, had become the biggest band in Britain.

So much of R.E.M.'s long-term success in the UK was due to the music press, the nation's equivalent of America's college radio. And the early Nineties found that UK press in a relatively healthy state. The 'Madchester' boom of 1989-90 had seen The Stone Roses, Happy Mondays, Charlatans and co. revitalise British rock by infecting it with the grooves and aesthetics of the 'acid house' dancefloor revolution. The 'indie dance' acts EMF and Jesus Jones conquered both the British and American singles charts. A group of more intellectual rock bands from the south of England such as Ride, Chapterhouse and Slowdive, collectively labelled 'shoegazing' for their tendency to concentrate on guitar playing and ignore the audience, filled a gap somewhere in between. To cater for the public's apparently insatiable desire to read about all these sub-genres, new rock monthlies *Vox* and *Select* joined the now-established *Q* magazine on the racks. The ageing weeklies *NME* and *Melody Maker* lost sales to these new monthlies, but sacrificed little of their credibility as the leading voices and opinion makers. And across all these publications, it was becoming increasingly difficult to find either editors, staff writers or young freelancers who didn't venerate R.E.M., a group which, in stark contrast to hyped-up British bands who collapsed on their second albums, had already proven their consistent brilliance for a decade.

As such, and given the phenomenal UK popularity of *Out Of Time,* blanket coverage was barely slowed by the news that Michael Stipe wouldn't be giving interviews; Warner Brothers simply flew the magazines out to Athens or to video shoots as compensation and the front covers duly appeared. And reviews for *Automatic* proved positively hyperbolic. Dele Fadele in *NME* gave the album a coveted 10-out-of-10. Keith Cameron in *Vox* likewise. David Cavanagh in a 5-star *Select* review called it "one of the greatest records ever made", adding in an accompanying feature that it was "an album to keep playing for as long as music means the world to you."

Over at *Melody Maker*, meanwhile, editor – and long-time R.E.M. champion – Allan Jones closed a glowing review by stating that "*Automatic For The People* is R.E.M. at the very top of their form . . . Listen to it, and let it stone you to your soul."

Near the beginning of his review, however, he stated the following: "It's almost impossible to write about the record without mentioning the recent grim rumours concerning Stipe's health. Variously, he's said to be dying with either AIDS or cancer."

The British media's gossip machine is a law unto itself, and never one to let simple facts get in the way of a good story. With rival publications tripping over themselves to gain an exclusive on R.E.M., yet with new angles few and far between – especially given that the enigmatic lead singer, the one everyone wanted to know about and talk to, was staying in America and refraining from interviews – the papers upped the ante by turning to rumour: Michael Stipe had AIDS.

Allan Jones, ten years later, insists of the rumour that, "*Melody Maker* didn't start it, I'm sure of that – but where we would have picked up on it completely escapes me." Regardless of who instigated it, the paper was taking it seriously enough that in the same issue as Jones appraised *Automatic* in the context of Stipe (not) having AIDS, it published an interview in which American correspondent David Fricke directly confronted Buck and Mills with the rumour.

"Bullshit," snorted Mills.

"What can you say about it?" challenged Buck. "We've all been tested. We have tons of insurance, millions of dollars worth . . . I know Michael passed the test just two months ago."

But rather than killing the rumour dead, so to speak, the pair's denials instead just fed it. Though other music magazines, perhaps knowing better, avoided the topic, the AIDS rumour quickly spread to the national tabloids as *Automatic For The People* entered the UK charts at number one, took up permanent residence in the top 10, and 'Man On The Moon' followed 'Drive' into the British Top 20.

There were several supposedly serious reasons for this rumour ever being given credence, and they should, for the sake of accuracy, be offered up and responded to.

Reason: Michael Stipe was thin, gangly and balding.

Response: So what else was new?

Reason: *Automatic For The People* was obsessed with death.

Response: True, there were songs about dying: one from the perspective of an old person, one that was patently anti-suicide, and another about burying one's parents. It was deep, dark and often depressing material for sure. Still, there were no songs that referenced AIDS, nor any that hinted at the singer's imminent demise. Mike Mills did mention in an interview that Andy Kaufman, subject of 'Man On The Moon' had died of "either AIDS or cancer" – it was the latter – but had probably not expected someone in the media to take that sentence and apply it to his friend and lead singer.

Reason: Michael Stipe had collected an award at the Grammys wearing a hat that read "White House – Stop AIDS".

Response: Good for him. Within the music and arts community, everyone knew at least one person who had died of AIDS in the Eighties and early Nineties. Most knew dozens. It was a plague. And the Reagan and Bush administration seemed blind to it; funding to find a cure was hopelessly inadequate.

Reason: R.E.M. were no longer touring.

Response: This was a disappointment for fans, but understandable given the context of the new album's restrained mood and sparse arrangements; the songs from *Automatic* would have been even harder to recreate on stage than those from *Out Of Time*. Still, the group was already announcing its intention to make a rock'n'roll record and get back on the road in '94, which would have been a tough promise to live up to if their singer was going to be dead by then.

Reason: Michael Stipe had stopped doing interviews.

Response: Who could blame him if this was what he would come up against? "He's a lyricist and everyone wants to jump inside his mind," Peter Buck told Q's Mat Snow in his friend's defence. "This record is pretty much what it is, with not a lot of metaphors, and I don't think he felt like explaining things. This year we want to be more low-key."

All of which means there had to have been another reason the British press invented and then perpetuated the story, one that had nothing to do with R.E.M., and there was. Freddie Mercury, the extrovert singer with Queen, Britain's most consistently popular band of the Seventies and Eighties, had died of AIDS-related pneumonia on November 24, 1991. Throughout that year, the media had charged that he was HIV-positive and in ill health, but Mercury denied both counts – and with them, by affiliation, his homosexuality – until the very eve of his death, when he finally issued a statement "that I have been tested HIV positive and have Aids." After he died the following day – the first major rock star to pass away from AIDS complications – the floodgates opened. The whole issue of homosexuality, AIDS and the celebrity's responsibility to honesty moved into the national arena. The British public's hunger seemed insatiable, and to keep feeding it, the media needed a new target. In Michael Stipe, the latest singing sensation, they found one. By asserting that Michael Stipe had AIDS – which he could deny if he wanted – the media was in actuality informing the public that he was gay. And that was something Michael Stipe would not deny.

It had always been known within R.E.M.'s circle that Michael Stipe was, as he would finally put it two years later, "of indecipherable or unpronounced sexuality". But that was considered to be his business, and for good reason. Though there was a gay scene at the Art Department in Athens, Georgia was still the Bible Belt of America, and an admission of homosexuality was an invitation to serious brutality. Even in the mainstream pop world, unless you were Boy George – who played up to and hammed up many stereotypical images of gay femininity – you simply didn't get up on a pedestal and announce yourself as being bi- or homo-sexual if you knew what was good for your career. Homophobia was rife across America throughout the Reaganite era, and while R.E.M. had never taken shit from anybody, neither were they were willing to be sacrificial lambs. Besides, rock'n'roll by its very nature attracts the misfits, the indefinables, the inscrutables and the undesirables, and there was an unspoken understanding among insiders that you didn't advertise each other's predilections, addictions or inflictions unless you intended owning up to your own.

Still, times change. And Freddie Mercury may well have been the last of the pop generation to steadfastly deny his sexuality. In the States, a benchmark moment occurred when David Geffen, one of the most powerful individuals in the entertainment industry, publicly came out in November 1992 – and was both commended and celebrated for his decision.

Interestingly, in August '92, while talking about the gradual acceptance and growth of punk rock, as epitomised by Nirvana's success, Peter Buck stated, "I always likened it to the way being gay is perceived. When I was a teenager, gay rights were just starting and the reaction was the most vitriolic, nasty beatings, and now fifteen years down the line everyone I know including my mom has gay friends. And that's what it was like with the whole punk underground thing. It was just out of the public eye for a long time and it was just going on, and eventually it just saturated public consciousness."

Yet still Stipe stayed silent on the subject. This seemed odd given the changing political climate and his own increased popularity; if ever there was a time to publicly 'come out' with a minimum of negative repercussions and a maximum of positive ones, this was it. And yet his reticence played into his contrary nature. It's fair to say that Michael Stipe has always had a considerable love-hate relationship with publicity. While he clearly enjoys the admiration that comes with fronting a great rock band, while he loves singing, dancing, entertaining, talking up issues and making videos and films, he has simultaneously remained a most private person. Given that he would barely talk about his parents or his upbringing, that he kept his home address a closely guarded secret – and given that he wasn't talking to the media at all in 1992 – he chose neither to confirm nor deny the rumours of his imminent demise.

And so they continued apace. On December 11, the Welsh band Manic Street Preachers were midway through a set at London's Kilburn National Ballroom when bass player Nicky Wire chose to issue the following unprovoked statement: "In the season of good-will, let's hope Michael Stipe goes the same way as Freddie Mercury." As the comment swept through the national tabloids, the rumour was dutifully reaffirmed to the point that it seemed confirmed. If anything intelligent can be gathered from Wire's pathetic outburst, it's that success attracts not just fame and fortune but hatred and jealousy too. If any moral can be accrued, it's that what goes around comes around: The Manic Street Preachers' manic depressive lyricist and second guitarist, Richey Edwards, disappeared in February 1995 and has never been seen since.

★   ★   ★

The possibility that Stipe was fatally ill could be easily disproven by taking one look at the singer's work schedule through late 1992. Immediately after mixing *Automatic* there were videos to shoot, B-sides and Christmas singles to record, C-00's first feature-length movie to make (though *Desperation Angels*, an American 'road movie' directed by Jim McKay, never saw release) and, Stipe being Stipe, political campaigning to conduct. On October 22, while Buck and Mills were in Europe doing radio interviews and Berry stayed close to ground, Michael Stipe introduced Democratic Senator and Vice-Presidential Candidate Al Gore at a rally in Athens. R.E.M.'s new album had just entered the American charts at number two, held off the top spot at a peak time of year only by country music giant Garth Brooks. In fact, at this juncture, R.E.M. probably had more in common musically with Brooks' layman approach to Americana than they did with the hard 'alternative' rock groups alongside them in the top 10: Pearl Jam, Alice In Chains and Red Hot Chili Peppers. And it was perhaps a sign of R.E.M.'s mainstream appeal within the political system that the future Vice President could get up and deliver, with a straight face, the excruciatingly opportunist sentiment, "George Bush is Out of Time and Bill Clinton and Al Gore are going to be Automatic for the People."

Still, what else would one expect from a career politician? A debate on the hidden meaning of Stipe's more impenetrable lyrics? A discourse on why 'Fuck Me Kitten' had been retitled 'Star Me Kitten'? The fact had not been lost on American observers of censorship, or indeed on other members of R.E.M., that Al Gore's wife, Tipper Gore, was a co-founder of the Parents Music Resource Coalition (along with Susan Baker, wife of Ronald Reagan's Secretary of State, James Baker – so much for political partisanship). The PMRC had risen to prominence during the family-values-conservatism of Reagan's second term, calling for the introduction of voluntary 'Parental Advisory' labels on albums that contained 'explicit lyrics'. While the initial spark for the campaign had been the Prince song 'Let's Pretend We're Married' from the album *1999* (on Warner Brothers), by the time the labels were 'voluntarily' introduced by the recording industry – under threat of legislation in 20 States – they were used mainly to stigmatise thrash metal and the hardcore rap music that was spreading in popularity from its initial black urban base into the white suburbs. In certain States and across many mall-based record chains, under-18s were not permitted to buy such albums. And the self-censorship reached alarming extremes in 1990 when Prince released *Graffiti Bridge,* an album entirely devoid of swearing, sexual vulgarity or violence, and still his record label (still Warner Brothers) placed a 'Parental Advisory' sticker to be sure.

Unlike their label mate, R.E.M. escaped the dreaded sticker on *Automatic For The People* despite the presence of the f-word in a lyric; by 1992, some of the hysteria had passed. Peter Buck had nonetheless voiced frustration at even having to change the song title: "I think it should either be called 'Fuck Me Kitten' on the inside or nothing. But I lost the vote." At a previous charity event in which R.E.M. had participated, Buck had met the Gores and voiced his frustration to Tipper. "I said first of all she's aligning herself with the book burners, and people who have a hidden agenda to establish America as a religious theocracy. It's all very well to just say, label records – OK, you won – but that's not all these people want. They want to have prayer in schools, they want to stop abortion, they want to make homosexuality illegal again, these people are going to be burning books, throwing Jews in camps in a few years, and you're aligning yourself with them. She was shocked."

If it seemed unlikely that Michael Stipe would host a political appearance by a Senator whose wife had been such a leading proponent of censorship, it was also a sign of desperation among the left-wing. After twelve years of Reaganomics, the American economy was now deep in recession and the people seemed ready for a change of leadership style. A renegade billionaire, Ross Perot, launched a Reform Party, and immediately attracted millions of members, many of them dissatisfied Republicans. This gave the Democrats a chance to regain the Presidency, and in Bill Clinton, Governor of Arkansas, they had plenty going for them among the younger alienated voters: Clinton had risen from abject poverty, he was clearly egalitarian, he promised attention to such issues as national health care (taken for granted across Europe but denied Americans), he was a rock'n'roll fan who could play a mean sax wearing shades on late night TV, and he had a certain insouciant decadence that marked him among his detractors as an habitual liar (Slick Willie), and among his supporters as a survivor (the Comeback Kid). Those on the left, like R.E.M., were willing to turn a blind eye to the failings of these potential leaders for the opportunity to wrest the major seat of American government from Republican control. In fact, once the campaign got under way, it was noticeable how Tipper Gore was kept to the sidelines, her statements about morality in music suddenly silenced by 'voluntary stickering' of her speeches.

At least this time Stipe backed the winner. Due in no small part to the Reform Party splitting the Republican vote, Bill Clinton was elected President in November 1992. The Reagan era was over, and the country had its first youthful leader since JFK. The Inauguration in January quickly became the focus for a vast number of celebratory 'Balls', of which the MTV Rock'n'roll Inaugural Ball was clearly the hippest.* Michael Stipe and Mike Mills headed to DC for the party; while there, they hooked up with Adam Clayton and Larry Mullen, bassist and drummer respectively from U2, where they rehearsed a version of the latter band's 'One' for the television special. It was the first public meeting between what were now probably the two most consistently successful and acclaimed rock bands in the world, and it went off just fine. On live television on January 20, Automatic Baby – as they named themselves after each of the group's most recent albums – performed 'One' to rapturous applause; Stipe then stayed on stage to perform with his friends 10,000 Maniacs their song 'Candy Everyone Wants' followed by the theme from the movie *To Sir With Love*.

---

* By launching a Rock The Vote campaign among its viewers, and by allowing Bill Clinton significant air time in a town hall question-and-answer format – an opportunity George Bush declined – MTV had significantly influenced the result of the election.

Sixteen

R.E.M. returned to Washington in May when Clinton passed the 'Motor Voter' Bill. Registering to vote had long been a complex process in the States, especially for the poor and uneducated. The Motor Voter Bill enabled people to simply register when applying for a driver's licence. Having spoken up on behalf of MTV's Rock The Vote campaign and the Motor Voter bill, the group were invited to witness its signing into legislation on May 19 and were even given a tour of the White House and invited to a photo op on the South Lawn. Stipe, Mills and Berry all made the most of the occasion. Peter Buck was conspicuous by his absence.

★   ★   ★

The decision had long ago been made to follow 'Drive' as *Automatic*'s 'difficult' first single with the 'easier' trio of 'Man On The Moon', 'The Sidewinder Sleeps Tonite' and 'Everybody Hurts'. Videos were duly shot for all three. One of them, 'The Sidewinder Sleeps Tonite', was probably the most inane video R.E.M. ever wasted good money on. Its editor Robert Duffy (there was no credited director) wisely avoided interpreting the stream-of-consciousness lyrics, but settled for some half-baked performance shots and a meaningless piece of rotating machinery instead. Was it mere coincidence that the single flopped in America, where MTV support was essential?

In compensation, the videos for the other two singles were cinematic classics. 'Man On The Moon', like 'Drive', was shot by British director Peter Care in black and white. Stipe starred, in a Stetson and jeans, striding through the desert as the screen split into variously shaped frames, getting away with literal interpretations of the lyrics (Andy Kaufman, a horrible Asp, a spinning apple, the game Twister) by the sheer purpose of Stipe's stride. Halfway through the song, Stipe hopped on board an 18-wheeler driven by Bill Berry; the pair then pulled into a truck stop where Peter Buck was bartending, Mike Mills playing pool, and a whole assortment of customers, from pretty young girls to wizened old men, were lip-synching to the final choruses as if the song was on the jukebox – but in a spoken voice, as if the words were their own conversation instead. A TV in the corner portrayed Kaufman wrestling and 'goofing' on Elvis, a homely blonde smiled to someone just off camera, and the clip closed with Stipe taking his leave, back to the desert. It was everything positive one associated with R.E.M. – evocative, wistful, intelligent, nostalgic, and familiar all at once. It depicted the song lyrically, yet left ample room for further personal interpretation. It helped visualise the song on the radio where it stood out as R.E.M.'s most articulate and intelligent pop single to date. 'Man On The Moon' rapidly followed 'Drive' into the British top 20 before Christmas; it was a top 30 hit in the States in the new year.

The outstanding 'Man On The Moon' video actually paled against the clip for 'Everybody Hurts'. Clearly aware of the song's commercial potential, no expense was spared by Warner Brothers and the group on this one: director Jake Scott (son of *Bladerunner* director Ridley) was hired and a section of Interstate 10 at San Antonio in Texas commandeered for two days. Hundreds of vehicles were gradually funnelled into a colossal traffic jam, including a car driven by Stipe, with the other band members as his passengers. The lyrics to the first verse were shown as subtitles, soon replaced by the (half-completed) thoughts of others on the road as the slowing traffic gave them the opportunity to ruminate: "17 years . . ." (a truck driver); "I had no idea" (a frustrated housewife); "they're going to miss me" (a teenager leaning out of a window). From above a flyover, a man ripped pages out of the Bible onto the highway below as the Holy words showed up in subtitles. The middle eight saw Stipe exit the car and start climbing boldly across other vehicles as the other band members were portrayed looking moody up against immobile cars. Finally, to the words "hold on", Stipe began actually lip-synching and all the passengers, hundreds of them up and down the highway, evacuated their vehicles at the same lazy moment, walking off, as if in a daydream, into the horizon. It was a dangerously messianic gesture on Stipe's part to portray himself as their saviour, but he pulled it off thanks to Scott's superb filming, the vibrant colours, the sense of melancholy, Stipe's own cinematic presence, and the dream-like pace of the editing. Without dumbing down the lyrics, the message came across exactly as intended – there's always a way out, however hemmed in you feel – and yet the clip succeeded as a mini-movie in its own right. R.E.M.'s lack of touring was no longer an issue; why bother when you could raise the audio-visual promo clip to a work of art instead?

'Everybody Hurts' was held for *Automatic*'s fourth single, one more than most albums can bear. But those on the business side of the band knew there was a market for this song outside the regular R.E.M. fan base. Released in the UK in April '93, 'Everybody Hurts' quickly rose to the Top 10, staying there for a five-week period, during which time *Automatic For The People*, now some seven months old, returned to number one on the album charts on three separate occasions.

You can measure a song's impact by its sales and airplay, or its effect on album sales; and you can measure a song by its cultural resonance. Three years later, on March 13, 1996, a gunman with a grudge walked into a primary school in the small Scottish town of Dunblane and shot dead 16 five- and six-year-olds and their teacher before turning the gun on himself. Britain was rocked to its very core by such a senseless massacre: surely this was the kind of event that only ever took place in America, where guns were as common as murderous tendencies? Perhaps it was fitting then, that when 'the nation's favourite', Radio 1, observed two minutes of silence on a day of mourning, it returned to music with a song by an American group. 'Everybody Hurts' was the record deemed most capable of emoting that indescribable pain.

Seventeen

Two years after *Automatic For The People*'s release, the point at which Peter Buck could usually be expected to announce his dissatisfaction with the band's last album as he introduced the new one, he stated exactly the opposite. "*Automatic* is the album that I think will hold up best, the one people may think is pretty good ten years from now," he told writer Greg Kot. "I was driving through the desert with a friend listening to it and saying, 'We should probably break up. This would be a good place to stop.'"

R.E.M. didn't break up. From the public's perspective they barely seemed to slow down, let alone stop. But after thirteen years' relentless hard work, the most industrious musical member decided to take a break. A lengthy one.

Peter Buck was older than the other band members; he had lived in Athens longer than any of them. He was peripatetic by nature, not easily assuaged by the lack of touring even though he fully supported and encouraged the decision. He had made a determined effort to settle down by marrying Barrie Greene back in '88, and for a while it had all worked fine – R.E.M. recorded, toured, and when they did neither, Buck did both with other people – but by 1992 the marriage was collapsing, and he had begun looking for a life outside Athens. As the group recorded in New Orleans, he bought a house there. As they returned to Woodstock and made more frequent trips to the business hub of New York, he bought an apartment in Manhattan. And when they went west to Seattle to mix *Automatic*, his friend Scott McCaughey from The Young Fresh Fellows took him to the Crocodile Cafe, the city's equivalent of the 40 Watt Club, and introduced him to its owner, ex-lawyer and ongoing music fanatic Stephanie Dorgan. Seattle was thriving as the Athens of the Nineties, and now he considered living there too.

In the meantime, he kept travelling. "I spend a lot of time in cars," he said in August 1992. "I take train rides. It's this kind of bohemian thing except I've got a gold card." During the latter half of 1992, Peter Buck fulfilled his familiar promotional duties as R.E.M.'s most eager interviewee and reluctant video performer. He joined in the recording of the Christmas single, a cover of the Spizz Energi post-punk classic 'Where's Captain Kirk?'. He took part in a one-off show at the 40 Watt Club on November 19 to record a song, via solar-powered console, for a Greenpeace album. And then he took himself, his gold card and his "bohemian thing" and headed south across the border, to Mexico, for the best part of six months, in an attempt to clear his head.

"It was more the external personal things that were making me unhappy," he explained many years later, by which point he was fully settled in Seattle, married to Stephanie Dorgan and the father of twin daughters. "When *Automatic* was this huge album, I was driving around in a car, sleeping in $19 hotel rooms, listening to cassettes, and so it was really good for me, because I didn't experience that huge fame thing. I think we sold 23–25 million records in the space of three years, but by the same token what I actually owned I was wearing on my back, and I had an acoustic guitar in the back of my car."

He was hardly the first rock musician to have reached a pinnacle of success – critical and commercial – and find that it didn't make for contentment. In fact, he was barely the first in R.E.M. "I know Bill was really depressed about certain things," he admits of the drummer who avoided both interviews *and* public appearances as *Automatic* went global. "It was a fairly bleak time for some of us. A lot of it comes out in the music, and some of it comes out in the lyrics, but then again, none of us were junkies, none of us died."

The last half-sentence is telling; R.E.M.'s personal problems were, in truth, no worse than the average record-buyer's – and they had far better personal resources to deal with them. And so, while some might look at Peter Buck's lengthy sojourn across the border as a mark of desperation, it was nothing of the sort. As far as he was concerned, the interviews had been done, the videos were stockpiled, and there were no shows to play. Michael and Mike could attend inaugurations, pick up European awards and visit the White House. When it became apparent that, with the success of 'Everybody Hurts,' the UK could afford a fifth single from *Automatic*, the task of a video clip was given to Jem Cohen, on the understanding the band members would not be involved. For 'Nightswimming', Cohen and friends visited various watering holes around Georgia and Florida, to tastefully recreate the nostalgic, nocturnal mood of the song.

The group finally caught up with Peter in April. In Acapulco. R.E.M. had incredible humility for such a global phenomenon, but they were not beyond the occasional lavish business expense. Besides, the impact of the ongoing success, the constant invitations to awards shows, the hobnobbing backstage, the deviations into movie-making and even Buck's temporary absence were all serving as constant distractions. A business conference utilising Warner Brothers property by the Pacific Ocean would provide a relaxed scenario to answer the 10 million album sales question: What the hell do we do next?

★   ★   ★

Just by asking that question, R.E.M. were tampering with the answer. This was a group, after all, that had generally recorded its albums by osmosis – writing songs on the road, writing more in the rehearsal room after an end-of-tour break, assembling them all in the studio, and then touring those songs and starting the process all over again. Even though there was no official tour for *Out Of Time,* the promotional acoustic shows clearly bore their influence in the mood of *Automatic For The People*, which was written and recorded as swiftly on its predecessor's heals as any R.E.M. album thus far.

That change of pace had also resulted in a crossover to the mainstream such as had genuinely gone unimagined, with the result that each of these last two albums had sold to several million people who now absolutely revered R.E.M. – possibly as their favourite act – and yet had never had the opportunity to see the group live. There was no evidence that the band had lost the couple of million fans it had acquired previously either. If R.E.M. were therefore going to go back on the road – and they had already assured their audience they had every intention of doing so – then to satisfy audience demand it would have to be on a scale that would make the 1989 arena tour look like a club jaunt. And if *that* was going to be the case, they'd need a seriously loud album to accompany it. "We did want to make a rock record," admits Peter Buck. "We wanted to be a big rock band, we knew we were going on tour."

For most groups in R.E.M.'s position, the result would have been an album of ready-made stadium rock anthems. But of course R.E.M. weren't most groups. Forced for the first time to confront audience anticipation head-on, to live up to their own expectations – and having been away from each other for such a long time, to accept that they were starting a new chapter in their lives – they nonetheless determined to toy with the possibilities as far as humanly possible.

In looking at the path R.E.M. subsequently took, it's worth considering the subtle influence of their fellow post-punk surviving superstars, U2. The Irish quartet had built steadily through the Eighties on the back of a similarly evident passion, honesty and bond with their audience; aided by their own insatiable appetite for success and voracious love of performing, they reached the very pinnacle of popularity in 1987 with *The Joshua Tree*. But a subsequent 'road movie' complete with double soundtrack album, *Rattle And Hum,* had demonstrated how tedious dealing with success on traditional terms could be to the public, and U2 went back to the drawing board. After a three year hiatus they returned, reborn with 1981's *Achtung Baby* (released in between R.E.M.'s two blockbuster albums), full of off-kilter beats, warped guitar riffs, filtered vocals, glam imagery – singer Bono sending himself up as the permanently beshaded The Fly – and a multi-media live show full of television sets, suspended cars and cellular phone calls. It was still rock'n'roll, just not as we knew it of them. And the global audience lapped it up

So it was probably no coincidence that R.E.M.'s 'comeback'/'rock' album would turn out to be a similar mix of artifice and artistry: equal parts glam and grunge, punk and trash, it was intensely post-modern, musically askew, lyrically sexual, self-consciously ironic and titled, with a wink-wink reference to their place in the rock'n'roll pantheon and the year of touring coming up ahead of them, *Monster.* And just like U2's *Achtung Baby*, *Monster* would serve as notice of successful reinvention while selling by the truckload and positioning its makers at the very centre of rock'n'roll superstardom.

But first they had to make it.

And before settling down to that task, each member had personal and professional tasks to complete. Peter Buck wrapped up his sabbatical by taking a six-week safari in Africa with new partner Stephanie. Mike Mills joined forces with fellow alt-rock superstars as The Backbeat Band, recording in three days the soundtrack to the movie *Backbeat*, a surprisingly effective biopic about the original fifth Beatle, Stu Sutcliffe, as played by Stephen Dorff. Michael Stipe helped out former Throwing Muses' singer Kristin Hersh in the studio, joined 10,000 Maniacs on tour, and in his new role as movie producer and familiar guise as R.E.M.'s video supervisor started attending film festivals. And Bill Berry upped and moved out of Athens – into the surrounding countryside, where he bought himself a farm, a tractor and cultivated a secondary job tilling the local land.

Collective concerts having been restricted to two charity performances at the 40 Watt in 1992 and prior to that, the select acoustic performances in support of *Out Of Time,* the news that R.E.M. would perform at MTV's Music Video Awards in early September '93 was greeted with considerable enthusiasm, confirmation that the group was indeed emerging from its self-imposed isolation. There's only so much you can glean from a short performance on a national awards show, but there were plenty of indicators that night as to R.E.M.'s refreshed state of being. First up, a freshly shorn-and-shaved Peter Buck, looking ten years younger than he had just a year ago, appeared on stage playing mandolin on that summer's crossover hit 'Runaway Train' by Soul Asylum – a Minneapolis band whose career dated almost as far back as R.E.M.'s and whose sudden elevation to the big time demonstrated the impact of grunge and all things alternative.

R.E.M. themselves performed 'Everybody Hurts', another of the summer's big hits. Michael Stipe announced his return to the stage as a glam beatnik, with heavily painted eyebrows and a sharp goatee; Mike Mills wore a loud and somewhat tacky Vegas-style jacket while seated at keyboards; Buck looked content to be back on the black Rickenbacker; a hired bassist and French horn player fleshed out the sound; and Berry gazed down on them all from his riser, the elevation of which seemed an indicator of the band's current stature. As 'Everybody Hurt' drew to its conclusion, R.E.M. ripped into a funked-up version of 'Drive' and Stipe started jerking back and forth, this way and that, clearly at ease with both the crowd and the cameras. The group went home without any statues ('Everybody Hurts' had only recently been released as a single, though the 'Man On The Moon' clip was more than worthy of awards), but with a renewed high profile.

R.E.M.'s celebrity status was further acknowledged during that visit to LA for the Video Awards, when Stipe and Berry jammed on stage with members of Pearl Jam (whose début album *Ten* was racing Nirvana's *Nevermind* towards the eventual ten figure American sales mark, twice more than R.E.M. would ever sell) at Johnny Depp's hipper-than-hip Hollywood club The Viper Room. Similarly, while Nirvana's bruisingly antagonistic new album *In Utero*, released that same month, appeared to be the musical antithesis of *Out Of Time* or *Automatic*, Kurt Cobain began talking up R.E.M. publicly as "saints" for their response to success. In private he sought them out for advice on how to handle his own new-found fame and fortune. Peter Buck had dinner with Kurt in Los Angeles, where the front man's well-rumoured drug problems were all-too-apparent, but as the pair were about to become close neighbours in Seattle, there would be plenty of opportunity to build on the relationship. Michael Stipe, who had suffered more public attention than he himself had wanted this past year, also extended the hand of friendship and hosted Kurt, his high-profile, high-maintenance wife Courtney Love of the band Hole, and their baby daughter Frances Bean to his Athens home. Cobain expressed public interest in following R.E.M. into the acoustic arena; he and Stipe talked privately, and seriously, about writing and recording together.

But R.E.M.'s own writing and recordings took priority. Sessions in Athens during the summer found the band members more than ready to return to their original instruments, which resulted in a number of loud and yet purposefully discordant instrumentals. In October, the group then followed *Automatic*'s fortune by moving, once again with Scott Litt, on to Kingsway Studios in New Orleans. Stipe got busy lyrically, and by the end of the month, half the songs that would make it onto *Monster* had been written and demoed. Things were looking good.

And then, late on the night of October 30, River Phoenix died from a drug overdose outside the Viper Room, and for Michael Stipe, the world stopped. He later described River as "my brother . . . I loved him a great deal" and cited the death as "the most shattering experience of my life." Distraught at the loss, Stipe found he couldn't write, couldn't sing, could barely focus. For the first time in the group's career, R.E.M. had to (temporarily) abandon an album. It would be almost four months before they'd be ready to record again.

The friendship between Stipe and Phoenix had never been widely publicised; in the world of music and movies, it's sometimes assumed that everyone knows each other but no one's really close. Phoenix, almost a decade Stipe's junior, was a child actor, and had encountered fame far younger than had R.E.M.'s singer – though at almost exactly the same period in time. They'd been brought together partly through a mutual love of each other's art form: Phoenix fronted a respected band (for an actor) called Aleka's Attic with his sister Rain, and his most acclaimed movie had been named for a B-52's song, 'My Own Private Idaho'; Stipe, of course, was getting into movie-producing. But they were more closely allied as celebrities with alternative lifestyles: committed vegetarians, each had just contributed a track to the album *Tame Yourself* on behalf of the charity In Defence of Animals.*

Phoenix's renowned penchant for clean living made his death from an overdose at just 23 all the more disconcerting. Had he been a hypocrite all along, taking hard drugs while he decried the use of even dairy products? Was it peer pressure, a desperate attempt at acceptance with a harder partying crowd that backfired in a body unused to the poisons? Or was he the unwitting victim of a practical joke, the unknowing recipient of a spiked drink? As can be the case in these most public of situations, the doors of privacy were drawn shut by those with plenty to lose by exposing the truth, and the media has never successfully pried them open. "It

---

* Stipe's was the haunting 'I'll Give You My Skin' with The Indigo Girls; River's was an Aleka's Attic song.

was just an awful, awful mistake," was all that Stipe would say about the circumstances.

Michael Stipe would end up dedicating *Monster* "for River". In the meantime, R.E.M. went back to Athens. By eerie coincidence, the British record label had decided to try to eke a sixth, Christmas hit out of the year old, near two million selling *Automatic For The People* and released the song 'Find The River' that November. A video was assembled using group footage from a year earlier. The single didn't sell.

★   ★   ★

One particular reason Stipe needed a break after River Phoenix died is that he still had songs to write, and he didn't want them to be about mortality and loss, fear and separation; he'd done that on *Automatic For The People* to the extent that people thought he himself was dying. For the rock'n'roll album with the mega tour, he had been determined to enact a change. He wanted the new songs to be more sexual, more trashy, more androgynous and even aggressive. He already had a reference point – 'Star Me Kitten' from *Automatic* – and given that the band were presenting him with far more assertive music, he could afford to take the subject matter several steps further. Having been effectively outed by the media in his absence but having stayed silent on the subject himself, he now decided to fuck with his public image by singing crudely, in various narrator's guises, about fucking.

For role-models, he turned to the music and lyrics of his Seventies youth: the glam-punk influence of Bowie, Iggy, Lou Reed and The New York Dolls was all over *Monster*. On one of his earliest lyrics, 'I Took Your Name', he even admitted as much, with the lines, "I'll be your albatross, devil, dog, Jesus, God, I don't wanna be Iggy Pop but if that's what it takes, hey." Another song written before the break, 'Crush With Eyeliner', included lines like "What position should I wear" and "We all invent ourselves and, uh, you know me."

These early songs all had an unusual creepiness. On 'Tongue', an ode to oral sex, Stipe delivered the harsh truth that "Ugly girls know their fate/anybody can get laid." The title 'Star 69' seemed like a dual sexual reference: to the word that should have been 'fuck' in the title of 'Star Me Kitten' and to the position well known by all enthusiasts of oral sex. It was, in fact, named after the call-back option on home phones in the States, but still the song was all about stalking and recriminations. Stipe sung-shouted how "three people have my number, the other two were with me/this time you have gone too far with me/I know you called," sounding unusually vicious in the process.

And so it continued. When finally Stipe came back to the fold, he was armed with more of the same explicit sexual-obsessive imagery. A middle line from 'I Don't Sleep, I Dream' asked, "Do you give good head?/Am I good in bed?" and replied, "I don't know, I guess so/I don't sleep, I dream." 'Circus Envy' closed with the lines, "You're mean, mean, mean you tease, tease, tease me/Do you smell jealousy?" while the title 'Bang And Blame' left little to the imagination. Some of the same themes even cropped up in different songs – meanness in 'Strange Currencies', blame in 'I Took Your Name'. "There's this weird sexual thing going on," Peter Buck would comment later of *Monster*. "Songs about stalkers and people following you. It's a record that is not us."

Only a couple of tracks veered away from these sexual connotations, and even they had a glibness quite unlike prior R.E.M. albums. 'What's The Frequency, Kenneth?' – a street phrase that had been practised on TV anchor Dan Rather during a mugging – allowed for all kinds of stream-of-consciousness about media overkill. And the hard-rocking 'Revolution' was a conscious throwback to The Beatles' song of the same name, right down to the sentiment "Your revolution is a stupid idea". But so dominant was the lyrical theme of sexual identity and post-modern consumerism that this last song was eventually dropped from the running order.

If Stipe was wreaking lyrical havoc, (gender) bending from audience expectations, the three musicians were thrilled to have the same opportunity. Perhaps the most noticeable item on *Monster*'s musical agenda was that Peter Buck, returning to electric guitar after years wedded to the mandolin, abandoned the arpeggios of old for bruising guitar chords and feedback-ridden effects.

"When we started rehearsing it was just the three of us and we wanted a big sound so I just kept turning up," recalls Peter Buck. "That's as simple as it starts. But the songs were written around that too, when we were doing demos in New Orleans – 'Crush With Eyeliner' and 'Kenneth' were things we just played live. They sounded just like that."

Coming back together in February '94, the band opted to record live on a soundstage in Atlanta, in an attempt to rediscover the dynamic that had made them such a phenomenal live act through-out the Eighties. And to help the band sound its best, Scott Litt recruited as engineer Pat McCarthy, a mid-twenties Dublin native who'd come to prominence by producing the first Counting Crows album, of which Litt had mixed several cuts and been impressed with what he heard. McCarthy would come to play a crucial part in the group's career, but for now he felt very much the new boy, somewhat overawed by R.E.M.'s status, and, as he put it, "concerned with staying on my toes, trying to get the job done, making it work."

He did notice that as the band performed in a live situation, they were keen to experiment – and that the enthusiasm to play with sound was coming from all quarters, Stipe included. "He would maybe not know technically how to suggest it," recalls McCarthy of the singer, "but he might suggest a definite direction, in his very descriptive way, and you would emerge with whatever permuta-tion. Or Peter and Scott would interpret it and I would try and facilitate it."

"There aren't that many overdubs on the album," notes Buck of how these sounds evolved. "But I was doing things like using two or three amps in tandem, or taking big water bottles and drilling holes in them and putting microphones in them and then milking amps along with four or five other amps. So I might have five or six sources for one sound. So it's got this reverby huge sound kind of done live."

Ultimately, Buck's new guitar techniques would be the album's hallmark: more than any other R.E.M. record, this one would have his name stamped all over it. And recording live clearly had an attraction for a band that thrived on the synergy of a collective per-formance. But although by March, many of the songs, and their lyrics, had been written, there was about to commence a whole series of interruptions that would mar *Monster*'s recording and con-tribute to its ultimately jarring mood.

The first occurred almost immediately the band convened in Atlanta. While recording 'What's The Frequency, Kenneth?' the others noticed Mike Mills slowing down slightly, grimacing in pain; by the end of the day he was in a hospital bed, divested of his appendix. Recording was duly halted while he recuperated.* Next, Bill Berry came down with a particularly nasty dose of the 'flu; work was halted again. The backing tracks were finally completed despite the rhythm section's medical crises, and the band reconvened in Miami at Criteria Studios. Michael Stipe had thrived there on *Automatic For The People* and was looking forward to starting on his vocals. Instead, he promptly came down with a tooth abscess and couldn't sing for days.

There were planned interruptions in the recording process too, the kind that occur as former road-dogs mature into adults and their families take equal priority to their careers. Michael Stipe's sister Lynda had a baby and the singer took time out to be with her. Peter Buck became a father – of twins named Zoe and Zelda – and he returned to Seattle at the end of April to be with Stephanie for their birth.

And there was one entirely unwelcome, unplanned interruption too, far more serious than the members' own individual illnesses. On April 8, but a few doors down from Buck's new abode by Lake Washington, the body of Kurt Cobain was found, his head blown apart by a shotgun blast. Unable and unwilling to cope with the pressures of his fame and fortune, unappeased by his own parenthood, hopelessly addicted to heroin, the Nirvana front man had apparently committed suicide.

The warning signs had been visible for months. Cobain's heroin problem was public knowledge even before the birth of his daughter; in a high-profile feature in *Vanity Fair*, Courtney Love admitted using the drug herself while pregnant. His suicidal tendencies were better hidden. Love had visited Cobain in Rome after Nirvana's European tour in March had been cut short, Cobain deliberately overdosed on prescription pills, leaving a suicide note in his hand; but the public was told it was an accident. Worried

---

* The recording of 'Kenneth', its slow-down almost imperceptible, was kept.

242

about this deadly combination, then, upon Cobain's return to America, R.E.M. sent him airline tickets to join them in Atlanta; "I wanted to get him out of Seattle," Stipe later told Anthony DeCurtis. "That was my attempt to get him enough out of the head that he was in that he wouldn't kill himself or hurt himself." Cobain never used the tickets.

Instead, there were interventions by Cobain's playing and business partners, which finally led to Kurt entering rehab in Los Angeles on March 30, only to escape two days later and go into hiding. Courtney Love, who was herself undergoing private rehab treatment while conducting interviews for Hole's new album at a Los Angeles hotel, stayed in that city while hiring a private detective, Tom Grant, to track down Kurt, but the detectives' time was wasted, mostly spent casing out the motels and drug dealers that Cobain was known to frequent; there were people staying at both the Cobains' private residences, the house at Lake Washington and a log cabin in the nearby town of Carnation, and it was assumed their occupants would notify Courtney should he show up. They didn't, and during that frantic first week of April, Courtney even phoned the eight-month pregnant Stephanie Dorgan, who barely knew the Hole singer, asking her to check in on the house down the block. But it was too late. An electrician made the grisly discovery of Cobain's body in a 'greenhouse' apartment attached to the garage; as the news broke of Kurt's suicide, thousands of Nirvana fans flocked to Seattle in a public display of mourning not seen since the death of John Lennon.

Michael Stipe mourned particularly hard. The two singers may have had little in common by way of upbringing, but they had each shared the enormous pressure of being labelled spokesman-for-a-generation – "something that I really, really did not want," as Stipe told *Rolling Stone* shortly thereafter. Stipe had proven too secure in himself, his band mates and his choice of friends to be easily thrown off artistic stride, and he'd felt that he could use his experience to help accompany Cobain through the worst if only the singer would let him in. But Kurt ultimately shunned all help.

The Nirvana singer remained an R.E.M. fan to the bitter end, however. *Automatic For The People* was the last album Cobain ever listened to: it was found in his CD player, which was switched on

243

with the volume up, in the room where he died. It was surely not lost on Michael Stipe that 'Everybody Hurts' had been hailed by so many as a song of hope; strangers would come up to the singer on the street and tell him how it had saved their life. Yet the message behind 'Everybody Hurts' failed to get through to one of R.E.M.'s most vocal and public fans at the very moment it mattered most. In the words of the song, Kurt Cobain "threw his hand".

Stipe chose to exorcise his own emotions by writing a follow-up to 'Everybody Hurts', entitled 'Let Me In'. "I was really working against anything to do with those topics," he explained later, but Cobain's death "profoundly affected me. I couldn't really ignore it much longer." While the title was a blatant reference to Kurt's inability to share his pain, the lyrics were far more oblique except for references to Cobain as a Pisces and, perhaps, the lines, "I had a mind to try to stop you/let me in, let me in/but I've got tar on my feet and I can't see."

Peter Buck draped a heavy wash of guitar reverb over Stipe's plaintive vocals for 'Let Me In'; an organ drone and some gentle tambourine were the only other accompaniments. The R.E.M. guitarist attended Cobain's funeral, but he was fatalistic about Kurt's death. "As a friend, you wish there was something that could have been done," he told David Cavanagh of Q. "But every-one tried. It wasn't like this poor kid was abandoned. Everything that could have been done was done. That was a thing that he planned, and it sucks and I wish that something could have been done, but he didn't want it to be done." Three years earlier, Peter Buck had commented that "we'd be dead" if R.E.M. had broken big as quickly as Nirvana; it proved anything but a rhetorical state-ment. With Cobain's death, Nirvana immediately broke up. R.E.M. were once again America's leading alternative rock band. Except that the word 'alternative' suddenly felt very empty and hollow; devoid of meaning, corrupted by over-use, it was aban-doned by the groups themselves.

On June 4, Michael Stipe accompanied Courtney Love down the red carpet at the MTV Movie Awards in Los Angeles. The move – a gesture on Michael's part of continued friendship – led to immediate media speculation about a possible relationship between the two, though among fans of R.E.M. it seemed a further example of Stipe's elevation to the superstar set, one hardly offset by his presentation that night of the top award to Tom Hanks. Mike Mills had his own superstar set to worry about: the Backbeat Band performed live on the same show.

Recording of *Monster* proceeded amidst all these interruptions, but at a perilously slow pace. The group had already decamped to Los Angeles for what was originally intended to be just the mixing process. But there was still too much else to do; without the orchestral arrangements that graced the last two albums, and because the songs had been recorded on stage in Atlanta, the tracks sounded brutally raw. In addition, many had been recorded back in Atlanta onto 8-track, with instruments bleeding across one track and onto another, leaving Scott Litt with a particularly difficult job in trying to accentuate one instrument without simultaneously affecting another. As the producer concentrated on this unenviable task, the group continued with overdubs at Litt's own studio Louie's Clubhouse. Given that the vocals were so different from past R.E.M. songs, not lending themselves to the familiar Mills and Berry harmonies, friends were brought in to add vocal texture: Thurston Moore of Sonic Youth sang on 'Crush With Eyeliner'; River Phoenix's sister Rain, and Michael's own sister Lynda, on 'Bang And Blame'. Yet even these collaborations created problems: the group's individual friendships with fellow musicians in Los Angeles, with actors, artists, film-makers, and industry movers and shakers, along with their own relationship issues – Buck was sleeping even less than usual whenever the twins were around – all seemed to diffuse R.E.M.'s usual razor-like focus. *Monster* was living up to its name in all the wrong ways.

"It was the first time we had trouble finishing a record," says Buck, looking back on the experience without much fondness. "That had never happened before. We had all these songs and no one knew which ones to concentrate on. I had my opinions. Mike had his opinions, Michael wasn't really sure. Literally the last two weeks of the record we were still going, well what's on this record? We had 17 songs in the running. It was getting to the point where we were going, *We've got to finish this record*."

The impatience was as much due to corporate deadlines as individual frustration. Being a mega rock band with its mega rock tour already booked for 1995, R.E.M.'s album release had been written into fourth-quarter marketing plans and budget expectations; there was simply no way of continuing work on the album without delaying its release all the way into the new year – and throwing the global tour into jeopardy with it.

Tempers understandably flared under the pressure. "We reached the point where none of us could speak to each other," Stipe admitted to Chris Heath of *Rolling Stone* two years later. "We just said, 'Fuck off!' and that was it. We were crazy, making that record."

Finally, a meeting was called to calm matters, to remind everyone of their responsibilities to each other, that this was above all a rock *band,* one that had never previously suffered the fist fights and name-calling so familiar to other groups. The four members agreed to knuckle down to the same daily schedule, ignore the call of LA friendships and midnight feedings, and get the album finished. Q magazine was flown in for one of the first of the all-important buzz-building cover stories at the start of July, and found the band in chipper spirits – with a perfectly healthy Michael Stipe in full-on interview mode – but only six songs sufficiently mixed so as to be deemed listenable.

Several more were at the final stages. But there were still all sorts of half-finished songs sitting around, under consideration for inclusion. Mike Mills volunteered to sing on one, "and it didn't really work", says Peter Buck, so it was abandoned. Then Michael Stipe mentioned an instrumental cut back in Athens, at which time it had been called, without much forethought, 'Yes I Am Fucking With You'.

"That song literally was not a song until the day we were supposed to mix that record," recalls Peter Buck. "And Michael said, 'I've got some lyrics for that.' And he sung it, and I was like, 'I dunno, I don't really like it.'"

Buck was overruled. Stipe finally gave the song a new title, 'King Of Comedy', but seemed to be keeping the facetious original title in his head. Among a litany of coolly spoken post-modern references ("Make your money with a power ply/Make your money with a buy out bribe") he threw in the lines, "I'm straight, I'm queer, I'm bi"; he must have been fully aware that this would become the most talked-about lyric on the album, at the expense of many a better couplet.

As the recording and mixing dragged through July, a restless Michael Stipe found a way to reintroduce himself to his audience while relieving some of the tedium. He borrowed a laptop computer from the studio, went online and started hanging out in the R.E.M. chat room on AOL, under his own name no less. (Stipey@aol.com.) His first posting, on July 16, stated plainly, "the records almost done and im bored." The R.E.M. fans were initially and understandably dubious that their hero would show up in their midst, but once they realised he was for real, there followed a week of warm to-and-fro correspondence right up until the last night of mixing.*

Of the new album, Stipe typed (and very badly) "there are 12 songs and its punk rock. like aftp punkrock but loud." He enthused about how "theres a cool niew song that im discoripping on l.cohen called >make your money.<" (He was referring to Leonard Cohen and the still untitled 'King Of Comedy'.) Though Stipe's 'mailbox' filled rapidly as fans wrote directly to him, he deleted all the personal mail without reading it and answered only questions posited to the group at large. And proving that R.E.M. fans were still the same loveable nerds they always had been, most of these questions seemed to be about lyrics. Asked to set the record straight about 'Sitting Still', he responded: "lets be reasonable here. youall know that there arent words,per se, to a lot of the early stuff. i cnat even remember them.let it be on those ones."

On July 18, two days after signing on, he typed how, "Ive gotta wrtie the last song and sing it so im outa here til later. its called >you< ." The song was subsequently chosen to close the album with its original drum parts still in mono as recorded, by accident, months earlier; there was no time to do anything else with them. There was no real drum beat anyway, no obvious chord sequence either, and as with much of the album, Stipe's newly completed vocals were thrown back into the mix, nearly indecipherable.

But finally *Monster* was finished.

---

* Courtney Love began doing likewise around the same time; the two rock figureheads were influencing each other heavily. They were also demonstrating that you could do the red carpet thing on national TV and still be at one with your audience.

Eighteen

Short of a military operation, there is little in the world to rival the rock'n'roll juggernaut for effective long-term planning, day-to-day precision, expensive weaponry and sheer might of force. As with a military operation, the rock'n'roll juggernaut leaves casualties along the way, and as with a war, its goal is often difficult to define. It can be about conquest, vanquishment, defence, spoils, cultural or spiritual superiority – and sometimes, it breaks out from the simple need to prove something. In 1994, for the first time in their career, R.E.M. became that rock'n'roll juggernaut with something to prove. And it was quite a sight to behold.

R.E.M. reintroduced themselves to the global record-buying public in the last four months of 1994 with the single and video for 'What's The Frequency, Kenneth?', which would also be *Monster*'s opening cut. From its fuzzy opening guitar chords through its media-crazed lyrics, funky-assed bass, tight-fit harmonies, four-to-the-floor beat and soaring, backward-sounding guitar solo, it presented the band almost verbatim to their promise of an upbeat, loud and trashy return.

The video was even truer to type. Directed by Peter Care ('Drive', 'Man On The Moon'), it introduced the members hesitantly, as if softening up the viewing audience for the shock of seeing them in a pure performance situation. Stipe was initially shown only from the neck down, in a T-shirt with single star (suggesting both fame and socialism); Mills likewise, in spangled flared trousers and then jacket to boot (suggesting rock'n'roll stardom). When finally seen up top, Stipe was bald and animated; Mills was sporting blown-out curls. Buck and Berry, reassuringly, seemed the same as they ever were, the former plugged into a Vox AC-30, the latter on a Pearl kit. It was a back to basics – but in vivid colours.

'Kenneth' pushed all the right buttons for audience approval, but nobody was heard to declare it the greatest single in the R.E.M. catalogue. Then again, neither had 'Orange Crush' been, nor 'Drive'. The first cannonball fired from an R.E.M. album was often just a warning shot. Proof of what might follow along the *Monster* single sequencing line came the week of the single's early September release when 'Everybody Hurts' walked off with five MTV Video Awards. The clip had been shot 18 months earlier, the song recorded over two years previously; R.E.M. singles were proving to survive way beyond the ephemeral fads of the pop marketplace. In the meantime, 'Kenneth' blasted straight into the UK top 10; in the States, it rose quickly up the Hot 100.

From September through to November, the R.E.M./Warner Brothers juggernaut gave a textbook lesson in how to handle the media. The major magazine cover stories that had been conducted during the chaotic last weeks of mixing in Los Angeles hit the stands on the album's release, further interviews were conducted in New York boardrooms for the American press, and then the band flew to Dublin with friends and families, and invited the rest of the world's media to come to visit them at their rented castle.

This merits a pause. There are bands one would expect to rent a castle in Ireland for a media junket. And then there's R.E.M., whose usual means of introducing an album consisted of kicking back in their Athens, GA hometown, where locals barely blinked at the sight of their most famous sons propping up the local bars and coffee houses. But times had changed: the band knew that Athens (or, more pertinently, their own reputations within it) could not easily survive a media invasion on the level at which they were now operating. Besides, Peter Buck didn't even live there any more. Flying to Europe enabled the band to re-familiarise themselves with travelling *en masse,* bringing equipment encouraged them to start writing new songs, and inviting the media to one easily accessible location also allowed them to announce, as fully anticipated, the world tour. The live section of the *Monster* juggernaut would begin in Australia in January 1995, head up to south east Asia, see in spring in Europe, and then spend early summer traversing America. The venues announced were almost exclusively and unapologetically arenas. The UK leg, two or three nights each in the country's biggest indoor halls – Wembley, N.E.C., that sort of thing – sold out in one day. With U2 back on sabbatical and Nirvana defunct, there was no longer any competition: R.E.M.'s was the biggest rock tour of the coming year.

It was into this media blitz that *Monster* was released in the last week of September. A band that had sold over 20 million copies of its last two albums in just over three years, without even touring, and was now hitting the global concert trail and promoting the hell out of itself in preparation, was not going to have problems selling its new record. In the States, *Monster* scanned a phenomenal 344,000 copies in that first week, far and away the band's most impressive one-week sales. At the start of October, the launch of the record industry's bonanza fourth quarter, *Monster* entered the charts at number one in countries all across the world, the UK and USA included. It was the first time R.E.M. had ever pulled off the transatlantic double. (It would, as of 2002, also be the last.)

The tour was still three months away; R.E.M. were playing the tried-and-tested major rock band tactic of allowing the album to sink in and spread around before taking to the road in support. While waiting, a video for 'Bang And Blame' (another performance piece) was shot as the follow-up to 'Kenneth'; the single went top 20 in the UK the same week of November that R.E.M. performed on *Saturday Night Live* in New York – their first public 'gig' since the MTV Awards of a year earlier and the first live airing of their new songs.

As they were beamed into millions of American homes performing three new numbers, R.E.M. were also filmed by an additional camera crew for a documentary. *Rough Cut,* shot tastefully in black and white, would serve as an advance guard for the travelling juggernaut, ideally to be broadcast in international territories around the time of the group's visit. Unfortunately, there is only so much excitement you can wrestle out of a rock group's promotional duties and tour rehearsals, particularly if you take any hint of debauched behaviour or controversy – and the concerts themselves – out of the equation. In lieu of excitement, *Rough Cut* accompanied Michael Stipe on a limousine ride through Manhattan, as the singer concocted a list of bald-headed pseudonyms (followed, as if *This Is Spinal Tap* had never been made, by an interview with the limo driver himself about Stipe's humble persona); it also offered viewers the problem of costume fittings for a national TV appearance. Even the band's performances, at rehearsal in Atlanta, concentrated as much on the group's choice of Jimmy Webb covers ('Galveston', 'Wichita Lineman') as on new songs like 'I Don't Sleep, I Dream'.

Rough Cut was unfortunate confirmation that documentaries should never be left in the hands of their subjects. If only R.E.M./Warners could have treated the concept with the same ingenuity as earlier promotional videos, hiring a director with both a vivid imagination and contempt for convention; if only the group could have better trusted their audience to sympathise with the banalities of the rock band's promotional duties; if only the band itself could have better displayed its genuine empathy for the fans on the other side of the frosted limo windows and TV camera . . . then they could have turned in an absurdist exposé of rock'n'roll boredom. Instead, for possibly the first time in their career, R.E.M. were shown to be playing the game – and it didn't suit them.

This is not to say that *Rough Cut* didn't offer moments of both insight and humour – mostly when the group was being interviewed by other journalists. It was hard not to smile when a camera panned to Peter Buck's incessantly twitching leg as the guitarist announced, quite cheerfully of his twin baby daughters, "Just like dad, they do not sleep at night! You'd think babies would have to sleep sometimes . . ."

Or when Michael Stipe summarised *Monster's* subject matter by saying, "A lot of records are cerebral, a lot of records are from the heart. This one is more from the crotch. It's kind of a dick record."

Or indeed when, with all four members huddled together on one couch, Michael Stipe reflected of the band dynamic that, "We're four very distinctive people and we admire and appreciate each other a good deal – usually. All the differences put together are R.E.M. If anyone of those persons were to leave this couch right now . . ."

At which Bill Berry interjected, ". . . It would be more comfortable."

And Michael Stipe laughed, thought nothing more of it, and finished his sentence, ". . . But it would not be R.E.M."

★   ★   ★

Amidst all the chart-topping celebrations and continued touring preparations, it was easy to overlook the critical reaction to *Monster*. After all, R.E.M. no longer needed glowing reviews to sell albums. As it happened, they weren't really getting them either. Critics in the group's two prime territories, the UK and the USA, were unusually guarded in their praise of *Monster*. Most of these reviewers were ardent fans of the group and few of them had any sour grapes to throw the band's way; there was a general sentiment in the media that R.E.M. had just come off two of the greatest albums made in recent times. Perhaps that was the problem: writing in *Q*, traditionally something of an R.E.M. bible, Stuart Maconie admitted how, "It's grossly unfair to use a group's own triumphs to browbeat them, but we have to measure *Monster* by the standards R.E.M. have recently set." And by those standards, most reviewers found reasons to be underwhelmed.

"Frustratingly, you rarely get the full picture here," wrote David Browne in *Entertainment Weekly* about the heavily drenched guitar sound that subsumed so much of Michael Stipe's vocals. "It's ironic that an album that seems to dwell so much on communication and misinterpretation often obscures its own communiqués with sonic gunk." This was a common complaint, as Stuart Maconie picked up on when he wrote how the last three numbers "pass by almost unnoticed apart from the grinding tremolo guitar sound that swamps the whole album," and that, "Strong songs have been sacrificed for an alienated mood that can quickly pall." Over at the *NME*, Keith Cameron made the comment that "The problem with *Monster* – for problems there are – is that it is, in substantial part, an incredibly coy, stylised rock album." He also shared Peter Buck's negative view of 'King Of Comedy', calling it "dumber than Devo dumb, a club-footed robot stomp that bizarrely sounds like a parody of U2's 'Numb', itself a parody."

There were glowing tributes, too, from equally familiar quarters, and offering equally justifiable praise. Andrew Mueller in *Melody Maker* described "a pumped-up, revved-up, messed-up, f★★★ed up classic." And R.E.M. were given the all-important all-clear from *Rolling Stone* with a four and a half star review by Robert Palmer, who noted rightly how, "R.E.M. make an album with such potentially grave subject matter so much fun," and that, "*Monster* could be guitarist Peter Buck's finest hour; he's all over this album, proving he can be just as effective without all those overdubs and acoustic fills, playing more from the gut."

Most reviewers observed that *Monster*, like many of its predecessors, needed repeated play to reveal itself. Yet that same majority listened over and over again, and bemoaned its lack of classics; when Roy Wilkinson asserted in *Select* that, "There isn't one song here that truly stops you in your tracks", he spoke for many, both the 'critics' and the 'fans'. *Monster* contained perfectly good singles – better than 90 per cent of what passed for rock music in the era of grunge – but it was devoid of its 'Fall On Me', 'The One I Love', 'End Of The World', 'Losing My Religion', 'Man On The Moon' or 'Everybody Hurts'. The closest *Monster* got was with 'Strange Currencies', and that seemed too stylistically similar to 'Everybody Hurts' (6/8 time signature, soulful vocal, arpeggio accompaniment) to truly distinguish it. Possibly the only other R.E.M. album to have lacked a song of both instant *and* permanent appeal had been *Green*, and interestingly enough, that was the last album made in the knowledge that R.E.M. would be going out on a full-blooded, major venue tour.

Speaking years later with the benefit of hindsight, Peter Buck observes of *Monster* how, "We did want to make a rock record, and the fact that we knew we'd be playing the biggest places on Earth probably did affect the way the record sounds a little bit. As it did with *Green*. And both of those records to me are a little too polished. I think we knew we were looking at playing big places and both those times I think the records, because of just small things, like the polishing level of the record, the reverb, the drum sound, were kind of big records."

In his defence, he notes how, "Everyone thinks, 'I'd like to wake up in the morning and be a different person, have a different job, live in a different place.' Being in a band, musically you can do that. Essentially we were just going, 'You know what, we're tired of being who we are, we're going to be someone different.' We weren't trying to make a hugely successful record, we were trying to make a noisy record that was our weird idea of rock'n'roll: collapsing guitars, and fuzztone and tremolo and not a big stadium record but a rock record. But that's not really where our strength lies. I don't know what we would have done if we hadn't done that record. I look at it as one of those transitional records that you skip through to get to the next one. It's not my favourite and it never will be. But when we do the box set one day there will be four or five songs that will sit cheek by jowl next to the other stuff and people will say, 'Gosh, that really makes sense in context.'"

That's a fair assessment. *Monster* is neither as great an album as R.E.M. intended it to be, nor as disappointing an album as some reviewers and fans came to believe. Certainly all the positive comments about Buck's guitar playing and Stipe's lyrical leap are every bit as valid as the negative ones regarding the constant swamp of reverb and the paucity of audible vocals. *Monster* starts strong, with 'Kenneth' and 'Crush', and somewhere in the middle it gains a real sense of self: the journey from punk-thrash 'Star 69' through the neo-soul 'Strange Currencies' and 'Tongue' back up to the buoyantly aggressive 'Bang And Blame' is as good an example of mid–CD dynamics as you're likely to find. But there's no doubt that *Monster* fails to hold the listener to the bitter end; R.E.M. albums had been edging up slowly in length as the CD format became ever more dominant, and at almost fifty minutes, *Monster* compromised by conforming to the unproven industry notion that more music meant better value. 'Let Me In', the mournful ode to Kurt Cobain, would have been an apt conclusion; following it with 'Circus Envy' and 'You' only prolonged the process.

With all the touring still to come, the videos still to be shown, the mainstream press still to run, none of this mattered for the time being. *Monster* was a self-perpetuating beast that would end up selling nearly 10 million copies worldwide. In the USA, it would, like its predecessors, be certified four times platinum. Curiously, its SoundScan figures remain under three million, far behind both *Out Of Time* and *Automatic,* which suggests that many copies went unsold in record stores. Tellingly, given that it was R.E.M.'s only true out-of-the-box global smash, *Monster* has become the one R.E.M. album you expect to see in the bargain bins – and that in itself has prompted a rediscovery among music fans picking it up for chump change and becoming immediately enthralled. By the turn of the decade, *Monster* was being reappraised – positively. "I can't tell you how many people tell me *Monster* is their favourite record," says Peter Buck, himself somewhat surprised.

★   ★   ★

"*Monster*, I just love that record," says Scott McCaughey. "There's more nuances on there than you think. People say, 'Oh, it's just a big loud guitar rock record,' well it is that but there's just amazing sounds on there. People think, 'Oh Michael's just tossing off a glam rock song here,' but some of the lyrics are really funny. And he doesn't get credit for being funny. He's got a great sense of humour. And you can find just delirious puns in some of the songs. That record I literally listened to fifty times non-stop with headphones."

Scott McCaughey had every reason to listen to *Monster* fifty times non-stop with headphones. Before the album's release, Peter Buck suggested to Scott that he might be the right person to flesh out R.E.M.'s live line-up. Buck and McCaughey had a long-standing friendship which had only grown closer since Peter had moved to Seattle to live with Stephanie – with whom Scott had made the introductions. Now McCaughey's band The Young Fresh Fellows had ground to a halt, yet another of the Eighties 'alternative' groups to call it a day in the face of ever diminishing returns, not to mention being relegated to local obsolescence by the onslaught of grunge. "I was hurting for money and I had a young daughter and I didn't want to get a normal job," recalls McCaughey, who took on the job of booker at Stephanie's club the Crocodile Cafe in the interim.

Buck might have felt tempted to take on his friend out of sympathy, but by this point the two had started playing together, firstly at the Crocodile with visiting musicians, and then, just after *Monster* was finished, on McCaughey's new musical project, The Minus 5. "We knew by then that we were musically compatible," says Scott, "and we knew we liked a lot of the same bands, and that we were freaks – about rock'n'roll." Indeed, Scott demonstrated the same passion for music and the same unrelenting work ethic as the R.E.M. guitarist, and he had similar all-round musical skills, being an accomplished but – importantly – not prodigious player on guitar, bass and keyboards.

The decision to adjoin McCaughey to the band was not Buck's to make alone, however, and Scott was flown down to band rehearsals for an audition. Having learned a requested set of songs, he arrived at rehearsals and was immediately asked to play along to 'What's The Frequency, Kenneth?' instead. "I think that was one of the things they wanted to test me on, to see how fast I could pick up songs." By the end of the day, as he swapped instruments to allow the R.E.M. members to fulfil their own favoured roles, McCaughey was in. He could forget about spending the rest of his days booking bands at a local club, looking on enviously from the wrong side of the stage, and, at least for the next year, he wouldn't have to worry about feeding his daughter either. The Young Fresh Fellows' biggest headlining show of a ten-year career had been to perhaps 2,000 people: McCaughey made his public début with R.E.M. in November, on *Saturday Night Live*, in front of an audience of millions.

As rehearsals for the *Monster* tour started in earnest, the group looked at their increasingly complex arrangements, considered the size of venues they would be playing and the need to fill the halls musically, and decided yet another guitarist was needed. Buck and McCaughey immediately thought of Ken Stringfellow, another Seattle band-leader who was part of The Minus 5's rotating line-up, but Stringfellow's group The Posies were themselves promoting a new record. It wasn't on the scale of *Monster*, but Buck wasn't about to split another group up for the sake of his own. R.E.M. hired Nathan December, an LA club veteran, instead.

The two extra musicians were put under contract, as is typically the case, establishing their salaries and duties. A couple of additional terms confirmed that R.E.M. remained, on paper at least, the same tightly knit four-piece it always had been. McCaughey and December were not to give interviews as members of R.E.M. Nor were they to make any claims to songwriting. To avoid even the possibility of such a scenario, they were to head off stage during soundchecks whenever the band started experimenting with new material.

And R.E.M. had every intention of doing just that. "We're going to tour and ideally record a live record of all new songs," said Peter Buck on the *Rough Cut* documentary. "I would love it if next

September we're touring America and we have ten songs in the set that no one's heard."

R.E.M. had always tried out new material on the road, but by publicising their intent to début a whole album's worth, the group were setting themselves an ambitious agenda. Part of it came from their belief that a group with R.E.M.'s devotion to integrity should, by rights, be at the peak of its playing powers on tour, capable of turning in renditions every bit as strong as future studio recordings. R.E.M. were also looking back at great rock acts of the Sixties and Seventies who, before the days of lengthy studio sessions, had frequently recorded in between touring dates, and often to devastating results.* The group were looking sideways too, at their peers. U2 had so revitalised themselves with *Achtung Baby* that a recording session in between tour legs, intended for an EP, turned out instead a whole new mega-platinum album *Zooropa,* in 1993. And R.E.M. were particularly impressed by how Pearl Jam had booked days in the studio after weekends on the road to lay down tracks for their 1994 epic *Vitalogy* at a time when R.E.M. were struggling to complete *Monster* for months on end. As much as anything, the plan to write and record as they went was a method by which to maintain interest and stay sane during a year-long tour.

★   ★   ★

The R.E.M. juggernaut set itself down in Perth, in early January, 1995. For its first real shows in over five years, the group had opted for as remote a location as possible, but that didn't stop the world's rock press descending on the northern Australian city too. "We haven't been out in the public eye to experience what that new stage of celebrity is going to be like," Bill Berry had said. "How wacko it's going to be on tour." The answer was simple: very wacko.

A diversion to the pre-tour nerves, if not from the media glare, was provided by Peter Buck's wedding on January 11, two days

---

* *Led Zeppelin II* was a prominent example, as cited by Mitch Easter at the time of making *Reckoning,* but Neil Young's *Time Fades Away* was very much on Peter Buck's mind.

prior to the first show. Buck's divorce from Barrie Greene had come through just before Christmas, and given that he was taking the twins on the road with him – no more dawn patrols in the hotel bars for the group's famed night owl – he could perform nuptials with his new family present, as well as his best friends and touring partners. Support act Grant Lee Buffalo fulfilled the role of wedding band – and, naturally, Buck joined them for a few songs. The entire group then played a handful of numbers and the next day was put aside for hangover relief.

The nine-date Australian leg of the *Monster* tour kicked off at the Perth Entertainment Centre on Friday, January 13, the group laughing off any premonitions of bad luck. "My grandfather was born on Friday the 13th," Michael Stipe told a local reporter the day before the show. "And if he hadn't been born . . ." Well, precisely. R.E.M. were less concerned with superstition than with living up to high expectations – especially their own.

The set list in Australia drew predominantly from the last three albums; on the opening night there was nothing that pre-dated *Green,* all twelve songs from *Monster* were performed, and the unreleased 'Revolution' was thrown into the set too. The flexibility of the line-up, which also included violinist Amanda Brown, allowed many of the quieter songs from *Out Of Time* and *Automatic For The People* to realise their potential. One of the few staples of the year's tour was the first encore, which began with 'Let Me In', Buck switching to organ and Mike Mills playing one of Kurt Cobain's guitars, donated by Courtney Love; it was routinely followed, as if out of poetic necessity, by 'Everybody Hurts'. The latter provided one of the few audience singalongs as, of course, did 'Losing My Religion'. A similar reaction to 'Man On The Moon' indicated that this song too had struck the "universal chord".

Most attention, of course, was devoted to Michael Stipe, who was now charged with the unenviable position of entertaining tens of thousands of people a night. To compensate for his long-standing insecurity and self-consciousness, he took to increasingly extroverted clothing. Coupled with his bald pate and frequent use of eye make-up, and slow-mo, almost mime-like movements, he came across as a combination of Peter Gabriel and (Australian band) Midnight Oil's Peter Garrett, albeit wrapped in his own distinct presentation. Mike Mills had clearly reinvented himself in the Vegas/Nashville/Gram Parsons tradition of loudly stated 'Nudie' suits. Buck and Berry rocked hard and pure as always, the former taking pride in his increasing ability to coax unusual sounds out of his guitar, the latter securing the foundations with his familiar nonchalant ease. Scott McCaughey and Nathan December were given free rein to display their own enthusiasm as long as it didn't encroach on the four founding members.

Film-makers ranging from Gus van Sant to James Herbert and Jim McKay had been commissioned to produce short clips for various songs, which were projected onto a vast backdrop – though this blocked the view of those seated behind the stage, given that R.E.M. had opted for 360-degree seating. Tongue-in-cheek acknowledgement that the group were involved in the business of mass entertainment came with a disco ball lowered during 'Tongue'; lighting rigs rotated and wriggled playfully during 'End Of The World', which would soon settle into position as the can't-follow-that final encore.

Yet even though many of these songs required meticulous timing from projectionists, backdrop operators and lighting designers, R.E.M. insisted from the beginning on experimenting with the set list. Three different opening songs were tried out during the first six shows alone ('Kenneth', 'I Took Your Name' and 'Circus Envy'). A rotating choice of older songs ('Disturbance At The Heron House'), obscure songs ('Fretless') and cover songs ('Wichita Lineman') all made an equally quick appearance.

For at least one of the extra musicians, the aversion to complacency was welcome. "I realised pretty quickly that the attitude in R.E.M. wasn't that different from The Young Fresh Fellows," recalls Scott McCaughey. "Which was, 'Let's go out every night, let's rock, let's change the set list every night, no big deal if someone hits a bum chord here or there, it's not going to be this slick choreographed arena rock tour.' They still had the garage band attitude in a way. Which isn't to say we weren't tight or rocking, because we were. We were really good."

And yet, at least as some of the Australian reviews went, audience expectations still exceeded the group's delivery. It's fair to say that nothing short of the second coming would have sufficed:

R.E.M. had always been one of the best live bands on the planet – especially in smaller venues – but they offered neither the shameless showmanship of The Rolling Stones, the destructive aggression of The Who, or the messianic-turned-superironic gestures of U2. Their appeal had always been primarily visceral, and it's hard to mass market something so intangible for impersonal arenas where most of the audience has never experienced that sensation before.

R.E.M. themselves seemed undeterred. They'd expected some of this, knew there was little they could do to prevent it, and they could only hope that by constant experimentation and the steady introduction of new material, they would prove to as many of their newly acquired mainstream audience as were willing to pay attention, that R.E.M. was a band that took risks.

As the group hit new territories, various singles were lifted from *Monster* to pave the way and heighten the buzz. The artfully made videos for 'Kenneth' and 'Bang And Blame' (a top 20 US hit in the new year) were both primarily performance pieces as befitted the touring rock band. 'Strange Currencies', the ballad, was being saved for the all-important fourth single (just like its soundalike 'Everybody Hurts' had been from the previous album), but as yet another performance set in yet another warehouse/abandoned building, its video was in danger of making R.E.M. look stylised, conformist. There was nothing wrong with these clips, and they accurately represented R.E.M. in its new-old role as a touring band, but they were hardly pioneering; nobody was putting aside the MTV statuettes for them.

Perhaps that's why Michael Stipe hired Spike Jonze, just 25 and part of the same hipster crowd as the R.E.M. singer, to direct a promo for 'Crush With Eyeliner'. Jonze had burst onto the video scene in recent months with hilariously inventive clips for Weezer ('Undone' and 'Buddy Holly') and The Beastie Boys ('Sabotage'), introducing a much-needed playfulness to the increasingly tired and overblown promo genre. For 'Crush With Eyeliner', Jonze replaced the R.E.M. members with a quartet of trendy young Japanese – including a girl on guitar – and filmed them miming a performance of the song on stage in a neon restaurant/nightclub, along with footage of the kids glamming it up around town and generally mugging for the camera. Only at the end of the clip were the real R.E.M. revealed, watching the performance from separate corner tables. Stipe looked intrigued; Buck appeared horrified.

The video was clearly playing up the lyrical theme that "we all invent ourselves"; it appealed to the glam ethic at the heart of *Monster*'s subject matter; it even latched onto the band's light-hearted fascination with karaoke. But for a Spike Jonze clip, it was distinctly devoid of humour, and R.E.M., a group long prided for humility and humanity, came across as conceited and distant. Fans winced at the sight of an R.E.M. video crushed by the weight of its merciless cool, and while Jonze would return to work with the band, pile up further video awards and make an acclaimed feature film début, 'Crush With Eyeliner' was one of his few artistic failures. Curiously, just like *Automatic*'s third single and worst video ('The Sidewinder Sleeps Tonite'), 'Crush With Eyeliner' flopped as a single in the States; it was also the album's least successful cut in the UK.

A cynic might conclude that between the new-found devotion to the mega tour and apparent indifference to the video format, R.E.M. was losing focus. Charles Aaron, who had attended the University of Georgia in Athens during R.E.M.'s early Eighties heyday and was now a senior editor at *Spin* magazine, opted to take on the role of that cynic. In 15 years of constant media coverage, R.E.M. had rarely, if ever, been on the receiving end of genuinely bad, high-profile press. So Aaron was breaking somewhat overdue ground when he penned a particularly unflattering cover story based around a performance he witnessed (and accompanying interview) in Italy in February.

"A fuzzed-up comment on arena-rock machismo, (*Monster*) doesn't project so well in an actual arena," Aaron wrote. "All the nuance and humor and coy sexiness fades into forced posturing. The tremolo loses its ironic twinge, and your focus wanders to Mills's hideously unironic, spangled cowboy costume." Of course, his negativity could easily be construed as the classic case of an early fan feeling betrayed by, isolated from, or merely jealous of his erstwhile heroes' elevation to the superstar stratosphere. But still, he had a point when he concluded how, "R.E.M., after proving it could be an inspiring international pop icon on its own unconventional terms, was now attempting to prove it deserved that status, but on everybody else's conventional terms."

Indeed, Peter Buck had virtually invited that very allegation. Back in July, talking to *Rolling Stone* while finishing *Monster,* he had asserted that, "I don't really feel that R.E.M. have to have any rules or boundaries. It's more important to do what we feel like. Once you admit that there are rules, then you've lost." All of which made perfect sense – especially considering that was the creed by which R.E.M. had made it to the top. Except that then Buck had added, "And one of those rules is that you tour to promote your record," which is exactly what they were now doing, and on a scale that made it look very much like they were playing by the rules.

"I can see his point," agreed Buck years later of Aaron's accusations. "When you do your big pop record you go on tour. On the other hand there hasn't been much invented that sidesteps that. I tend to think that a band that doesn't play live at all isn't going to last. That's one of the glues that holds you together."

R.E.M. certainly didn't need to offer excuses for spending a year on the road. But now and then, they needed to clarify their reasoning. Michael Stipe stated it perfectly in a filmed interview included in *Rough Cut*. "I think all of us realise that we're probably never going to be in a position like this again. We're probably never going to be this popular again and able to do a world tour on this scale." In other words, every rock star, however ill at ease he feels with the role, deserves the occasional opportunity to live like one.

And it would be wrong to discount the financial incentive. "We'd never made money touring," says Peter Buck, by which he means, "We'd paid our bills, paid everyone else's wages, but not given ourselves a cheque. And we wanted to get paid too."

But the scale of the tour provoked something of a vicious cycle. There were six tour buses – including a travelling nursery for Peter Buck – and a 47-man crew.* There were the extra musicians to accommodate. Scott Litt was regularly flying in to supervise live recordings. And as they travelled on to New Zealand, Japan, Taiwan, Hong Kong, Singapore and then to Europe, they found

---

* R.E.M. were even using U2's soundman, Joe O'Herlihy.

their travelling operation treated with an awe that rendered them distinctly uncomfortable.

"The 1995 tour was the one weirdly unpleasant tour of all the tours we've done," says Peter Buck. "It was the kind of tour where you checked into a hotel and there would be hundreds of people waiting for you. And in the past that would happen and we'd say, 'There must be someone famous staying here,' and there would be. But this time it was for us. Your phones would be ringing at weird hours and people would camp in the hallways."

Buck's reaction was, by his own standards, drastic. "It was so fucked up and chaotic I quit drinking. I stopped drinking in February and didn't have another drink until the end of November. I was just like, This is too insane. I have to be sober for this whole thing to keep it together."

For Michael Stipe, the pressure was particularly acute. Months earlier, he had commented, "I love my job. I love the position I'm in. I love all the benefits that come with being what I am and doing what I do. I've got everything. Within that, I hate touring." In another interview around that time, he had hardly sounded enamoured of the concept when he talked of "throwing ourselves to the dogs for ten months."

Stipe's return to the interview table around the release of *Monster* had only increased the attention, forcing him to discuss both the AIDS rumour and his sexuality. Of the former, he suggested initially that by refusing to respond to it in his role as a celebrity, he hopefully provoked people to question their own attitudes to the disease and their own chances of catching it.* He also stated that the rumour was so ludicrously inaccurate and based on spurious observations he didn't see why he should dignify it with a reply, which made more sense.

Of the latter subject – accentuated by that line "I'm straight, I'm queer, I'm bi" in 'King Of Comedy' – he quipped that "labels are for canned food" and that sexual identity was a "slippery" subject.

---

* It was a dubious response given that Freddie Mercury might just as easily have thought the same, and Stipe usually accompanied his comment with the caveat that it was "unbelievably naïve".

If people were meant to conclude from this that he was bisexual, that appeared to be fine with him.

In subsequent months, as his celebrity status grew, his confidence with it, and the press pushed for fresh comments, he elaborated. Sometimes under duress. Charles Aaron from *Spin* confronted Stipe on the "games you play in the press with your sexual preference . . . It sometimes comes off like a put-on to get attention." To which the singer replied, "I've never played the game of arriving at big media events with supermodels to try and prove that I fuck women. If I suck dick or suck pussy or if I alternate between the two, it's my business and nobody else's. People can make whatever assumptions they want, and they have. I think a lot of people just assume that I'm queer and that's fine. I've never been ashamed of anything and I've never denied anything."

It wasn't the last word. It never is. But a month earlier, talking to Michael Goldberg of the pioneering online magazine *Addicted To Noise* in Sydney, he gave possibly his best quotation on the subject when he stated that he wanted "to retract that thing I said about the canned food" and went on to explain:

"Some people feel real comfortable saying, 'I'm queer', or, 'I'm straight', and 'that's all that I am and that's all that I'll ever be' and that's great for them. I'm just saying that I think there's a world of people out there that don't feel that way. And I'm not dictating to anyone that they can't be whatever they want to be or identify with whatever they want to identify with. I'm just saying, don't project that onto me or onto the entire world. I don't like that. Doesn't that make sense? Cool."

Cool.

By the early Nineties R.E.M. had emerged as America's premier rock'n'roll band, though they would soon be reduced to a trio with the departure of Bill Berry. (*LFI*)

Toying with his celebrity status, uncompromising in his political views and determined to push the boundaries, Michael Stipe often exhibited a bizarre dress sense on stage. Among Michael's strangest costumes (below, right) was the sarong he chose to wear at the Concert For Tibet in Washington DC, on June 14, 1998. (*Rex, LFI*)

Michael and Peter on stage during the Nelson Mandela South African Freedom Day concert in London's Trafalgar Square in 2001. (*Redferns*)

In October 2004, R.E.M. joined Bruce Springsteen and the E Street Band on a brief tour of electoral 'swing states' under the banner 'Vote For Change.' The half-dozen shows alongside the Boss quickly turned into a mutual appreciation society. (*Contographer/Corbis*)

R.E.M. were inducted into the Rock and Roll Hall of Fame in March 2007. The all-star finale in New York saw R.E.M. join fellow inductee and influential friend Patti Smith and her band to perform 'People Have The Power' alongside Keith Richards, Eddie Vedder, Steven Stills, Ronnie Spector, Sammy Hagar and more. *(Kevin Mazur/WireImage)*

The ever dapper Mike Mills on stage at the Isle of Wight Festival, June 2005, during the group's largest ever world tour. *(Louise Wilson/Getty Images)*

Peter Buck on stage at the Olympia Theatre in Dublin, July 2007,
during the five nights of 'Live Rehearsals' for the album *Accelerate*. *(Chris Bilheimer)*

R.E.M. continued to frequent and perform, collectively and individually, at their Athens home-town venue, the 40 Watt Club, over the years. Top. Mike Mills joins the Baseball Project in September 2009. *(Chris McKay/Retna Ltd.)* Bottom: Steve Wynn, Peter Buck, and Scott McCaughey at a Baseball Project show in March 2011. *(Chris McKay/WireImage)*

R.E.M. in March 2011. "We built something extraordinary together," said Stipe in September of that year, announcing their split. "We did this thing. And now we're going to walk away from it." *(Minneapolis Star Tribune/ZUMA Press/Corbis)*

Nineteen

Given R.E.M.'s popularity, the level of media scrutiny they were touring under, and the fact that you need to be a devoted fan to read this much about them, there can be few who don't know what happened on stage in Lausanne, Switzerland on March 1, 1995, two weeks into the European leg of the tour. The group were performing the disco ball song, 'Tongue', when "all of a sudden it slowed down and started dragging", as Peter Buck recalls. The guitarist turned to check on the time keeper, Bill Berry. He knew the drummer wasn't drunk when they went on stage, but something was clearly wrong. At the end of the song, Berry "came out front and just collapsed into my arms. He said, 'My head hurts.'"

The road crew carried Bill Berry off stage and the group huddled together for a quick conference. R.E.M. had never been in this position before: for 15 years they'd ended each night with the same line-up they started with, and they didn't want to break with the formula now. Then again, the show was already well under way and they had an arena filled to capacity in front of them. The Swiss are not noted for impetuous behaviour, but walking off stage in the middle of a show is usually the best way to test a crowd's patience. Working on the belief that Berry had just taken ill for a night – a mid-winter flu bug was doing the rounds and Bill occasionally had migraines – they called Joey Peters from Grant Lee Buffalo in to fill Bill's seat. Fortunately, having been with R.E.M. for the last seven weeks, there was probably no drummer on the planet, other than Berry of course, who knew the new songs better. Peter Buck, having no vocal duties, conducted Peters through a truncated set, one that included an acoustic rendition of Chris Isaak's 'Wicked Game' to give Peters a rest.

Backstage afterwards, they found Bill shaking, and an on site

265

doctor confirming that the drummer had a migraine. They returned to the hotel, uneasy at suffering a mishap so early in the global proceedings, but feeling professional pride at finishing the show. In the middle of the night, his headache no better, Berry was taken to hospital, where a scan revealed that he had two aneurysms on the right hand outside surface of his brain – one of which had already ruptured. Up to five per cent of Americans have brain aneurysms and live normal, healthy lives, but among those who suffer a ruptured aneurysm – referred to as a subarachnoid haemorrhage – as many as half die rapidly from internal bleeding. (And among survivors, complications such as memory loss can seriously impede recovery.) Fortunately for Bill Berry, there was no internal bleeding. With additional good luck, Lausanne was one of the best cities in the world in which to find himself with a ruptured brain aneurysm. "If it had been in any number of other cities we'd just been in, Bill would have died," says Peter Buck. "The guy who did the operation has probably done it more than anyone else on Earth."

The operation itself – known as 'clipping' – is not desperately complicated by modern medical standards: it involves removing part of the skull bone and, via microscopic surgery, blocking off the balloon-like aneurysm with a tiny metal clip, akin to a miniature clothes-peg. This keeps blood from entering the aneurysm, which in turn protects nearby brain tissue. The bone plate is then wired securely into place, the wound closed, and the patient kept in intensive care for a few days. A statement put out by Warner Brothers on March 3 announced that in Bill's case, "The operation was uneventful and 100 per cent successful and the doctors are happy with Berry's recovery."

The group, however, were in complete shock. "He was a lot sicker than people knew," says Peter Buck. "He was paralysed for a few days." The seriousness of the aneurysm was perfectly apparent to those fans who held tickets for any of the remaining 32 sold-out shows across eleven European countries, including Britain, all of which were immediately cancelled. This was not the way R.E.M. had scripted their long-awaited comeback tour.

But being the group of close friends who'd spent 15 years effectively sharing each other's lives, business concerns and career moves were the least of R.E.M.'s worries. Working on the theory that they were meant to be on tour together anyway, the entire band and its immediate crew and management stayed in Switzerland while Bill recovered. Three weeks after the Lausanne show, on March 21, Bill was discharged from hospital. The next day, according to a fan club card sent out on this announcement of his recovery, Berry played a full 18-hole round of golf. It looked like he was going to be OK.

But for a few weeks, there had been a very real chance that R.E.M. might no longer exist. As Michael Stipe had said during the interviews included on *Rough Cut,* "If anyone was to leave the couch. . . . It would not be R.E.M." Peter Buck confirmed, at the time, "We would never play without him as the drummer." And, at the time, he surely meant it.

In regard to what causes an aneurysm, medical experts suggest anything from alcohol and smoking to a severe head injury suffered earlier in life. Bill Berry had once been laid flat by a baseball to the head. It could well have been that. It could have been something else. It's fair to say that in the immediate aftermath of his life-threatening attack, Bill's primary concern was to his band mates and their employees. When he learned that he was going under the knife and there was a chance he might not come back, he recalls thinking, "I just didn't want it to end that way. I at least wanted to be able to walk out of a band meeting in disgust or something, and slam the door behind me. Not that way."

"I was ready to quit," recalls Buck of the tour, "but Bill said, no, we're going back, I'm not going to let this happen." The R.E.M. juggernaut would keep going for the time being. The true severity of what occurred, how close to death any of us are at any chosen moment in time, and how we decide to make best use of our remaining years, would only gradually implant itself on Bill's brain.

★   ★   ★

To allow Bill Berry full opportunity to recover, the first eight shows of the American tour were also cancelled, pushing the recommencement date back to May 15, in California. Perhaps that's why hoaxers were able to get away with sending a carefully fabricated fax on Warner Brothers stationery (with accurate phone numbers and contact information) on Sunday, April 30, stating that Berry had actually died. Word spread rapidly across the country, aided by the speed of the Internet and its various R.E.M. chat rooms and user groups. It was, as they say, adding insult to injury.

The group had in fact returned to their Athens rehearsal studios, partly to ensure they were in gear for their high-profile return to the American stage, but equally to work up fresh material: for all the talk of recording an entirely new album while on the road, the first month of the tour had seen only the constant inclusion of 'Revolution' (a hangover from *Monster)* and the handful of European dates the occasional try-out of the brand new 'Departure'. Set to a bluesy guitar riff that would have been at home on a ZZ Top album, 'Departure' kicked off with subject matter considered equally taboo by iconoclasts like R.E.M: on-the-road reportage. "Just arrived Singapore, San Sebastian, Spain, 26-hour trip," Stipe half-shouted, half-sang, before veering into fragmented references to *Rolling Stone* economics reporter William Greider and the chemical ptomaine. The title 'Departure' was shared with a poem by Arthur Rimbaud, Patti Smith's favourite poet; not so coincidentally, Stipe spoke for the first time to his icon Patti Smith from "an anarchist book store in San Sebastian", and, completing the circle, R.E.M. introduced 'Departure' in that same city, on the opening night of the European tour. 'Departure' could be seen perhaps as a counterpart to 'Little America' from 1984, the group's travelling perspective having shifted over a decade from a beleaguered van following the highway to first class cabins crossing entire continents. "I like the way that song particularly captures the feeling of being on tour," says Peter Buck. "You're always looking out a window somewhere. For me, it always brings back other trips I've taken."

'Departure' was still the only unrecorded song in the set when the band belatedly began its American tour at the Shoreline Amphitheater on May 15, a show opened by the seminal Sonic Youth and attended by many of the LA rock royalty. But within a week, a snarling number called 'Undertow', with verses in the brooding tradition of Michael Stipe's favourite R.E.M. song 'Country Feedback' and a chorus straight out of the group's hard-rocking textbook, was also making itself heard.

Nineteen

The group was regaining its stride and, in particular, the soundchecks started turning into the creative force that the band had intended them to be. Rather than routinely running through the same half-dozen songs to ensure all equipment was functioning properly, the group would treat each afternoon's on-stage time as a rehearsal and songwriting opportunity.

For Scott McCaughey and Nathan December, the original official policy of heading off stage as soon as they heard something 'new' at soundcheck was quickly forgotten. As McCaughey recalls, "Those guys might bash through something once and Peter might say, 'Scott, why don't you play organ on this?' or Mike might say, 'Why don't you play piano, but only on the bridge?' Really quickly it became that we could start playing along and with their guidance would come up with a part that they were happy with." McCaughey, who took solo songwriting credit in The Young Fresh Fellows, felt that he was performing a distinctly different role with R.E.M. "To me, whoever writes the words and the melody and the chords, that's the song. It's written. Everything else is arranging."

★　★　★

It's fair, if not exactly polite, to say that by the time R.E.M. made their American 'comeback' through May and June, in essentially the exact same venues they had played in 1989, some of the excitement surrounding *Monster* had dissipated. Both 'Kenneth' and 'Bang And Blame' had been sizeable hit singles, and the album was certified triple platinum in February, but neither 'Crush With Eyeliner' nor, surprisingly, 'Strange Currencies' made much of an impact as singles, and the album was in the nether regions of the top 100 as the tour moved east. To use industry parlance, *Monster* was lacking 'legs'.

But being free of the mass-media microscope they'd been under elsewhere in the world made the American shows more fun. Content with their work-rate and their status, they ended the six-week run of arenas with a three-night stint at New York's Madison Square Garden, where the usually stiff and staid Dan Rather was filmed performing 'What's The Frequency, Kenneth?' and the group turned in a performance of 'Crush With Eyeliner' on *The David Letterman Show*.

That same week, a new home video collection, *Parallel*, was released, collecting the promos from both *Automatic For The People* and *Monster* and demonstrating, rather clumsily, the group's audio-visual shift over the course of one album. For while *Parallel* included a previously unseen and quite thrilling black-and-white on stage clip of 'Star 69' from the show in Singapore, and an alphabetical end sequence (mostly comprising *Rough Cut* footage) that was R.E.M. self-expression at its best, there was simply no way to compare the communal harmony of 'Man On The Moon', or the epic elegance of 'Everybody Hurts', with the performance pieces from *Monster*. The era when R.E.M. bestraddled the video genre as both darlings of MTV and yet purveyors of the form's finest art, had come and gone, and *Parallel* was its witness.

At the end of June, R.E.M. returned to Europe, where their star status remained unquestioned. The original European tour tickets had sold out so rapidly that the group were now booked to grace not only the same annual festivals they'd appeared at in 1985 and '89 (Belgium's Torhout and Werchter), but also to headline their own outdoor shows. In stadiums.

It's all too easy to throw Peter Buck's 1987 comment, "If we ever did a stadium tour, I would imagine it would be about the last thing we'd ever do together," back in his face. Even as recently as on *Monster*'s release, he had still considered the scenario unlikely. "I have real trouble with those big places," he told Jim Sullivan of the *Boston Globe* when asked specifically about stadiums. "Preferably, I'd like to play in front of 150 people in a blues bar in town."

But he knew that the latter was impossible, and on the former, he was outvoted. There were, after all, legitimate reasons of popularity for moving to the outdoors – especially in the UK, where the cancellation of the British arena tour in March left tens of thousands of fans disappointed and the tight scheduling prohibited the original shows from being rescheduled. (Many of the continental European shows cancelled in March had been successfully rescheduled for July.) The band had already publicly stated that it didn't imagine being so in-demand ever again; combine that with the understandable ego gratification of selling 70,000 tickets to your own show and the financial pay-off too, and it's not surprising the group decided to do it while they still had the chance.

Besides, while stadium shows carry a certain negative stigma when orchestrated around one touring act – such as R.E.M.'s British shows in July – this is offset by a general European enthusiasm for the annual outdoor festival season as a whole. For a visiting American band, even one with over a decade's experience touring the continent, the credible difference between playing, say, the annual Roskilde Festival in Denmark alongside Jimmy Page and Robert Plant, and headlining their own event at Cardiff Arms Park with a hand-picked support including Belly and The Cranberries, would have been too slight to lose sleep over.

But before playing the British stadiums, R.E.M. had to make it through the continent again. And no sooner had they landed in Europe and started playing the festivals there than Mike Mills took ill. Initial medical inspections failed to reveal the cause, and given that the group was travelling every day, it was difficult to run a full gamut of tests. Mills opted to keep the tour going.

"We were doing shows in front of 80,000 people," recalls Peter Buck, "where Mike would stay in a hospital after a show, then they'd get him on a stretcher, put him on a plane, fly him to the show, then the doctor would give him a shot that would loosen him up enough that he could play. By an hour and a half he couldn't sing any more so they'd put him on a stretcher and take him back to the hospital. So we did that for about two weeks, 'cos we didn't know what was wrong with him. The doctors couldn't find out what it was."

They finally found out on July 11, while in Prague, which had already been cancelled once. Soundchecks had been conducted and Peter Buck was at the hotel, when he received a call. "We've found out what's wrong with Mike," he was told. "The good news is it can be remedied by an operation. The bad news is we're going to do it today. We're going to cancel Prague again." Fully anticipating a riot from twice-disappointed Czech fans, Buck called for his tour bus and he and his family made straight for the German border.

As it turned out, Mike Mills was suffering nasty complications from his appendectomy during the *Monster* sessions. Scar tissue had affixed itself to his intestines, ample explanation for why singing and moving around on stage had become so agonising. The next ten days' shows were cancelled and the British fans (along with the promoters) panicked that R.E.M. were doomed not to make it across the English Channel at all. But Mills, like Berry before him, bounced back quickly from surgery – and with equal determination to keep the juggernaut rolling. "The law of averages caught up with us," was his nonchalant view of the medical crises.

R.E.M. duly played their outdoor summer shows across Britain and Ireland. With the likes of Blur and Oasis opening (though not on the same bill!), blessed by unusually perfect weather, and with 'Tongue', the fifth single from *Monster,* riding high in the top 20, they took in Slane Castle outside Dublin, Cardiff Arms Park, the McAlpine Stadium in Huddersfield, Murrayfield Stadium in Edinburgh, and finally, two shows at the National Bowl in Milton Keynes, an hour's drive north of London. Precisely ten years earlier, R.E.M. had appeared here during their most musically dour and personally depressed period, halfway up a bill headlined by U2, and spent most of the rain-soaked set dodging bottles of piss. Now they shared U2's stature. They had sold over four million albums in the UK in less than five years. The final show of the UK stint, at Milton Keynes on July 30, was broadcast live on Radio 1. Six of their albums graced the charts that year. Without stooping to hyperbole, R.E.M. could barely have been any more popular in the UK.

Still, the stadiums were not R.E.M.'s natural domain and the group knew it. "When it was great, it was really good," says Buck looking back at that week. "But it was easier to not be as good. I doubt if the audience noticed when it wasn't as good. But also, you get such a wave of affection and stuff coming that it boosts you up."

A freshly boosted R.E.M. returned to the Continent to play some of the halls cancelled back in March – and again in July. Another new song, 'The Wake-Up Bomb', was introduced. A throw-back to *Monster*'s glam obsession both in its dirty guitar riff and lyrical references, it was written about a night spot in Manhattan, where the protagonist "could practise my T. Rex moves" and "get high on my attitude" from the glam heyday of "1973". With its resounding chorus and classic Mills harmonies,

'The Wake-Up Bomb' became an instant live favourite.

A new territory was added to R.E.M.'s lengthening list of conquests when the group played the Ramat Gan Stadium in Tel Aviv, Israel on August 9, though by now it was Michael Stipe complaining of stomach illness. The band returned to Prague for its final European show on August 11, planning to make it third time lucky for that city's beleaguered R.E.M. fans. It turned out to be a close call: Stipe had discovered he was carrying a herniated diaphragm, which also needed an immediate operation. Determined not to let Prague down yet again, Stipe saw the show through in some pain, flew straight back to Georgia and straight into an Atlanta hospital for surgery. A suddenly superstitious Peter Buck was heard to remark that he was looking both ways before crossing the road.

There was a temptation to look at the group's injuries and suggest that, like an ageing sports team, their bodies were starting to fall apart on them; that spending a year on the road after five years away had proven beyond their stamina. Scott McCaughey, the oldest playing member, points out of the various hospitalisations, "None of them were the result of abuse or rocking too hard. Mike had appendicitis while making *Monster* and it came back to haunt him. And then Bill? You get an aneurysm you get an aneurysm. Michael is the only one I could see that might have been related to singing, because he had a hernia in his diaphragm and that's a muscle that you use a lot when you're singing for two hours every night, night after night. And man, he doesn't slide on the shows. I can't believe how resilient that guy's voice is. Michael had to have a pretty strict regimen. You really wouldn't see him before the shows. He would be in his dressing room having tea, or maybe a massage, psyching up for the two hours. And have a glass of wine on stage – not red wine, because red wine is bad for your voice. So just white wine. He was very strict to the regimen."

Stipe also recovered quickly, and although it must have felt to the band like they'd already been on the road for a year and a lifetime, they still had one more substantial leg to complete – a two-month north American arena tour. With *Monster* off the charts, they signalled their intention to look forward by performing 'The Wake-Up Bomb' on the eve of the tour, live on the MTV Video Awards; they brought their friends Radiohead, Grant Lee

Buffalo, and Luscious Jackson along to open for them; they introduced another new number, 'Binky The Doormat' (the title lifted from a 1991 movie *Shakes The Clown)*; they introduced more songs into soundchecks. And they invited their friends to join them on stage. In and around her home state of Michigan, Stipe's idol Patti Smith joined the group for a version of her own 'Dancing Barefoot' and the Cobain ode 'Let Me In'. There were appearances too by Ed Kowalczyk from Live in his group's home state, and by Lindsay Buckingham of Fleetwood Mac, with whom Peter Buck had developed a friendly relationship.

As always, the tour ended in Atlanta. After a year of unrivalled success and unexpected injuries, no one was quite certain what the future would hold for live work, except that it wouldn't be this. So for the last three shows of '95, all at the Omni, R.E.M. brought in the film crews and recorded themselves on camera for posterity.

The 1989 video was called *Tourfilm;* this one was called *Roadmovie.* It was pointless trying to be too clever about what was essentially a concert souvenir. Watching the two films back to back, it's easy to see how much the group had changed over one tour separated by five years – and yet how much remained the same.

There were more projections behind them now and more projecting coming *from* them. The show was brighter, more visual, more concerned with entertaining and filling big rooms with sound. The crowd, barely visible in the 1989 movie, looked older now than it had seemed in the past, more mainstream too. Michael Stipe was less animated, and bald as well, but more likely to keep his shirt on. Mike Mills, who still sported the college boy haircut and clothes back in 1989, now dressed and acted every bit the rock'n'roll star, hamming up audience participation on 'Losing My Religion' like he was born to the task. And in some ways, he seemed all the more vibrant for coming out of his shell. "Those suits are beautiful," he told *Rolling Stone*'s Chris Heath of his colourful stage gear. "And anyone that doesn't like them can kiss my ass."

The filming was different, too. In 1989, the shows were shot in 8mm and 16mm, with the tapes farmed out to different directors for artful editing. This time, Peter Care directed the entire event in standard video format. In 1989, all cameras were on the band; when viewers saw the crowd, it was mostly just the back of their heads as viewed from the mixing board. In 1995, under much brighter lights, the audience appeared to be everywhere – not surprising given that the group was even selling the seats directly behind the stage, but a perpetual distraction all the same. Peter Care did his utmost to take the experience of the concert arena and bring it into the living room, but it was hard work. Only on the final encore, 'It's The End Of The World As We Know It', did the director let loose with the sort of rapid, quick-fire edits that truly captured the information overload appeal of a riveting performance.

In both its strengths and its failures, *Roadmovie* was an accurate portrayal of R.E.M. in 1995. "That was a fun tour in the sense that we reinvented ourselves as a band," says Peter Buck. "I remember the playing and actual soundchecking being really great. All of us getting together and playing every day. The last day of the tour we played an hour and a half soundcheck."

But still, "I thought it was going to be the last time we were going to do something like that on that level – and it has been."

★   ★   ★

Considering the trials and tribulations of the year on the road, it would have been understandable had R.E.M. taken a lengthy respite from each other. But their solidarity, musical and personal, was stronger at the end of the tour, in Atlanta, than it had been at the start, in Australia; the thrill of writing, rehearsing and performing new songs over recent months provoked a collective desire to finish them while still in everyone's minds. In fact, Peter Buck and Mike Mills were so enthused – and so completely undeterred by any of the *Monster* tour's setbacks – that they suggested getting the album finished and released in time to play the European festivals again the following summer. But Bill Berry was emphatic: "No way am I going to tour again." The emotional fall out from the aneurysm was taking a toll way beyond the physical recovery.

And so, after a short holiday – Peter Buck went to Hawaii and bought a house there – they returned to John Keane's in Athens in the new year. Most of March and April 1996 was spent at Bad

Animals studios in Peter Buck's new home city, Seattle, recording, overdubbing, tweaking and mixing.

This is not to over-glorify the band's sense of motivation. The original intent, after all, had been to record the entire album on the road, and yet by the end of the year, only five unreleased songs were being regularly featured in the set. One of these, 'Revolution', itself a hangover from *Monster,* was considered unrepresentative of the group's new direction and dropped from contention. Its inclusion on *Roadmovie* remains its lone official release.

That left 'Departure', 'Undertow', 'The Wake-Up Bomb' and 'Binky The Doormat'. All four had a big, boomy, somewhat anthemic sound, very much influenced by the arenas they were composed in and the songs that surrounded them in the set; versions were retained from performances in, respectively, Detroit, Boston, Charleston and Phoenix. Having already acknowledged that the new album would not be entirely 'live', the group reserved the right to re-record parts where necessary. On both 'The Wake-Up Bomb' and 'Departure', for example, Scott McCaughey's organ track had "crapped out" on stage and Mike Mills replayed it in the studio; Nathan December's secondary guitar parts stayed.

December was given the task of whittling down the 100-plus hours of soundcheck recordings to a shortlist. Several of the songs finally selected were in the same vein as those performed in public. 'So Fast, So Numb' offered classic rock piano tinkles and a blistering, simplistic fuzz solo; it was lyrically reminiscent of *Monster*'s harshest moments. 'Low Desert', which would follow toward the conclusion of the new album, had been sitting round in various forms since *Monster,* when it was called 'Swamp'. This might explain its musical proximity to a southern rock jam, all bluesy guitar squawls and organ overdubs. Lyrically, it was obsessed with the great American theme of the highway, of "the ashtray cities and the freeway drives, broken casinos and water slides, the 18 wheeler and the payback dives, gravity pulls on the powerlines," as Stipe's lyrics so evocatively put it. The title 'Low Desert' was reflected in the album sleeve: a Michael Stipe photograph of a semi-blurred desert landscape as seen from a speeding tour bus.

'Leave', like 'Low Desert' taken from the band's last soundchecks in Atlanta, clocked in at seven minutes; it would have been the longest R.E.M. song to date even without its one-minute acoustic introduction. (And even longer if the band hadn't edited it down.) Marrying the dark tension that had infused parts of *Green* and *Out Of Time* with an edgy repetitive synth line performed by Scott McCaughey, it became something R.E.M. had never really allowed of themselves: an epic. "We always finished the sound-check with it," recalls Peter Buck. "And people would be cheering. I felt like smashing the guitar at the end of it, it was such a powerhouse."

These seven songs all reflected the road experience: many of them lyrically, all of them musically. They fused the looseness of an on-stage recording with the cohesion of an intuitive unit. To put it in simple American parlance, they rocked. But collectively they pushed R.E.M. into an area that was never really their strength, which Peter Buck recognised when he stated the need to avoid becoming Grand Funk Railroad singing "We're an American band". Fortunately, the rest of the new material spread out in all manner of different directions.

'Bittersweet Me' best melded the studio and the stage, the ballad and the rocker. Though the sleeve states it was pulled from a soundcheck in Memphis, much of it was recorded in Seattle, including Buck's many guitar overdubs, Mills' organ and mellotron parts and Stipe's completed lyrics, which suggested the betroubled rock star ("I don't know what I'm hungry for/I don't know what I want anymore") but were in fact set inside a fictional relationship.

On the album's ineffably gorgeous finale, 'Electrolite', Stipe described a sensation that was everyone's to share – standing atop of Mulholland Drive in Los Angeles, from where "Hollywood is under me/I'm Martin Sheen/I'm Steve McQueen/I'm Jimmy Dean." Born of a Mike Mills piano sequence eerily similar to 'Nightswimming', 'Electrolite' ended up with acoustic guitars galore, Nathan December playing the guiro (a dried-out, percussive gourd), Andy Carlson on violin, and Peter Buck on several electric overdubs. Many instrumentals had also been toyed with on tour, of which 'Zither' was mixed almost intact from a dressing room in Philadelphia; the delightful and uncharacteristically upbeat 'Tricyle', a throwback to 'Rotary Ten' from R.E.M.'s early days, was saved for a B-side.

Ten songs could have been enough. But once settled in Seattle, the band found themselves recording others from scratch. 'New Test Leper' had been played just once on the entire tour, recorded by Stipe on a portable cassette recorder and more or less forgotten about. When Stipe came in the studio one day with the tape, the band were pleasantly surprised and decided to re-work it. Though conforming to the R.E.M. cliché in which all the best ballads are in 6/8 time (and vice-versa), 'New Test Leper' turned into something unique. Over simply strummed acoustic guitar, an arpeggiated electric played through a Leslie speaker, some stunning feedback and Mike Mills' organ overdubs, Michael Stipe delivered lowly vocals that took on religious theocracy with apparently bold intent. ("I can't say that I love Jesus, that would be a hollow claim," remain among his strongest opening lines.)

The same theme cropped up on 'Be Mine', written and demoed on the tour bus as an instrumental by Mike Mills and re-recorded in Seattle. After referencing the trivialities of Easter bunnies and Christmas trees, Stipe offered the lines, "If you make me your religion/I'll give you all the room you need," which suggested a Messiah complex for those who forgot that Stipe sang from character's perspectives, not his own. 'Be Mine' built steadily and slowly over five and a half minutes, like an archetypal power ballad, which explains why the group fuzzed it up beyond all likely airplay acceptance. "It really depends what kind of band you want to be," says Peter Buck. "My feeling is that if we had gone and got Steve Lillywhite or Bob Rock to produce it, it might not have been a hit anyway and then we'd just look stupid. It's better being this weird little jam that's surrounded by all this stuff. It's a good song but it's not too saccharine."

Also recorded afresh in the studio was the *Monster* era 'E-Bow The Letter', for which Michael Stipe, as big a rock celebrity as they now came, engaged in his own idol worship, and finally convinced Patti Smith to duet. The words were classic Stipe scattershot approach, notes from a 'letter never sent', as per the song on *Reckoning*. The title prefixed the name of the instrument Peter Buck played to cello-like effect; worked up further with synths and sitar, and with Patti Smith's equally yearning voice floating in the ether, 'E-Bow The Letter' was a beautiful, brooding, uncommercial album track. In a move of typical perversity, R.E.M. decided to make it the album's lead single.

With similar disregard for audience expectation, *New Adventures* would open with the song that least sounded like R.E.M. 'How The West Was Won And Where It Got Us' was also the only number both written and recorded in the Seattle studio. With its classical piano flourishes, synth overdubs and gently grooving acoustic guitar, it was so slow as to make 'Drive' sound like 'Stand'.

At 65 minutes and with 14 songs, *New Adventures In Hi-Fi* – titled with good-natured tongue-in-cheek after all those stereo-era high-fidelity discs – would be R.E.M.'s longest album by a stretch. It was also their most disparate collection to date, or at least since *Reckoning*. Michael Stipe was particularly proud of "being able to somehow cross-graph the live stuff with the studio stuff and make it so you couldn't tell what was live and what wasn't." After the problems that arose recording, and particularly mixing, *Monster,* R.E.M. had been determined to enjoy the experience this time around, and by the speed of the Seattle sessions and the subsequent enthusiastic comments, they would seem to have succeeded.

"This is the kind of band we are," says Peter Buck. "We went on the road, people almost died, we had all kinds of injuries, we had to cancel shows, and still we wrote and recorded about 25 songs on the road. Spent a month in the studio afterwards finishing them up, and played five or six of them live. I'm really proud of the fact that we did it under adverse cirumstances, and full speed ahead and damn the torpedoes and all that."

Mike Mills was more sanguine. "It was partly motivated by laziness," he quipped. "If we could do as much as possible on the road, that's stuff we didn't have to do in the studio. That's one reason why this album was so easy to make."

Twenty

The recording of *Monster* in 1994 had been hampered by a breakdown in R.E.M.'s internal communications. The touring of *Monster* in 1995 had been riven by serious individual illnesses. The recording of *New Adventures In Hi-Fi* in 1996 was not dented by any such upheaval – at least not amongst the four band members. But R.E.M. worked on their tenth studio album under the disconcerting realisation that the key relationships around them – the ones that supposedly cemented them – were all in a state of flux. There were serious question marks hanging over their involvement with producer Scott Litt, manager Jefferson Holt, and record company Warner Brothers, and each partnership's future was seriously affected by the outcome of the others.

By the time the dust had settled – and that's assuming it ever really has done – R.E.M. would have dissolved two of these partnerships and renewed the third. Their motivations and aspirations would have been severely tested by their decisions. And they would receive enough bad publicity from their choices to make up for several years' worth of prior media protection.

By far the most shocking of their decisions – though it was later dwarfed in terms of media attention – was to part company with Jefferson Holt. Though it has been said before, it is almost impossible to overestimate the importance Jefferson Holt played in the rise of R.E.M., throughout the Eighties and on through the band's mainstream breakthrough in the early Nineties. His early, unyielding belief in – and friendship with – the group had quickly escalated him to 'fifth member' status, paid accordingly, and afforded non-typical managerial roles such as taking lead vocals (on an unreleased 'Windout'), being name-checked in song ("Jefferson, I think we're lost" from 'Little America.'), and appearing prominently in videos ('Can't Get There From Here', the intro to *Succumbs* and

280

more). These public confirmations of his honoured status were amplified daily in music industry offices, where Jefferson's unique combination of intellect and intuition, humour and honesty – combined with an enviable ability to always get his band the best deal and highest profile their credibility required and could afford, while seemingly making out like *he* was the one granting the favour – made him one of the most beloved managers in the business. R.E.M. succeeded because of the music, for certain; because of the four members' own engaging and complementary personalities, absolutely; but as many a bitter, badly managed band member will tell you, especially those who were once part of R.E.M.'s peer group, such success would not have happened – *could* not have happened – without management that acted less as a business division of the group than as an extension of the music.

Bertis Downs was equally integral to the group's success: his level-headed legal mind ensured the paperwork was always in order, the percentages added up, and R.E.M. retained ownership of its intellectual property wherever and whenever possible. Jefferson was fortunate to have such a partner not just for these reasons, but also because Bertis' presence in Athens allowed Holt to attend every show, check in on every recording, be involved in almost every presentation and media appearance, serving as the group's highly visible intermediary and guide. In the process, he became as familiar to the fans as to the industry; his standing with both was as close to impeccable as a music business manager can ever aspire to be.

"He knew everybody at the record company," says one former Warner Brothers executive. "He knew my assistant's name. He had a way of knowing people and their likes and dislikes. He would know that the radio guy at such-and-such company loves dogs. He knew how to work the music business – not just the record company, but the whole music business. He was really good at making a sense of community about R.E.M. He was the most popular manager I knew, hands down. I would say Paul McGuinness (of U2) is the only other person who has that popularity, and he never did it in quite as good a way as Jefferson."

Holt's status peaked during the early years with Warner Brothers. The record company, long known as the family label among the corporate giants, was staffed by music enthusiasts, from the interns on up to the legendary leadership of Mo Ostin and Lenny Waronker, and those who were not already R.E.M. fans rapidly became such. There was a joke around the industry that R.E.M. always had five record companies working for them, because every division of Warners, even those officially uninvolved in R.E.M.'s career, would put in a good word for the band at any given moment. The success of *Out Of Time* and *Automatic For The People* were a peak period for those who believed you could buck convention in the increasingly corporate entertainment industry and still make money. As it turned out, those years were the swan song too. For a number of reasons, it would never be the same again.

There are those who saw Jefferson Holt gradually start to lose interest somewhere after the early Nineties breakthrough – and that includes the band members. "He was not on the team for quite a while," says Peter Buck, "but we were all kind of willing to let it slide. It didn't really matter if he never showed at the office."

The *Monster* tour, given its scale, would appear to have been the one mountain left to climb, the last thing left for a manager to prove he could pull off, but instead his absence was increasingly noted around this time – if not physically, then perhaps emotionally. A clip on the A-Z of R.E.M. that rounded out the home video collection *Parallel* takes on an interesting relevance in hindsight. Jefferson's mobile phone rings; he misses the call. He jokes about it to camera, the familiarly goofball manager playing entirely to type. Unless the group, who oversaw the production, were trying to send a signal.

There was the fact, too, that *Monster* was less an old-fangled rock'n'roll tour than a juggernaut; once the itinerary had been planned, it needed hardhearted generals and bull-headed commanders to ensure that it went off as planned, rather than a creative manager who thrived on personal relationships. Though Jefferson no doubt got the same kick out of watching 'his' band sell out stadiums as did the musicians themselves, there were pressures that had never come up before – do-gooders intruding into the members' personal space, businessmen trying to make deals, outsiders wanting a piece of the pie. And then of course there were the illnesses that saw the juggernaut splutter round Europe rather than roll right over it – hardly Jefferson's fault, but the sort of calamities that stretch a complex personal-professional relationship to the hilt.

R.E.M. have always conducted their business like proper southern gentlemen. Whether schooled by their parents, teachers – or managers – they have learned not to insult other musicians or professionals in public. Try to find a cutting where Peter Buck, the band's most opinionated member, bad-mouths a fellow musician. It will always be accompanied by the quote, "nothing against [so and so]" or, "I mean, I like some of [so and so's] records." The same with the other members, who are less likely to even hint at disparagement to begin with. Their animosity is saved entirely for the political right wing, which only furthers the ideal of R.E.M. among their fans as communal, committed, politically correct.

The upside of being such proper southern gentlemen is apparent then – a reputation for civility and honour. The downside is an unwillingness to truly speak one's mind. R.E.M. have rarely fought with each other largely because they love each other, but also because they've learned to abide each other, faults and all. The personal problems that interrupted *Monster* were allowed to fester longer than they should have done for this reason. The same with the group's frustrations with Jefferson. They felt he was losing interest, they suspected he may even be losing grip, but they failed to confront him on it. It was like a troubled marriage, hobbling painfully along, each side nursing its grievances, yet refusing to communicate them out of some desperate hope that personalities would revert to the type that had attracted each other in the first place.

Such marriages usually end up in divorce. And that's what happened between R.E.M. and Jefferson Holt. When word escaped in May that the parties had split, it caused the same kind of disappointment and shock among fans and industry as when a favourite wedded couple announce their break-up. The manner in which the divorce played out in public was then no less damning than finding out that one of the supposedly enamoured couple was a serial adulterer. On June 21, 1996, the *Los Angeles Times* published a cover story on its entertainment section by reporter Chuck

Philips. It was titled, startlingly, 'R.E.M.'s Former Manager Denies Allegations of Sex Harassment'.

The story, which started out by questioning why a long-term manager would choose to break with a group at the peak of their earning powers, included statements from both sides. Jefferson Holt announced, "I've agreed to keep the terms of my agreement with R.E.M. confidential," and ended, "I'm happier than I have been in a long time." For their part, R.E.M. announced, "The reasons for this decision and terms of the termination are private and confidential, and no further discussion of these matters will be made by any of the parties."

But the headline clearly revealed something more sinister at work. And Chuck Philips, who had written a major exposé on the serial sexual harassment of female employees within record company offices back in 1991, was experienced enough to work his way around these statements and present the few facts as he understood them. They could essentially be boiled down to this one sentence. "Sources say that Holt was asked to leave after members of the group investigated allegations that he sexually harassed a female employee at R.E.M.'s tiny Athens, Ga., office."

To the extent that the sexual harassment allegations are true – Philips stands by his story, which he notes was never legally challenged – they relate very heavily to a further sentence in the *LA Times* story: that R.E.M. was "long considered one of the nation's most liberal and politically correct rock groups."

Precisely. By 1995, R.E.M. were the very embodiment of moral rectitude, the pillar of virtue by which others set their standards. Many new fans would assume they always had been this way. But look back to their Eighties roots. This was the band whose original catalyst, Kathleen O'Brien, felt she was held back from becoming manager by her status as a female. The group of whom first office employee (and Jefferson Holt's then-girlfriend) says "always made sure I was treated like a secretary – and paid like one." The former college boys whose rhythm section – and their best buddy manager – helped establish the Athens Men's Club, from which women were banned, or forced to serve as topless waitresses.

On the road during those early years, R.E.M. indulged in many a rock'n'roll cliché, and they've no need to apologise for it. It's not as if they were The Beastie Boys, employing hydraulic penises as stage props and insisting that girls in the audience bare their breasts. But the fact that by the mid-Nineties The Beastie Boys were also seen as a totem of political correctness demonstrates that, generally speaking, boys will mature into men. R.E.M. had, by varying degrees over a fifteen-year period, grown up, settled down and left their carefree days behind them.

To what extent Jefferson had similarly matured remains as open to question as to what extent the allegations held true. Certainly, what may have been considered 'passable' behaviour among equals back in the early Eighties would have been considered 'unacceptable' in a management-employee relationship by the mid-Nineties. And while sexual stereotyping remains a constant within the entertainment industry – from which sexual harassment is by nature only a step away – it was strictly forbidden within the R.E.M. home office. Michael Stipe had publicly confirmed his bi-sexuality these last 18 months, and that rendered him particularly vulnerable to accusations of male sexism within his camp. He and the rest of the group were actively involved in social causes, from voter registration to pro-choice, environmental protection and animal rights. (As indeed was Jefferson Holt.) They could not afford public accusations of failing to practise what they preached.

And they never were. As Chuck Philips wrote, "The employee did not file a lawsuit or register a claim with the Equal Employment Opportunity Commission, but complained to the band that Holt had verbally harassed her with lewd remarks and demanded sexual favors."

The precise truth – as far as there can be one – will probably never emerge. The 'muzzle' clause of the settlement contract ensured that whatever dirt the two sides may have had on each other would stay permanently private and, presumably, Jefferson's pay-off was sufficient to cushion the assault on his character. Nonetheless, there are some who believe that the sexual harassment charges were an attempt to find 'for cause' – a legal reason to sack a manager who otherwise had contractual right to the band's past and future earnings. Katherine Dieckmann, who directed the group's 'Stand' and 'Shiny Happy People' videos, went on the record to state that she believed "the allegations were something of a smokescreen."

And there are those who firmly believe that the allegations were true, and that they were but the final straw in a long declining relationship, a breaking point upon which the band would not yield. "The incidents that actually heralded it," says Peter Buck of this final blow, "I didn't know anything about." Then again, he was in Seattle, as, thankfully for the sake of their artistic concentration, were the entire band for most of the investigations period, which apparently began in February and continued until the firing took place in May.

This is not to suggest that the band weren't distracted by the matter. Expelling a member of their gang, after fifteen years unbroken solidarity, was far more painful than the routine sacking of rock managers that goes on daily elsewhere in the business. "It was a very hard situation we had to deal with," says Peter Buck. "There was a huge sense of let down on our parts. We were all depressed about it. We had to deal with it for months. We had to finish this record. Bill had been sick. He had recovered fully but you could tell it had changed him. I never thought when I was writing songs when I was 15 that I would be sitting in a room deciding who could keep their job, how much we pay people, you never think about that. And it's hard. I hate doing it, I hate being a boss. All these people are dependent on the four of us to decide what goes on, and sometimes you just think, 'Fuck, I'm supposed to be the guitar player.' But on the other hand, one of the reasons we're in the position we are is that we've always watched ourselves. We've never been one of those bands that says, 'Just give me a pile of cocaine and do what you want to.' We've made every decision ourselves."

In the months after Holt's departure, the group were tight-lipped on the subject; the 'muzzle' clause of the termination clearly carried weight. As befits his role as the band's garrulous spokesman, Peter Buck was the only member who would issue more than a 'no comment'. Talking to Chris Heath of *Rolling Stone*, he fell back on the southern gentleman metaphor. "We want to do everything we do in a moral manner," he said. "And I feel that the four of us have . . . comported ourselves to the very best of our honour that we can handle."

Twenty

To *Q* magazine's Tom Doyle, he spoke another truth. And it's harsh. "Things change, people change, situations change . . . There are people who jump off the boat, there are some people that get left behind, and there are people who, y'know, we write out of the books or whatever."

R.E.M.'s ability to close ranks has already been noted. Except that this time, there was one less of them closing ranks. Bertis Downs IV, who would say nothing on the record but instead handed out a laminate with the band's official statement on it (a very Jefferson-like antic) assumed managerial duties. Jefferson's name was conspicuous by its absence from *New Adventures In Hi-Fi*. So was that of another long-serving office employee, management associate Brooke Johnson.

★   ★   ★

Over at Warner Brothers, there were enough break-ups, firings, law-suits and resignations taking place to make the situation between R.E.M., Jefferson Holt, and their office staff look like a tea party. The Nineties heralded a new era of corporate mergers, and as record companies became but floating assets for a select handful of multi-national corporations, the old, maverick days of the 'music biz' became but a memory. 'Bean counters' took over from 'music men' in positions of authority; a constant round of memos, e-mails and boardroom meetings replaced the old fly-by-the-seat-of-your-pants tactics. Corporate management was put under pressure from shareholders to improve the stock price; label bosses were put under pressure to produce instant results in turn. Artists that couldn't pay for themselves after one album – two at the most – were dropped to make way for fresh blood. Hit singles became more important than ever, even as the actual format of the single was made less available to the public. Marketing costs exploded as glitzy videos became ever more important to the 'breaking' of an artist; budgets began being allocated according to worldwide expectations, not domestic. And those executives that couldn't stomach the new way of doing business were quickly, and unapologetically, shown the door marked 'way out'.

Warner Brothers suffered the upheavals more than any label.

And more than made sense. For so many years the record divisions of the Warner Brothers empire had stood apart from the financial avarice that passed for common practice at other multi-nationals, had avoided the body count that was the daily price of commerce at other conglomerates. If it seemed like Mo Ostin and Lenny Waronker had been at Warner Brothers forever, well that's because they *had* been. Their utopian ideal that you could be music men first and foremost, from which loyalty would follow and profits would flow, became a self-fulfilling policy, and it brought groups like R.E.M. on board as a result. In the early Nineties, the 'W' in the WEA triumvirate – that is, the actual Warner Brothers label (which included Reprise and Sire, all of which fell under Mo and Lenny's domain) – was home to such commercial favourites and/or critical darlings as Madonna, Prince, Elvis Costello, Eric Clapton, The B-52's, Neil Young, David Byrne, Lou Reed, Enya, Erasure, Depeche Mode, Morrissey, Paul Simon, Rod Stewart, Tom Petty, Green Day, The Red Hot Chili Peppers and Dire Straits. And of course R.E.M. Add in the Elektra and Atlantic components of the WEA triumvirate and that list also included Natalie Merchant (and before she split from them in 1993, 10,000 Maniacs), Bjork, The Cure, Tracy Chapman, Metallica, Tori Amos, Hootie & The Blowfish, Jewel, and Jimmy Page and Robert Plant. WEA distributed other labels as well as its own, and it was the biggest in the business. The year R.E.M. signed to Warner Brothers, 1988, WEA distributed no less than 44 of that year's *Billboard* Top 100 albums.

But in 1989, Warner Brothers attempted to merge with Time, Inc. – an old-fashioned publishing empire that had expanded successfully into cable TV with the likes of HBO – and in the shareholder uproar that followed, ended up being bought *out* by Time, instead. Time had to borrow heavily to complete the deal. The new company, Time Warner, was therefore born with horrendous debt. Profit margins immediately came under close scrutiny throughout the increased empire – the money-making WEA being no exception. A new power structure emerged from the combined corporations: Jerry Levin from Time, Inc. and Robert Morgado from the Warner Music Group. Both were what the 'music men' derogatively call 'suits', but it was the suits now calling the shots.

And the first sights in their target were the ageing executives atop the music labels.

Though the hits kept coming, especially for R.E.M., Mo Ostin, who turned 67 years old in 1994, was being urged to name a successor and retire. Similar advice was being given to Ahmet Ertegun at Atlantic (71 years old) and to Bob Krasnow at Elektra (59 years old). When the three refused to abdicate their kingdoms, Morgado (a youthful 50) promoted Doug Morris (a mere 54), at the time the co-chairman of Atlantic, above their heads to oversee the entire empire. The move had the desired effect. Krasnow took a $7 million pay-off; Ertegun appointed a successor. And in August 1994, a month before *Monster* was released, Mo Ostin announced he would retire as Chairman/CEO of Warner Brothers Records when his contract ran out, at the end of the year. To this last move, there was uproar within the music business, and several artists threatened to jump ship; the most prominent was R.E.M., who had a particularly strong relationship with Ostin – and only one more album to deliver under their five-album contract.

To appease the outraged artists, Ostin was maintained as a consultant through 1995, and Warner Brothers President, Lenny Waronker (52) was asked to assume his mentor's role. Except that Waronker then decided instead to follow Ostin on to pastures greener at the end of *his* contract. Rob Dickens, who had successfully run Warner Brothers UK for two decades, was flown in on Concorde by Morgado to take over the US company; Morris vetoed the appointment, sent Dickens packing and swiftly elevated Danny Goldberg, the 44-year-old former manager of Nirvana who had only just started running Atlantic, to become Chairman/CEO of Warner Brothers Records instead. Under Morris' watch, Goldberg took over the reins in the first week of January 1995.

That same week, R.E.M. went to Australia to concentrate on what they did best – playing music. By the time they returned, the bloodletting at 75 Rockefeller Plaza in Manhattan read like a Stephen King novel. Jerry Levin had fired Bob Morgado (who got a $60 million golden parachute) and appointed Michael Fuchs from HBO in his place overseeing the Warner Music Group; six months later, Levin then fired Michael Fuchs (who, likewise, got a

$60 million pay-off) and hired Bob Daly and Terry Semel, from the Warner film studios, to run a new, combined, Movies and Records division called 'Entertainment'. In between hiring and firing Fuchs, Levin had also fired Doug Morris (who was sacked 'for cause', related to $150,000 worth of missing Atlantic stock; there were few who believed that this was not a smokescreen) and tried but failed to reinstate Mo Ostin in *his* place. As part of a wholesale clear-out of Morris acolytes, Danny Goldberg was gone too, with a rumoured $5 million pay-off for his seven-month stint. His former Vice-Chairman, Russ Thyret, became the new Chairman/ CEO of Warner Brothers Records, the man now answering to R.E.M.'s career in the role formerly held by Mo Ostin. Another insider, Steven Baker, was appointed as President, the role once held by Lenny Waronker.

Thyret and Baker knew full well that after delivering *New Adventures In Hi-Fi,* R.E.M. could walk. And as the most consistently successful and critically respected rock band of their generation, they could name their price at any of the other labels that came knocking. Thyret, who had been part of the Warner Brothers team that broke R.E.M. into the mainstream, therefore tried what Miles Copeland and Jay Boberg had attempted, unsuccessfully, towards the end of R.E.M.'s I.R.S. contract: renegotiate in the band's favour before the period was up.

For the time being, the band declined the offer. They had enough on their hands. Up in Seattle, the group were attempting to finish their new album. They were going through personal, professional and legal nightmares with Jefferson Holt. There was absolutely no way they were going to sign a new contract with any record company before signing a termination agreement with their former manager. "We wanted to get the Jefferson thing past before we committed to anything else," says Peter Buck, "because we didn't want him to have any part of it. I'm not stupid."

R.E.M. finished *New Adventures In Hi-Fi* around early May. Release was scheduled for September. Unlike the rush-released *Monster,* Warners had a solid four months to prepare for the release. And they appeared to be ecstatic about its potential. "The record company heard *Hi-Fi*," says Peter Buck, "and said, 'There are five top 10 singles on this record.' We said, 'Well you know we're not touring it,' and they said, 'Yeah, fine.' They were sure that it was a huge monster album the way *Monster* was."

There's no reason to doubt any of this. But there's every reason to think that Warner Brothers needed to *believe* that it had another monster album. The label was suffocating under the weight of bad press, and R.E.M. was its showcase band. What if the new hierarchy passed adverse comment to a group notorious for self-control – and proven, until now, to have accurate artistic instincts? What if this last album on R.E.M.'s contract did fail to match its predecessors upon release – and everyone in the industry blamed the label? Any negative noises, and R.E.M. might be tempted to move on to pastures greener themselves.

At the start of 1996, their own contracts with Warner Brothers having expired, Mo Ostin and Lenny Waronker were hired to run DreamWorks SKG, an entirely new label formed out of the heavily publicised partnership of entertainment moguls Stephen Spielberg, Jeffrey Katzenburg and David Geffen. Between SKG's start-up capital and Ostin and Waronker's hands-on stewardship, DreamWorks could very possibly provide R.E.M. with the best of all worlds. Mo and Lenny voiced their interest in taking the band on; R.E.M. listened attentively.

Scott Litt, meanwhile, was also moving into label ownership. His Outpost label, which would include as a partner the early I.R.S. employee and R.E.M. champion Mark Williams, was to be funded and distributed by Geffen Records.* Litt's was a familiar route for a successful record producer, and he no doubt had his eyes on former U2/Tom Petty/Bruce Springsteen producer Jimmy Iovine's success with Interscope as a blueprint. Peter Buck remembers Scott Litt telling him, during the *New Adventures In Hi-Fi* sessions, that, "If things work out the way I want, this is the last record I'm ever going to produce."

The R.E.M. public looked at Outpost and assumed that Litt would be trying to lure R.E.M. on board as his showcase act, but quite apart from the prohibitive costs of such a deal for a boutique

---

* That's the old Geffen Records, which David Geffen had sold several years earlier, and not to be confused with DreamWorks SKG.

label, the band's relationship with its producer of six albums' standing was on the verge of collapse anyway.

"I love Scott," Peter Buck prefaces with his usual southern gentleman manners. "But he was so not into it. When we went to LA to mix the last song (for *Hi-Fi*) he forgot to send the tapes. I was saying, 'You mean I just flew in from my family vacation in Hawaii, left my wife and kids in Hawaii to sit in the studio 'cos we don't have the tapes?' He was like, 'I was doing other stuff.' "

The problems with Litt ran deeper than that. It's been reported elsewhere that Litt fell into the 'pro-Jefferson camp' and that a childhood friend of his wife was apparently dating Jefferson Holt at the time, which can't have made the overdubs and mixing as easy a process as was claimed. And while it's fair to say that Scott Litt's stewardship of Outpost would have prevented him taking on another lengthy production job with R.E.M. regardless of his standing with the band, it's equally likely that had he *not* started Outpost, *New Adventures In Hi-Fi* would still have been his last album with the band. The ten-year working friendship between Litt and the band seems to have survived its fall out, but the band's former producer, once such a vocal champion, nonetheless declined to be interviewed for this overhaul of their biography.

Of the other major labels, surprisingly only Sony and Capitol were ever seriously in the running. Conspicuous by its absence from the bargaining table was MCA/Universal, where Jay Boberg was now President. One might have imagined Boberg holding an open chequebook, inviting R.E.M. to renew their relationship. Then again, MCA/Universal was distributing DreamWorks SKG.* And R.E.M. had not been enthralled at the manner in which I.R.S. kept repackaging its old albums and issuing new compilations. Boberg stayed hands-off, trusting that his corporation would get the band through Mo and Lenny.

On the face of it, there was absolutely no reason for R.E.M. to sign with anyone at this point. They could release *New Adventures In Hi-Fi*, go on holiday, and return to consider their future thereafter. A cynic might suggest that R.E.M. chose to sign at this point

---

* It also owned Geffen, which meant it was distributing Outpost too.

because they were fearful that *New Adventures* would not match its predecessors' sales – something that would certainly harm, though hardly destroy, any future deal. An optimist would instead look at the noises Warner Brothers made about signing now and consider it madness to refuse.

And Russ Thyret played the exact same ace card as Miles Copeland and Jay Boberg had attempted almost a decade earlier: higher royalties on the back catalogue. In 1987, R.E.M. had said no to I.R.S. on that score, understanding, with their usual solid instinct, that they had more to gain from future income than past sales. But in 1996, R.E.M. were at their commercial peak. Their four albums with Warner Brothers so far had sold 30–35 million copies worldwide. On an incredibly simplistic assumption that each royalty point is worth about 10 cents (of which, more later), that meant an extra $3 million-plus for every retroactive royalty point they could squeeze out of the label. And it was money already recouped: pure profit.

Certainly there were other reasons to stay with Warner Brothers. R.E.M. would not just earn more from their back catalogue with the label, but they would keep control of it, too. There was the fact that much of the middle management that worked so hard on the group was still at Warner Brothers in America. And outside the States, the label had performed a phenomenal job, justifying R.E.M.'s primary reason for coming off I.R.S. in the first place. Leaving now for another label would mean establishing new contacts in every single foreign territory, some of which the band was only just being discovered in. In fact, were it not for the corporate upheaval and revolving door of label heads at Warners, it would have been a no-brainer.

But that very problem played into R.E.M.'s hands. Warner Brothers needed R.E.M. to re-sign. Desperately. And immediately – so that the reign of Baker and Thyret could get off to a confident, positive-press generating start. The band and Bertis recognised that they would never be in a better bargaining position. They decided to milk it for every last drop.

To negotiate the new deal – and renegotiate the old one – Bertis Downs employed Donald Passman, an LA-based heavyweight who in 1991 had secured Janet Jackson an unprecedented $40 million advance from Virgin for three albums. Downs, Passman, Russ Thyret, and Steve Baker huddled in an office for two fourteen-hour days, hammering out the details.

In the third week of August WEA held its 25th annual convention, in Anaheim. It was the opportunity for the executives to sell their employees on the blockbuster releases for the all-important fourth quarter, and R.E.M.'s *New Adventures In Hi-Fi* was high on that list. On Saturday, August 24, a ten-minute audio-video promotion was aired for the album, after which, in a perfectly choreographed moment, Bertis Downs walked on stage and handed Russ Thyret a telegram. Thyret read it out to the staff.

"We've always said we'll only do this as long as it's still fun, and right now, it feels like we're just getting started, so let's keep going. R.E.M."

The 2,000 strong crowd of WEA employees jumped to their feet in exhilaration and relief. Some actually started crying. Watching from the stage, seeing how there were people in the music business who still put the music before the business, Thyret broke into tears, too. It was Steve Baker who got to release the official statement. "This is a watershed moment for Warner Bros. Records – an incredible new beginning for the company," it read. "R.E.M. embodies everything important about the culture of this company. They are a tremendously hard-working, successful band with integrity and vision. I can't describe how proud we are that R.E.M. is allowing Warner to continue our association with them."

Thyret's tears might have been of pain. He and Baker had just okayed the most expensive deal in recording history.

★   ★   ★

It was the *Los Angeles Times*' Chuck Philips who broke this story too. The morning after the deal was announced in nearby Anaheim, the paper printed the headline, "R.E.M., Warner Records Sign $80-Million Deal; Grammy-winning band will produce five albums under largest recording contract ever." Few readers took much time to read further – especially once the gross figure was bounced around the world's media without the small print. From that moment onwards, R.E.M. became known as 'the $80 million band'.

Understandably, it grates with them. "We didn't send out a press release," sighs Peter Buck. "Basically, one guy guessed, picked a number and he wasn't right."

But ask Buck whether it was indeed the 'largest recording contract ever', at that time, and he pauses. "I think it was," he says. And then he laughs, nervously. "It was pretty damn big."

Philips didn't get all his facts right on this story. Inaccuracies included the statement that R.E.M. "recently delivered the last of six albums under its previous contract" (it was the last of five), and that, "The band already had negotiated reversion of ownership rights to its current six-album Warner catalog." (As stated much earlier in this book, the original contract – for five albums – already *guaranteed* reversion of ownership to the band.) So the band are justified in disputing the financial figures put forward in the *LA Times*: "a $10 million signing bonus plus a $20 million royalty advance on future sales of its six-album Warner catalog. The band is also guaranteed an estimated $10 million advance per album plus a blue-chip 24% royalty on the retail price of each record sold."

But those who know the deal don't disagree that as ball park figures, these sums are just about correct. Of no dispute is that *New Adventures In Hi-Fi* was the fifth album in what would ultimately become a ten-album deal. Of less dispute is the 24% royalty – or that it covered *all* sales on the original five-album catalogue. In some dispute are the amounts of the advances. But add up $20 million paid against the back catalogue, $10 million guaranteed on each of five albums in the new deal, and $10 million against *New Adventures In Hi-Fi* under the same terms, and the career advances would indeed add up to $80 million.

This sum of money – or rather, the announcement of it – has probably done more to harm R.E.M.'s credibility than anything else in their career. And there are reasons why that was bound to have been the case. But first, let's look at the positive aspects, of which there are many. For in extracting such a stupendous deal out of Warner Brothers, R.E.M. made a statement on behalf of successful artists everywhere: that if you can time your negotiations correctly, you can get paid what *you're actually worth*.

There's enough history to fill a book – and there are plenty already in print – on how the music industry has routinely ripped off its artists over the years. Such violations extend from pathetically low royalties*, through to nonsensical deductions (such as 'packaging' and 'new technology', which combined can strip away 30% of an album's percentage base, though that money still goes to the label) through to outright theft, as the number of court cases in which artists sue labels for non-payment or accounting irregularities are testament. In his book *Exploding: The Highs, Hits, Hype, Heroes and Hustlers of the Warner Music Group*, former Warners executive Stan Cornyn breaks down a 15% royalty on a $16 CD to show why an artist receives, not the $2.40 you would expect from doing the basic maths, but $1.22 instead. Former Nirvana producer Steve Albini has published an excellent essay that shows a textbook case of how a four-piece band selling 250,000 albums on a major label ends up with only $4,000 per member for a year or two's work, while the label has banked over $700,000 profit.†

R.E.M., of course, were smarter than most other acts signed to major record companies. They came to Warner Brothers in 1988 as a platinum act still on the upswing, and negotiated one of the best deals in the industry at that time. Most notably, they retained ownership of their master recordings, leasing them to the label for a specific period of time.‡ But the scale of R.E.M.'s success in the Nineties rendered that 1988 deal so much small fry. Here's why – and why the new deal was justified.

THE BASICS:
By 1996, R.E.M. had sold, as previously stated, some 30–35 million copies of its four Warner Brothers albums worldwide. (Approximate sales: *Green,* 4 million; *Out Of Time,* 12 million; *Automatic For The People* 10 million; *Monster,* 9 million.) Warner Brothers owns its distribution company, WEA, which means the company receives income from record and CD sales right up until the record

---

* The Beatles are reputed to have received half an old penny per track on their early singles and albums, rising annually by a farthing – a quarter of an old penny – and there were 240 old pennies to £1.
† http://www.negativland.com/albini.html
‡ Prince, who had spent years trying – and failing – to get a similar deal, took to wearing the word 'Slave' on his face in protest.

stores buy them. Using dollar figures, because that's the currency R.E.M. get paid in, the country where they were selling most records, and the home of the Time Warner corporation and their contract – and ignoring the fact that CDs actually retail for more outside the USA – it's fair to say that WEA banks at least $10 for CD sales to record stores. Basic maths says that R.E.M. had therefore generated well over $300 million in direct income for its label with those four albums – and that doesn't include the considerable single sales or home video sales. According to the original deal, R.E.M. were receiving guarantees of between $2–$3 million an album, meaning they'd been fronted a total of approximately $10 million in advances across the four albums. The Warner Music Group had banked over $300 million. That's over a 3,000% gross return on investment. No wonder R.E.M. were given free use of the Acapulco hide-away.

ROYALTY RATE

The 24% royalty rate has not been strongly denied. In his *LA Times* story, Chuck Philips suggested that this would average out to $2.50 an album. Perhaps so for a lesser artist, but given R.E.M.'s shrewd business sense, that seems low. As R.E.M. did not have new technology deductions, and had surely snubbed out the inexplicable packaging deductions too (were albums meant *not* to be packaged?) they were probably receiving their 24% based on the standard 90% of a CD's $16 recommended retail price. This would put their income per CD album closer to $3.45. Allow for further deductions from foreign sales (unjustifiable, given that Warner Brothers had the band for the globe), allow that some fans were still buying vinyl, consider that Warner Brothers was probably fronting video costs that required recoupment and so on, and split the difference. Assume that R.E.M. were now going to be paid $3 a CD sale. It's more than almost anyone else, but Warner Music Group, remember, was grossing $10 per CD. And on a mega-platinum act, that leaves a lot of room for profit.

FUTURE ADVANCES

R.E.M. had averaged 10 million sales on each of their last three albums. To make back a $10 million advance at their new 24%

royalty ($3 a CD) meant selling around 3–3.5 million albums a time, worldwide. It must have seemed near impossible to the record label that their fan base could fall away so rapidly for those figures to not make sense. Admittedly, such sales estimates would apply all the way to the band's fifteenth studio album, unproven territory except for perhaps The Rolling Stones and Aerosmith. But for the time being, R.E.M. had merely ensured their advances saw them receive perhaps half the sum up front of what they had previously waited two years or more to receive down the line.

BACK CATALOGUE

Miles Copeland had suggested, back in 1988, that R.E.M.'s royalty rate on the first Warner Brothers deal was going to break 20%. Perhaps that's what the band wanted him to believe. Insiders have since claimed the band signed for 18%, still an extremely high rate.* Again, no one seriously disputes that the new royalty rate, as of 1996, became 24% of retail. Those same insiders insist that royalty was applied, retroactively, to the band's back catalogue, which makes sense; this was the ace card by which Warners successfully gambled on keeping the band. Working on the 'Royalty Rate' maths that each percentage point was worth about 12.5 cents to the band ($3 divided by 24), multiplying that by the extra six royalty points (the jump from 18%–24%) and applying that retroactively to the 30 million-plus album sales easily accounts for the $20 million 'advance' on back catalogue earnings. Were R.E.M. to apologise for being in a strong enough position to get an increased back-dated royalty out of their label? "Of course you're going to pay us more money, that's the way it works," says Peter Buck. "That said, they have a thousand lawyers, they're a huge corporation, one of the biggest companies on earth. I certainly don't feel we took advantage of them." When all was said and done, the bottom line for the back catalogue was that for the $300 million-plus income that Warner Brothers had banked from the band thus far, it would ultimately, over a delayed period of

* Even Madonna was only able to extricate a 20% royalty when renegotiating at the peak of her own powers, in 1992.

time, be paying R.E.M. approximately $100 million. That's *still* a 300% net return on investment.

COMPARATIVE INCOME

R.E.M. were now going to get paid $10 million an album, up front. It's a lot of money. Then again, they were only releasing an album every two years, which brings the guarantee down to $5 million a year. There were four of them plus management. As owners of their recordings, they should have been paying their own recording costs – and producer fees too. Warner Brothers was guaranteeing them considerably less than a million dollars a year each.

Compare that to the salaries of the top executives at Warner Brothers. When Doug Morris was fired 'for cause', Time Warner leaked the details of the short-term CEO's income since taking over at the start of that year: it was almost $10 million – not including stock options, chauffeurs, access to the corporate jet and the kind of unlimited expense accounts that are routine for the top dogs. That was the same year that Robert Morgado was seen off with a $60 million compensation package, followed just a few months later by a similar farewell to Michael Fuchs. Those still running the labels would have to get by on seven-figure salaries, middle and senior management on six-figures. Against such pay-offs and pay-outs, the $60 million guaranteed to R.E.M. for delivering six albums over twelve years doesn't look so exorbitant.

Of course R.E.M. can count on plenty of other income besides the record label advances. Publishing alone – given that they own that too – could easily double the figure of $10 million on a hit album, and merchandising is always a cash cow. The *Monster* tour was intended to make money, and R.E.M. had started contributing songs to soundtracks too. Still, they avoided all sponsorships, had withdrawn from the road again and refused to sell their songs to TV commercials. They employed a full office staff working solely on their behalf, kept select members of the road crew on retainers, paid hefty legal and accountancy fees, covered health insurance, and though they could write off all manner of these expenses against tax, they were still the ones signing their own expense accounts at the end of the day. R.E.M./Athens Ltd. had grown to be a significant corporation with an eight-figure annual income by 1996, but it was not Time Warner.

⋆　⋆　⋆

For all these reasons, the band should have been praised for forcing a corporation to ante up to its clients what they were actually worth. Instead R.E.M. received a tidal wave of negative publicity that painted them as greedy and complacent; the fall out has never really subsided. "It did affect the way people look at us," says Peter Buck. "I understand that. It went from being here's this band who makes really cool records, to here's this band who makes really good records – and are they worth it? Well, probably not."

The public is routinely subjected to media reports of high income – it's part of the celebrity culture we live in. We know that Arnold Schwarzanegger and Julia Roberts each get paid $20 million a movie, even if the film turns out to be a dog. We know that top footballers in the UK are now on £50,000 a week plus bonuses, even though many of them are prima donnas with no loyalties to the working-class fans who earn less in a year than their supposed heroes earn in a week. We know too that supermodels "don't get out of bed for less than $10,000 a day" – and that was a decade ago. TV personalities get paid millions a year, often just for being blonde. Superstar DJs can make ten grand a night. All of this we excuse for any number of reasons: they have limited years of earning potential; they'll bring home a cup for 'our' team; their employers can afford it; their peers are getting it; it's the nature of capitalism. But mostly it's because we consider all these people 'entertainers' and we don't expect much from our entertainers in the way of scruples.

Artists are different. Artists are not meant to get rich. Be they working in the visual, literary or musical fields, those who profess to care about their output are meant to suffer for their art, not get paid millions up front for it. The alternative music culture reinforces this perception with particular acuteness: from the blues on through rock'n'roll, psychedelia, folk and punk, the culture grew out of the working class and/or social protest. The idea of such artists making millions seems to negate their purpose.

Deep down, we know full well that anyone who sells millions of records (or books, or paintings) is either making millions – or needs a new agent. And we don't *really* begrudge our artists their income as long we don't hear about it. R.E.M. on I.R.S. were a prime example of going about it the credible way. By taking low advances and high royalties, the band could claim a certain altruism even as they banked healthy royalty cheques from year one. R.E.M. during their first tenure at Warner Brothers upped the ante considerably, but the public face of the band was still that of a group engaged in charity and social causes, eschewing the mainstream and the big payday; we knew that those millions of album sales were being accounted to them at a high royalty, we just didn't sit down and figure out what they were actually making.

Once the group was exposed, however, for taking the biggest up-front payday in the history of the music business, the perspective changed. They were seen as being greedy at best, hypocritical at worst. And it's true, the huge advances went very much against the philosophy of a band that had always insisted you focus on the back end. (Then again, you couldn't do much better than a back end royalty of 24% either.) Short of setting up their own label, or going into a 50–50 partnership with a company – engaging in their own financial risk for greater profits – the band couldn't ask to have it both ways. R.E.M. were in the spotlight like never before, and they had a better opportunity for renegotiation than ever before. But each aspect fed off the other so that for the first time, R.E.M.'s business – including the fall out with Jefferson – was conducted in public. It's fair to say that the whole experience soured their relationship with a number of their long-term fans.

Twenty-one

The media push for *New Adventures In Hi-Fi* was the antithesis of *Monster*. No rented castles in Ireland, no sojourns in Nice, no grand tour announcements or self-financed TV documentaries. Almost the entire publicity campaign was conducted in Los Angeles, during the same few days that the group made their first two videos for the album, 'E-Bow The Letter' and 'Bittersweet Me'. This meant TV cameramen filming the video shoots, magazine journalists reporting on satellite TV interviews, band members wondering aloud why they'd agreed to such a circus, and as drunken respite, a members-only party at Mike Mills' new holiday home in the Hollywood Hills.

Somewhere in the middle of it all, Michael Stipe managed to talk a little bit about the new album. "If there is something thematic to this record," he explained, "it's that it is very similar to our first album, *Murmur*. When we were on the road the first time, in '82 and '83, travelling from town to town and playing small clubs, the songs that emerged were about travel and movement and being away from home, wherever home is. And this record has at least a little bit of the same feel. The songs we wrote on the road have a feeling of movement, of passage, a feeling of being distant, whether it's geographic distance or otherwise."

There were religious sub-texts as well, but that too was nothing new for R.E.M.. "More dark, sad songs about death and anxiety," he joked to *Rolling Stone*, referencing *Automatic For The People*. And just as with that album, the group welcomed the release with near silence. There were no more photo ops, almost no interviews, not a TV appearance, acoustic show or secret gig in Athens. *New Adventures In Hi-Fi* was going to have to stand on its own merits.

The same August week that R.E.M. re-signed with Warner Brothers, they released 'E-Bow The Letter' as a single. Aided by the amiable instrumental 'Tricycle' and the Richard Thompson cover 'Wall Of Death' as two of the group's more collectable B-sides in recent years, it crashed into the UK charts at number four, the band's highest position to date. Celebrations were curtailed when the next week it dropped to number 15. It was out of the top 30 before *New Adventures In Hi-Fi* made it to the shops. In the USA, 'E-Bow The Letter' ambled slowly up the Hot 100 to its peak of 49, and drifted quietly away again. The video, a dry Jem Cohen clip with the band shown playing in Los Angeles and Patti Smith shot in Prague, did not get the kind of heavy rotation R.E.M. had once taken for granted.

Still, the hit singles world is a notoriously fickle one. The albums market is more reliable and on that score R.E.M.'s popularity seemed well secured. *New Adventures In Hi-Fi* was released worldwide the second week of September and promptly went to number one in some fifteen countries, including Germany, Holland, Australia and Canada. In the UK, it followed its three predecessors by going straight to the top spot, selling well over 100,000 copies that first week. In the USA, *New Adventures* SoundScanned an admirable 227,000 copies in seven days; unfortunately for R.E.M., New Edition's *Home Again* SoundScanned 1,000 copies more. It wasn't considered a major disappointment: *Automatic For The People* had also stalled at number two, and nobody was griping about *that* one all these years later. Then again, *Automatic* had been held off the top spot by America's most popular artist, Garth Brooks, not by the reunion of Bobby Brown's boy band.

As important as initial sales undoubtedly were, equal focus was being placed on the album's critical reaction. After the guarded praise for *Monster,* and on the understanding that *New Adventures In Hi-Fi* was a hard-sell to the mainstream, it was vital that the press resumed its infatuation with the band. And they did, wholeheartedly. "A triumph," wrote Bill Prince in a five-star *Q* magazine review, "easily the most diverse set of tunes R.E.M. have yet chosen to deliver." "There's a sense of spontaneity here that's rarely been heard on an R.E.M. record. . . . a sense of ambition and liberation," commended David Fricke in another four-and-a-half-star *Rolling Stone* review. *NME* accurately called it "not an easy album but . . . a great one." *Entertainment Weekly* came back around, writing that "if the arena-designed, occasionally forced *Monster* felt like a midlife crisis, *New Adventures In Hi-Fi* finds R.E.M. returning to their joyful idiosyncrasies." The *New York Times* talked of "a beautiful hodgepodge", and the *LA Times*, which had inadvertently caused the band so much grief these past few weeks, concluded that R.E.M. "not only competes creatively with the best of the new '90s outfits, but ranks favourably when measured against the greatest bands ever."

'Bittersweet Me', with a Dominic De Joseph-directed video that juxtaposed a band performance with a spoof movie set in Rome, where Stipe had followed Patti Smith on tour during the summer, was released as the second single in November. It only edged into the UK top 20 and like its predecessor barely brushed the US top 50. 'Electrolite' – once more the soft song for the third single – was rushed out in the UK for Christmas; it but grazed the UK top 30 and sank without trace in the States. The video was entrusted to Spike Jonze, who replaced the song's inherent melancholia with a desert storm of dune buggies and comic costumes. The result, like his 'Crush With Eyeliner' clip, was most un-R.E.M., but at least this time it reflected his humour – and yet it still didn't go into heavy rotation.

The truth is that the musical marketplace had shifted again and while R.E.M. had looked down upon the last sea change – the ascendancy of American alternative – from a position of authority, they were now being viewed by many taste-makers, editors and programmers as part of the old guard, the establishment. In the UK, 1996 was the year of Cool Britannia, the country turning in on itself in a self-serving celebration of Britpop, the European football championship and the inevitable collapse of Conservative rule. One of last year's R.E.M. support groups, Oasis, was now spoken of as the biggest British band since The Beatles, its *(What's The Story) Morning Glory* album outselling R.E.M.'s *Out Of Time*, even in America. The week that *New Adventures In Hi-Fi* was released, the number one single in the UK was 'Wannabe' by The Spice Girls, who by the end of '96 would be sweeping American culture too as part of the wholesale introduction of a new fabricated pop boom. Meanwhile, the white American suburban audience was lapping up the gangster rap of Snoop Doggy Dogg, Tupac Shakur and Notorious B.I.G. – assassinations and murder trials notwith-standing – and the industrial-Alice Cooper shtick of Marilyn Manson. Grunge was on the ropes, with Pearl Jam heading to the margins, Alice In Chains and Stone Temple Pilots boring with their rumoured heroin addictions. The only album from the once-known-as college culture to rightfully break the mainstream was Beck's masterpiece *Odelay*. Musically, R.E.M. were trapped between rock and a hard place.

The generation that had grown up with R.E.M. in the Eighties, that had enthusiastically shared and applauded the maturity of *Out Of Time* and *Automatic For The People*, many of whom had stuck around for *Monster,* was ready now to move on. Not to new artists, but to their home mortgages, car payments and children's birthday parties. They'd still be there if the group wanted to tour the hits, they'd probably be back if the band released another single that struck the 'universal chord'. But they would no longer maintain their obsession.

Ironically, the fact that *New Adventures* was, in most respects, a better album than *Monster* was one of the reasons it didn't do so well. There's no denying that many fans who'd been in for the long haul – and especially those who came on board with the pop cross-over of 'Losing My Religion' or 'Everybody Hurts' – had been disappointed by the forced grunge-glam of *Monster*. A large number decided to pass this time around. They were hardly encouraged to change their minds by the lack of a strong single. R.E.M. fans who wanted to see 'their band' succeed were left scratching their heads at the choice of 'E-Bow The Letter' and 'Bittersweet Me' when 'The Wake-Up Bomb' and 'Departure' seemed so much more like, well, *singles*.

The band seemed nonplussed on that one. "We thought we were at the position that we could put out a single that was a little difficult but was really great and beautiful," says Peter Buck of a song whose title never featured in the lyrics. "It's one of the favourite things we've done, the way it floats into that chorus and with Patti, I thought it was a great thing. Maybe I overestimated the patience people have with us."

Maybe. Although one shouldn't discount overkill either. *New Adventures In Hi-Fi* was R.E.M.'s fifth album of the Nineties; the band had barely been off the radio or out of the press for more than a few months since early 1991. Had *New Adventures In Hi-Fi* been your usual live souvenir, it would simply have marked the closing of a chapter; two years later, absence making the heart grow fonder and all that, the audience would have been ready to welcome the band back with open arms. But as a 'proper' album release – it was, after all, 65 minutes of new songs – *Hi-Fi* followed so soon on the heels of the band's *Monster* year that some fans (especially the fairweather ones) felt overwhelmed. The sense of overkill was hardly helped by the negative publicity surrounding the break-up with Jefferson and the out-of-proportion new record deal; it could even be suggested that Jefferson's careful control of the band's public image was notable by its absence.

R.E.M. understood just about all of this. They'd fully expected, even encouraged, a drop-off from the *Monster* mainstream and they got it. In the UK, where the band had played to half a million people in one week just the summer before, *New Adventures In Hi-Fi* never sold more than half a million copies in all. (*Automatic* had done two million in the UK, *Monster* around one million.) In the USA, the drop-off was even more pronounced: though certified platinum out of the box, five years later it had still not SoundScanned one million. That meant a no-show by two-thirds of the people who'd bought *Monster*; Warner Brothers executives who'd expected to reach their three million break-even in America alone, began crossing their fingers that they'd get there in total global sales.

On the upside, R.E.M. noticed that in the countries that had only recently taken to them, sales held more than steady. By the time it was all done, *New Adventures In Hi-Fi* would sell close to five million copies worldwide, and the band would have stood by it with total pride. "Mike, Peter, and I all feel like *New Adventures In Hi-Fi* was as close to a perfect record as we've ever made," said Michael Stipe two years after its release. "That record, if anything, was a rock band playing together live."

Equally, it remains many a fan's favourite; just as the first generation holds up *Lifes Rich Pageant*, released on the cusp of the mainstream breakthrough, as their cult classic, so the second generation came to favour *New Adventures In Hi-Fi*, released at the eclipse of the mainstream period, as both the one that proved their loyalty and as 'the one that got away'. For R.E.M., given their complete lack of commercial expectations when they started fifteen years earlier, then the millions of sales, and the hardcore fans' enthusiasm for an album recorded largely at soundchecks, provided more than sufficient succour. The cup of life remained more than half full.

*   *   *

Following the release of *New Adventures In Hi-Fi*, the R.E.M. members returned to their own worlds. Bill Berry holed up on his farm in Watkinsville where, he explained, "I've worked out a lot of problems on my tractor." Mike Mills flew round Europe for some *New Adventures In Hi-Fi* listening parties, sang 'The Star-Spangled Banner' at the start of an Atlanta Braves game (no small honour), continued perfecting his golf game with his well-heeled Republican friends, and showed up at the occasional gig in Athens.

Michael Stipe stumped for Bill Clinton, who was easily re-elected in November '96 against last-of-the-World-War-II candidates Bob Dole. (It was further confirmation of R.E.M. as the establishment now that they were backing the incumbents rather than the challengers.) He sang with Patti Smith and Natalie Merchant at a Tibetan benefit at New York's prestigious Carnegie Hall. And, undeterred by the failure of *Desolation Angels*, he put his film producer's cap back on and, under the auspices of his new company, Single Cell Pictures, set about getting *Velvet Goldmine* into production. The Todd Haynes script was a continuation of the glam rock obsession that had fuelled *Monster,* an unapologetically ambitious reworking of the relationship between a fictionalised David Bowie and Iggy Pop with particular focus on the concepts of personal and artistic reinvention, and (bi)sexual experimentation – in other words, a perfect cinematic project for Stipe.

Part of Michael's task as Executive Producer was finding the right musicians to play both on- and off-screen roles, and he flew to London in the new year of 1997 to check out glam revivalists Placebo, among others. It seems somewhat surprising that Stipe would so enthusiastically take on a job that is a constant round of phone calls, pitches, faxes, letters, e-mails and face-to-face meetings; one can imagine Stipe preferring to act, direct, or merely photograph – anything that allows him to concentrate on making the art, as opposed to conducting the business. But this was clearly no dilettantish diversion; Stipe pursued the project with blind dedication, and *Velvet Goldmine* finally went into production with financing from Miramax among others. Jonathan Rhys Meyers would play Bowie as the fictional Brian Slade; Ewan McGregor, looking much like Kurt Cobain, would play Iggy as the fictional Curt Wild. The musical cast would only further blur lines between fact and fiction, past and present. Under Stipe's encouragement, two different all-star house bands were assembled. The Venus In Furs featured Thom Yorke from Radiohead, and Andy McKay from Roxy Music; The Wylde Rats included, among other American post punk notables, Don Fleming and Thurston Moore, who had performed similarly in the Backbeat Band.*

Peter Buck was undertaking a similarly pivotal role in Seattle. Having played with Scott McCaughey in The Minus 5, and brought McCaughey into R.E.M.'s touring band, he was also playing regularly with The Screaming Trees' drummer Barrett Martin. When Martin formed an instrumental act Tuatara with Luna's bass player Justin Harwood, Buck quickly volunteered his services. "First day together I wrote two songs," he remembers. "So I was in the band." Tuatara's début album, *Breaking The Ethers,* was recorded in late 1996 and released through Sony in '97; it would confound expectations by incorporating Asian and African influences into an ambient ethic. Buck also found both time and enthusiasm to help co-write an album for Seattle-based American Music Club vocalist Mark Eitzel; when it came time to record, the Tuatara collective was brought in as backing band.

This was all in character; Buck hated to sit still. And it was equally Peter Buck's nature to announce his main band's future intentions; by doing so, he set the group public goals that all four of them then had reason to meet. "I like to lead from behind," he explains. "It's like, 'Here's a bunch of demos, this is where I'm going,' as opposed to saying, 'This is what I'm gonna do, what do

---

* If Mike Mills seemed notable by his absence from this project, it was largely out of an unspoken understanding that R.E.M. members would not involve themselves in each other's off-duty projects.

you think?' I'm always the one who has the first ideas, that's my job." Upon *Out Of Time*'s release he'd stated that he wanted to make a chamber record, something more overtly orchestral, and the result had been, suitably enough, *Automatic For The People*. On release of that album, he announced enthusiasm for a trashy rock'n'roll record with a full-blown tour, and *Monster* had followed in due course. During the promotion for *Monster,* he advertised the intent to record new songs on the road, which Michael Stipe has claimed caught him by surprise; still, *New Adventures In Hi-Fi* came about, and out, more or less as planned.

In August 1996, conducting interviews for the latest R.E.M. album, he was already on to the next one, implying the others would come out to his house in Hawaii, write a new crop of songs, engage in their own activities for a few months, then return to the studio and maybe head back onto the road. He reasoned that by recording constantly, the band never had to lose time second-guessing its creativity, or worrying about the peaks and valleys of record sales. He admitted to an obsession with working "while I still have the time"; he would turn forty that December.

The other R.E.M. members, still in their mid-thirties yet often left breathless by the oldest member's relentless musical ambitions, agreed to his timing, thankful as always that someone else was willing to set the agenda. The four of them reconvened at Peter's house on the island of Maui, in Hawaii, in late March.

Buck, as usual, brought the most ideas to the table. He had set up a simple studio in the attic of his Seattle home, and filled it with first-generation beat boxes, analogue synths and primitive key-boards like the Mellotron, the Baldwin Discover, the Kitten and the Univox. Unable any longer to pop down to the West Clayton Street rehearsal room in Athens and jam with Bill and Mike, he would use the drum machines for rhythmic backing. By the time he'd added other instrumentation, often with Scott McCaughey by his side and frequently using his new-old electronic gear, it sounded less like R.E.M. than anything he'd ever written. And he liked it.

So, it seemed, did the others. In Hawaii, Peter, Mike and Michael spent most of each afternoon and evening recording on to a four-track tape deck in Peter Buck's living room, trying out the drum machines, vintage synths and effects units with the wide-eyed enthusiasm of unattended kids in a toy store. Michael Stipe saw in the electronic-ambient sparseness of the demos the opportunity to follow his favourite R.E.M. songs like 'Country Feedback', 'E-Bow The Letter', 'New Test Leper' and 'Undertow'. "There were places that I went to in those songs, whether it was the loose, thematic style of writing or the subject matter, that I wanted to take off from to make this record," he explained a year later.

It was soon obvious that the fuzzy arena rock that had dominated their last two albums would be confined to the past; the new songs brought back R.E.M.'s love of pure melody and immediacy, while the instrumentation suggested they would be anything but conventional. A little like Elton John as performed by Suicide, as Peter put it.

Bill Berry was physically present for the Hawaii sessions, but in other ways, he was entirely absent. If this sounded like Jefferson Holt a couple of years earlier, the comparison was apt. Berry had taken the legal fall-out with Jefferson particularly badly. "It was hard for all of us," said Peter Buck, "but it was soul destroying for him. He was just shaking." Buck had felt a lack of interest from Berry during the final stages of *New Adventures In Hi-Fi*, but then the band was used to his cutting out early. On the first tour of Japan, back in '84, Bill had earned the nickname 'I Go Now' for his tendency to excuse himself prematurely. Since settling on his farm, his hours had moved even further forward; in direct contrast to the typical rock drummer, Bill was rising at dawn and setting off for bed at dusk.

Berry came to Hawaii with the additional pressures of a divorce upon him, and a total unwillingness to tour again. "I found myself wandering out to the beach and looking at the waves and stuff while the other guys were inside working away," he said a few months later. "I put some things on tape, but my heart wasn't in it."

"We noticed," said Michael Stipe of Bill's emotional distance. "He just wasn't as involved. And maybe personally we were trying to gloss over that. Like maybe he was just having a bad week or something."

"I knew something was going on," says Buck. "I didn't know

what. I always tried talking to Bill, like maybe you want to see a therapist or a marriage counsellor, but he didn't want to do that kind of stuff." As with Jefferson, the friendships – foibles and all – were so deeply ingrained that there was an unwillingness to sit down and confront any personality problems.

The Hawaii sessions finished in April and the band went their separate ways for a few months. Mike Mills engaged in writing a movie soundtrack, though his compositions for the film *A Cool Dry Place* never saw release. He and Stipe graced the stage at an outdoor Tibetan Freedom Concert in New York City at the start of June, playing a few *New Adventures* songs acoustically before sharing vocal duties on some covers with Pearl Jam's Eddie Vedder and The Beastie Boys' Mike D. In the process, they volunteered the whole band's services for a similar but bigger event next year.

Peter Buck took his floating Seattle line-up on the road throughout the month of May. The Magnificent Seven versus The United States was an old-fashioned revue in which different per-mutations of the entourage (Tuatara, The Minus 5, Mark Eitzel and Peter Buck) performed brief sets during an all-night show that lasted a good two hours. The seven musicians were Buck, McCaughey, Martin, Eitzel, Harwood, Skerik Walton (of Critter's Buggin' and Tuatara) and Dan Pearson (of American Music Club). As with an R.E.M. tour, the last date for the Magnificent Seven was in Atlanta, and the other three members all came out to watch. Mike and Michael duly stepped up to play some R.E.M. songs and cover versions for the encores; Bill Berry left before he could be called upon.

★   ★   ★

R.E.M. settled on Pat McCarthy to replace Scott Litt. The genial, 30-year-old Irishman had worked on a couple of *New Adventures In Hi-Fi* sessions at Scott Litt's studio in Los Angeles – what he calls mere "fixing and mixing" – and had just come off engineering Madonna's latest, *Ray Of Light*, and mixing k.d. lang's *Drag*. Michael Stipe was particularly taken by McCarthy's mixes for Patti Smith's *Gone Again* album, Peter Buck by his production on Joe Henry's *Trampoline* and Luna's *Pup Tent*. Such were his impeccable credentials that he was hired over the phone.

311

McCarthy flew into Athens that first week of October. Peter Buck came down from Seattle with both Scott McCaughey and Barrett Martin; the inclusion of the additional all-rounder musicians was intended to encourage further experimentation with the instrumentation. In conversations with Pat McCarthy, there had been much talk about stripping down the drum sound, about using beat boxes, maracas and suchlike rather than a conventional drum kit. It turned out to be prescient thinking.

The Seattle trio booked into their hotel late on Sunday night, October 5. Mike Mills called Peter there and then to let him know that, "I just want you to walk in to rehearsal tomorrow to be prepared. Bill's going to tell you something and you're not going to want to hear it." Mills and Berry having been friends since high school, the bass player had been given advance warning by the drummer as to his intent.

Curiously, neither Peter Buck nor Michael Stipe expected the worst. "This is the best job on Earth and you make a ton of money doing it," reasoned Peter. Bill would have to be not right in the head to quit.

But that's exactly what Bill wanted to do. He gathered the other three together in private and told them that his heart was no longer in it, that he wanted out of R.E.M. He was going to quit the band. To their pained and dumbfounded expressions, he added if his departure meant they would break up, he'd stay – but only for their sakes.

"I'd be lying if I said my brain surgery two or three years ago didn't have a little to do with it," Bill told hometown newspaper the *Athenaeum*'s Rich Copley three weeks later. "I think that while I'm physically in good shape – my brain works fine – just going through that process of being really that sick and coming out of it and lying in a hospital bed for three weeks made me kind of look at things a little differently and shift priorities. It's not a tangible thing. Why would I want to quit? Why would anyone be wild enough to do something like this? I don't know. It's just what I feel in my heart."

The others begged him to reconsider. R.E.M. had been together for almost 18 years without a line-up change: of all the major rock bands since The Beatles, only U2 could claim a longer unbroken relationship. They would therefore bend over backwards to accommodate his issues. "I was saying, 'Well God Bill, if you don't want to travel, make the records in your barn,'" says Peter Buck. "'You don't come to the mixing anyway. You don't want to tour, well, do we have plans to tour?' [Actually, they did.] But for him, it just weighed on him. Every bit of it. He dreaded doing demos, he dreaded doing a record, he dreaded travelling, and he would think about it for the six months previous. One interview and he would worry about it for a month. We could see all that happening, and my feeling was that he would just say, 'I don't want to do these things anymore.' Theoretically for him, he could have done the whole record in Athens, three weeks of taping, gone home and not thought about it again for a year and a half. Basically he just didn't want to think about it."

Bill remained adamant that he wanted to leave. Not that he had any plans other than tending his farm. His divorce from Mari was being finalised at almost exactly the same time; it was as if he wanted to start his life all over again. Yet he reiterated his willingness to keep going if the band were going to break up over it.

This put the other three in a quandary. They'd frequently stated that if one member went, it would no longer be R.E.M. – so if they let him go and continued the band, they'd be called on their hypocrisy by both the media and the fans. Then again, they'd also stated they'd only keep going for as long as it was fun. For Bill, it had stopped being fun. Yet for the other three, R.E.M. was as enjoyable now as it ever had been. They didn't want to stop. They had the best record contract in the world, they had a fan base of five million worldwide, they'd just come off what they considered one of their finest albums, and they'd regained their critical respect after an intensely difficult two years. They also had forty new songs that they didn't want to abandon. Particularly as these songs circumvented the conventional rock line-up.

"I was already geared up," Peter Buck told Rich Copley. "It's one of those weird coincidences in life that I've been getting into using drum machines and building loops and samplers and stuff, and I have a little sampler in my house and then all of a sudden we don't have a drummer so I'm kind of semi-prepared. It's also really weird, but I was kind of liking the spareness and the sparseness, and

I was talking to Michael about how we could possibly break down the idea of the band as a four-piece and Bill could play guitar and bass and keyboards. Maybe Bill could play lead guitar and I'll play maracas." Buck, clearly, was not one for ending the band.

Over at John Keane's studio, Keane, McCaughey, McCarthy and Martin remained in the dark as to what was occurring. "Bill just *wasn't there*," recalls McCaughey, "and nobody was saying anything about it." The other three R.E.M. members were still desperately hoping to change Bill's mind. "But after talking to him for three weeks," said Michael Stipe at the end of October, "I know that he doesn't want to stay and we have to respect that." The band decided to continue without him.

"It made me the happiest guy in the world," said Bill. "Because I didn't want to be the schmuck who broke R.E.M. up."

★   ★   ★

Once the decision had been accepted, the group had to figure out how to break the news. As a partner, Bertis Downs had been privy to all but the first discussion. The others over at John Keane's were notified now too, in person by Bill, after which the sessions were abruptly cancelled, with barely a demo for a song 'Falls To Climb' completed. It was now only a matter of days – perhaps hours – before word spread around Athens, and with it, the world. The group had learned from its experience the previous summer with Jefferson's firing and the new deal with Warner Brothers how important it was to control publicity, and they didn't want people to think the band was disintegrating. On October 30, Warner Brothers issued a press release, announcing Bill's departure in the softest terms possible, stressing the word 'amicable'. It was just the kind of announcement that usually hid bitter acrimony, and so, to their credit, the four members of the band gathered together at their office that same day, invited local press to visit them and presented a united, if disappointed, front to the world.

"It's incredibly sad," Michael Stipe told the *Atlanta Journal-Constitution*. "I won't pretend that it's not. It's going to be really weird for us to be a three-piece. But I'd much rather be a three-piece and deal with the change than have Bill stay in the band and be unhappy."

To home town paper the *Athenaeum*, he elaborated on the importance of honesty and friendship. "There are too many bands in this world that are going through the motions. It's very courageous for him to say, 'You know, it's not really in my heart, I don't want to do this anymore.' We've never been about faking it. The reason we're calling people together to see the four of us here at this table is that we have nothing to hide."

Mike Mills had eight years of friendship in Macon to add to the seventeen years in R.E.M., and that enabled a more positive attitude. "I have to look for some perspective on it," he said, "and when I do I say, well he's not dead, he's still around, and that sort of shrinks this particular situation to a very small size. At the end of the day we still have the band, we still have Bill, just the two things are not conjoined. That's fine."

"We are still the best of friends and we still love each other a great deal and respect each other a great deal and that, as far as I'm concerned, is what R.E.M. is," Michael Stipe told *Addicted To Noise*'s Gil Kaufman. "The music is almost a by-product. I know that sounds really stupid, but our friendship is what makes R.E.M. – R.E.M. We could not make the music that we wanted if we did not really mean it. Three of us still really mean it."

Bill Berry repeated his own uncertain mantra: that he wanted out but couldn't really explain why. "I think I'm just ready to not be a pop star anymore," he told the *Athenaeum*. "It's been great, it's been a wild ride but I'm ready to get off." He said he would stay in the neighbourhood, tending his farm. "My friends are here. And the thing is I'm going to feel distanced enough from R.E.M. after this anyway. I don't want to leave. I want to have at least that connection, so I can run over to Michael's house and pet his dog if I want to. There's no reason to leave."

The last words Bill Berry spoke – or typed – as a member of R.E.M. were at the end of an MTV/AOL online chat with their fans, on October 31, 1997.

"Let this whole thing go. Leave these guys alone so they can continue to make great music."

★   ★   ★

At face value that might have seemed easy enough. The drummer, legend has it, is usually the most dispensable member. Bill's loss of interest after the *Monster* tour hadn't stopped *Hi-Fi* being a critical success; besides, the new songs barely called for a drum kit, and there were two more all-round musicians on board already. If he was ever going to quit, this was probably the perfect moment.

And yet R.E.M. had been a band for almost eighteen years. They'd been friends for just as long. It was no coincidence that U2 and R.E.M., the two groups with the permanent line-ups, were the two most consistently successful acts of their generation; bands were not called bands for nothing. So while you could take away the drummer, and possibly even remove the drums themselves, taking away the cornerstone of a long-standing creative partnership was another issue entirely.

Bill's contributions, after all, had encompassed so much more than mere percussion. In those early days, he'd supplied the group with their leadership. When the other three might have settled for popularity in Athens, Bill was the one who booked gigs further afield. When the others may have contented themselves with part-time income, it was Bill who provoked their ambition by threatening to leave for Love Tractor. R.E.M. were always too good to have failed outright, but without Bill's contacts with Ian Copeland – and his willingness to work them for all they were worth – it would have been that much more of an uphill struggle.

Over the years, he'd proven himself an able musician, coming off the drums after the *Green* tour to play guitar and bass. Along the way, he'd laid the foundations for some of R.E.M.'s best songs, including 'Everybody Hurts' and 'Man On The Moon'. He shared Peter Buck's enthusiasm for getting things done quickly and moving along, rather than worrying about the finer points of detail. And he had the group's keenest ear for pop music, which showed both in his songwriting and in his demand that recordings be kept concise. "If I wrote something that was seven or eight minutes long," says Buck, "he'd just throw his sticks up in the air after five and a half minutes." The fact that the songs were so long on *New Adventures In Hi-Fi* possibly confirms Buck's claim that Berry had lost interest before the mixing of that album.

Yet none of this accounts for his spiritual contribution – his presence as the band's soul. Bill Berry had a down-to-earth nature that was a pleasure for everyone who came across it and a sense of humour that was a delight for anyone who shared it; he rooted the group in so many more ways than just playing the drums. If it's true that one reason for R.E.M.'s lasting popularity was because, like The Beatles, they had such different, complementary personalities, then R.E.M. had just lost its Ringo.

The others knew as much. Considering how eloquently they spoke during the interviews around his departure, it's a surprise that Michael Stipe allowed the following comment to make it to the official press release. "Are we still R.E.M.? I guess a three-legged dog is still a dog. It just has to learn how to run differently."

Twenty-two

R.E.M. fans got an idea of what a three-legged dog might sound like when they received their Christmas Fan Club single in the mail at the end of 1988. 'Live For Today' juxtaposed two seriously distorted guitars against a heavily reverbed lead twang and a vibraphone; Michael Stipe delivered a spoken vocal along the lines of 'Belong', except that it was almost entirely buried in the mix; the rhythm track was supplied intermittently by what sounded like beat box drums filtered through a tin can. The 'song' was credited to all four R.E.M. members, though apart from Michael's brief vocals it bore all the hallmarks of a Peter Buck demo from his La Casa del Elefante Studio – i.e. his attic. It was, without doubt, further removed from R.E.M.'s catalogue than even their most random B-side; fans of Sonic Youth, Sebadoh, and Fugazi were going to need to re-evaluate what had until now still been considered one of rock's more mainstream acts.

Whether Bill Berry had actually played on the last song to bear his name as a composer was uncertain. It was, however, clear that he wouldn't be playing on any other new recordings in a hurry; he auctioned off his drum kit for charity prior to Christmas.

The trio that was now R.E.M., with Scott McCaughey and Barrett Martin in tow, went to work at Toast Studios in San Francisco the first week of February, determined not to let Bill's departure slow them down. The drummer's absence was in fact seen as a golden opportunity. "They were just like, 'We don't know what we're doing, we have nothing to lose, we don't even care if we don't have drums on half the record,'" recalls Scott McCaughey of the mood at those sessions. "'Anything goes' was the attitude. 'We don't have any agenda, try anything, in your wildest imagination, just go for it.'"

The first indication that things were different in practice as well as theory came when Peter Buck arrived at the studio at noon every day with his Seattle friends. "Bill was always the guy who would show up with me, first," says Peter Buck, "and we would have all the things worked out when Mike would come in." But Bill wasn't there any more to join Peter in early afternoon work and, rather than waste time, Buck decided to start recording without waiting for Mike Mills. "One of the reasons I play bass on most of *Up*," he says of an album that would eventually be titled by looking at a packing crate when they were almost out of time, "was because Mike wasn't really there for the beginning of it. It would be me, Scott and Barrett working out the track and getting it almost finished. Then Mike would come in and I'd be playing bass, and I've already worked out the bass parts, so he would play keyboards."

That might be why Mike Mills was heard to comment early on that R.E.M. was now sounding more like the ambient-ethnic-electronic Tuatara, with him and Stipe as guest musicians, rather than the other way around. "Some people have ideas relatively fully formed before we start to record," Mills commented acerbically a year later.

Working earlier hours than Stipe and Mills, the Seattle trio thrived off each other's input. As far as they were concerned, the San Francisco sessions were a pleasure. "I was having the time of my life," says Scott McCaughey. "And I thought we were making a fucking masterpiece too. I was just so excited every day by the stuff we were putting down."

"I was thinking, 'This could very well be our best record,'" confirms Peter Buck of the six weeks spent at Toast, where the group worked in two studios simultaneously. "There was just tons of stuff that was unbelievable." Many of the tracks kept elements from Peter's attic demos, especially the drum machines and "these crazy guitar parts that you put on without even thinking . . . and you could never redo," as McCaughey describes them. Reports that were leaked out to the press – by the Seattle trio of Peter, Scott and Barrett while conducting interviews for the second Tuatara album, *Trading With The Enemy* – warned R.E.M. fans to expect a complete overhaul. "You can't really tell it's us on most of the songs," insisted Peter, elaborating on how, in lieu of conventional percussion, they'd taken to recording the sound of a duffle bag filled with percussion instruments dropped rhythmically on the floor, the slamming of a piano lid, and the crinkling of M&M wrappers.

"There's definitely a lot of Peter in those sound ideas," says Pat McCarthy. "Peter's pretty spontaneous, not someone to sit around and tweak sounds for very long. Michael's the same, he's not into the finer points of recording. He's into big strokes as opposed to little, dainty touches."

As for Mike Mills, "I'm much more reactive," he told Q magazine a year later. "I tend to wait. To me, the songs tell you what they need after you start playing them . . . I fully respect Peter's ability to see all this in his head and to hear it beforehand and have his ideas formed like that – in a way I wish I could do that – but that's just not how I work." With Buck's demos being used as backing tracks as well as templates, and with McCaughey and Martin (who Mills greatly admired) recording with Buck every day before he got there, Mills saw his long-term partner starting to lead from the front, and he wasn't sure he liked it.

Michael Stipe, initially excited by the new musical direction, came to San Francisco with half-a-dozen lyrics already prepared: he recorded the vocals to such new songs as 'Suspicion', 'Sad Professor', 'Parakeet' and 'Airportman', all of which seemed more literal in nature, more driven by narrative than many of his past obfuscations. (Not that any of these songs' characters seemed particularly happy.) He got the inspiration for the more uplifting 'Hope' – which would owe so much to Leonard Cohen's 'Suzanne' that a co-writers credit would be included for Cohen – while driving to San Francisco, and for another, 'Lotus', from walking through the city. His lyrics-in-progress taped on the studio wall as always, Mike Mills commented that they were the best Stipe had ever written and that they should be included with the album this time out. On the understanding that R.E.M. was effectively a new band, the lyricist agreed.

In between sessions, the band busied themselves by attending gigs in one of the nation's more active music capitals. Those R.E.M. fans at an Apples In Stereo show that month were stunned to see not just Buck, Mills and Stipe hanging out, but Bill Berry too. What he was doing in town has never been fully explained, but asked whether he'd rejoined R.E.M., he replied nonchalantly that the group had a new drummer already, in Barrett Martin.

But it was never R.E.M.'s intention to replace Bill Berry. And while Barrett Martin did record drums on a couple of songs (including 'Lotus'), so did Mills and Buck. Besides, Martin had the Tuatara album and tour to prepare, and there was also talk of Screaming Trees re-forming and getting another deal. So when the San Francisco sessions ended, Martin went back to Seattle (as did McCaughey) and Buck, Mills and Stipe – that is, R.E.M. – moved down to Athens to overdub at John Keane's.

The location was a mistake. Bill's ghost was too obviously in the air and Michael Stipe, unfamiliar with having to finish an album in his home town, suddenly hit writer's block. With dozens of half-finished songs floating around, Mike, Peter and Pat McCarthy took to constantly touching them up and trying out different mixes while waiting for Michael's words to come through. For Buck, the spontaneity of San Francisco disappeared in the process.

"We weren't communicating real well," says Peter Buck. "Michael had real severe writer's block because he was so stressed out. Things were not getting worked on. We'd mix something then remix it because there was nothing else to do that day. I'd walk in and hear a remix and say, 'Didn't we mix this a month ago?' and someone would say, 'But it sounds better now,' and I would say, 'No it doesn't.'"

In retrospect, Pat McCarthy considered a lot of these problems as "down to a delayed reaction with Bill. The relationship that had developed between the four of them over twenty years was suddenly not there. And because there wasn't a new member to fill that void, whether it was making decisions or even giving input, it was more responsibility on the other three."

In short, while San Francisco was a liberating experience, the realities of recording in Athens without Bill's grounding presence suddenly brought his departure home. Especially for the group's singer and lyricist. "I'm sure Michael would be inhuman if he's not listening to this music thinking, 'This is different, this doesn't have Bill,'" says McCarthy. "I'm sure he realised, 'This is probably going to be scrutinised.'"

Stipe admits to feeling anger at this point towards Berry, for leaving the band and fucking with the long-standing dynamic. The anger only increased his lyrical constipation. "Some of them just stand up, cross their arms and say, 'Quit fucking with me,'" Michael Stipe would explain afterwards of his lyrics, citing 'Hope' as a notable example. "Others are always inviting me to come back in, and I have to decide whether I'm willing to do that or not." On *Up*, he kept going back in.

"Michael always likes to save his words until the very end," explains Peter Buck. "That's just the way almost every singer I've ever known has worked. I've worked with a bunch of bands in the studio. Doesn't matter if you've been playing the song on the road for a year, when you come into the studio, the third verse is never written."* Frustrated at the lack of progress, Peter went back to Seattle.

"When it's down to lyrics then you are waiting," says Pat McCarthy, "and Michael definitely felt the wait. I also think that while he loves Athens, it might have been tough for him to focus. I was there for a lot of it and he's probably feeling the pressure of me being there, and Peter up in Seattle waiting to hear from him." The distance between Seattle and Athens only increased the paranoia. Buck felt the other two were teaming up against him; they felt he was ganging up on *them*. For some reason, in the four-piece band, they'd never had that problem.

Compounding the tense atmosphere was R.E.M.'s long-standing commitment to perform at this summer's Tibetan Freedom Concert. Now the date was upon them, scheduled for the weekend of June 13 at the RFK Stadium in Washington, D.C. and they simply weren't in the mood. But nor were they going to renege on a promise. And so their first show since 1995, their first ever without Bill, the first for which they'd interrupted a recording session (discounting their gig at a pizza bar during *Reckoning*), was now also going to be in front of 65,000 people. R.E.M. rapidly went from rejoicing in the freedom of a three-piece to panicking about a high-profile 'comeback' gig.

---

* This probably explains why the third verse is so often the same as the first!

Enter Joey Waronker, drummer with Beck and son of the former Warner Brothers President, Lenny Waronker. The 28-year-old Joey had grown up surrounded by his father's famous musician friends and fellow executives, and had duly spent his early teens immersed in the underground sounds of The Minutemen and Hüsker Dü in typical revolt. From those bands he progressed to The Replacements, "who were a touch more pop and a touch more sophisticated" and then onto R.E.M, "which was really pop and really sophisticated." By 1987, both Hüsker Dü and The Replacements were signed to Warner Brothers, and when Lenny Waronker took Joey to see R.E.M. at the Fox Theater at Atlanta that same year and asked whether he thought Warner Brothers should sign them too, "I realised that my dad was really cool and that I was really lucky." In college, Waronker joined the band Walt Mink, which released albums and toured nationally; he ended up in LA, playing with Beck on the lauded album *Odelay*, recorded without thought to its potential given that everyone in the industry wrote Beck off as a one-hit 'Loser'. After four years as Beck's side-man he was ready to expand his horizons; when Bill Berry left R.E.M., Waronker's manager had the sense to contact Bertis Downs.

R.E.M. flew Joey into Athens for a short meeting and an even shorter rehearsal. As a passionate fan of R.E.M.'s early albums, Joey was bowled over by the experience but dared not expect anything else from it. Then he got the call asking if he was available to play with the band for the Tibetan Freedom Concert. As it happened, he would be at RFK stadium anyway that weekend: he was playing with Beck at the same event, on June 14.

Waronker had but a half-day rehearsal in DC, on June 12, along with McCaughey and Martin, the latter performing in his accustomed role as percussionist. The set was to be mostly new songs; they ran through them twice. "From my point of view I was not being given a chance to learn the songs," says Waronker. "I felt I just had to be professional, and then I could take it all in later." The drummer, who likened his task to replacing Charlie Watts in The Rolling Stones – an apt comparison given Berry's inimitable simplicity – ended up playing with a crib sheet.

On the day of the show, lightning struck. Literally. A dozen people were injured, and the event was called off before R.E.M. or co-headliners Radiohead could play.* Both bands were re-scheduled for the next day – when Beck would also be appearing.

For Waronker, who had recently recorded with Smashing Pumpkins and was not immune to pressure, this meant the début from hell. And yet, for all his experience touring with Beck on a hip hit album, he remembers how, "The level of excitement and love from the audience was so amazing" when R.E.M. hit the stage. "I had never experienced that."

The excitement was short-lived. The band had decided to open with 'Airportman', by far the most inaccessible and perplexing song from their new album, with minimal drum box hi-hats, vibra-phone, fuzz guitar and post-modern near-spoken vocals. "As long as we were going to give them songs they've never heard," Mike Mills reasoned to a documentary crew, "let's give them something they really don't expect. We hadn't played live in three years, it was our first show without Bill, there was every reason to make the differences as pronounced as possible – and sink or swim." They sank. One reviewer described 'Airportman' as "so incompre-hensible that it's unclear whether they may simply be doing a strange Tibetan chant to keep in the spirit of things." R.E.M. briefly roused the crowd for 'Losing My Religion' and again, later, when Thom Yorke joined them for 'Be Mine' and 'E-Bow The Letter' but between an atrocious sound, Michael Stipe's sarong, and uncertain renditions of other new numbers, 'Suspicion', 'Sad Professor' and 'Parakeet', the comeback was a damp squib.

Away from RFK, the weekend was more fun. Michael Stipe guested with Radiohead at a surprise, last-minute show at the 9:30 Club on the Saturday night, Tuatara performed on the Sunday night at the same club, and the trio played 'Fall On Me' and 'Losing My Religion' on the West Lawn of the White House on Monday 15. Still, it had been a frustrating use of five days' valuable studio time, and R.E.M.'s profile had actually suffered in the process.

---

* Radiohead had now been elevated to the same saviours-of-rock status that R.E.M. had endured a few years earlier, and front man Thom Yorke would later publicly thank Michael Stipe for helping pull him back from the madness that such a role can lead to.

324

The one silver lining was that Joey Waronker had acquitted himself admirably; he was brought down to Athens almost immediately to add drums to 'Daysleeper' and 'Suspicion'. He was surprised that not all the band were on hand, but otherwise "it was relatively copaseptic and the recording sounded beautiful."

In private, however, frustration abounded. Peter Buck was meant to be touring with Tuatara in July. "I'm going, 'Guys, I've got stuff to do, this record was meant to be done a month and a half ago, we've *got* to be finished by the third of July, right?' 'Yeah, we'll be finished.' Third of July: two finished vocals."

"There were moments of complete breakdown of communication between the three of us, or the four of us, if you include Pat McCarthy," Michael Stipe reflected when it was all done. "There were moments that were very horrible, difficult for each of us. The darker sides were much darker than ever." Stipe even says that at one point, morale was so low that he thought he was making R.E.M.'s "last will and testament".

"We were certainly grouching at each other," confirms Buck, who credits the calm confidence of Pat McCarthy as "probably the reason we got the record finished." McCarthy says he felt no responsibility to anybody but the band (he was, after all, hired by R.E.M. and not the record company), yet all the same didn't want to be the producer that the group broke apart on. "I tried to say, 'This is inevitable and maybe it would be a good thing to accept it and understand it.' And in fairness to them I think they realised this themselves."

In July, along with Bertis Downs, R.E.M. retired to Idaho for a group confab; Pat McCarthy joined them on the last day. Having learned the hard way with both Jefferson and Bill that silence is not necessarily golden, they aired their grievances without holding back.

"Basically we just talked it out," Mike Mills told Q a year later. "Do we wanna keep doing this? Can we make this enjoyable for everyone? If we can't, then maybe we should consider that it's time to move on. The essential thing is that you've got to realise that the band is more important than your hurt feelings. And if it comes to the point where the band is not more important than those particular personal feelings, then maybe it is time to move on."

Buck recalls that he'd been close to doing just that, but that his wife appealed to his common sense. "I remember she said, 'I know you're mad at them right now but those two guys are your best friends and you love being in this band. You're pissed off now but a year from now you're going to miss being in the band. You have got to give it one more shot.' "

"We sat in a room for several days and vomited on each other," said Michael Stipe in the same interview, presumably using a metaphor. "And we emerged much much stronger, realising that, Yes, these are the people that I wanna do this with and, No, I'm not ready to give up on this and, Yeah, this has sucked and it's been really really hard. But let's try and move forward from this."

On their return, the group knuckled back down to work and got the overdubs and half the mixes finished by the end of July. At Pat McCarthy's suggestion, they farmed out the other half of the album to Radiohead's producer Nigel Godrich. "I just thought it had been such a difficult record that it probably would be good to get a different perspective," says McCarthy. Godrich's mixes, the first time the band had entrusted their sound beyond their album's immediate producer, were scattered throughout the finished album, sounding suitably similar in tone and texture.

When *Up* was completed, the band finally accepted, in Michael Stipe's words, that, "Bill was very present by his absence on this record", and that, "Our next record will be our first record really as a three-piece because of that." The upside was that, according to Stipe, "I feel like we leapfrogged over what would have been the next two records in terms of experimenting and getting to a place."

"We ended up finishing the record under a lot of stress," Peter Buck told Tabitha Soren of MTV. "Then sat down and talked about the experience – what was bad about it, what was good, who was the biggest asshole, that kind of thing. And having done all that we just realised, you know, we made a great record, we're still good friends. We kind of walked through the fire on this one."

Such was the sense of upheaval that Michael Stipe even told the *New York Times*, "I don't even know if we're a band anymore. I almost feel like we're a musical collective at this point." Mike Mills bristled that the word 'collective' "sounds pretentious". Peter Buck offered the interpretation that, "We are three guys who write songs together, and then there are other guys who help record it. And we don't know who the other guys are from record to record."

Continuing the *New Adventures* and *Automatic For The People* tradition of opening a new R.E.M. album with a curve ball, the group took stubborn pride in placing 'Airportman' at the front of the record. "It's like a signpost," said Mike Mills. " 'This way lies madness.' "

★   ★   ★

The band's honesty about the recording difficulties on *Up* hardly came across as a confident endorsement. Audiences were prepped for low expectations. There was a further dent in the armour when the much-heralded plans to tour were scrapped. "It was a tumultuous time," elaborates Buck. "We said, 'The way we're feeling right now we can't go on the road for a year, we're not ready.' "

R.E.M. fans therefore found it something of a surprise when the airwaves started filling with the sound of 'Daysleeper' towards the end of September. Clearly more Elton John than Suicide, it balanced familiar acoustic guitar patterns with Stipe at his most melodic and discernible, singing sympathetically about a night shift worker; the song moved from a pensive verse through an uplifting bridge and into a rolling chorus within forty seconds, it had real drums, some pleasantly ethereal keyboard textures, and its three verses, with a minimal middle eight, were all done within three and a half minutes, before fading away via a descending keyboard flute line reminiscent of mid-period Beatles.

It was R.E.M.'s most overtly pop single since the days of *Automatic For The People* and it was not entirely unrepresentative of the new album as a whole. Yes, *Up* was deliberately difficult to get into, thanks to the atypical opening trio of the ultra-minimal 'Airportman', the awkwardly rocking 'Lotus', and the electro-ballad 'Suspicion'. (The latter was Buck's original choice for single, but after the commercial disaster that was 'E-Bow The Letter', he'd agreed to "Let the guys who know about this stuff decide.") But for forty-five minutes after that, *Up* was a constantly inventive, albeit slow-paced, post-modern pop record.

'Hope', which followed 'Suspicion', was a perfect example of all these motivations coalescing: the quiet drum boxes and space-age keyboard sounds providing an innovative foundation for a beautiful vocal melody, with a classic Stipean lyric of a lost soul looking for a way out.

'At My Most Beautiful' was a total Beach Boys tribute. The line "I've found a way to make you smile", was Michael Stipe's way of referencing a Beach Boys album (the unreleased *Smile*) as a gift to the other R.E.M. members who, Bill Berry included, were all big fans. Peter and Mike needed little prodding to imitate the Brian Wilson school of production, from the drum patterns through the ascending bass lines, and onto the perfectly harmonised backing vocals. The song stood out as much for Michael's openly romantic lyrics ("I count your eyelashes, secretly, with every one, whisper I love you") as for its evident love affair with the past.

'The Apologist' and 'Sad Professor' were of a pair, each musically taut, each finding Stipe in the body of a negative character. The first protagonist was a cynic, bellowing "I'm sorry" with far less sincerity than when Stipe had previously used that chorus line on 'So. Central Rain'; the second protagonist was a self-pitying drunk who hates "where I've wound up". 'You're In the Air', 'Why Not Smile' and 'Parakeet' all straddled the thin line between love and optimism; 'Walk Unafraid' rose magically from dark verse to uplifting chorus, and for Stipe was the centrepiece of the album. (His Patti Smith obsession at higher levels than ever now he'd befriended the artist, he wrote the song after Smith's insistence that Stipe should "be unafraid" going into this first album without Bill Berry.) A short hidden track, 'I'm Not Over You', found Stipe accompanied by his own guitar playing for the first time; 'Diminished' was bare-bones R.E.M., Stipe as narrative defendant singing to the jury from the dock; and 'Falls To Climb' ended the album with the same sense of beautiful hesitancy as 'Me In Honey' or 'Find The River'. Throughout these ballads, the possibly disconcerting dominance of ancient keyboards and drum boxes was frequently offset by Mills' charming piano lines, Buck's calming acoustic strains, and now familiar string accompaniments.

Up was not a rock record, that was for sure. But for an established four-piece band attempting to find a way forward after the drummer's departure, it was remarkably cohesive. It was too long again, somehow clocking in at over an hour for its fourteen songs, but *Up* had soul, it had melody, it had spirit. It even justified Stipe's sometimes sloth-like pace with the lyrics. As printed on the album sleeve, they seemed longer than ever, but more coherent too.

"Topically speaking, a lot of the record is kind of dealing with classification and categorisation of different things," he told John Sakamoto of *Jam!* "Particularly religion and spirituality versus science and technology and where those two clash and how, culturally and sociologically, in this period of time in history, a lot of people are not able to recognise that science and religion are essentially the same thing, and that they overlap more than they're really separate."

Given that R.E.M. were musically more *Out Of Time* now than when they'd released the album of that name, that much of the early Nineties fan base had dropped off, and that a number of the newer fans were ill-at-ease due to the group's own voiced reservations – perception so frequently equals reality – *Up* was destined to be the band's hardest sell yet. For the 'Daysleeper' video, in which Stipe wore a suit like the night-time worker of the song, Iceland's Snorri brothers were hired for their technique of shooting thousands of still frames and then editing them. The effect was beautiful and unworldly, like a futuristic animation – or a hi-tech version of James Herbert's 're-photography'. Aided by the airplay and the quality video, the single entered the UK charts at number six – only to drop even quicker than 'E-Bow' did, straight out of the top twenty the next week. In America, despite positive initial reaction at radio – especially the growing adult alternative market designed precisely for people like ageing R.E.M. fans – 'Daysleeper' stalled at 57. It was the first time a trailer for an R.E.M. album had failed to make the top 50 since *Lifes Rich Pageant*.

It was a similar story when the album was released at the end of October. Initial chart positions – number two in the UK, number three in the USA – indicated that the group still had a fanatical following, but first-week sales were only half those of *New Adventures* in *its* first week, and in both countries, *Up* dropped out of the top 10 in only its second week. In the States, its first four week chart positions were calamitous: 3-16-33-63.

Bang in the middle of this downward spiral, Warner Brothers Records in America laid off 15% of its staff to "bring overheads in line with profits" (i.e. the label wasn't selling as many records).

Among those let go were two Senior Vice Presidents, Karin Berg and John Leshay, who just happened to be R.E.M.'s point people for A&R and Marketing respectively. A year previously, around the time Bill Berry left the group, Steve Baker had departed as President, and a new top man brought over from Virgin, Phil Quartararo. With the latest round of cuts, the only chief executive left who'd been heavily involved in R.E.M.'s glory days was Chairman/CEO Russ Thyret, and though he desperately wanted R.E.M. back at the top, if only to justify the lucrative deal he'd given them, he was hardly able to attend to their day-to-day needs.

The group looked overseas for comfort once more. *Up* went straight to number one in Germany, and in Italy, where it sold 90,000 in its first week, far more than in the UK and almost as many as in America. Those Italian sales doubled within a month.

Reviews for *Up* were mostly positive. This was no enormous surprise insofar as critics will usually reward a left-field turn such as R.E.M. had just made. Still, given the band's admitted problems with recording *Up,* then the sight of four stars in both *Q* and *Rolling Stone* must have come as quiet relief. But the reviews were far from unanimous, and there were no claims of perfection as had previously been bestowed on almost every R.E.M. album to date somewhere in the media. And while good reviews maintained all-important critical respectability, they weren't translating into new sales at the stores.

Years later, *Up* remains a source of frustration for the band, particularly for Peter Buck. "*Up* never really did get finished. That's why we had such a big to-do about it. We had all these meetings and talked about it, yelled at each other, but my feeling was, we're just not getting what we should out of this stuff. We take my home demos and stuff we do in Athens, and we play them for people and they just drop dead on the floor, and say, 'This is going to be your best record.' And then half the songs everyone points out as the best songs don't make the record because they just don't get finished. And that was painful."

At the same time, he acknowledges its strengths. "One of the things we were trying to do was push ourselves into new territory and be a different band and given all these things I think it's a really cool record. And if I was a fan of the band it's one of those records I would really like because it's totally different from all the things we've done."

Put it down to a fan's wilful obduracy then, but for this author, *Up* remains the best R.E.M. album since *Automatic For The People*.

★   ★   ★

As always, R.E.M. feigned disinterest in chart positions and record sales. There was some truth to this: unlike other mega-rock acts who worked hard to get to the top and even harder to stay there, R.E.M. always saw themselves as a left-field band that had fortuitously made it big for a while. Rather than trying to increase their income each year, they used their personal fortunes to ensure themselves complete creative independence.

But of course, they still wanted to sell records. And though the idea of a proper tour had been scrapped in the wake of *Up*'s problematic recording, they stuck with the plan for a run of promotional concerts, TV appearances and select gigs that would challenge the 'either'/'or' approach to live work. Joey Waronker and Scott McCaughey were both retained, and now that The Posies were inactive, Peter Buck recommended Ken Stringfellow as the additional all-round musician. If eyebrows were raised back in Athens at the preponderance of Seattle musicians being invited into R.E.M., there was also acceptance that as the most constantly gigging and recording member of the band, Buck had the best connections. Such was Buck's confidence in Stringfellow that an audition was deemed unnecessary: he could meet Mills and Stipe for the first time in San Francisco, where they would rehearse before their two appearances at Neil Young's annual Bridge School benefit.

Like Joey Waronker, Ken Stringfellow had been part of R.E.M.'s original fan base, buying the early albums almost on the day of release; The Posies had even covered 'Sitting Still' at their very first show. "If they'd broken up after *Reckoning*," he says of R.E.M., "I would still have had interest in hooking up with Peter when he moved to town," which is what happened with their mutual involvement in Minus 5. Just like Joey Waronker, Ken had lost touch with R.E.M.'s music during their early Nineties peak, largely as a result of his own band's activities. In fact, despite having

331

been Peter's friend in Seattle these last few years, when it came time to learn the songs, he had the office send him copies of both *Out Of Time* and *Automatic For The People*, the group's biggest sellers. He found *Out Of Time* "basic" but *Up* he considered "astounding". And the opportunity to play with his former favourite band was, like Waronker, complemented by the fact that as a now-experienced musician, he was far beyond being star-struck.

"I would say that my aesthetic and their aesthetic are fairly compatible," says Stringfellow, citing the same garage/folk background. This made it easier to play songs from *Up* even without advance rehearsals. "*Up* has a lot of overdub components," he says, and "you're not going to be able to re-create that, but you can figure out the general vibe and tone of a song, what you can pull out of it to get something that works live."

The R.E.M. promo gigs for *Up* were the band's first shows since the *Monster* tour ended in '95 (the Tibetan Freedom disappointment aside), and the Bridge benefits – an annual garden party of sorts in aid of the disabled children's school that Neil Young helps finance – were thereby an ideal way to ease back in. R.E.M. had always been ardent fans of Neil Young's and though they'd shared a record label this past decade, they'd never shared a stage. They did just that when Young joined them for 'Country Feedback' over both shows that October, and Buck and Mills joined Young for his 'Ambulance Blues'. Reviews were far warmer for the Bridge School benefits than for the Tibetan Freedom Concert; then again, the group didn't risk disaster by opening their set with 'Airportman'.

The next month was a whistle-stop global tour of high-profile appearances, often in low-profile settings. In New York, a secret gig at the tiny Bowery Ballroom in lower Manhattan for an MTV special (though their videos no longer made heavy rotation, the band was still considered a major draw for special broadcasts); *The David Letterman Show*; the *Storytellers* show for VH1. In London, a concert for BBC Radio, a John Peel session of all things, *Later With Jools Holland, Top Of The Pops, TFI Friday* – and a conveniently timed appearance to pick up their Lifetime Achievement trophy at the Q magazine awards. On to Germany, Spain, Switzerland, Austria, Sweden and Italy, the latter visit coinciding with the MTV

Europe Music Video Awards in Milan – and then back to New York for more TV. Considering how many times R.E.M. performed 'Daysleeper' on American television talk shows that fall it's a mystery that the song was not a bigger hit. When R.E.M. participated in a *Behind The Music* special for VH1, it was clear that they were doing *everything* possible to sell the album. The documentary show relied on a band's torrid past of drink, drugs, debauchery, divorce, and hopefully death; the nearest R.E.M. could offer to any of this was Bill Berry's aneurysm and departure, and Bill gamely took part to help the group milk his past for all it was worth. Mike and Michael had earlier driven out to Watkinsville to take their former partner a copy of the new album in advance of its release; he seemed a little put out that he hadn't been able to walk into a record store and buy it like any other R.E.M. fan.

Actually, it was when R.E.M. recorded 'Furry Happy Monsters' for *Sesame Street* that it looked like they were doing not just everything possible to sell records, but far more than was necessary. At least that's the way the cynics portrayed it. From R.E.M.'s perspective, having gone through the wars these last few years, it was all part of their new-found determination to simply enjoy themselves, to do all the things they'd ever dreamed of – whether that be sharing a stage with Neil Young or sharing a TV studio with the Cookie Monster.

Or, indeed, simply playing together as a six-piece rock'n'roll band. Frequently during these radio and TV appearances, the group found themselves continuing their sets after the television cameras switched off. Without the pressure of ticket sales or the expectations of a public audience (the fan club arranged priority seating for its members in each city), R.E.M. were getting back to what they knew best – being a band. For the three hired hands, consummate R.E.M. fans each, the shows were the antithesis of session work. "Scott, Joey and I would learn songs," says Ken Stringfellow. "We'd go down and soundcheck first at some of these TV shows. The band would walk in and we'd be playing something, like 'Cuyahoga'."

Inspired by the enthusiasm of the secondary trio, the group agreed to include older material. 'Perfect Circle', 'Pretty Persuasion' and 'So. Central Rain' soon showed up in the sets, along with older cover versions like Wire's 'Strange'.

Joey Waronker was finding as he learned his way through the catalogue that Bill Berry's sticks were harder to replace than he had thought. "Bill's style is crucial to a whole period of pop music. I think it's definitive. But it can be deceptive for drummers. The rhythm side of most older R.E.M. songs is so straightforward and simple, it's actually really hard. The beats might be similar enough to where you would think, 'Oh I know this song really well' and I would play the wrong simple beat and it would just sound completely *wrong*. That was a really big deal for me."

But not for the band. Joey, fully versed after four years with Beck as to the pressures of the touring outfit, felt a wave of relief sweep across the R.E.M. trio as they crossed Europe that November. "I could just tell everyone needed to have an amazing time and remember why they were a band in the first place," he says. The attitude being: "Let's just all have a good time with this and then the pressure is off. I think everyone united in that spirit and then it just took off and became its own thing."

"We ended up playing a lot during the promotional things and it was really good fun," recalls Peter Buck. "There was a real good chemistry, all the shows were real loose and we thought, Okay, let's continue."

And so, having proven themselves in a public-promotional capacity, having established that they were enjoying themselves once more, having regained their *raison d'être*, R.E.M. decided that they *would* tour after all. The announcement was made at the start of the new year. 'Lotus' had been released as a single in December and despite bringing in esteemed photographer Stephan Sednaoui for the video, had fared poorly in both the UK and USA. The media in those countries rapidly seized on the group's turn-around from its original U-turn and concluded that they must have been pressured by Warner Brothers to help shore up sinking sales.

"We don't tour to prop up albums, we tour because we like to play," bristled Mike Mills at that suggestion. "If you know anything at all about R.E.M. you know that the record company doesn't make us do anything."

"The fact is that the record was totally dead when we started booking the shows," says Buck. "We just wanted to go out because it felt good to do it. I don't know if it sold one record. But doing it is its own thing too. Rather than doing a promo tour that takes six weeks I'd just as soon play. And we're good at it too."

There was no Bill Berry to veto the decision this time. The friendship between the trio had been reinforced on the promo tour. The group was relieved in many ways that its drop in mainstream acceptance meant they could tour with less tabloid scrutiny and without invasion of personal space. Playing through the summer felt, simply, right.

In February '99, just after the dates were announced, the group undertook another round of TV shows, benefits and the continual award ceremonies that herald the new year, performing from Los Angeles to New York to London and halfway round Europe again. Contrary to Buck's assertion, *Up* was not "totally dead". 'At My Most Beautiful' was lifted as – yes, yet again – the ballad for third single, and re-established the group's status in the UK by hitting the top 10.

Nor did the group downsize its venues for its first tour in four years. The summer shows instead reflected R.E.M.'s confidence in themselves as a perennial live attraction: major stadiums, auditoriums and festivals throughout Europe, the summer shed circuit in America. And for the first time ever, Britain's premier outdoor gathering, Glastonbury. Headlining.

Twenty-three

As evidenced by its immediate reaction on the *Monster* tour, and then its success as a hit single, 'Man On The Moon' was one of those R.E.M. songs that struck the universal chord – even if audiences outside America initially had no idea who this Andy Kaufman character was. The mystery was partly cleared up in interviews – and when that beautiful and timeless Peter Care video included footage of Kaufman wrestling and "goofing" on Elvis, then R.E.M. found they had unintentionally launched an Andy Kaufman revival.

In 1994, a documentary on Kaufman was aired, featuring R.E.M.'s song and video among interviews with family and friends. A couple of screenwriters, Scott Alexander and Larry Karaszewski, then decided to write a movie based on Kaufman's surreal life and death, and, figuring that they should milk the pop culture tie-in for all its worth, entitled the script *Man On The Moon*. Actor and producer Danny DeVito fell in love with the script and called Milos Forman, suggesting he direct it. Forman, a Holocaust survivor and Czech émigré whose last film, *The People vs Larry Flynt*, had made an unlikely movie star out of Courtney Love, promptly called R.E.M. and asked if they would care to score the movie.

R.E.M. said 'yes' in a heartbeat. They had been contributing songs – many of them exclusive recordings – to movies for several years now. 'Fretless' had been included on Wim Wenders' *Until The End Of The World*; 'It's A Free World, Baby' on the outdated *Saturday Night Live* off-shoot, *Coneheads;* beat pioneer William Burroughs had distinctively vocalised 'Star Me Kitten' to R.E.M.'s original backing for *Songs In The Key Of X*, an *X-Files* spin-off; and an ambient-electronica reworking of 'Leave' had been included on the soundtrack for *A Life Less Ordinary*, a 1997 comedy starring Ewan McGregor and Cameron Diaz.

Michael Stipe had, of course, been getting involved in Hollywood himself through Single Cell Productions. *Velvet Goldmine* had been released around the same time as *Up;* it was overly ambitious, blindingly confusing, far too long, and like all rock movies, struggled for success at the box office. But when it was good, *Velvet Goldmine* was brilliant, and even when it wasn't, it remained a visual tour de force. For the second Single Cell movie, Michael Stipe had successfully campaigned for Spike Jonze to direct a surreal script called *Being John Malkovitch*; it was already in production by early '99. While Jonze may not have been the right person for R.E.M. videos, he was absolutely perfect for *Being John Malkovitch* and ended up with an Oscar nomination for Best Director, not bad going for a first movie made on the youthful side of 30. Stipe was in the Hollywood big time.

Of the other members, Mike Mills had composed for *A Cool Dry Place* though it hadn't come out and Peter Buck was writing increasingly avant-garde instrumentals. Now a major Hollywood movie was being named after one of their songs, directed by one of the industry's finest, and it was telling the life story of one of their heroes.* Jim Carrey, the most bankable comic film star in America, was slated for the lead; Courtney Love was in line to play Carrey's wife. Agreeing to provide the music was the easiest decision R.E.M. had ever made.

R.E.M. had already written one song about Kaufman and it would obviously be included in the movie. But Milos Forman now asked the band to write a "sisterpiece" for which Michael Stipe chose to "self-cannibalise" 'Man On The Moon', as he put it. He moved into Kaufman's character, taking the line, "There's nothing up my sleeve" from the chorus to the 1992 song and including it in the new song, 'The Great Beyond'. The seemingly incongruous chorus lyric "I'm pushing an elephant up the stairs" referred to what Stipe called Kaufman "trying to achieve the impossible", as did the line, "I'm looking for answers from the great beyond." As Stipe explained, "Andy's whole thing was breaking down the

---

* In his teens, Stipe had seen Kaufman singing along to Mighty Mouse on his *Saturday Night Live* début, and become a life-long fan. On tour in the Eighties, Kaufman was a cult hero for the likes of R.E.M. and Hüsker Dü.

fourth wall to such a degree that the audience never really knew whether he was for real or not. And I wanted to capture a little bit of that in the song."

To record the single, the group convened at John Keane's. Joey Waronker was brought in on drums; Scott McCaughey and Ken Stringfellow were each invited to take part; Pat McCarthy returned to the producer's chair; inspired by the recent promo shows, the atmosphere was calm and the entire group felt inspired. 'The Great Beyond', a lush ballad with heavily scripted strings and a resonating chorus, and Mills harmonies such as hadn't been heard for years, harked back to the *Automatic For The People* era and yet it was also looking forward; it sounded as if *Up* had never happened.

R.E.M.'s instrumental contributions to the movie were less finite. The trio, along with Scott McCaughey, flew out to Los Angeles with Pat McCarthy in April, where the film was still in production. Mills and Buck set about composing their little snippets of sound with gusto, Stipe directing traffic from the sidelines, Pat McCarthy loving every minute of it. Orchestras were hired, tracks were taped, entire segments ended up on the cutting room floor. This was, after all, Hollywood.

"On a big movie there are so many people involved and none of them know anything about music," says Buck. "Literally nothing. Whatever they say on Tuesday goes on Tuesday night but on Wednesday they change their mind. Halfway through the movie we realised that if we send them all this stuff they would just reject it, so we just sent them everything on the last day and said 'here's your score' and they said 'great'."

★   ★   ★

The scoring completed and the new song recorded, R.E.M. were able to approach their summer tour with even more enthusiasm than when they booked it. Though not quite on the scale of *Monster,* the travelling R.E.M. entourage was still some 40+ people, and a backdrop of neon signs had been incorporated, everything from the *Up* logo to a banana, a lotus and the word Praha in honour of the Prague audience that had suffered two cancelled shows back in '95.

338

This time there would be no cancellations, no personal injuries. The tour started in Portugal, concluded in Slovenia – which along with Greece and Hungary were new territories for the group – and the shows were pretty much triumphant throughout. A big part of this was down to flexibility with the set-list: while concerts routinely started with 'Lotus' (after a taped instrumental introduction of 'Airportman'), finished with 'End Of The World', and understandably highlighted the songs from *Up* in between (Stipe playing 'I'm Not Over You' unaccompanied, then joined just by Mike Mills for 'Why Not Smile'), over fifty songs in all were rehearsed for possible inclusion. Some of these were the group's own choices from recent years – 'Find The River' and 'Sweetness Follows' for example, which had barely been played before – but several older classics were down to the secondary trio of McCaughey, Waronker and Stringfellow angling for their personal favourites. 'Cuyahoga' finally made it in, as did 'Pilgrimage', 'Life And How To Live It', 'Wolves, Lower' and a song Ken Stringfellow was most familiar with, 'Sitting Still'.

The downside of such freewheeling experimentation was the occasional pacing problem. The fourth and fifth dates of the tour found R.E.M. at the cavernous Earl's Court, their first official indoor shows in Britain in exactly, get this, ten years. With almost every rock band in the country having taken the night off to check out the masters of their game, an admittedly nervous R.E.M. followed 'Lotus' with 'Crush With Eyeliner', 'Suspicion', 'New Test Leper' and 'The Apologist' – hardly a running order guaranteed to excite a 15,000-strong indoor crowd, many of whom had been on their feet all day queuing up for front row honours. The second night at Earl's Court, 'Lotus' was followed by 'What's The Frequency, Kenneth?' and 'So Fast, So Numb' in an attempt to catch the crowd quicker.

Those same three songs opened the show that following Friday, June 25, when R.E.M. headlined Glastonbury, their first ever appearance at one of the traditional British festivals. With 95,000 people in the audience, it was also R.E.M.'s biggest crowd ever, and it was a runaway success. R.E.M didn't pull from their very earliest albums, but instead played to their hardest-rocking strengths, delivering 'The One I Love', 'Cuyahoga' and 'Finest Worksong' from the back catalogue alongside the newer numbers. "It was one of the coolest things I remember doing," says Peter Buck, happy to have ticked another item off the group's 'must-do' list.

After return visits to the Roskilde and Werchter festivals, and indoor stop-offs in central Europe, R.E.M. came back across the Channel for an outdoor show at Dublin's Lansdowne Road and an indoor one at Manchester's Evening News Arena that was among the more memorable of the tour, both for the band and the audience; one local paper concluded that, "R.E.M. just might be the most exciting and stimulating rock band in the world right now." Three nights outside Stirling Castle wrapped up the British shows and left the group in no doubt that they were still on top of their game. Even though 'Suspicion' had been released as a single at the start of the British dates and failed to chart, the effects of the shows had been felt on album sales. *Up* was platinum now in the UK, and had topped a million sales across Europe. Compared to *New Adventures In Hi-Fi* this was relatively good going.

It was a similar story in the States, where *Up* was above half a million by the time the group started their summer shed tour. Considering that only a third of the Americans who bought *Monster* committed to *New Adventures In Hi-Fi*, it was in some ways quite reassuring that two-thirds of *those* were sticking around for *Up*. But casual observers would hardly have been sent rushing into the record store if they caught the belated broadcast that August of the documentary *This Way Up*. Unlike *Rough Cut,* this time the camera crew had a story: a group falling apart in the wake of a founding member's departure. As the band were followed from the contentment of their initial recording sessions in San Francisco to the writer's block that was Athens, on to DC for the Tibetan Freedom debacle, and then up to the New York final touches and video shoot, they proved painfully honest about their problems and palpably relieved to still be together at the end of it. Each of them came across as intensely intelligent, enormously sympathetic and desperately human. Just four years after *Rough Cut*, viewers got to see how *un*fun the life of a famous rock band could be; though it didn't make pleasant viewing, *This Way Up* is a key document in the group's visual library.

R.E.M.'s commercial decline in its home country was reflected

in ticket sales. The venues in the summer shed circuit accommodate anywhere from 5-15,000; R.E.M. averaged around 10,000 a
night, with the best seats held back for fan club members. Rather
than worrying about the empty seats or lawn spots at the bigger
venues, the group concentrated on those who were in attendance,
and the band's first run of outdoor American shows since 1985
were uniformly excellent. The 'new' R.E.M. – still a guitar group
but with more tenderness and eccentricity than almost any other
group wearing the rock mantle – seemed well-suited to the
outdoor spaces, where the atmosphere is generally more convivial,
if sometimes less attentive, than the indoor arenas. There can be a
negative association with this summer circuit, given that it is
usually dominated by middle-aged artists who long ago stopped
selling records but can still command a summer audience to come
hear the hits, and that's not an association R.E.M. would have
wanted. Nor was it one they acquired. For as much as the set lists
themselves varied, so did the performances of the songs: 'Sweetness
Follows' benefited from keyboard strings, 'Cuyahoga' from twin
guitars, 'Pilgrimage' from the folk-rock root of McCaughey and
Stringfellow. Joey Waronker, the only member filling anyone else's
shoes, was rarely singled out for special attention but nor was he
criticised: he seemed perfectly able to ape Bill's strengths without
exposing any weaknesses. Reviews of the shows were as good, if
not better, than on the *Monster* tour; even those who walked in
cynical usually came out sharpening their praise for the morning
edition.

For once, the tour didn't end in Atlanta: three nights in that
city's Chastain Park came in the middle instead. As had been
expected, Bill Berry chose to attend the first of these shows, and
watched from the wings throughout. The others had debated for
weeks whether to ask him to play a song with them, and concluded
that if they did make the request, he'd stay at home instead. During
'Find The River', the audience saw Bill Berry standing stage left
and started calling his name. The chant rose to a cacophony at the
end of the song, at which Bill walked across the stage, waved, got a
kiss from Mike Mills, strode over to Joey Waronker and shook the
new drummer's hand, then waved again and walked off. "Got in
his car and drove home," as Peter Buck recalls. Michael Stipe

dedicated the next song, 'At My Most Beautiful' to "our friend Bill". Whether Berry was still in the building to hear it has never been clearly ascertained.

As the band wound its way north along the east coast, Ken Stringfellow received an end-of-tour gift. For almost a year, as a *Reckoning* fanatic, he'd been pushing to include 'Camera' in the set. "We were told to forget it," he recalls, understanding there were bad memories attached to the song's lyrics. Undeterred, he and the other two hired musicians "just kept doing it and one day at soundcheck they said, 'Okay, let's do Camera.'" It was at the Merriweather Post Pavilion in Maryland, the penultimate night of the tour.

The next night, the group played the Tweeter Center in Massachusetts and Bertis Downs stood in the wings with a sign asking for 'Radio Free Europe'. Just before the final encore of 'End Of The World' the band obliged. It was the perfect conclusion to an entirely enjoyable experience.

"'99 was as fun as we've ever had on tour," says Peter Buck. "We played well. We did different songs every night. Everyone had a really good time. And we thought, 'This is fine, we're in a really good place.'"

★   ★   ★

Under normal circumstances, that would have been it for the year. But in November 1999, the *Man On The Moon* soundtrack was released, a month ahead of the movie, during which period Michael Stipe gamely appeared on some American talk shows and the band performed 'The Great Beyond' on *The David Letterman Show* and *Saturday Night Live*.

Their publicity presumably helped the movie, which was a success in so far as Jim Carrey managed to subsume his own ego to portray an Andy Kaufman equal parts hilarious, sad, baffling and frustrating. Courtney Love pulled it off too. Thematically, artistically, cinematically, it was an excellent movie, and reviews were highly positive. But biopics are notoriously difficult sells at the box office, and *Man On The Moon* did little to change that. "I think they realised they were in trouble when they did one of those Q tests," says Peter Buck, referring to someone's recognition quota, "and 70% of people didn't know who he was, and of the 30% who did, 50% didn't like him. And I think they did that a month before the movie came out. And everyone realised, 'Holy Shit!' Because all us musician types were all saying, 'Oh, Andy's a genius, everyone loves Andy.' But no, that's not really true." Indeed, as the film ably portrayed, at the height of his controversial fame, it was put to public vote whether Kaufman should continue on *Saturday Night Live* – and the public duly voted him off. It had been left to musicians like R.E.M. to carry his candle through the following fifteen years.

The soundtrack album was not a best-seller either, nor should it have been. Apart from 'The Great Beyond', there was little to attract an R.E.M. fan, let alone a casual buyer – some dialogue snippets, the original version of 'Man On The Moon', an orchestral version too, R.E.M.'s alternately jazzy and orchestral incidental music (attractive enough, certainly, and fun for the musicians, but nothing to worry the likes of John Williams or Danny Elfman), and a couple of oldies. Oh, and Jim Carrey and Michael Stipe 'duetting' on the oldie 'This Friendly World', backed by Mills, Buck and Waronker, with Carrey jumping in and out of Kaufman's violent Tony Clifton character and alternating single words with Stipe on a whole verse. Such pleasant diversions didn't bring the album above thirty-five minutes in length.

Still, the soundtrack did have that unreleased, especially commissioned R.E.M. song on there, and at the start of the year 2000, 'The Great Beyond' was released as a single, with its own promotional video. In the USA, 'The Great Beyond' was the first R.E.M. single to top 100,000 sales since 'What's The Frequency, Kenneth?' – though it still failed to chart. In the UK, both video (directed by Liz Friedlander as a Kaufmanesque take on a video shoot) and single went into heavy rotation, and for the first time R.E.M. found themselves playlisted at Radio 2, once considered an oldies station but gradually trying to reposition itself as a credible proposition for *Q*/*Mojo* readers. Single sales in February are far lower than in October or November, but that's not to take away from 'The Great Beyond's achievement: it entered the UK charts at number three, R.E.M.'s highest singles position ever, and unlike the group's other recent top ten hits, it stuck around those single digits for three weeks, staying in the top 50 for two months.

R.E.M. could hardly have asked for a better way to start the new century.

*   *   *

'The Great Beyond' portrayed a comfortably mature R.E.M. quite at home with the lusciously orchestrated ballad. For the band's upcoming twelfth studio album, recorded at a very gentle pace throughout the year 2000, the group continued in precisely that vein, recording a dozen numbers of almost universally similar style. Gone were the weird sound effects for the sake of it, the reliance on drum machines, and the ventures into Radiohead territory.

Absent, too, were the miscommunications and frustrations that had hampered *Up* to the point that it was nearly the group's swan song. The band entered the studios with a new-found confidence, a freshly honed harmony, and a rich understanding of each other's needs and desires. Giving interviews for *Up*, Stipe had used the old adage that, "What doesn't kill you makes you stronger," and in R.E.M.'s case, never had a cliché contained more truth.

The biggest difference going into the new album was deciding, in advance, on an unrestricted recording schedule. Rather than setting a release date and then struggling to meet it, or planning a tour and then worrying about not being up for it, they would work on the record until it was finished. Only then would they allow themselves to be concerned about the business of promoting it.

"That was me and my needs," admitted Michael Stipe to *CD Now*, "because I'm the one who drags my feet and has writer's block, and can't always deliver when I'm supposed to and what I'm supposed to – to my satisfaction."

This meant Peter Buck re-evaluating his sense of urgency and spontaneity, but after the fall out over *Up*, it was a compromise he was willing to make. And for his part, Michael Stipe made every effort to be fully present during all the original recording sessions to get a greater start on the lyrics and a bigger input on the mood.

Rehearsals took place in Athens as always, working with Pat McCarthy once more – given that he'd gotten them through *Up*, there's no way they weren't going to reward him with an opportunity to oversee a more pleasant experience. There were no pre-conditions, no set agendas, just a desire for everyone to bring their strengths to the songs. That 'everyone' included Joey Waronker, Scott McCaughey and Ken Stringfellow. The presence of a drummer at such an early stage, and using the six–piece as had worked so well live, initially suggested that the new album would move the band back towards a rock direction, but as the songs took shape, it was apparent that they were leaning instead toward the famed R.E.M. melancholia.

The bulk of the initial recording for the album that would be called *Reveal* (after a line from a song called 'I've Been High') took place in Vancouver throughout May. The city was chosen partly just because it was a city they hadn't worked in before, but also because it was conveniently close to Seattle to allow the three working members from that city – particularly Peter Buck and Scott McCaughey, who had children – to drive home for the weekend.

In the studio itself, the initial ideas flowed freely. "Everyone was just having a really good time in Vancouver," recalls McCaughey. "It was a real nice place to work. The Warehouse is in a really old brick building and the studio is on the second floor and it's got real high 40 foot ceilings, so it's a really spacious room, and there's almost floor to ceiling windows. Not that you necessarily get a lot of sun in Vancouver, but it was like working in daylight. You didn't have the feeling that you were working in some basement studio, you were in this spacious atmosphere that at least had some natural light coming through. It had a real good feeling, real relaxed." Bill Berry had complained upon leaving R.E.M. that he'd never been in a studio with natural daylight; "He would have loved the Warehouse," admits McCaughey.

The synths that had dominated *Up* were reassigned to comple-ment rather than replace the more conventional instrumentation. The thinking, explained Buck, was "Let's use a lot of the technol-ogy we've been using in the past because we should keep going with that – it's a fascinating, interesting way to work, and it's pushing us in ways we've never been pushed. But we should also use these real instruments, making a real lush, kind of beautiful statement around it."

"Some of these songs are actually very sparse," Mike Mills confirmed. "But they have some beautiful sounds within the sparseness. We're working on using synthesizers to get sounds that maybe really haven't been heard before, certainly that don't exist from within the natural patches that come with the synthesizer. We try to screw it up a bit and it's something we've been doing all along, but it really kicked into high gear with *Up* and this is just a continuation of that."

Ken Stringfellow discovered what Mike Mills was describing when he started making his own contributions, "a nice piano part or organ part" as he recalls, and got word back through Pat McCarthy that what the band actually wanted was "more Ken". As he explains, "The more off into my own personal vision of the deep end, the more they liked it. All sorts of messed up crazy distorted things run through pedals, they were loving that."

So while Michael Stipe's agenda was "to be really melodic", Stringfellow was asked to provide a counterpoint. "Maybe I would try to do something rhythmically or tonally that pushes it left in a big way. The premise of R.E.M. as I understood it was that their songs, even on *Murmur,* are not exceedingly weird in chords or rhythm, but they layer this stuff on top."

Joey Waronker also understood this ethic. He recalls how Peter Buck was still bringing in demos on drum machines, "but the drum machines are often their own parts. They might be really cool but would have nothing to do with what I would add. My favourite thing as a musician is knowing when not to play. Sometimes it's not necessary or maybe I'm adding another percussive colour."

Although Waronker had not been in on the initial recording stages of an R.E.M. album before, he had enough experience with the band to recognise the difference in mood from the *Up* sessions. "Everyone was very present, everyone was very much involved," he recalls. "Michael was there and I think that made a huge difference, at least spiritually. He would have lyrical ideas or melodic ideas while we were doing the record. It was really, really powerful."

"He had a little more of the lyrics when we went in there," says Scott McCaughey of Stipe. "So we tracked a lot more of the songs with him singing, even if they weren't final words or were just melodies. And that was great, to be playing with five people and Michael singing, really performing a song. *Up* was a lot more pieced together and we didn't use drums that much. By the time we did *Reveal*, Ken and Joey and I – and Mike and Michael and Peter – were like a real band and it *felt* like a real band making a record."

Most of the dozen songs that became *Reveal* were formulated and tracked during this period, with a certain amount of joyful chaos passing as inspiration. For 'Saturn Return', Peter Buck played piano, not his strongest instrument. "I just told everyone what the chords were, showed them how one passage goes, and told them what the bridge was," he explains. "Then I said, 'OK, everyone get like an obscene sound and don't worry about playing the right chords, just play.'" He and Waronker built up a loop, then tracked some of it backwards and used it as the song's foundation.

'Chorus And The Ring' grew out of an impromptu jam, recorded in one take, with Peter on electric guitar and Ken Stringfellow "on super distorted keyboard," as the newest musician recalls, "doing a big echoey blurry bagpipe explosion in the chorus and then Michael singing some weird impromptu thing." After Stringfellow found himself stumbling rhythmically they went for a second take. It didn't have the same feel, so they kept the 'stumbling' one.

'Imitation Of Life', which would become the album's lead single, provided an ideal example of how a song would take shape. It had been born backstage at Roskilde the previous year under the typically R.E.M.-like demo name 'Trumpet Chorus'. As McCaughey recalls, "It was much slower with these horn parts that ended up being the strings on the record. We switched instruments around, we would track it. One of the times we did it I just played tambourine, one time I played piano, I played acoustic a lot of the times. The version we ended up using we told Joey not to play drums, we just got a drum machine going to keep the rhythm steady, Joey playing tambourine, the other four of us all sitting round a microphone playing acoustic guitars. The four Amigos, as Pat McCarthy calls us. That was it. That was great. But it just took a real long time before we got the feel we thought was going to work out. Michael had the lyrics for the verses by then probably but he rewrote the chorus like three times."

"We were overdubbing something on the final version," says Stringfellow, "and I walked over to this cheap synthesizer, and played this little solo on the bridge. I couldn't even really hear what I was playing and kind of guessed what notes would fit. It turned out to be the keyboard solo in the bridge." It was after this that Peter Buck removed his own burbling synth sound from that part over to another song, 'I've Been High'. Frequently Buck would take tapes home to Seattle for the weekend and record his overdubs in his attic after the kids were asleep.

By the end of May an album was taking thematic shape – mid-paced songs that could easily pass as ballads, full of ethereal sound effects. With everyone thus far satisfied, the album moved into its second stage; for lyrics and vocals, Michael Stipe got as far away from Athens as he could ("Distance brings clarity and I didn't want to fall into writer's block by being in familiar surroundings," he explained), moving into a rented house in Dalkey, outside McCarthy's native Dublin, for the months August through to October.

"It cost like three days of studio time," says Peter Buck with typically eager over-statement. "With the new technology it was just basically Pro Tools, a few mikes, a few outboard effects and a board." More important than the equipment or the budget was peace of mind. Mike Mills and Peter Buck would fly in and out from America, fine-tuning the songs as necessary, but without rushing Michael to complete his vocals.

"It was really hard work," recalls McCarthy of this period. "Michael might be working for eight hours a day with pen and paper on the other side of the house, and then after dinner he'd be there for another three hours trying stuff or whatever. He was enjoying it and it was great to see. I was really impressed with his output. But he kept me up every night."

In what could be interpreted as a grand example of rock star excess, Stipe claimed that, "I followed the sun round Europe for most of the summer. I would hole up in a hotel for a couple of days and finish the song and then come back to Dublin until I got stuck again. Then I would go back to the airport and fly off somewhere else."

"I encouraged him," says Pat McCarthy of these flights of fancy.

"And I think that was part of the Athens thing that there it was seven days a week, whereas this way he would at least go off and come back. Also, going from *Up* to this, I think everyone was concerned about enjoying the process."

There were three or four such trips in all. One of them was to Tel Aviv, to meet his parents who were travelling there. There were other more purely hedonistic sojourns in Italy, France and Denmark. But as McCarthy points out, "Michael likes to travel. He's not going to sit still for six months for work. He's an observer, he's a traveller, he loves it, whether it's for pleasure or for work."

The primary benefit of the travels was felt in the seasonal mood of the resulting album. "Most of the records we have made have been put out in early autumn," Stipe explained to journalist Neville Kitson. "This time I wanted to write a summer record that reflected my love of warm weather and the promise that summer offers." His success could be easily ascertained in such song titles as 'I'll Take The Rain', 'Beachball' and, especially, in 'Summer Turn To High', another Beach Boys tribute in the vein of 'At My Most Beautiful'.

The trip to Tel Aviv had a specific influence; Stipe attended a rave there, where a suitably surprised fan asked what the singer was doing there. "I came to disappear," said Stipe, hitting on the core lyric of what appeared to be an unusually personal song; for all the frequent flier miles, the singer concluded that, "The only thing worth looking for is what you find inside."

The change in atmosphere surrounding the recording of *Reveal* was also apparent in Stipe's singing, which came across more laid-back, more relaxed. "I think he was experimenting with a softer side of his voice," says McCarthy, "which is very popular with a lot of people." As the vocals were completed, Peter Buck and Mike Mills maintained a heavier vigil, finalising their own overdubs, and in early October they brought an orchestra into Windmill Lane in Dublin. Even then, they recognised the importance of imperfections. For the song 'Beachball', they used the human strings for the verse and kept synth ones for the chorus. "It sounded too stiff," said Buck of the orchestra. "They were playing it really well, while I was playing it really badly on the keyboard."

After a stop-off back in Athens, mixing took place in Miami.

There was a recognition that *Reveal* was dominated by slower songs – one reason that the faster 'Imitation Of Life' was included, if only at the last minute – but the upside was a sense of self. "I like it when I find an album that I can put on and leave on through dinner or through a party," Michael Stipe told MTV. "So I consciously tried to steer stuff toward something that was cohesive from beginning to end. And then of course each song has its own thing . . . and is its own piece. But I like the idea that you can put it on and leave it on, that there wasn't one song or two songs that stood out or made you want to change the record."

It was like night and day. After the torment of recording *Up*, *Reveal* was pure pleasure. No arguments, no misunderstandings, no pressure, no writer's block. And even some overseas travel thrown into the bargain. Best of all, unlike the doubtful conclusions issued upon release of *Up*, the prognosis on *Reveal* was positive from the start.

"We were very happy to be making this record," Mike Mills confirmed to *CD Now* at the time of its release. "We had gotten through a bunch of crap in the last few years and we had no ongoing crises at the time. And I think that's what shows up and makes it kind of summery and fun."

"It sounds a little insincere because every time we make a record, I say it is the best we have ever done," said Michael Stipe, "But I have to believe that. And I genuinely happen to feel that way about this album."

Twenty-four

"One of the things we're realising is that if there's anyone this is supposed to be fun for, it's us," said Peter Buck after the release of *Reveal*. The second half of the Nineties had seen R.E.M. desperately try to make the process of being in one of the world's biggest rock bands a fun experience and, for much of that time, failing. The music would survive the bad memories, but the experience of recording and promoting the albums *Monster, New Adventures In Hi-Fi* and *Up* had been off-set either by internal friction, personal health crises, external deaths, business break-ups, departing members, corporate confusion and/or falling record sales. Only with the 1999 world tour had the group rediscovered their love of performance – and of each other. Having transfused that joy and harmony back into the studio, initially with 'The Great Beyond', and now with *Reveal*, R.E.M. could once again continue along the path of self-fulfilment. The year 2001 would see their first album of the new decade, their first recorded under the recently established two-tiered line-up, and the first for which they would either tour, or not tour, but determine to find a satisfactory path somewhere in between.

In January, the group visited South America to headline the Rock In Rio festival, their début performance in Brazil coinciding with their biggest audience ever, some 190,000 strong. The ninety-minute set found the group on top form, undaunted by the size of the crowd, playing a primarily greatest hits set but pausing to introduce 'The Lifting' and 'She Just Wants To Be' from *Reveal* along the way. Coincidentally, the Rock In Rio show came just 24 hours after Time Warner completed a merger with America Online, which had in the meantime used some of its spare stock-market evaluation cash to sponsor Rock In Rio in an unapologetically heavy-handed manner; the famously anti-corporate

351

R.E.M. inadvertently found themselves performing surrounded by their new owners' logos.*

A second outdoor show, in Argentina, another new territory for R.E.M., followed a few days later. Increasingly comfortable with open-air concerts, R.E.M. responded positively to a request to perform in London's Trafalgar Square as part of the South African Freedom Day Concert, an anniversary celebration of the end of apartheid that would be graced by Nelson Mandela himself. The concert date, at the end of April, tied in perfectly with the mid-May release of *Reveal* and could be used as a springboard for other European promotion. The concept of playing in city squares across the world – for free – suddenly resonated with the band, and feelers were put out by promoters across America and Europe. The reaction from city authorities was typically tepid, citing crowd control issues, insurance problems and a general mistrust of loud music and young people in close proximity: apart from the London show, such concerts would take place only in Cologne and Toronto. For the rest of *Reveal*'s performing promotion, R.E.M. would take the exact opposite tack, playing in front of pocket-sized audiences for the television and radio broadcasts they could command upon request – but at least they would do so right across the world. In advance of all this, Mike Mills and Michael Stipe undertook European interviews in March while Peter Buck contentedly toured the States with The Minus 5.

The mood in the R.E.M. camp was one of considerable excitement as the group planned to reconvene in London on April 21, a week ahead of the Trafalgar Square concert. The buzz on *Reveal* was already considerably higher across Europe than it had been for the last couple of R.E.M. albums, and 'Imitation Of Life' was blaring from radios across the continent as a perfect accompaniment to spring weather. In Seattle, Peter Buck had been hard at

---

* One of the most bizarre mergers of modern times, Time Warner's Gerald Levin agreed to what looked very much like a take-over by AOL based on the two companies' stock prices at the time of the deal; within months, AOL would be back to trading under the value of Time Warner, the dot.com balloon would have burst with a bang heard around the financial world, and Levin's days at the top would be numbered.

work assembling music for a theatre project *Dinner With Friends* alongside Scott McCaughey and Bill Rieflin, which allowed him to experiment with instrumental compositions and not worry about commercial appeal. But the project ran particularly close to his departure for the UK, and when the inveterate insomniac went out to dinner on the eve of his departure, he voiced his wish to be able to just sleep through the impending ten-hour, 5,000 mile flight to London.

Hoping to help him get through the journey, a dinner guest gave Peter two Zolpidem sleeping pills – known commercially as Ambien – from a private prescription. On the evening of April 20, Buck and tour manager Robert Whittaker boarded British Airways Flight 048 – first class – for London, while Scott McCaughey and Ken Stringfellow travelled business. According to the best interpretation of published and discussed accounts, Buck took one and a half of the pills, Whittaker the remaining half. Not having been personally prescribed the Ambien, Buck may have been unaware that the sleeping pills were not to be mixed with alcohol; he may have assumed as much and figured he could handle the combination; he may not have cared. And again, without having been personally prescribed the pills, he may have had no knowledge as to their possible adverse side effects, including memory loss and hallucinations. (Though according to a story published in *R.E.M.: An Oral History,* Buck had engaged in strange activity of which he later had no recollection after taking Halcion, a predecessor to Ambien, back in '86.) Regardless, he downed at least three glasses of complimentary, first class red wine before the pills took effect.

What then happened over the course of the overnight flight will forever remain in some dispute given that Buck himself claims to remember none of it, but it seems safe to say that the guitarist 'turned', and went on what looked and sounded very much like a drunken rampage. Buck is a big man, and in a confined space such as an airborne passenger plane, any aggressive action under a combination of alcohol and/or prescription pills was likely to have induced considerable fears for the safety not just of fellow first class passengers but of the entire flight. According to subsequent court evidence, Captain Tom Payne held a cockpit crisis meeting during which he considered landing at the nearest airport, but eventually decided to fly on to Heathrow and have police detain Buck there. The guitarist was arrested upon landing and charged later that day, Saturday, April 21, with two counts of common assault, and one charge each of criminal damage, disobeying an aircraft commander, threatening behaviour and being drunk on an aircraft. He appeared at Uxbridge Magistrates Court the following Monday, looking extremely sober in every sense of the word as he was set free on £30,000 bail pending a return date at the end of the group's promotional duties. Outside the court, Bertis Downs read a statement in which Buck seemed to advertise some guilt by saying that he was "very sorry for the incident and, of course, very embarrassed about the whole thing."

It was a sign of R.E.M.'s enormous UK popularity that in between his arrest and his court appearance, Buck's 'air rage' incident made all the Sunday newspapers, with big bold headlines in the tabloids promoting the famously amicable guitarist as some modern day Keith Moon figure. On one hand, the entire event looked ridiculous, a rare loss of faculties blown out of all proportion, but just the previous year, the former Stone Roses' singer Ian Brown had served jail time after an airborne incident, also on British Airways; although Peter Buck commanded greater public respect, and had more money to pay for better lawyers than Ian Brown, the price for 'air rage' was evidently running high. The bizarre episode, which would haunt Buck for the following year, was brought into some perspective once it was noted that this was the first time any of the band had been in publicly acknowledged trouble with the law – a rather mundane claim for one of the world's leading rock'n'roll bands.

The Trafalgar Square concert went ahead the following Sunday, April 29, though not entirely as planned. It rained for much of the day, which can usually be expected at an open-air British event, and after some of the stage scaffolding was pronounced dangerous, R.E.M. were forced to cut their set down to seven songs – which had not been anticipated. The event was a success, but for R.E.M. something of a muted one.

Still, between the city centre concert and the air rage headlines, R.E.M. were very much in the public eye as 'Imitation Of Life' was released on April 30, further aided in the UK by the various

TV and radio appearances the band had recorded during the rest of their stay in the country. (And also by a curious and ambitious Garth Jennings directed video, in which the pan and scan technique was employed over a 30-second loop of a garden party, the members of R.E.M. scattered amongst the hand-picked cast.) The single entered the British charts at number six the following week, R.E.M.'s second UK top ten hit in a row. By then the group was in mainland Europe, where the open-air concert in Cologne on Saturday, May 12 was broadcast live across the continent by MTV Europe, garnering the network its highest ever figures outside of its annual awards shows. A better advertisement for *Reveal*, released the following Monday, could not have been bought with all the record company advances in the world.

Reaction to *Reveal* proved to be united on many fronts. Those whose job it was to review the album all seemed to agree that this was R.E.M.'s most straightforward collection of mainly slow-paced songs since *Automatic For The People*, and far less depressing with it. There appeared to be no dispute either as to *Reveal*'s melodic maturity, its lyrical complexity, and its overall consistence, cohesion, commerciality and contentment. The Beach Boys and Burt Bacharach were the acts most frequently cited by reviewers as primary influences; 'The Lifting' was complimented as a wise and optimistic choice of opener – especially after the last two album's deliberately off-kilter introductions – and 'Imitation Of Life' was lauded as a single that captured much of what had always been best about R.E.M., especially the rare reappearance of the famed Buck jangle. Michael Stipe's vocals were noted for their softness; Mike Mills' traditional harmonies were widely commented upon for their absence. There was a general agreement that with *Reveal*, the three-piece that was now R.E.M. appeared to have gotten over the hump of Bill Berry's departure and with the input of Messrs Waronker, McCaughey and Stringfellow could look forward to a harmonious future.

Opinions as to what this all meant were divided, however; more than any other R.E.M. album, *Reveal* was what the listener made of it. For example, there were those who took all of the above and concluded that R.E.M. had made possibly their best album ever. In an influential five-star review in *Q* magazine, David Cavanagh repeated some of the praise he had previously heaped on *Automatic For The People,* observing that after alienating so many fans in recent years, "*Reveal* is such a thoughtful gesture of reconciliation that it virtually comes with ribbons and a bow." Andy Gill at the *Independent* talked of "depth, variety and subtlety" and how "Michael Stipe had rarely written or sung better than he does here." He singled out 'I've Been High' for being "as close as R.E.M. will ever get to composing a standard." Over in the States, *Rolling Stone* was just as loyal as *Q*. In a four-star review, Rob Sheffield talked of a "ceaselessly astonishing beauty" and likened *Reveal* to U2's recent "spiritual renewal rooted in a musical one." (R.E.M.'s peers had returned the previous year with the equally straightforward *All That You Can't Leave Behind*.) Similarly, *USA Today* noted that "sheer beauty . . . makes a glorious comeback in this lush and mellow dreamscape."

But then there were those who looked at what was undeniable about *Reveal* and concluded that R.E.M. had sold themselves – and their fans – short. Interestingly, most of these disappointed reviewers were in the States. David Segal at the *Washington Post* slated *Reveal* as "the dullest R.E.M. effort in many years, with a lulling, mushy sound that seems fogged in by a computer-generated haze," and concluded that "the album's title seems ironic: *Reveal* hides the band's best parts." Similarly, Mac Randall of the *New York Observer* commented that, "*Reveal* isn't a terrible album . . . but it is painfully dull. Its title is amusing, too, because *Reveal* essentially reveals that, despite R.E.M.'s pretense to depth, there is ultimately nothing of interest beneath the facile surface of its music." Stipe's lyrics, once famed for vagueness, were now found guilty of over-elaboration. Writing in the *Boston Globe* Jonathan Perry noted how Stipe "indulges his tendency toward the precious with foggy lines about dragonflies, seahorses, and starfish butterflies." Sam Jeffries at *SonicNet* cited for similar reasons the following lines from 'She Just Wants To Be' – "It's not that the transparency / Of her earlier incarnations / Now looked back on, weren't rich / And loaded with beautiful vulnerability" – and added how, "To make things worse, he sings every verse on an even clip with the metronomic beat, strengthening the snoozy effect."

Finally, there were those who listened and listened to *Reveal*'s sophisticated pleasantries and could only damn the result with faint praise. "What's missing from *Reveal* is any sense that R.E.M. have anything left to prove or kick against," opined Adam Sweeting in the *Guardian*. "*Reveal* is the slippers, fire and photo album," wrote April Long in *NME*, "a place to sit back and take stock." *SonicNet* wound up noting how, "*Reveal* is mostly nice for putting on in the background." (Ouch!) And *Entertainment Weekly* concluded that, "One can imagine the band making records like this, sweet and sad, graceful and marginal, for years to come. Whether that's a good thing remains to be seen."

The last was a fair point. The benefit of hindsight and the tone of future albums would indicate whether *Reveal* marked a permanent shift in direction or just a brief moment of calm reflection. In the short term, and especially in the countries the band was working hardest in, *Reveal* was propelled forward by sheer force of promotional momentum, renewed fan loyalty, good press and recent singles success. In the UK, *Reveal* entered the album charts at number one, the fourth R.E.M. album out of the last five to do so; it did the same in Italy, Austria, Ireland, Norway and Switzerland. *Reveal* débuted at number two from Brazil to Belgium; it quickly rose to number one in Germany; it went top ten in Japan, Thailand, Australia, Canada, France and at least six other major countries. As impressive as these chart positions were, the sales figures were even better. 110,000 in the first week in the UK was a return to *New Adventures* levels; the 130,000 shifted in Italy was about 50% more than *Up* and enough to earn a platinum disc in its first week. Within a month, *Reveal* had sold a million across Europe. In some twenty territories *Reveal* outsold *Up* before the release of a second single.

The USA was not among them. In their home country, where R.E.M. had been arguably the most important band of the Eighties and certainly one of the biggest of the Nineties, 'Imitation Of Life' sold a paltry 15,000 and peaked at number 83; *Reveal* entered the album charts at number six, the group's lowest entry since the introduction of SoundScan. As *Reveal* plummeted out of the charts with almost as little fanfare as accompanied its arrival, R.E.M. were left in an incredibly curious and only partially enviable position. They had reaffirmed their status as one of the world's leading rock bands, admired and adored from Bangkok to Bangor, from Tokyo to Torquay, yet in the land they loved and where they lived, the biggest market in the world, where they had sold over 20 million copies of their previous eleven studio albums, they now struggled to top a mere 300,000.

"We can't sell less records than that, it's just not possible," commented a somewhat baffled Peter Buck at the end of the year. "I mean, we used to sell 300,000 records within fifty miles of Atlanta."

Talk to the people around R.E.M. and you hear a multitude of reasons why the band is so much more popular in Europe, Asia, Australasia and South America these days than in America. And while every reason has a kernel of truth, at the same time none of them really make sense. The most frequently cited explanation is the state of American rock music, dominated in the early 2000s by rap-metal punk: for example, the albums that topped the American charts in June 2001, when *Reveal* saw limited U.S. chart action, were by Tool, Staind and Blink 182. At the end of his glowing *Rolling Stone* review, Rob Sheffield wrote that "the rock world of 2001 looks so much like the one that (R.E.M.) were rebelling against twenty years ago; once again, the radio is full of interchangeable metal gomers who never met a rule they didn't obey, and once again R.E.M. are totally out of step with the times." True enough, but still it seemed odd that R.E.M. couldn't find some kind of audience outside of the "metal gomers" as they had done all those years ago. For if it was understandable that such mature and melodic songs as 'Imitation Of Life' and 'Daysleeper' were not going to sit comfortably alongside Slipknot and Staind, why was it that U2's *All That You Can't Leave Behind,* which represented *that* band's similar return to straightforward songwriting, was rewarded with multi-million sales and Grammy awards? How come that in a year when a freshly rediscovered Beatles could sell eight million albums, when Coldplay could sell a million, when a middle-of-the-rock-road band like Train could dominate the airwaves, that there was no room among all the radio formats for R.E.M.'s elegiac classic pop?

Changing tack, the loyalty of British audiences towards their favourite bands has also been cited by the R.E.M. camp as explanation for continued UK success, though in reality the British tend to jump from new sensation to latest hype with all the attention span of a new-born kitten, while it was once a given that American audiences stayed with their favoured bands for eternity. In this area, R.E.M. appeared to be an anomaly. Likewise, the European's willingness to embrace left-field music is offered as explanation, yet it's hard to consider *Reveal* as anything other than a mainstream pop-rock record made by a highly accessible and uncontroversial trio of good-natured Americans; in the meantime the top of the American charts are frequently fought over by a revolving door of envelope-pushing hip hop and R&B producers. And Radiohead were topping the American album charts with overtly experimental recordings. And sure, the US charts had been dominated for five years by boy bands and girl pin-ups, but then so had the Europeans.

Ultimately then, given the sheer implausibility of R.E.M. being *so* unpopular, the explanation for the band's calamitous American slide is repeatedly laid at the door of the record company. Ironically, the group that had once been Warner Brothers' cash cow was now considered the black sheep. "We were spoiled," says Buck of the first few years with Warners. The attitude back then, he explains, was, " 'They're Lenny and Mo's band,' so people went the extra mile. We didn't realise that when Lenny and Mo go, everyone's going to look at us and go, 'They're Lenny and Mo's band, fuck 'em.' "

It's true that by the new decade, just about everyone who had been involved in R.E.M.'s glory days with Warner Brothers had moved on. Not just the famed duo of 'Lenny and Mo', and not just the group's point people Karin Berg and John Leshay, but as importantly, those associated with the band's lucrative 1996 contract, namely Russ Thyret and Steve Baker, and their overseers Bob Daly and Terry Semel. Now there was nobody left to take responsibility for the "$80 million" deal, nobody whose job was dependent on selling R.E.M. records above any other act.

In Daly and Semel's place as head of Warner Brothers' entire music division came the Trinidad-born Roger Ames, who had been phenomenally successful in the British music business, initially with London Records, then with the entire Polygram conglomerate before it was bought by Universal and the 'Big Six' majors became the 'Big Five'. Ames, appointed to Warner Brothers in late 1999, was considered a 'music man' through and through, but he was taking the helm of a sinking ship: Warner Brothers had slipped from its once unshakable perch as the top-selling label to a previously unimaginable number four. Ames tried to halt this slide by advocating a $20 billion merger with EMI, which would have shrunk the number of majors down to just four; the move met with such fierce resistance among European regulators as Time Warner entered negotiations with AOL that it was abandoned. In the meantime, Ames appointed another respected industry executive, Tom Whalley, to run the Warner Brothers label, but Whalley was contracted to Interscope until January 2002. Phil Quartararo continued to head Warner Brothers in the meantime, though he had not been around for R.E.M.'s heyday.

In defence of their diminished status, R.E.M. rightfully point out that they are not the only major act on Warner Brothers to have suffered in the States over recent years; such luminaries as Neil Young, Paul Simon and Eric Clapton all released records at the start of the 2000s to uncharacteristically low sales. Yet it wasn't as if Warner Brothers had forgotten how to sell music: with five million American sales of Linkin Park's début *Hybrid Theory,* the label had the biggest selling rock album of 2001 – and a bigger record than they'd ever had with R.E.M. The implications then were clear: audiences had moved on, and the big money was to be found elsewhere. R.E.M. were not just out of time, they were out of favour.

But if it's true that the record company had fallen out with and/or given up on R.E.M., then so the band may equally have given up on the label. R.E.M.'s initial American promotion for *Reveal* was slotted into a single week in between the three-week blitz of Europe and visits to Japan and Australia; during that seven-day stint the band also played the open-air concert in Toronto (Canada being a different country) and undertook a video shoot for the album's second single, 'All The Way To Reno'. There was not a single public concert in the USA around *Reveal*'s release, merely an appearance on *The David Letterman Show*, an MTV *Unplugged* special, and a couple of invite-only shows at the

Museum of Television and Radio (one in New York, one in LA) for radio broadcast. The band complained that that was all the interest the record label was able to drum up; the label complained that was all the interest they could generate. Behind the scenes, there were rumours of pressure on the band to sell songs to TV commercials, to hook up with more recognisable hit producers, to release a greatest hits album. R.E.M. said no to all of it. As for a proper live run, R.E.M. had not toured America upon the actual release of a new album since 1987, and this year would be no exception.* It was stalemate.

"No one should feel sorry for us," asserted Peter Buck on his 45th birthday. "I make records in my attic. Then I take them to the guys, we rehearse and we make records and we turn them in to the record company. And record companies have dropped the ball on plenty of great records in the past. *Pet Sounds* didn't sell anything. My feeling is, we've made consistently good work, these records could be on CD when I'm dead. We sell a lot of records each week, we sell a million records a year just on catalogue alone. I'm proud that at this stage of our careers we're still making records that people think are on a par with our best work. I know a lot of people who think *Reveal* is our best record. I think it's equal to *Automatic*. I don't care how much it sells."

All this was fair comment – apart from the last sentence. R.E.M., like any other band, want to be rewarded for their hard work. They like to be loved. They just insist it be on their own terms. For *Reveal*'s second single, 'All The Way To Reno (You're Gonna Be A Star)', a promo CD was issued in America under the unusually apologetic title *Not Bad For No Tour*, in which sales figures and chart positions from the rest of the world were listed as if it was necessary to prove to American media that the band were no failures. 'Reno', with an uplifting video shot at Bishop Ford High School in Brooklyn under the auspices of outspoken television and film commentator Michael Moore (but with the students doing

---

* U2, taking no chances after the disappointment of their 1997 album *Pop*, toured almost constantly for 18 months upon release of *All That You Can't Leave Behind*. To which Peter Buck notes, "They really want to do it. They want to be the biggest. But I just want to make records."

most of the filming as per the song's bracketed subtitle) was a moderate hit across all R.E.M.'s major markets; in the States, it continued their run of misses.

The disparity between the American homeland and the wider world at large was not just commercial. When Q magazine (which came close to becoming an R.E.M. fanzine after publishing a one-off special on the band in June, and then hiring Peter Buck as a guest columnist) celebrated its 15th Anniversary with a chart of the top albums of the last decade-and-a-half, the two R.E.M. releases to make the list were *Automatic For The People* – and *Reveal*. In the States, when the annual *Village Voice* Pazz and Jop Poll was published at the start of 2002, with a record 600+ critics voting, R.E.M. were absent from the top 20 albums list for the first time in their history. In fact, *Reveal* was absent from the entire top 50.

★　　★　　★

Within weeks of *Reveal*'s release, R.E.M. stopped working for the rest of the summer. The lone group activity consisted of ticking off another item on the rock-star's wish-list: being immortalised in cartoon form for Fox TV's classic series *The Simpsons*, in which R.E.M. would become Homer's house band when the hapless Simpson father opened a bar in his garage. Otherwise, the group sat back as 'All The Way To Reno' charted around Europe, *Reveal* sold steadily – outside of America, that is – and a documentary film based around their Scottish shows of 1999, *A Stirling Performance,* made its way into select cinemas.

For Peter Buck, it was a difficult summer. He twice made the 10,000 mile round trip to show up in British court, once in June as agreed, upon conclusion of the promo tour, and then again on July 31 for his first appearance at Isleworth Crown Court, where he pleaded not guilty to five charges, was again given bail, and set a trial date for November. The realisation kicked in that, should he be found guilty of all charges, he was looking at up to four years in jail and it inspired him to work on music as hard as ever. The demos recorded in his attic, often with Scott McCaughey alongside him, reflected his sobriety. Rather than rotating between verses and choruses, they either reflected his continued interest in electronic music, which is more about the repetition of a motif and the development of texture, or leaned towards classical structure, in which Theme A segues to Theme B, C and so on. Clearly, if Buck was going to have anything to do with it, *Reveal* would be but a relaxed reflection before another sharp left-turn.

R.E.M. had already agreed to make October their 'charity' month, with concerts announced for the Bridge School Benefit again near San Francisco, and for a global hunger organisation called Groundwork at the Key Arena in Seattle; both all-star benefits would include their friends Pearl Jam. In the meantime film director Cameron Crowe had already arranged to include 'Sweetness Follows' in a new movie, *Vanilla Sky*, starring Tom Cruise and Cameron Diaz, and now asked the band if they might have a new song for a particular early sequence against which he was struggling to place appropriate music. The band agreed to dip way back into its past for 'All The Right Friends', one of the six songs recorded for the group's first demos in Atlanta back in 1980, and which had occasionally poked its head up over the years as being a little too good for eternal avoidance. There were also discussions with Warner Brothers for some other promotional events in an attempt to kick-start the stalled *Reveal*.

The events of September 11 threw many of those plans into turmoil, just as they played havoc with the diaries of so many others in the west. That terrible morning found Michael Stipe at his home in Greenwich Village. After the first hijacked airliner hit the World Trade Center, Stipe was instantly roused, and was watching directly from his window as the second hijacked plane tore into the South Tower. Like thousands of his neighbours he took straight to the streets; he was seen by many on Manhattan's West Side Highway gaping in horror as the Twin Towers collapsed and three thousand people were killed at the hands of Osama Bin Laden's terrorists. In the midst of the death and destruction, confusion and chaos, many people on the streets approached Stipe – who used his cell phone for as long as it worked to call the families of panicked workers and relay assurances as to their safety – to thank him for all the music over the years, for the solace and companionship that R.E.M. had given. By the end of the day, 'Everybody Hurts' would be pining softly from radio sets across America (and indeed the world) just as it had done after previous tragedies. In weeks to come, a 'remix' that included news broadcasts from that morning edited in between Stipe's vocals would make its way onto the Internet, and the requests would come in from record company departments across the world for permission to reissue the song as a single. R.E.M., probably the last band on Earth to contemplate profiting from tragedy, said no to that, but yes to most requests to use the song for charity and benefit purposes. "We feel it belongs to the people," says Peter Buck of the song.

Back in 1991, when George Bush was President, and R.E.M. cancelled its promotional visit to Europe at the start of the Gulf War, Michael Stipe had told this writer during a conversation about the war that, "I'm a total peacedick, there it is." A decade later, with Bush's son, George W as President, and America suddenly gearing up for a new war after this attack on home soil, Stipe's attitude remained unchanged. Two weeks after September 11, he joined Bertis Downs in an anti-war protest on the grounds of the University of Georgia in Athens. At the end of October, by which time a war was indeed raging in Afghanistan, he appeared unannounced at a New York Against Violence benefit organised by The Beastie Boys, performing The Velvet Underground's 'All Tomorrow's Parties' with Moby accompanying him on acoustic guitar, moving into a version of Neil Young's 'Helpless' on which Bono joined in on vocals.

During the weeks in between, R.E.M. played a handful of American shows that took on a new poignancy in the light of worldwide events. Peter Buck wrote in his column for Q magazine that, "As we all talked on the phone after 11 September we felt it would be good to throw in a few impromptu performances, not so much to raise money but more to focus on our own lives, on what it is we do. We're musicians after all, and we thought performing in public would be kind of a sign of solidarity as well as being fun."

Heading to Athens for a week of rehearsals, Buck pressed manager Bertis Downs for the opportunity to play in his former home town. As it transpired, a local charity much favoured by R.E.M., Community Connection, had arranged a screening of a Jim McKay movie Our Song and a performance by local band The Possibilities on October 18. The event provided perfect cover for R.E.M.'s first home-town performance since the Greenpeace benefit at the 40 Watt Club in 1992, and the secret was so well kept that there were but 200 people in the audience when Buck, McCaughey and Stringfellow joined The Possibilities on stage following the movie. So sparse was the attendance that Downs and Community Connection organisers took to the Athens streets handing out wrist bands for "a really cool show"; locals spoiled by musical choice and unaware that it was R.E.M. on offer mostly rejected the opportunity. The band played 15 songs to a half-full Georgia Theater, following their usual encore of 'It's The End Of The World' with Patti Smith's 'People Have The Power'.

For the Bridge School Benefits R.E.M. performed a nine-song acoustic set as a six-piece; Michael Stipe concluded 'Everybody Hurts' with bowed head and a raised peace sign. For his own part, Neil Young played 'Blowin' In The Wind' and 'Imagine', but he also had a new song of his own entitled 'Let's Roll', written from the perspective of the passengers on board United Airlines Flight 93 on September 11, those who overpowered the hijackers and caused their plane to crash in the fields of Pennsylvania. It was a more militant stance than R.E.M.'s, and reflected the new conservatism sweeping across many of rock's elder generation in the wake of September 11 – a stance that R.E.M. side-stepped as they stuck by their 'peacedick' attitude.

Moving up to Seattle for a third show in three days, R.E.M. begged Pearl Jam to close out the Groundworks Benefit on October 22; despite being on home turf, Pearl Jam instead insisted that R.E.M. took the honour. R.E.M. turned in an especially powerful set for their only indoor arena show of the year, covering Pearl Jam's 'Better Man' and having Eddie Vedder join them for an encore of 'People Have The Power'.

The next night, The Minus 5 'Plus Friends' were billed to appear at the Crocodile Cafe and unlike the Athens surprise show, there was little doubt as to who those friends might be. The Crocodile stripped back a moving partition to double the size of the venue, and the band pulled out all the stops, including a rendition of Catatonia's 'Dead From The Waist Down' sung by Scott McCaughey, the frequent addition of Eddie Vedder, and the first performance of 'All The Right Friends' since 1983. "It was as good as we've ever been," asserted Peter Buck, and such was the band's exuberance that they went into a local studio the next day and cut 'All The Right Friends' in six hours. The rendition was a delightful throwback to an R.E.M. sound so many had known and loved – with Buck's Rickenbacker jangle, Mike Mills' prominent harmonies, and those dumb-but-endearing Stipe lyrics. The *Vanilla Sky* soundtrack was released just six weeks later, with the R.E.M. track in pole position, ahead even of Paul McCartney's specially written title track. Reaction from the people at Paramount Pictures was so enthusiastic that there was talk of commissioning a video for 'All The Right Friends' and releasing it as a single, but over at Warner Brothers, where Tom Whalley was finally going to take over in the new year, there was trepidation about starting a new relationship with R.E.M. on anything less than the very strongest footing. The idea was nixed and 'I'll Take The Rain' was released as *Reveal*'s third single instead. As per the last couple of albums, it proved one single too many.

There was just one more scheduled performance for R.E.M. in 2001, at the MTV Music Video Awards in Frankfurt on November 8, where the band performed 'Imitation Of Life' – though both R.E.M. and U2 lost out on their Best Group nomination to Limp Bizkit. The Frankfurt trip at least paid Peter Buck's airfare to Europe, where his court case started at Isleworth Crown Court on November 12. Other band members followed him over to offer moral support and Mike Mills, Scott McCaughey and Ken Stringfellow joined Robyn Hitchcock at Dingwalls on November 11 for a night of R.E.M., Beach Boys and Minus 5 songs. Prudently, Peter Buck stayed at home.

The case of 'Regina vs Mr Peter Lawrence Buck' opened on November 12 and was almost immediately adjourned when it was learned that an American Airlines plane had crashed in New York; once initial worries that this was another terrorist attack appeared to have been allayed, the case resumed with prosecutor Mr Edward Lewis QC delivering a rambling speech detailing Buck's activities on the flight. The guitarist had supposedly consumed 15 glasses of red wine in three hours, made grabs for champagne when told (untruthfully) that wine and whiskey had both run out, ran up and down club class where McCaughey and Stringfellow were seated, fell over and got wedged between two seats from where he began fumbling with the controls, mistook a hostess trolley for a CD player, tore up the Captain's yellow card warning, punched a wall in frustration, and after trying to claim a total stranger as his wife in club class then apparently assaulted the cabin services director with a container of yoghurt, which exploded over the hapless director (a Mr Agius) and a stewardess (Ms Holly Ward). After the altercation, according to Mr Lewis, "Mr Agius's jacket and trousers were covered in yoghurt" and, threateningly, the defendant said to him: "I can fucking take you out any time", which if it was true would suggest that Buck's British success had rubbed off to the extent that he had perfected the Friday night pub vernacular.

After the yoghurt incident, he was then escorted by another member of the crew back into First Class, where, according to the prosecution, "in his fury (he) bent down, grabbed the bottom of the trolley, flipped it over, sending all the breakfast paraphernalia flying – 20 side-dishes, 15 plates, 15 soup, and so forth, honey, marmalade, sugar cubes, the lot." Hence the classic charge of damage to British Airways crockery. As the stewards tried to pick up the mess, Buck joined in apologetically, only to apparently be seen slipping a knife up his sleeve. At this point, Captain Payne came back out to warn Buck that he would be met by police at London, a comment allegedly met with the hilarious – if only for the fact it's the last thing a sober Peter Buck would ever say – retort, "I am R.E.M."

McCaughey and Stringfellow apparently did their best to calm Buck down, and succeeded: he finally fell asleep for the rest of the flight. As for why Bob Whittaker, as tour manager, wasn't able to do the job, it appeared that Whittaker was also derailed by the combination of wine and half a sleeping pill, at one point taking his shirt off as he and Buck kept wandering into business class to join their companions.

It might have seemed an open–and–shut case of woeful misconduct under the influence of drink, prescription drugs and lack of sleep. However, as Mr Lewis admitted at the start of his speech, "It is right to say that identity is, to an extent, an issue, and therefore we will have to hear what the witnesses say as to whether it was Mr Buck, in fact, that was the person who was misbehaving. The Crown say that on hearing the evidence and the totality of it you will find as a fact that the person we are talking about was Mr Buck and not Mr Whittaker." Mr Lewis then closed his comments by acknowledging that "there is an issue, clearly, on identity which you will have to deal with."

The next morning, Judge Crocker dealt with that issue promptly, discharging the jury. "Matters have arisen which necessitate that this trial cannot proceed at the moment," he told them, which was taken by the lawyers and defendants to mean that there was too much confusion over who had done what. He announced that a date would be set for a retrial – and while the affair would therefore hang over Buck's head for several more months, the guitarist was at least home for Christmas. Being Buck, he grabbed Mike Mills and headed off to Hawaii for a working holiday of maximum songwriting.

★   ★   ★

The retrial date was set for early March, which at least allowed R.E.M. to welcome in the new year by performing a couple more charity shows. These were not the group's usual non-profit appearances either at small clubs (à la the recent Georgia Theater show in Athens) or the great outdoors (e.g. the Bridge School Benefits or Trafalgar Square) but high ticket price, black tie VIP affairs such as R.E.M. had steered clear of for many years. Perhaps it was something about the new line-up allowing a new beginning, perhaps it was the onslaught of middle age and the familiarity with wearing suits in and out of court appearances, or perhaps it was easier to say yes than to say no, but R.E.M. went ahead with two of their most unusual shows of all time.

The first was at the venerable Carnegie Hall in Manhattan for the 20th Anniversary of the Gay Men's Health Crisis – which on the face of it, was a perfect charity for the group to support.* But the event was also honouring Gerald Levin and AOL Time Warner for his and the company's continued support in the fight against AIDS. While it was true that Warner Brothers, back in the old

---

* There had been a splash in the British press the previous year after Michael Stipe announced he had been in a three-year relationship with another man, as if his sexuality needed further confirmation.

days, had been one of the most liberal and open-minded of all the major music conglomerates, and that this was clearly a good thing, the notion that R.E.M. would be honouring the same person who had dismantled the most successful record company of all time, and in the process be publicly supporting the record company that they claimed no longer publicly supported them, seemed somewhat contradictory. Perhaps it was an attempt to kiss and make up: Levin was departing AOL Time Warner, handing over the chairmanship to Richard Parsons, and this event was a 'golden watch' kind of farewell gala. There would be plenty of high-powered AOL Time Warner brass in the front row seats, whose costly tickets would also be funding a well-deserving charity. R.E.M. may well have figured that their first concert at Carnegie Hall could serve the best of many purposes.

With Jewel and Sweet Honey On The Rock also on the bill, the concert was publicly advertised, and as R.E.M.'s first indoor New York City concert since the Garden in 1995, one could have imagined it rapidly selling out. Yet as a black-tie charity event, tickets ranged from $100 for the nosebleed seats up to $250 and above for the 'parquet'. This was beyond most R.E.M. loyalists' budget and the balconies were therefore far from full when the band took the stage for a 45-minute set – directly after Gerald Levin's thank-you speech and an introduction by Whoopi Goldberg along the lines that "R.E.M. rock shit." Which they did. Michael Stipe played into the role of Andy Kaufman inviting the audience for "milk and cookies" by continually advertising the band's after-show party at the Russian Tea Rooms.* The group took advantage of Carnegie Hall's famed acoustics to have Mike Mills play a previously unheard grand piano part on 'The One I Love' which, as with a hard-rocking 'Walk Unafraid' and a funked-up 'Let Me In', seemed an apt choice for the occasion. 'All The Right Friends' got only its second airing in almost twenty years, and of course they closed, as intimated all night long, with their Kaufman tribute 'Man On The Moon'. As intimation of where the group might be

---

* In the movie *Man On The Moon*, Carnegie Hall was the site of Kaufman's performance swan song, complete with The Rockettes. Only at soundcheck did R.E.M. grasp that the scene in the movie had been shot at Radio City Music Hall instead.

headed on a future indoor hall tour, it was mesmerising, but it was still a strange occasion, with the suits leaving the front rows in ever increasing numbers as R.E.M. turned up the volume. That a million dollars was raised for charity and that R.E.M. were seen to stand by their label's commitment to the fight against AIDS no doubt rendered it sufficiently successful for the band.

Two weeks later, the group played an even stranger benefit on the west coast – the first ever Love Rocks, celebrating U2's Bono as Humanitarian of the Year for his work on Debt Relief. The night of mutual back-slapping also included No Doubt and Lauryn Hill, and was hosted by Drew Carey in front of an A-List Holly-wood crowd. R.E.M. had already intended to ham up the occasion by covering Sonny and Cher's 'I Got You Babe' as a deliberately misleading tribute to a different, (Sonny) Bono, and when they found out that Cher herself would be at the event, Michael Stipe talked the legendary singer-actress into joining them for the spoof. Her surprise appearance was sandwiched between 'Imitation Of Life' and 'Losing My Religion'; Tom Cruise then introduced the living Bono, whose speech was followed by R.E.M. performing U2's 'One', with Bono, not surprisingly, joining in. For a band that had spent its early days playing 'I Got You Babe' in Georgian bars, singing with the real Cher while honouring Bono alongside Tom Cruise in front of Hollywood players must have been as strange an occasion as they come.

"There is no way to put something like this in perspective," wrote a clearly star-struck Peter Buck in Q, "except to say: I'll see you in jail next month."

★   ★   ★

Peter Buck's retrial began on March 18, 2002. Once again the British media showed up in droves to cover the case in as much lurid detail as possible. When a new Crown prosecutor, David Bate QC, set out precisely the same claims against Buck as Mr Lewis had the previous November, it was clear that the high-profile 'air rage' case had begun in earnest. Since September 11, flight crews, fellow passengers and law enforcement all seemed to be pushing for zero tolerance of in-flight misbehaviour in the interest of overall safety, and while Buck's incident had taken place several months before those terrorist attacks, still the pall of that awful day hung over the court proceedings as if Buck might be made a suitable scapegoat.

On the opening day, the jury listened as Cabin Services Director Mario Agius, whom Buck was accused of assaulting, detailed Buck's conduct and the 'yoghurt' incident while admitting to having taken out a £5,000 civil suit against Buck; a flight attendant, Nara Incecchi, also talked of grabbing Buck's hand away from a control panel as he announced his desire to "go home". Day two saw a succession of British Airways employees, including Ms Holly Ward (the other staff member Buck was accused of assaulting), take the stand and tell correlating stories regarding the seemingly ceaseless incidents and their steady progression from childish insolence to threatening behaviour, via Buck's pissing over the floor of the toilet and Whittaker's smearing himself with ice cream. Steward Ravinder Singh talked of physically restraining Buck after his assault on Agius; Nara Incecchi admitted she was "scared to death" when she saw Buck slip a knife up his sleeve; and an American woman, Linda Christianson, confirmed that Buck had tried claiming her as his wife.

On the third day, Captain Tom Payne verified every worst detail, including Buck's reaction to the 'yellow card' warning: "When I served the document he took it, tore it into pieces and dropped them on the floor. It was as though what I had done was irrelevant. He was just standing there in front of me with very little expression, trying to ignore me, as if I had not done anything." Finally it was Buck's turn to take the stand. He described downing a sleeping pill with a glass of red wine, and then, as he told the story of waking up in a Heathrow jail, "I recall . . . there were bright lights overhead. I wasn't really awake. I had this fear I had had a heart attack and was in a weird hospital in Disneyland. I don't mean I was seeing characters or anything like that. I was just struggling to get conscious." Clearly taking the recalcitrant approach, he announced how, "To me it was just incomprehensible . . . I have never been in trouble before . . . I will go miles away to avoid confrontation. I really don't like it." The following day, under cross-examination, Buck said that he couldn't really explain why he hadn't told police at the airport that he'd taken the Ambien pills. "It didn't really occur to me. I felt scared, kind of terrified, kind of foggy . . . I was just trying to deal with a very difficult situation. I didn't know exactly what was going through my mind at the time."

Robert Whittaker took the stand to confirm that he had taken half an Ambien pill himself, and could also remember little of the subsequent journey. Called for the defence, Professor Ian Hindmarch from the University of Surrey explained that clinical trials on Ambien had revealed serious side effects, especially when the intended heavy sleep was interrupted; such effects included confusion, forgetfulness, loss of balance and "bizarre behaviour". Mixing Ambien with alcohol would only "enhance" such effects, he asserted.

In turn the prosecution called its own psychiatric expert who testified that Buck's actions were not those of an "automaton" under the influence of drugs but those of a regular drunk: the fact that Buck knew the purpose of an exit door indicated as much. (Though the question would then beg as to why he mistook a hostess trolley for a CD player.)

The trial finally lived up to its rock'n'roll promise at the start of its second week when U2's Bono returned R.E.M.'s support from a couple of months back and showed up as a character witness for Peter Buck. Wearing a black suit, black shirt and a single gold-and-silver earring, the rock star assured the court that in 17 years of friendship with Buck, since the Milton Keynes concert of 1985, "I have never ever seen him drunk." To many who knew both men, this comment suggested either Buck's considerable capacity for alcohol or Bono's own high threshold for drunkenness, and it was a comment that QC Bate worked hard to trip Bono up on under cross-examination. But without success. "Most people that are in bands don't drink if they're serious and professional about what they do," the U2 singer insisted with a straight face. To Buck's own barrister David Ferguson, Bono proved typically garrulous. "It's very strange behaviour and I just wanted to stand up and be counted and say this is ridiculous really . . . It's hard to get him to go on tour, he loves his kids so much."

Court crowds got a further celebrity sighting the next day when both Michael Stipe and Mike Mills took the stand. Stipe, who early on in his testimony apologised for being nervous and explained to the judge that, "I'm kind of shy," referred to Buck as his "big brother". "When I was 19, he was the only person who would talk to me." Denying that he had ever seen Peter act aggressively, he explained how Buck was the definition of "a southern gentleman, someone who is considerate of all people, and genteel, and polite." As for Buck's blackout, Stipe elaborated how "he has a photographic memory, an account of every single thing", implying that something unusual must have taken place for Buck to have no knowledge of it. When Stipe concluded that, "He's a gentle, kind, incredible person, he would never be rude to anyone", his sincerity was such that even QC Bate could not see the purpose of cross-examination.

Mike Mills then described Peter as "honest, straightforward, kind, and calm" while acknowledging that when R.E.M. were not working, he might see his partner only two or three times a year. Mills, known as "trouble" within the R.E.M. camp for being the last at the bar, acknowledged that he and Buck both liked red wine with dinner, but insisted that Buck would stop drinking at the end of a meal.

We should all be so lucky as to have Bono and Michael Stipe (and Mike Mills, of course) testify to our great character while on trial for air rage. But probably the most valuable witness on Buck's behalf was his wife, Stephanie Dorgan, who before putting her money into the Crocodile Cafe and marrying Peter had been a lawyer. She was the last witness and her description of Peter as a "very gentle man . . . shy . . . very self-effacing", and her insistence that "I would not be married to him if he was anything like" (the person he was accused of being on the British Airways flight), probably carried considerable weight. The case was adjourned until after the Easter holidays, and just as R.E.M. had stuck around in Switzerland when Bill Berry was in hospital, so the band now stuck around in London while awaiting closing arguments and the jury's verdict.

The more it had gone on, the more ridiculous the whole case seemed. It was clear that nobody on either side was deliberately lying, but that events had proceeded as Buck had indicated – unwisely mixing a potent sleeping pill with too much alcohol in an attempt to relieve stress – followed by the unpleasant actions as described by the British Airways staff. Buck was clearly embarrassed, apologetic and suitably chastened, while the Crown Prosecution felt the need to clamp down firmly on air rage regardless of mitigating circumstances or the 'guilty' party's public popularity. Even the most loyal R.E.M. fan on Internet forums found it difficult to claim Buck's innocence and yet no one could see the point of sending a well-liked, generally agreeable, highly successful rock star – and doting father – to jail. It seemed clear that Buck and his family had already suffered personally, that the drawn-out trial had cost considerable amounts of time and money and that it was unlikely that Peter Buck, or any other halfway intelligent rock star, would mix sleeping pills with free-flowing booze on board a British Airways flight again. (And perhaps British Airways and other airlines would be forced to rethink the effects of offering continual alcohol on long-haul flights to first-class passengers.) Aghast at the waste of time and money, and the crap shoot of a jury vote that could lead to jail time, American fans wondered why Buck's lawyers hadn't plea-bargained, acknowledging guilt on lesser charges to get the case out of the way. The answer was because the British legal system didn't work that way.

Closing arguments were made on April 4. The jury returned with its verdict on April 5, 22 years to the day since R.E.M. had made their live début at the Oconee Street church in Athens. No one knew that morning whether R.E.M. would be celebrating their anniversary proudly or sadly.

It turned out to be the former. The jury found Peter Buck not guilty of all charges. Buck sighed audibly, his wife burst into tears, and Michael Stipe gave Mike Mills a bear hug. Outside the court, Buck stood by as lawyer Neill Blundell read a statement: "I am grateful to the court, the jury and my lawyers, to my family, friends and supporters who have stood by me throughout this experience. I am obviously relieved to be finished here and I look forward to be returning my attention to my family, my band and music." Buck confirmed that he would be flying home on British Airways. The airline confirmed it was happy to have him as a passenger.

R.E.M. went out that Friday night in London and celebrated, reminiscing about their début concert half a lifetime ago that night. Had they really called themselves Twisted Kites – or was that just revisionist history? Why *not* Cans Of Piss instead of R.E.M.? What cover songs had they really played? 'God Save The Queen' for sure. 'Honky Tonk Women' too. 'I Can't Control Myself' and 'Roadrunner' were definites. 'You Really Got Me' seemed familiar, but why were they now thinking they had also included 'Sweet Home Alabama'? Would that really have been a sensible choice, even by the uncomplicated standards of 1980? How were they supposed to remember it all anyway? They'd been riotously drunk, given that they'd been neither "serious or professional" back then. How would they ever have imagined they'd be sitting together trying to piece it all back together, from their perch as one of the most consistently popular and acclaimed rock bands of all time, yet still united by their love of music and of each other, some 22 years later?

★   ★   ★

When this author visited Seattle, in December 2001, for interviews with Peter Buck, the guitarist was dealing with two different, conflicting facets of R.E.M. On the positive side, he had just wrapped up a couple of days' work with Scott McCaughey in his bare-bones attic studio (mainly filled not with recording equipment but a vast library of rock books), where they had recorded enough demos of basic song ideas to fill an R.E.M. album. On the negative side, the guitarist then spent over an hour of his 45th birthday on a conference call with Michael, Mike and Bertis, expressing his frustration with the increasingly slow process of decision-making, let alone that of recording and touring. The fact that Buck now lived in the Pacific North West, while Stipe spent most of his time, when not globe-trotting, in New York City on the East Coast, hardly helped matters, of course, but the problem was equally due to the absence of Bill Berry. The drummer had always been R.E.M.'s taskmaster *and* peace-maker, ensuring that neither recording sessions nor the songs that they produced went on for too long. With Buck sharing Berry's sense of urgency, and Mills and Stipe tending towards deliberation and perfectionism, this had created a natural equilibrium within R.E.M. Following Berry's departure, Buck had embraced the experimental sessions that resulted in *Up*, and he was proud of the album *Reveal*, but it was evident that he felt

375

outnumbered by his long-term partners and their slow working methods. Hiring Seattle-based friends had provided some comfort along the way, but did not fully serve to redress the balance, given that they did not have voting rights. The 'three-legged dog' – a metaphor Michael Stipe must have wished he had never uttered – was walking with a pronounced limp.

Buck's clearance in the air rage trial did not serve to speed matters up. The year 2002 would have gone by without a single release from R.E.M. but for Stipe's executive production of *r.e.m.IX*, for which six songs from *Reveal* were given over to eight primarily electronic music producers/engineers to reinterpret at will. R.E.M. had dipped a toe in the remix world way back as 1988, when 'Finest Worksong' was given 'Lengthy Club Mix'. With typical R.E.M. contrariness, they then shied away from the concept even as the electronic remix – whether aimed for the dance floor or the bedroom – became almost ubiquitous through the Nineties, not only as a commercial selling point for singles, but as an alternative presentation for entire albums. R.E.M.'s historic aversion to the usual corporate games might explain why, now that they finally decided to embrace the latter concept, they opted to give the results away quietly, as a free download via their website. But that decision might also have been due to the project's modest artistic merits and commercial potential, Michael Stipe having assigned duties instead to such minor names as Andy LeMaster, Her Space Holiday and the aptly named Knobody. Only respected electronic producer Matthew Herbert, and *Reveal* engineer Jamie Candiloro, had any kind of real name recognition for the group's fans. Stipe appeared unconcerned, declaring that his expectations "were met and surpassed by every single remixer" and expressing his hope "that music lovers who are not R.E.M. fans or pop music fans might hear one of these and having never heard the album version take it as the definitive mix."

If so, few such listeners stepped forward. A handful of the ten remixes warranted repeat listening, especially Knobody/Dahoud Darien's trip-hop treatment of 'The Lifting', Herbert's grand aural sound-scaping on 'I've Been High' and the lone up-tempo workout – a dirty, grinding and thoroughly audacious rendition of 'Beachball' by Chef that eschewed vocals until the last few seconds and as such, bore almost no resemblance whatsoever to the original. But the truth was that the *Reveal* material didn't readily lend itself to such endeavours to begin with, and that listening through four consecutive experimental remixes of 'I've Been High' was tough on both fans of the original version *and* those of the avant-garde remix format. The free price sticker didn't seem to increase *r.e.m.IX*'s value; reviews were few and far between and not desperately complimentary.

While Stipe engaged in these electronic experiments and Mills kept a typically low profile, Peter Buck countered his ongoing frustrations and celebrated his ongoing freedom by hitting the road for three months with The Minus 5, including a prestigious theatre tour in September opening for Wilco, whose *Yankee Hotel Foxtrot* album was being hailed with the kind of accolades once reserved for R.E.M. (While awaiting its release, Wilco had lent their talents to the new Minus 5 album, humorously entitled *Down With Wilco*; its intended release to coincide with the three months' touring was now in limbo as The Minus 5's label, Mammoth, was swallowed up by a major and most of its acts unceremoniously dropped.)

When Buck then went into a Seattle studio with McCaughey to record more polished demos of five possible R.E.M. songs, they brought drummer Bill Rieflin with them. Rieflin had come to prominence through his powerhouse drumming with the industrial Chicago rock outfit Ministry, their various Wax Trax! Records offshoots, and other prominent industrial acts, but he had been known to McCaughey from his residence in Seattle as far back as the late Seventies, at which time he played in a band called the Black Outs. Rieflin had recently returned to Seattle to live; he was of similar age to Buck (and McCaughey), had come of age in the same post-punk period of eager experimentation, and had played as many different styles and substances as anyone around. Buck knew Rieflin's talent from the *Dinner With Friends* project, and Rieflin's subsequent performance on the Seattle demos was instantly noted by all in the R.E.M. camp, including Pat McCarthy. After further discussions and meetings, a decision was made to bring him into the studio to record with R.E.M., and though it was not the original intent, he soon replaced Joey Waronker, who preferred to leave the fold than share the drum stool. Rieflin's insertion into R.E.M., alongside McCaughey and Ken Stringfellow, gave Peter Buck his own band within a band, with which he could continue to rehearse and record in Seattle. This, at least, might help scratch the itch while he waited around on his official R.E.M. partners. There was an inadvertent additional bonus to the change: R.E.M. once more had a drummer who answered to the name of Bill.

Twenty-five

In retrospect, it's easy to understand why R.E.M. would have chosen to try and replicate the success of *Reveal* by continuing to work with Pat McCarthy for another set of lusciously produced, semi-acoustic mid-tempo songs. After all, *Reveal* had proven an unqualified commercial and near-unanimous critical success not only across Europe, now the group's main commercial territory, but in any number of other countries where R.E.M., 20 years into its albums career, was still making fresh inroads and winning new fans. The fact that it had bombed in the group's American homeland had been written off for a variety of reasons, many of them laid at the door of the increasingly dysfunctional relationship with the record company. Besides, the one time the group had previously maintained course across two albums – after the unexpected success of *Out of Time*, when had they stayed off the road, moved further into semi-acoustic mode, and maintained a producer (Scott Litt) for what was then an unprecedented third consecutive album – they had been rewarded with their most popular and lauded record of all, *Automatic For The People*. Why not adopt a similar mind-set of consistency a decade further on?

And yet in hindsight, it's equally obvious why this plan was destined for disaster. With that aforementioned exception, every R.E.M. album had almost wilfully set out to upset or offset its predecessor, to challenge audience (and band) expectations, to maintain a constant forward motion that ensured the group's reputation as the most creative of major bands on the planet. In fact, back in the days when they had recorded an album annually, they had clearly articulated their unpredictable approach: If you don't like our new record, hey, we'll have a different one for you next year.

But R.E.M. were no longer recording an album a year; they had moved into that stage of middle-age where everything in life – but

379

especially recording albums – seems to become a more complicated, more protracted process. And for all that *Reveal* was constantly cited by the band as their best album to date, there were enough long-term fans who had expressed disappointment with what they saw as a frustratingly pedestrian R.E.M. that the band ought, by rights, to have sat up and taken notice, to have taken *Reveal*'s impressive international success and turned it in a different musical direction. The global audience would likely have followed regardless; the older American fanbase that had recently abandoned the band might well have come back on board. There would have been, surely, nothing to lose.

And yet, for the first time in their career, R.E.M. chose security, comfort, familiarity. In the process – however inadvertently – they opted for stasis. And that was not a word one readily associated with R.E.M.

So, at least, reads the convenient perspective of history. The real problem with the album that became *Around The Sun*, released in late 2004 and unanimously derided as R.E.M.'s one and only true dud, was not necessarily that of intent, for although the band stuck with its producer, they didn't consciously set out to replicate *Reveal*. Nor was the dilemma, despite an easy assumption of such, the songs themselves: taken individually, the material on *Around The Sun* was not merely similar to that on *Reveal*, but, in many cases, better. The problem was one of process. For if *Reveal* had found R.E.M. slowing down in the studio, *Around The Sun* saw them grinding to a halt. Never had they spent so long tinkering with one set of songs; never would they do so again.

Two months of on-off recording at the Warehouse in Vancouver at the end of 2002 was followed by a longer stint there in early 2003, easily enough time for the R.E.M. of old to record a couple of great albums. Instead, it produced an awful lot of ideas but not many complete songs. Talking it up, Buck told *Rolling Stone* in February, "I always like to leave a demo sound, so we're trying to pretend we're making demos, and it's working really well . . . And everyone's just willing to try anything new." But in the same interview he emitted a warning sign. "We have so many songs right now, it's a little frustrating for everyone because we can't figure out what exactly the record is."

Still, some firm fruit from these sessions was made public on March 23, 2003, three days after the American-led invasion of Iraq, when R.E.M. played a surprise in-store gig in Vancouver, and unveiled the song 'Final Straw', a studio version of which they simultaneously streamed on their website. 'Final Straw' was, in essence, an old-fashioned protest folk song, light on the rhythm section, propelled predominantly by a swiftly strummed acoustic guitar, and dominated by its vocalist. Stipe's melody was quietly delivered – indeed, almost whispered – and partially defiant: "If the world were filled with the likes of you/Then I'm putting up a fight." And yet Stipe, who would come to call himself "the world's angriest pacifist" over the next couple of years, knew better than to fight fire (power) with equal violence. "Love will be my strongest weapon," he insisted instead in the same song. "I do believe that I am not alone."

He was not alone, certainly, but it was a tough time for anyone of a peaceful nature to try and hunker down and embrace their creativity: the American government, just 18 months after the horrors of 9/11, was embarking now on a war of choice, and unlike the invasion of Afghanistan in the aftermath of the Al Qaeda terror attacks, this time the world was not falling into step behind it. "Every sensible person knew that there was no reason for us to attack Iraq," said Buck later down the line. "It didn't accomplish anything and we knew it wouldn't. We finished ['Final Straw'] the week before the bombing started and put it up on the website . . . It didn't stop the war and I didn't expect it to, but if nothing else, if my kids ask me, 'What did you do when all this crap was going on, dad?' it's like, I did what I could."

"This is the strongest voice I could think of to send out there," Michael Stipe wrote on R.E.M.'s website upon the song's unveiling. "We had to send something out there now." And so they did, and it was an appropriate gesture, testament to R.E.M.'s continued political activism. Still, as an example of the problems that befell the album it was recorded for, it would be 18 months before 'Final Straw' saw official release on *Around The Sun* – properly mixed and mastered, and cleaner for sure, its fuzzy electric guitar more audible in the mix. But it was not necessarily much *better*. More so, the song had lost some bite in the interim: though the Iraq war remained ongoing in late 2004 – indeed, though the group might have felt somewhat vindicated by what looked suspiciously like a civil war in that country, were they the vindictive types – 'Final Straw' no longer seemed so significant.

To their credit, R.E.M. had always been acutely aware of the pitfalls of making political commentary by way of topical journalism, and a good song remains a good song regardless of its subject matter or its release date. But it's worth noting that Bruce Springsteen was inspired to write and record a dozen songs about the post 9/11 world and have them out in the form of the acclaimed album *The Rising* by the summer of 2002. Had R.E.M. reacted with similar speed, their own album might have reflected that urgency and been met with equal high regard; instead, right at the point that they should have hunkered down to complete such a record, they packed up the studio instead and hit the road to tout a compilation.

The decision to do so in support of what was called, without enormous imagination, *In Time: The Best Of R.E.M. 1988–2003,* could not have been an easy one. Though R.E.M. had actively championed the B-sides collection *Dead Letter Office*, and had quietly sanctioned I.R.S.'s *Eponymous* and *The Best Of R.E.M*, all of which comprised various music from the years 1981–87, they had never toured to specifically *promote* a compilation, let alone break an album session for such a purpose. But the band appeared to recognise the need to appease Warner Brothers, at least in the band's troubled American homeland – to build bridges, mend fences and at least *try* and return the relationship to where it had stood in the better part of the Nineties. It helped that Warners' new label head, Tom Whalley, who had been appointed before *Reveal*'s release but only started work at the company after it had tanked in the States, was a fervent R.E.M. fan: he even held a party at his house to launch the compilation, which the band attended along with the label staff. Besides, a compilation did not require additional advances from the label, it did not typically necessitate recording costs, and if promoted properly, its likely high sales would help ensure the band's positive bank balance with the label – not only in terms of royalties due but respect afforded. To further satisfy the corporate hand that fed them, R.E.M. not only embarked on its first proper world tour in five years but, whilst in Vancouver, allocated two new songs, 'Bad Day' and 'Animal', to the 18-song compilation for the specific purpose of exclusivity.

'Bad Day', as evident to anyone who had their hands on the Athens demos from *Lifes Rich Pageant*, was a hold-over from 1986. In that initial form, the singular bad day had laid the musical and lyrical foundation for what would expand into the apocalyptic 'It's The End Of The World As We Know It'. (One can easily phrase the words of either of those Eighties recordings over the other.) The arrangement was only somewhat updated in 2003 to avoid these comparisons, and not to the total extinction of the original lyrics, which still opened with the concept of "a public service announcement [that] followed me home the other day", continuing the theme of unwelcome news and general disarray through a chorus that, fortuitously for its placement on a compilation, recycled the best of R.E.M. It wasn't their most original song, but it was immediately one of their more anthemic.

'Animal' represented the more significant creative leap. With verses set to a pumping Eastern-style electric guitar/backwards drums riff, very similar to that of the Chemical Brothers' 1997 block-rocking epic 'The Private Psychedelic Reel', it offered an enticing hint at a drugged-up R.E.M. before reverting to a more conventional arrangement in its chorus. The original mix was hazy, opaque, Mills' backing vocals unusually muffled, Stipe likewise fighting to keep his voice (resplendent with lines like "I'm vibrating at the speed of light") above the instrumental waterline, and in holding back like that, it threatened to restrict the song's commercial potential as a single. Nonetheless, this pair of songs – pre-declared to represent *The Best Of R.E.M.*, despite no clear consensus from the public – suggested, in stark contrast to 'Final Straw', that R.E.M. were back to their brash, experimental old selves.

As the *In Time* compilation ramped up in apparent importance, with a summer European festival tour and American fall arena tour announced to preclude its October 2003 release, so it became important to produce equally high-profile new promo videos. For 'Bad Day', director Tim Hope succeeded in dressing not just Stipe but Mills and Buck in suits and ties, flattening down the latter pair's hair in the process and employing the trio as a TV news team, Stipe comfortably playing the role of anchor, Mills and Buck gamely adopting that of a weatherman and roving reporter respectively. If there was a welcome display of humour in this rare piece of play-acting, there was also a serious underlying comment on the public's growing addiction to news feeds, with the 'crawl' (which had only taken hold on television screens post 9/11) threatening at one point to engulf the whole screen. The video for 'Animal', shot later in the year by Motion Theory, was essentially a solo vehicle for Stipe, who wore the metaphorical mask of the modern-day actor starring in a futuristic, claustrophobic urban Hollywood thriller, revealing a six-pack stomach in the process of de-robing his upper body. Profoundly over-the-top, a universe away from the understated videos of Eighties R.E.M., it nonetheless matched the power of the song's later, louder single remix and, again, emphasised that R.E.M. were every bit the modern day monster rock band – when they wanted to be.

And through their tour of Europe in the summer and America in the fall, they appeared relatively desirous of that role. With Rieflin settling in on drums, McCaughey and Stringfellow augmenting on guitars and keyboards, and the necessary special effects and bright lights providing comfort of sorts for those at the back of the vast audiences, the group attacked and conquered many of Europe's largest stages, including the headlining slots at the major outdoor festivals of Glastonbury and Move (in England), T in the Park (Scotland), Werchter (Belgium), Neapolis (Italy), Les Côtes du Rock (France), Paléo (Switzerland), and other indoor and outdoor shows in Denmark, Austria, Poland, Ireland and Germany, where an outdoor performance at Wiesbaden's Bowling Green town square was filmed for future release. The tour having originally intended to serve as an advertisement for the forthcoming Warners compilation, it was therefore with typical contrariness that R.E.M. used the concerts to revive material from their I.R.S. days, return-ing such songs to the set as 'Maps And Legends', 'Little America', 'Exhuming McCarthy', 'I Believe', 'These Days', 'Feeling Gravity's Pull', 'Crazy', 'Carnival of Sorts' and 'Talk About The Passion', none of which had been played since the Eighties.

In fact, going a step further (backwards), a nostalgic R.E.M. even dug up the unreleased pre-*Murmur* song 'Permanent Vacation', introducing it in Vienna in time to have it nailed for the concert film shot in Wiesbaden a week later. The idea may or may not have been seeded at pre-tour rehearsals in Athens in June, when Bill Berry stopped by in chef's whites to prepare sushi for his former bandmates. (An invitation to scrap rehearsals the following day and spend it at his farm was gratefully accepted.) He then showed up to the tour's penultimate concert in Raleigh, North Carolina, on October 10, where he not only joined the group for backing vocals on 'Radio Free Europe' but took his place behind the drums for 'Permanent Vacation', his first live appearance with R.E.M. since leaving the group in 1997. A memorable night concluded with The Minus 5 – Buck, McCaughey and Stringfellow from the touring R.E.M. along with Mike Mills and support act Pete Yorn – playing a club gig in nearby Chapel Hill.

That North American tour, which opened in Vancouver on August 29 and concluded in Atlanta on October 11, focused almost exclusively on amphitheatres and arenas (with the occasional daytime stop off for a radio exclusive), suggesting that the group's concert draw had not been deeply affected by the drop-off in album sales – although, and especially with the impending release of *In Time*, this equally indicated that R.E.M. were in danger of slipping into the nostalgia circuit, where adult audiences show up to hear the hits from their youth and use the introduction of new songs as an excuse for a visit to bar or the bathroom. R.E.M. strived to keep that danger at bay by, as ever, changing up the set list each night, re-introducing more and more old songs ('Shaking Through' showed up for the first time since the Eighties late in the tour), and throwing in unexpected cover versions, such as Stipe's solo interpretation of Interpol's powerful post 9/11 song 'NYC' in New York, on which he accompanied himself on acoustic guitar. For sheer emotion, the New York and Raleigh concerts were rivalled by the one at the Hollywood Bowl, where the band celebrated Ken Stringfellow's marriage the previous day and commemorated the death of Warren Zevon, who had passed away, not unexpectedly, just two days before that; in dedicating 'Find The River' to his former Hindu Love Gods partner, Mike Mills visibly and audibly choked up. Under the circumstances, the planned disruption of 'Man On The Moon' by a Tony Clifton impersonator, who argued with Stipe, threw the singer's lyrics sheets in the air, poured cups of water over the band members' heads and got into a deliberate fight with security, seemed perfectly par for the course.

Perhaps the most poignant moment of that North American tour, however, took place not on a concert stage at all, but at the David Letterman Theater in New York City on October 2, where R.E.M. performed 'Bad Day' 20 years to the month since their memorable first national television appearance, playing 'Radio Free Europe' for the same late night host. Presumptions might well have been made about a loss of energy over the years; they would have been wrong. Peter Buck still ducked and dived on his guitar, indeed was still playing the same black Rickenbacker, and if he and Mike Mills had fleshed out somewhat in the middle, Stipe appeared to make up for them; the art student who had stood motionless at the microphone in 1983, deliberately mumbling his words, now stood resplendent, confident and charismatic, deliberately dressed down in a black hoody (Mills likewise eschewing his Nudie suits for a leather jacket), but dancing to the song's coda with sufficient grace for Manhattan's trendiest nightclubs. The overall volume and velocity of the performance was phenomenal; few other acts in the world could still claim such presence and power over two decades after forming. The only disappointment in this significant Anniversary was Letterman's own complete failure to reference it, as if oblivious that it was his show that had first introduced R.E.M. to the masses, back when he, too, was a cult rather than a colossus.

The American tour had barely concluded a week later before the band were back on a plane to Europe, performing on that continent's own high-profile television and radio shows (adding a 250-capacity lunchtime concert in London for fan club members); barely a pause for breath and they were doing the same again in the States – for Jay Leno, for Ellen DeGeneres, and for a low-key theatre show at the Avalon in Hollywood, which R.E.M. had known back in 1983 and '84 as the Palace. No stone appeared to have been left unturned in building anticipation for *In Time*, and the dividends paid off when the compilation topped the charts in the UK (where 'Bad Day' also made the top ten), Germany, Australia and other countries, and, significantly, made the top ten in the USA. Bolstered by a limited edition second compilation CD that gathered a host of rarities and even a couple of previously unreleased exclusives, *In Time* sold an impressive 130,000 copies in its first two weeks in the States. It would eventually be certified platinum, the band's first American million-seller since *New Adventures In Hi-Fi*. In other territories, it performed even more emphatically: five times platinum in the UK, four times platinum in Australia, two times platinum in Germany and so on. It had, it would appear, achieved its goals, confirming the band's phenomenal global status – as a live band as well as a catalogue recording act – and, presumably, setting them up perfectly for the next studio album. Under the circumstances, the somewhat dismal sales of the single 'Animal', released at the start of 2004 (even in the UK, it failed to make the top 30), could readily be put down to familiarity.

Only with the benefit of hindsight would it become apparent that with *In Time*, R.E.M. reached a point in their career where their past started to overtake their future. Almost every group of longevity reaches this mixed blessing of a milestone, but few come into it carrying the credibility of R.E.M., whose focus had always been so fixated on the future. Yet from here on in, there would be a higher number of sanctioned R.E.M. compilations and live releases than there would be new studio albums. Indeed, barely had the dust settled on *In Time* than it was announced that the outdoor concert in Wiesbaden's Bowling Green would be released in the spring as a DVD – officially, R.E.M.'s first concert movie since *Road Movie* back in 1995, yet their second catalogue release in a row – entitled *Perfect Square*. Musically, there was nothing wrong with the package; the set ran the full gamut of the group's career, as far back as that unreleased 'Permanent Vacation'. But visually, it bordered on the offensive. The frenetic editing jumped, literally every couple of seconds, from the Jumbotron screen-shots of the band to the face-painted superstar Stipe, to guitar fret close-ups, vast crowd sweeps and repetitively, relentlessly, tediously returning to shots of beautiful young Germans singing along to every (recent) hit single. Unwitting or inadvertent though it may have been, the filming and editing crudely played up every cliché of the stadium rock act. 1990's *Tourfilm* had been a triumph because it was so damn weird a concert souvenir – representative of an Eighties group that had grown into arenas without compromising its

387

presentation. *Road Movie* was more faithful to movie-making convention, but there were still enough unusual angles and edits to render it interesting. About the only thing weird or interesting about *Perfect Square* was that R.E.M. had allowed its release.

★   ★   ★

The *In Time* tour completed, R.E.M. did not resume immediate work in the studio – as if they needed time off from each other first. Mike Mills joined the Tell Us The Truth tour, initiated by Billy Bragg and Steve Earle; an attack on "media consolidation" and "corporate globalisation", the short American tour also featured Tom Morello, formerly of Rage Against The Machine, Boots Riley of The Roots, and Lester Chambers among others. Michael Stipe, meanwhile, showed up on New York's Lower East Side when MTV filmed the act Dashboard Confessional's 'Album Covers' taping of *Automatic For The People*, joining in on 'Drive'. And The Minus 5 checked back into their home town venue, the Crocodile Café in Seattle. (*Down With Wilco* had been released earlier in the year; the group had taken off in the midst of the Vancouver sessions to promote it for two weeks.) Finally, a few days before Christmas, Mills came up to Seattle to join Buck, McCaughey and Rieflin in recording a few fresh demos, and in January 2004 the entire group met back in Athens with Pat McCarthy to further resume work.

The approach was, now of necessity, somewhat scattershot, with the group listening back to the material that had been started over a year earlier in Vancouver, adding in the newer songs that had been worked up in the interim, and then attempting to re-define the record they were making. Typically, the reason behind breaking up album sessions into separate chunks was to allow for ongoing evaluation – by all the band for sure, but by Stipe in particular. "It makes sense to record a bunch of things and take a nice break and let Michael listen to the music and come up with lyric ideas and decide which ones are inspiring for him," says Scott McCaughey.

Occasionally, however, that would mean re-recording a song once Stipe had figured out what he wanted to do with it, as was to be the case with the eventual album's lead single, 'Leaving New York'. "When it was first demo'd," says McCaughey, "Michael

388

came up with the words but he said, 'I want the verse to be the chorus', so we had to re-record it, reconstruct it so it fit his idea for the melody and the lyric." In that specific case, it could be said that the exercise was effective, but it was an exercise that needed to be contained. Yet when R.E.M. flew down to the renowned Compass Point Studios in the Bahamas for two solid months in the sun, an e-postcard from Bertis Downs to the fans inadvertently revealed the shift in tempo for both songs and process: "The pace around what you'd expect – slow, relaxed." In the middle of May, R.E.M. headed back to the States, to equally heated climes, finishing off the recording and taking in the mixing at the Hit Factory in Miami. The album may have been titled for one of its songs (the first ever R.E.M. record to do so, incidentally), but *Around The Sun* also spoke to the group's recording, touring and working mindset of 2004.

"We had a great record on our hands before we spent six months playing with it," a frustrated Peter Buck later told *Q*. "The rough mixes and the songs that didn't make the album are just weird and fucked up and it would have been cool if that record had come out." This was an accurate enough observation. 'Animal' and 'Bad Day' might have done much to alter the album's eventual mood had they been saved for a studio album, but they were not the only alterations and omissions. An early version of the song 'Aftermath' was considerably faster than the ponderous re-recording that made the final cut, 30 seconds shorter as a result, and was propelled by Buck playing a 12-string guitar that was absent from the final recording. The songs 'I'm Gonna DJ' and 'Man-Sized Wreath', both of which would re-emerge on the band's subsequent album, were left on *Around The Sun*'s cutting room floor, as was an instrumental of what would become 'Living Well Is The Best Revenge'. The original version of 'I'm Gonna DJ' "was really cool", says Scott McCaughey. "It's weird, it's a little slower, it's not as loud and crazy, but it's got a really interesting feel." Initially inspired by the 1999 WTO riots in Buck's Seattle home city, the final lyric from 'I'm Gonna DJ' – "Music will provide the light you can not resist" – would be used as a sticker line on *Around The Sun* promo CDs, indicating the extent to which it had influenced the sessions. But all the faster songs were ultimately rejected. "They just didn't seem like they fitted in," says McCaughey. "It would have presented a change in tempo but they also likely would have been sore thumbs. We weren't consciously trying to make a mid-tempo slow record; it just turned out that way."

Apparently, some of R.E.M. didn't realise that they *had* made a "mid-tempo slow record", even once it was done. Michael Stripe crowed to *Rolling Stone* in July, as the group resurfaced and embarked on the promotional merry-go-round, that "It may be the most chaotic bunch of songs we've ever thrown together. They're going to surprise our fans and shock others." They did, though surely not in the way he had intended.

Several years later, Stipe tried to explain the disparity between intent and content. "We poached the two howling and primitive songs from the album we were making and put them on the best-of," he told Jack Rabid of *The Big Takeover*. Of the songs that were left, "All of us loved the material," he insisted, "but we watched it kind of disappear over the course of the recording."

Mike Mills concurred: "The songs are good. What happened was we tried to do too much. We stopped and did a greatest-hits record, we did a tour and then tried to finish the record. That was a disservice to the songs because it made it hard for us to focus."

But it was far too easy to blame the tour for the subsequent mess. What was really at fault was the group's method of working. As they had grown comfortable with Pat McCarthy, they had developed one laudable tendency – to share dinner together at the end of the recording day, complete with wine – but were increasingly combining it with a debatable one: going back in the studio, well-fed and perhaps a little tipsy, and continue *trying* to work. "That's when we discovered a lot of the tinkering happened," says Scott McCaughey who had been convinced they had the makings of a great record. When he says that "Too much time was spent on it," he is clearly stating the obvious, but when he compares the albums to their predecessors, he introduces an interesting observation. "It was the third in a trilogy, with each of them being long records with a lot of medium tempo things and a lot of layering of instruments – and very little rock'n'roll, basically. To me they're the trilogy of R.E.M. trying to become a band again, or not worrying about being a band per se without Bill. There's a law of diminishing returns there, and with *Around The Sun* we played out that approach and it became less exciting."

"It was really about myself, Mike and Peter being unable to sit together and talk about the music and what we wanted it to be," said Michael Stipe, with far less tact – after the event. "We didn't talk to each other for a couple of records – as friends or as bandmates."

Peter Buck was yet more blunt than this, and within weeks of the album's release. Speaking to the band's home-town newspaper, the *Atlanta Journal-Construction*, he declared of *Around The Sun* that "It sounds like what it is, a bunch of people who are so bored with the material that they can't stand it any more." This was not mere revisionism: he had become so frustrated with the endless recording process that he packed his bags and left Miami – before the album was mixed. His withdrawal became a self-fulfilling prophecy when the final mixes came back with most of his electric guitar low in the mix, if present at all. The absence of an electric Buck was to be well noted by all who didn't hear him, and though any elimination or reduction in the mixing process may not have been an act of spite, it would surely not have occurred had the group been properly communicating, and working at a sensible enough pace that Buck hadn't felt the need to flee the fold in the first place.

"Michael tends to think that the longer you work on something, the better it can be," said Peter Buck further down the line. "But it doesn't work that way for us. It just kept getting weirder and weirder and worse." In an interview with Michael Azerrad for *Spin*, he drew on the Bush Administration's American imperialism as a metaphor for the mess. "It was kind of like the war in Iraq – we don't know why we got in there, we don't know how to get out, and we don't know what we're trying to accomplish. If it had been the best record we'd ever made and everyone said it was *Pet Sounds*, I could put up with the eight months in the studio and the frustration. But it wasn't."

The finished record sounded as if someone *had* been trying to make an album as perfectly polished as *Pet Sounds*, and the question therefore remained as to whether Pat McCarthy was partly culpable for the album's over-production, the layers upon layers of hi-tech gloss that might have sounded good in the comfort of the

Nassau and Miami studios, but served to alienate the listeners from the songs they were intended to serve. With classic southern gentlemanly decency, the band refused to point the finger at him ("I want to stress that it was no fault of the producer – Pat McCarthy," said Stipe in the midst of his apologies for the final album), but McCarthy had always been known for taking his time in the studio, to the extent that he had earned the nickname "Speed Brake" amongst some in the R.E.M. camp. Yet even if McCarthy *had* recognised that, for whatever reasons, R.E.M. were in danger of making a muddled, over-cooked album, he was not necessarily in a position to change things.

"I wouldn't have wanted to be in Pat's shoes at that point," says Scott McCaughey. "I think he had a hard time saying, 'No, we have to move on. This is not the way we should be.' I think he was probably just as frustrated as anyone else might have been that *Around The Sun* was going on so long. And I think he would have liked to have been the guy who said, 'This is done, let's move on,' but I don't think he felt like he could do that, that he could over-power the other three. A producer has to be that guy."

Around The Sun would be McCarthy's final album with R.E.M.

★　★　★

Around The Sun was prefaced to the public by its opening track, 'Leaving New York', released as a single in September, 2004, a few weeks ahead of the album's early October global release. It was, transparently, a love letter from Michael Stipe to his adopted home city, the place of which he had dreamed as a misfit child, the city to which he had been emotionally betrothed since his first visit with Peter Buck back in 1980, a week or so before R.E.M.'s debut gig. Understandably enough, he declared of it that, "nothing can compare", and went further, insisting, with no hint of irony or disclaimer, "I love you forever". As for the 'leaving' part of the title, it was easy to consider that a reaction to documented post-9/11 flight from the metropolis, but studied closer, it spoke to the painful truth that New York could be a cruel mistress, always ready to move on to the next new suitor of an inhabitant, and that many of its most promising paramours had found themselves buried, even destroyed, by her constant demands on their time, their energy, their finances and emotions, and by the multifarious temptations of her 24/7 life-style. As such, suggested Stipe, "it's easier to leave than to be left behind." (The bad grammar of the follow-on line, "leaving was never my proud", became a source of internal debate, but was kept, he said, because "it worked, and the idea came across.")

Though clearly not breaking any ground that hadn't been thoroughly mined on *Reveal* (or, for that matter, on Aerosmith's epic 'Dream On'), 'Leaving New York' was essentially mid-tempo R.E.M. balladry at its best, Buck's barely electric guitar picking its way through a friendly arpeggio over a sea of strummed acoustics, an organ tugging at the heart strings by evoking violins, and a chordal piano accompaniment forming the comfortable bedding for a pleasantly formulaic chorus of backing singers. Its slow pace somehow belied its perilous five minute length, and the package was completed by a rather literal, glossy promotional video showing Stipe in white suit at an airport terminal, in a limousine crossing an East River bridge, and walking the streets of the Lower East Side as was indeed often his wont, concluding with a suitably multi-cultural hipster crowd in attendance at a downtown party. If fans noticed that the few clips of the three band members playing together showed Buck looking not just bored strumming his acoustic guitar, but genuinely put out to be doing so, nobody made a fuss about it. 'Leaving New York' leaped straight to number five in the UK, R.E.M.'s biggest hit in terms of chart placement since 'The Great Beyond'. Fans and critics alike promptly unwrapped their copies of *Around The Sun* with enthusiasm.

They had no particular reason for fear from its second track, 'Electron Blue', a stripped-down, structurally simple piece of synth and piano, programmed drums and glossy effects, similar to the experimental nature of *Up*, that provided a perfect vehicle for Stipe's increasingly mature and majestic voice. The lyric appeared to be calling upon its subject to remain very much in the moment, an increasingly common Stipe precept, but the singer, ever wary of overplaying his intent, stated that 'Electron Blue' was a fictional drug and left it there. It was later released as a single, with a polished artsy video that featured two hipsters lip-synching on Stipe's behalf.

Around The Sun started to reveal its deficiencies with 'The

Outsiders'. Clocking in at almost precisely the same tempo as its predecessors – the low 90 beats per minute – and using the same structure and arrangement (minimal chord changes, atmospheric sound effects, and a minimum of electric guitar), it should still have been distinguished by the fact that it was the first R.E.M. number since 'Radio Song' to feature a guest rapper. And yet, most frustratingly, the restrained, reflective, laid-back vocal style of Q-Tip (formerly of A Tribe Called Quest, though a star in his own right in hip-hop circles) proved just *too* perfectly suited for what was already, just ten minutes in, much too much of a restrained, reflective laid-back album. After all, the genius of KRS-One's presence on *Out Of Time*'s opening song was that it was so unexpected, and so angry with it; for all his own talents, Q-Tip's presence on 'The Outsiders' was almost straight out of *Around The Sun* casting central. It wasn't just R.E.M. lite; it was hip-hop lite, and the combination made for something out of a bad jam band nightmare.

At this point, *Around The Sun* desperately needed to ratchet up a gear, and some strong sequencing might yet have saved it, but instead, the album just slowed down further with the overwrought ballad 'Make It All Okay,' saved – if at all – only by Stipe's fine vocal delivery. That the follow-on final mix of the familiar 'Final Straw' seemed almost positively upbeat by comparison spoke volumes about the album's desperately dour mood, something not helped by the decision to pair it with 'I Wanted To Be Wrong', which contained one of the album's best melodies and strongest sentiments – a meticulously crafted attack on an alienated America in which "we can't approach the Allies 'cause they seem a little peeved." Heard in isolation, placed in a different position on previous or subsequent R.E.M. albums, and produced with even just a vestige of imagination, 'I Wanted To Be Wrong' might well have been hailed as a classic. Instead, accompanied by that predictably simple synth string line, it felt lost in the midst of an album that desperately cried out by this point for side one to conclude and for the listener to have the freedom to put on something else, something more uplifting, before resuming the potentially maudlin musical plot line of the remaining seven songs.

If heard as the opening track of that side two, 'Wanderlust' would at least have served to start afresh, upping the tempo, lightening the musical mood, and offering a positive lyrical outlook on a post 9/11 frame of mind. Yet its arrangement felt forced in a way that R.E.M. had never previously exhibited, its jaunty melody but one step short of a nursery rhyme, the combination offering none of the *joie de vivre* that had saved the likes of 'Stand' or 'Shiny Happy People'. The subsequent claim from inner circles that the follow-on ballad 'The Boy In The Well' was under-rated and would have carried its weight on *Automatic For The People*, would only have applied had it been afforded an appropriately adventurous production, rather than the now painfully repetitive sound of acoustic bedrock guitar, synth string sounds, four-four drums, and an uninspired grungy solo halfway through.

'Aftermath' offered some respite, though frustratingly so for anyone who had heard the original, faster, livelier version. It was a well-crafted song, with perhaps the only unpredictable chord changes of the entire album, lively lyrics ("now the universe left you for a runners lap/it feels like home when it comes running back"), and something close to a traditionally untraditional R.E.M. chorus – which was then pummelled into submission by an uninspired guitar solo that sounded like it had been phoned in from Seattle. Understandably marketed as the album's second UK single, it failed to make the top 40.

'High Speed Train' likewise offered – and failed to live up to – promise. Yet another song to clock in slower than 90bpm, and to run a full five minutes, there was a genuine darkness to it that was absent from the rest of the album, with ominous guitars sounding like they'd at least been recorded with some forethought – until a Spanish acoustic guitar solo stepped in, in this case providing unnecessary frivolity. By this point, there was perhaps a sense that *Around The Sun* couldn't win.

As such, it would be easy to mark 'The Worst Joke Ever' and 'Ascent Of Man' as two of a pair, both equally slow, both conforming to the predictable verse-chorus format, both buried in a sea of stifling production gloss that sounded as far away from the concert R.E.M. as imaginable. Yet 'The Ascent of Man', in particular, had considerable merit, both lyrically ("I try to float like a telegram Sam/I'm trying to divine you") and phonetically, as Stipe – whose strong delivery was generally *Around The Sun*'s lone saving grace –

embarked on a series of high-pitched "yeah yeahs" under which his spoken word counterpoint sounded like something closer to 'Country Feedback', oft-stated as his favourite R.E.M. song of all. And yet, once again, the song was snuffed out by what had now become the ballad band's obligatory solo – this time on a big swirling organ. To hear R.E.M.'s multiple individual and collective talents succumb to formula like this was positively painful.

Under the circumstances, the final, titular track didn't stand a chance, although, oddly, 'Around The Sun' was one of the album's few optimistic numbers. A cautious gaze into the future of a world that, at the time of recording, may have seemed one step short of imploding, it was Stipe – the angry pacifist or, as he also called himself, the 'cynical optimist' – refusing to quit, to give in to his darker desires. "Hold on world 'cause I'm not jumping off/hold onto this boy a little longer." For once, the piano sought to do something more than provide a plodding chord accompaniment; for once, Buck remembered to plug in and turn up; and though those damn synth strings fought to ruin the song as they had so much of the album, they were kept at bay by a psychedelic arrangement reminiscent of 'Animal'. Of course, the song should have ended at the 3:30 mark, when it broke down as if to do so, but if *Around The Sun* signified any one constant fault over its many others, it was that R.E.M. had misplaced their self-edit button. It seemed somehow appropriate that the title track should doodle around for a final minute of meaninglessness before finally fading into the distance.

Twenty-six

Bolstered by the promise of 'Leaving New York', propelled too by the success of *Reveal* and *In Time* and the previous summer's festival headliners, *Around The Sun* shot straight to number one in the UK, the sixth of their last seven official albums to do so. It entered the charts similarly high in seven other countries that had become R.E.M. strongholds over the past 15 years (Australia, Germany, Sweden and the R.E.M. bastion of Norway among them). Disappointment with the album quickly set in, however – in about as long as it took most fans, and especially reviewers, to struggle through the hour-long CD and to offer their verdict.

"The first R.E.M. album to really disappoint," observed the previously loyal *NME*. "The first out-and-out dull R.E.M. album," agreed the band's former British champion, *Mojo*. "Relentlessly, frustratingly slow," concurred sister publication *Q*. "A tired collection of R.E.M. Lite," surmised the increasingly influential blog *DrownedInSound*. And in the culturally pre-eminent British newspaper the *Guardian*, Dorien Linsky offered an especially harsh but accurate critique. "The CD cover, portraying a blurry, indistinct Stipe, Buck and Mills," he wrote of the first R.E.M. studio album to feature *any* image of its band members on the front sleeve, "turns out to be an all-too-accurate reflection of the music." Referring to the album's "creative torpor", he concluded that, "*Around The Sun* is REM's first truly redundant album."

Reactions were even more negative in the United States, difficult though that might seem to believe. "Every word, every note, and every instrument sounds dry, sapped of most of their personality," concluded *Pitchfork*, the newly omniscient online bible of hipster-dom. *Rolling Stone*, *Pitchfork*'s print predecessor, predisposed from decades of practice never to speak ill of a major label release, offered a lukewarm three stars and damned the album with faint praise, concluding of an R.E.M. "that refuses to fake a full recovery in the wake of drummer Bill Berry's departure", that "They'd rather struggle on their own terms." The influential *Filter* magazine saw no reason for such niceties: "Weak poetry set to any music sucks, let alone this plodding folk-lite." "A low-spark affair," observed Will Hermes in *Spin*. "R.E.M. have never seemed so directionless," opined AllMusic Guide. And so on.

Inevitably, the hostile reaction impacted on what was already a shrinking fanbase. 'Leaving New York' was to prove only the second lead single from any R.E.M. album not to make the American top 100. The first week sales figure of 60,000 was less than half that of *Reveal*, low enough to ensure that *Around The Sun* also became R.E.M.'s first album to stall outside the American top 10 since *Green* and their first ever not to go gold; it barely eked out the 200,000 in sales that *Murmur* had managed during its year-long climb back in 1983. In terms of album sales, R.E.M. were, quite literally, back where they had started.

★   ★   ★

Fortunately for their collective psyche, R.E.M. were positively engaged as the damning reviews came in, having gotten in and out of Europe on a promo tour just in time to embark on a 'Vote For Change' concert tour across American 'battleground' or 'swing' States ahead of the November 2 Presidential elections that pitted Senator John Kerry against the incumbent George W. Bush. Vote For Change was a positively ambitious attempt to steer half-a-dozen concurrent tours featuring a couple of headlining acts a-piece, into different cities of the same swing State on the same night. (The tour served as a fund-raiser for Americans Coming Together, which proclaimed a grass-roots, non-partisan effort to get out the vote in 'battleground' States; because ACT was a Political Action Committee, tickets were considered campaign contributions, and their purchase limited to proven US citizens.) The six-legged tour attracted such significant names as Pearl Jam, Bonnie Raitt, James Taylor, the Dave Matthews Band and the Dixie Chicks, but R.E.M. (and opening act Bright Eyes) had surely the best touring partner of all – Bruce Springsteen and the E Street Band.

398

The half-dozen shows alongside the Boss quickly turned into a mutual appreciation society. If it had seemed beyond the realms of possibility, back in 1975 when Peter Buck first saw Springsteen perform 'Born To Run', that he (and Mike Mills) would one day be playing that song alongside its composer and his E Street Band on a nightly basis; if it had seemed ludicrous for Michael Stipe, the consummate Patti Smith fan, to imagine back in 1978 that he'd be singing her hit collaboration 'Because The Night' with its co-writer Springsteen every night for a week; then how could anyone in R.E.M. have dreamed, back in 1982 when they dropped the power-pop song 'Permanent Vacation' from their set because, frankly, they had better, less overtly obvious material, that, of all people, *Bruce Springsteen* would be joining them on stage every night for a week to sing a verse and take a solo on his famed Fender Tele, all in the name of influencing a Presidential election? Under such circumstances, Bruce's nightly presence on 'Man On The Moon' was almost to be expected. (Shared stages were very much a part of the tour, and something that R.E.M. would become increasingly familiar with over coming years. The tour ended in Washington, D.C., for a concert filmed and shown by the Sundance Channel, with R.E.M. singing 'People Have The Power' alongside such diverse and not always complementary luminaries as Kenny 'Babyface' Edmonds, John Mellencamp, Keb Mo, Dave Matthews, the Dixie Chicks, John Fogerty and Jurassic 5. Plus Bruce Springsteen and the E Street Band of course.)

Unlike Springsteen, whose support for John Kerry via the Vote For Change tour represented a shift in his public profile, and alienated some of his blue-collar, conservative fans, R.E.M. had never been opaque in their politics. They worked their set list to include 'Exhuming McCarthy' and 'Walk Unafraid' as well as the two most overt protest songs from *Around The Sun*, 'Final Straw' and 'I Wanted To Be Wrong'. They 'donated' the song 'Around The Sun' to a pro-Kerry documentary. And Mike Mills wrote a powerful editorial that was published in the *Orlando Sentinel* (to coincide with their date in the Florida city on October 8), in which he was emphatic about the group's collective stance: "If there were ever a time to speak out, this is it. We want America to put a new president in the White House."

"We wanted George W. Bush the fuck out of the White House and we wanted John Kerry in," said Stipe, with even less restraint, a couple of years later. "And it didn't work." It did not. On November 2, although John Kerry won three of the five swing States that R.E.M. had performed in alongside Springsteen, George W. Bush not only took the Electoral College but, this time around, won 3,000,000 more registered votes than his Democrat challenger. The USA – and the world – was to be subject to four more years of the war-mongering, surplus-spending Bush Administration.

R.E.M. played their first show following the Presidential election on November 4, at Madison Square Garden in New York. It was to prove particularly challenging. "I was so fucking pissed off that night," Stipe later admitted. "The last thing I wanted to do was my job, or even attempt to be an entertainer. I was so very devastated by the results of that election." The group opened, for the first time ever, with 'It's The End Of The World As We Know It'. Officially, the song had a sub-title: '(And I Feel Fine)'. That particular night, the positive sentiment seemed hard to believe.

★   ★   ★

In rock music, once an act reaches iconic status, the quality and quantity of their studio albums often proves irrelevant to their popularity as a live act. Springsteen himself has proven testament to this; a series of patchy LPs in the late Eighties and a frustratingly erratic career in the 2000s has had little impact on his ability to maintain his Godlike status and sell out stadiums – or at least arenas – with little more than a press release. The Rolling Stones and The Who don't even need to release new records any more (and when they do, few pay attention) to command top dollar across the world. And, five years on from *Around The Sun*, there would prove almost no correlation between the comparatively poor sales of U2's 2009 album *No Line On The Horizon* and the tour that accompanied it, which over the course of two years saw more than 7,000,000 people pay an average of $100 a head for tickets; the gross attendance and receipts were each the highest in history.

And so it was with R.E.M.: the almost violently offended/offensive reaction to *Around The Sun* proved entirely at odds with the band's continued popularity as a touring act. On their six-week American tour of late 2004, though not all venues sold out, still R.E.M. played to considerably more people than bought their new album. In the first three months of 2005, they then took on the most ambitious schedule of their lives, visiting almost 30 different countries, from Austria to Australia, England to Estonia, Hong Kong to Hungary, South Africa to Serbia (where they were invited to the Presidential Palace), and Japan to New Zealand. In the nations they were visiting for the first time (including, somewhat surprisingly, Northern Ireland, where as a mark of respect for the small country's national pop-punk anthem, they treated the audience to an encore of The Undertones' 'Teenage Kicks'), it was surely to be predicted that they would play sold-out shows, but the size of the sold-out venues across the more familiar territories of Europe suggested that if R.E.M. fans were as disappointed by *Around The Sun* as the critics, they were willing to forgive the group their sins for the chance to see them play the hits live.

Whether this indicated a complacency on the part of the blindly loyal fans to match that of R.E.M. in the studio of late would have been a conversation worth pursuing – had R.E.M. proven equally lacklustre in concert. But the stinging rebuke for *Around The Sun* appeared, if anything, to galvanise the group, to force them to come together, engage in the communication that had clearly been sorely lacking in the studio, and better yet, to push the *Around The Sun* material out front and centre. The best songs came alive – quite literally – in the process. 'Leaving New York' morphed into a crowd sing-along, complete with Stipe yelping words he barely intoned on record and Mills offering a highly-pitched chorus of his own towards its conclusion. The apologetic pairing of 'I Wanted To Be Wrong' and 'Final Straw' gained a desperation and defiance that had been sorely lacking from their recorded versions; 'Electron Blue' married its pop sensibility with an underlying *nastiness*; even 'Ascent Of Man', 'The Worst Joke Ever' and 'Boy In The Well' dropped their balls and developed some welcome testosterone. Admittedly, none of them became the high point of the set, and not *every* song came alive onstage to begin with – the rap in 'The Outsiders' was equally stultifying coming from Stipe's lips – but, wisely scattered across the evening, they could be (and were)

treated as individual compositions of merit, not as part of a mutu-
ally maudlin album.

Indeed, on any given night through the tour, post-*Reveal*
material – counting the *In Time* additions 'Bad Day' and 'Animal',
and the frenetic 'I'm Gonna DJ' – provided well over a third of the
set, and the crowd lapped it up. Stipe had now moved into the
comfort zone of the mature rock star who knows precisely how to
work a crowd, his bright suits and painted face serving to exagger-
ate his increased athleticism, his easy humour, and his moments of
self-deprecation alike. Not that it wasn't work. "The degree to
which I apply myself as an artist, as a songwriter," he explained
while in Australia, "is at the very least absolutely sincere and giving
everything that I can. And that counts for something." Mills had
similarly mastered the art of crowd-pleasing, and if Buck had scaled
back his onstage dynamism over the years, McCaughey's bounding
enthusiasm helped compensate. The scale of the shows demanded
that R.E.M. bring extensive effects with them, and the stage set
was particularly well thought out, with a series of seemingly
random vertical light strips behind them providing colour-coordi-
nated lighting for each song. The recruitment of Blue Leach and
his British company XL Video, with whom the band had been
impressed on first encounter at their headlining Manchester Move
Festival show of 2003, additionally supplied a "Warhol on speed"
random look to a horizontal LED video screen running across the
top sliver of the backdrop, as likely to portray lyrics (e.g. 'Final
Straw') or splinter into four separate camera shots mixed with
effects, as to provide the typical video screen backdrop of the lead
singer in all his projected glory. The group's faith in Leach was
such that in Dublin they hired him to simultaneously direct a
multiple camera concert of the show whilst triggering all the video
effects and accompanying colours for the concert itself.

Unlike the *Monster* tour, R.E.M.'s globetrotting was bereft of
brushes with death – at least within the band and crew. When
Mike Mills took ill in the UK, it was only with the flu, and necessitated but two shows to be rescheduled. A planned first concert in
Russia was also called off when the group was delayed at the
border. Visits to the continents of Africa, Asia and Australasia went
off without an apparent hitch; R.E.M. celebrated their 25th

birthday during a day off in Adelaide, the dinner and drinks interrupted by a congratulatory phone call from Bill Berry from 17 time
zones away. "At this point we love each other very deeply," Stipe
told TV talk show host Andrew Denton just the day before the
silver anniversary. "There are immense amounts of respect for each
other. We also know each other better probably than anyone else
on this living earth."

The return to Europe to play not just the festival circuit, as in
2003, but a series of stadium shows at some of Britain's bigger football grounds, represented exactly the type of mass gathering that the
band had decried back when they had opened for the Police at
Shea Stadium 20 years earlier. But R.E.M. were now in that same
premier league of major international acts, and if *Around The Sun*
was hardly their *Synchronicity*, it nonetheless seemed as if the bigger
the venue, the more likely they were to fill the seats: in the space of
one week, they were to play the grounds of Hull City, Nottingham
Forest, Ipswich Town, the Welsh national stadium in Cardiff and,
additionally, London's Hyde Park. They were, in fact, to play
Hyde Park twice: on the afternoon of July 2, a week before their
scheduled headline show, and before flying to Switzerland and a
headlining appearance that same night, R.E.M. played three songs
there at one of the day's many all-star Live 8 performances.

Live 8 was the successor to Live Aid of 20 years earlier, although
this time around, organisers Bob Geldof and Midge Ure sought not
so much to raise funds as to put pressure on the G8 states – the
world's main economic powers, who were set to meet in Scotland
the week following the concerts – to support the platforms of
organisations such as Make Poverty History. Live 8 appeared to
have achieved some of its goals when, on July 8, the G8 leaders
pledged to increase aid to developing countries by $50 billion over
the next five years. Sadly, the noble call for global community had
received an enormous set-back the previous day, July 7 (or 7/7, as
it came to be known), when coordinated terrorist attacks on public
transport across London killed 52 people and injured hundreds
more. The attacks were the work of home-grown Islamists – influenced by Al Qaeda and Osama Bin Laden perhaps, but British
citizens for the most part all the same, which made the collective
reckoning all the more difficult. It also spoke, tragically, to the fact

403

that the invasions of Iraq and Afghanistan had not yet brought an end to Islamist terror.

R.E.M.'s Hyde Park concert, their most high-profile British headline show ever, was understandably postponed from its July 9 date, although only for a week. The group's history with the English capital dated back to 1983, when they sold out the Marquee and Dingwalls on their first overseas visit. It was where they had recorded *Fables Of The Reconstruction*, and regardless of that particularly dismal experience, London had served as their launching ground for increased popularity in Europe. As such, R.E.M. felt the terrorist attacks personally. After taking advice, the group did go ahead with their show in Ipswich on Friday July 8, where Michael Stipe introduced the set with a particularly eloquent discourse: "We came here today from London. It's an understatement to say that this has been a difficult couple of days for everyone. Music is, at its best, about catharsis, about epiphany, about feeling, about remembering, about community and about celebration – about celebrating life. The intention here tonight and with this gesture is to honour that; not to forget but to remember and to honour the sanctity of life. Together, tonight, let's raise our voices up in celebration and in remembrance."

Perhaps the small saving grace of the week-long Hyde Park postponement was that the rescheduled show became the global tour's finale. (It would otherwise have concluded at the vast Millennium Stadium in Cardiff, Wales.) The concert, performed in an emotional atmosphere of grief, fear and unity (and trailed by a fourth and final UK single from *Around The Sun*, 'Wanderlust') replaced a couple of the *Around The Sun* songs with deep catalogue cuts, 'Sitting Still' and 'Me In Honey', but ended with the three fixed finales, 'It's The End Of The World As We Know It', 'I'm Gonna DJ' and 'Man On The Moon.' A jubilant Michael Stipe was carried offstage by his bandmates.

A couple of days later, Stipe wrote an end-of-tour ramble and put it up online. It was a fair portrait of a global rock star attempting to come down from an incredible emotional high, trying to grasp what had been achieved and what lay ahead: "I think this has been the most fun and most fulfilling tour for me personally," he observed, cognizant of his matured stage personality. "I tried really

404

hard to be in the moment and let the moment be whatever it was going to be . . . starting with the vote for change tour, the sometimes arduous but finally fulfilling north American tour, the enthusiasm for 'I'm Gonna DJ', the older songs that we seldom play, the every night songs that we still love to play . . . it all amounts to a certain resolve and a beautiful humanity that playing music brings, to me anyway."

Reflecting, perhaps, on the calamity that had been *Around The Sun*, he added: "We are each of us moving through this world and figuring it out as we go. We are all sometimes great and sometimes really dumb. We all fall down and we all get up. We all listen sometimes to our instinct over our insecurities, and that makes us wiser and better people."

And allowing, in that case, that the fans appeared to have forgiven R.E.M. already, he concluded, with charm: "I am a cheeseball but I feel like the luckiest guy in the world."

Or, as Peter Buck would put it two years later, "On the last tour we played better than we ever had. Unfortunately, we didn't have a good new record to play live."

★　★　★

It was understandable that the three band members would want time away from each other following such a long period of close contact, and the following year would see them re-engage in their own individual musical, social and artistic activities.

Mike Mills came up to Seattle in August 2005 to play piano alongside Buck and the usual suspects at an art opening, and almost a year later he showed up in Pittsburgh at a Celebration Concert for the baseball legend and philanthropist Roberto Clemente as part of the night's Clemente All-World Band, playing alongside the bassist's bassist Tony Levin. But otherwise, as always, he kept the lowest profile of the three.

Peter Buck continued his multifarious activities with Scott McCaughey: together they recorded and toured an eponymous album with The Minus 5, and recorded and toured the Robyn Hitchcock album *Ole Tarantula* as part of Hitchcock's backing band the Venus 3. But Buck flexed his musical muscles in a different direction too, recording along with David Sylvian, Ryuichi

Sakamoto, Brian Eno and Bill Rieflin for a multi-media project, *Quadri + Chromies*, that combined experimental/electronic musician Hector Zazou's compositions with artist Bernard Caillaud's digital paintings; Buck and Rieflin then teamed up again with Zazou, the renowned guitarist Robert Fripp, bassist Fred Chalenor and drummer/percussionist Matt Chamberlain for an improvisational project called Slow Music, which grew out of a conversation between Rieflin and Fripp during a day off from R.E.M.'s world tour. The initial Slow Music collaboration proved sufficiently enjoyable that the musicians then toured it for a week down the West Coast in May. Sets were divided into long sections of ambient, spatial improvisation, with Buck seen using a plastic fork on his strings. One might presume that Michael Stipe approved.

In the wake of the devastating Hurricane Katrina of August 2005, and the Bush Administration's abject reaction to the disaster, Michael Stipe teamed up with Chris Martin of Coldplay to record a version of the Joseph Arthur song 'In The Sun', which would show up in the New Year as one of six renditions of the song (all featuring Stipe in some capacity) for a fund-raising, downloadable iTunes EP. The night after their recording session in Athens, Stipe also joined Coldplay on stage in Atlanta, where he sang 'Nightswimming', Chris Martin performing Mike Mills' piano part. Stipe had a well-known habit of befriending and frequently mentoring the newest of rock stars, from Natalie Merchant and Kurt Cobain to Thom Yorke; in that sense the new relationship with Martin came as no surprise. But Coldplay were in an odd position: they were one of the foremost and most successful bands on the planet, and yet their anthemic sing-along lite rock was widely reviled by critics in a way that R.E.M. had managed to avoid – at least up until *Around The Sun*, of which more than a few comments had been made of similarities to Martin's Grammy-winning, chart-topping, and ultimately *nice* group. In addition, Martin's marriage to actress Gwyneth Paltrow, and her evident desire for credibility as a tastemaker, had made them not just the kind of celebrity couple that graces supermarket checkout magazines, but an easy target for ridicule. Stipe's seemingly sudden and very close friendship with Martin and Paltrow was therefore taken by some R.E.M. fans as another slide away from his former status as an outsider art student and closer to that of Inside Hollywood.

Stipe emphatically had his heart and conscience in the right place, but the rarefied atmosphere of his celebrity lifestyle – especially when removed from the grounding presence of his bandmates – was such that he did sometimes float in a bubble of A-List self-importance. When he attended a New York City fundraiser hosted by the French jewellery firm Cartier on behalf of Mercy Corp's Gulf Coast Recovery, he posted a morning-after report on the R.E.M. website, listing those at his table as if accepting an award at the Oscars: "Donna Karan who is awesome and brilliant and talked a lot about Africa, Helena Christensen, Iman, Liv Tyler and Roy Langdon who I love. Ed Norton who I love, and Scarlett Johansson who is super cool . . ." And while it might have been churlish to dispute Stipe's claim, "It's awesome that a giant company like Cartier are committed to raising much needed cash and awareness for the issues and organisations that were represented here," his gushing praise for the jeweller and its glittering clientele ignored the fact that the closest most of R.E.M.'s fans ever got to a Cartier watch was from flicking through the ads of a glossy lifestyle magazine.

And these were hardly one-offs. During his year off, Stipe became the subject of a television tribute by celebrity chef Mario Batelli; he appeared on the cover of American Airlines' in-flight magazine talking about his favourite city, Paris; he posted a picture of himself hanging backstage with Dolly Parton, whose concert he rated as one of the best of 2005; he went to Austin to promote 'In The Sun' with Chris Martin, but couldn't help name-checking that he hung out with Lance Armstrong and Sheryl Crow, and that the mayor of Austin came to their show at Austin City Limits.

Fortunately, Stipe was also always willing to confront the issues at hand beyond attendance at charity functions. When the 'In The Sun' EP came out in the New Year of 2006, he helped set up a foundation of the same name to channel monies to Gulf Coast Relief, and he took his message to CNN, NBC and Air America. In March of that year he appeared at a 'Bring 'Em Home Now' concert in New York, an event that purposefully used the refrain of the Vietnam era for fear that the ongoing Iraq war was leading the United States into a similar quagmire. And almost a year later he struck the right balance when he appeared at the Annual Tibet House Benefit Concert at Carnegie Hall, sharing the bill with the likes of Sigur Rós and Ray Davies, where he performed the *Reveal* song 'Chorus And The Ring' for the first time (alongside Tony Shanahan of Patti Smith's group), and carried out a duet with Smith on 'Everybody Hurts'. And while away from R.E.M., he also found time to deliver vocals on 'L'Hôtel Particulier' for a Serge Gainsbourg tribute album – and to join a reformed New York Dolls on the song 'Dancing On The Lips Of A Volcano'. All things considered, it was no wonder he considered himself the luckiest guy in the world.

★   ★   ★

Time away from R.E.M. as the global enterprise that released and toured studio albums, however, turned out not to be time away from R.E.M. as they had originally existed. Far from it. On October 8, 2005, three months after the world tour concluded, the group's career guitar tech Dewitt Burton got married in Athens, and was gifted the dream wedding band for the occasion: the original R.E.M., with Bill Berry on drums. The set was only seven songs long (all from the I.R.S. era), but it was enough to bring tears of joy to the 300 guests of the wedding couple – especially given the apparent musical cohesion and personal camaraderie displayed by the original quartet, who were playing a proper set together for the first time since the *Monster* tour closed out in Atlanta back in November 1995. If it was not enough to induce Berry to return to the fold, at least not yet, the reunion served to remind R.E.M. of what they once had been – and perhaps what they could become once more. Their contract with Warner Brothers still had another two albums to run, and the advances were so famously high that they would be foolish not to go ahead and try to make a record worth the investment. But if *Around The Sun* was an indicator of their contemporary creative calling, was it worth the cost? Evidently, the group had no intent of repeating such a calamity. The dust had hardly settled on *Around The Sun*'s failure before Bertis Downs was meeting with Warner Brothers, assuring the executives that the band was aware of its misstep and that the next album would be a rock record. Michael Stipe was more circumspect about the music but equally adamant about the band's continued existence when he informed fans at the start of 2006, "I look forward to whatever we're going to do next; for now, it's a time to gather, reflect, draw together those things that bring inspiration to its explosive point, its necessary release. I look forward to the next record and what this time now may bring to it."

What was to be brought to it was the spirit of the original quartet, and it came about because, in large part, R.E.M. had reached the point where they were being celebrated for their quarter century career. They knew that in September 2006, they were to be inducted into the Georgia Music Hall of Fame, and they knew, too, that there was every likelihood of a similar and much larger honour the following year. So when Bill Berry agreed not only to attend the Georgia induction ceremony, but to perform with the group onstage – in a public, televised environment – it seemed almost too good to be true. That, for sure, was how the audience at the 40 Watt Club in Athens must have felt on September 12, when they came to attend a community benefit concert under the banner, 'Finest Worksongs: Athens Bands Play the Music of R.E.M.,' only to find a suspiciously large amount of top quality musical equipment lined up by the toilets. Sure enough, after local singer-songwriter Claire Campbell opened proceedings, none other than R.E.M. themselves took the stage. And any doubts as to Berry's chops after so many years away were dispelled with the opening cascade of drums on 'Begin The Begin', and the ease with which he followed on with 'So. Central Rain'. The memorable reunion, all the better for the band tipping off and inviting their families, was replicated on a larger scale four nights later at the Georgia World Congress Center in Atlanta. "This is going to be loud," Michael Stipe warned the black-tie audience at their banquet tables as Berry took his place on the riser, and the band ripped into 'Begin The Begin'. On the TV broadcast, by accident most likely though one hoped it was someone's design, just about all that could be heard were the drums.

It was hard not to come away with the impression that R.E.M. was – were – suddenly complete once more. It wasn't that Bill Berry hit the drums harder than Bill Rieflin, who had perfected his own physicality with Ministry. It wasn't that he necessarily hit them with greater dexterity than Joey Waronker, whose skills had never been called into question. It was just that he hit them the way Bill Berry had *always* hit them – as if he had been born to play alongside the three people in front of him, in a group called R.E.M. Following additional performances of 'Losing My Religion' and 'Man On The Moon', the group was inducted by former Georgia Senator Max Cleland and promptly put away their old southern rock enmities to back Duane Allman, who was also inducted that night, on a performance of 'Midnight Rider'.

R.E.M. had always been a walking contribution, of course. That same week, Bill Berry recorded with R.E.M. for the first time since *New Adventures In Hi-Fi*. Jeff Ayeroff at Warner Brothers was putting together a John Lennon tribute album, *Instant Karma*, on behalf of Amnesty International (with Yoko Ono's support), aimed at alleviating the humanitarian crisis in war-torn Darfur. The original R.E.M. quartet (plus McCaughey) headed into the comfortable confines of John Keane's studio in Athens to record their contribution, '#9 Dream'. Laid-back, luscious, arguably even lazy, it could as easily have hailed from the *Around The Sun* sessions; nobody would ever have known that it represented R.E.M.'s lone official studio reunification with Bill Berry. Ho hum.

Still, in 2007 it would be 25 years since R.E.M.'s first proper release, 'Chronic Town', and as such, they had "qualified" for nomination into *the* Rock And Roll Hall of Fame, the one set up in part by *Rolling Stone*'s Jann Wenner and now marked by a physical museum of the same name in Cleveland. R.E.M. were not only nominated – i.e. short-listed – at first go, but promptly voted in for full membership. It was not lost on anybody that Patti Smith, who had released her first album back in 1975, had been 'denied' entry for seven consecutive years; ironically, she was now finally voted in, the same year as R.E.M., a group whose founding members literally came together over her early music. (Others inducted in 2007 included the Ronettes, who had been knocking on the door for the full 15 years of the Ceremony; Van Halen, whose first record was released in 1978; and the Hall of Fame's first hip-hop act, Grandmaster Flash and the Furious Five.) R.E.M. had always been critics' darlings, but it was evident by the ease of their induction process that they had long ago become insiders.

The original R.E.M. quartet was inducted at New York City's Waldorf Astoria Hotel in March 2007 by their friend Eddie Vedder, whose speech struck just the right balance of humility, honorific and humour. It was an emotional occasion for all concerned, and Mike Mills treated it with all due reverence, thanking in his acceptance speech not just his bandmates for "changing my life", but also "the older brother I never had", Ian Copeland, who had passed away after a short battle with cancer the previous year. Michael Stipe then took the microphone to deliver what was quite possibly the strongest speech of his life. He told an anecdote about his grandmother, who thought of R.E.M. as "Remember Every Moment". He pointedly thanked (and asked to stand up) "our girl-friends – and boyfriend". (Stipe had by now identified his partner, with whom he shared their Tribeca apartment, as Thomas Dozol, an art photographer.) He had additional table after table of R.E.M. associates, friends and family stand likewise to honour their own part in the band's success – and thanked every producer of every album, even the disenfranchised Scott Litt, and Jay Boberg and the original IRS team. The only people relevant to the group's success story who were notable by their absence were Peter Holsapple and Jefferson Holt; otherwise, it was a veritable reunion – all the more so for the presence of Bill Berry, stood silent behind Stipe and Mills, alongside an equally muted Peter Buck who slugged at a glass of red wine, appearing typically nonchalant about the importance of the occasion while simultaneously providing an emotional shoulder for the former, now re-present-ing drummer.

It was further tribute to R.E.M.'s standing that their award – and subsequent set – should prove the last of the night. But when the group stepped up to (again) perform 'Begin The Begin', the back-slapping insider celebratory nature of the occasion fell away and R.E.M. were once more revealed as a band worthy of the night's honour. Never ones to rely on the hits, regardless of the occasion, R.E.M. followed up with 'Gardening At Night', Stipe successfully still mumbling his words even at full volume. Eddie Vedder then joined them for their lone hit of the three-song set, 'Man On The Moon', after which, Patti Smith and her guitarist Lenny Kaye came on stage for a protest version of 'I Wanna Be Your Dog' by the Stooges, who had *still* not been inducted into the

Rock And Roll Hall of Fame some 38 years after releasing their debut album, an act of gross disregard on the part of the same people who had no qualms inducting R.E.M. at first attempt. It might have been for that reason that at the song's conclusion, Peter Buck picked up his Vox AC30 amplifier and hurled it into the front row of what did not quite constitute an 'audience', where it landed harshly up against some poor suit's shins. It might well have been because the sound at such events was notoriously poor and he was just frustrated. It might well have been all that red wine. And it might have just been in memory of the night, up the road at the Beacon Theater, back in 1985, when R.E.M. performed its first awards show, for CMJ, and Buck felt sufficiently dissed by the sound crew as to throw his guitar across stage and walk off prematurely. Those who thought his actions disrespectful perhaps forgot that, black ties and gracious acceptance speeches aside, they were at an event honouring the tradition of Rock And Roll.

Buck then switched to acoustic for the all-star finale, the kind for which R.E.M. had had plenty of practice over the last few months and years, but which was still to serve as the most bizarre line-up of their lives. For Patti Smith's 'People Have The Power', Stipe traded verses not only with its composer, but with Eddie Vedder, Ronnie Spector and Sammy Hagar; when Steve Stills swapped guitar solos with Keith Richards, Stipe crouched on the floor and looked on at them with an expression that suggested that he couldn't quite believe his place in things.

Given Bill Berry's involvement in the Hall of Fame shows and other recent activities, there was, perhaps, expectation from the fans that the drummer might be reconsidering his options. It wasn't to be. His behaviour was almost like that of the ex-spouse who keeps climbing back between the sheets for great sex, but rules out an official reunion. "I love Bill and I miss him intensely," said Peter Buck just three months later. "I still feel like he's a member of the band. But it would pretty much take an act of Congress to get him to leave his house for more than a day or two at a time. The whole business is hard on him. He's a very sensitive person. Just doing the Rock And Roll Hall Of Fame, he worried about that for seven or eight months. I mean, he made phone calls every day to people, 'What should I wear; what should I do?' 'It's eight months away

Bill, let's not worry about it until the week before we go do it!' As great as it was having him there, I feel almost bad dragging him into that."

That night at the Rock And Roll Hall of Fame Induction Ceremony in New York would prove to be Bill Berry's final performance with R.E.M.

Twenty-seven

Throughout the world tour of 2005, R.E.M. had resumed the habit of developing songs at soundchecks, a process that had been absent during the *In Time* tour, when they should have been working on the material for *Around The Sun*. They knew from these soundchecks (and out of sheer necessity) that their next record was going to be a rock album, and to that end, that they would politely exclude their friend Ken Stringfellow from the sessions, lest there be too many temptations to excessive keyboards and unnecessary overdubs. In effect, R.E.M. was to declare itself a band once more – a five-piece now, with Scott McCaughey and Bill Rieflin taking on the mantle of permanent (if not equally paid) members.

Some of these decisions emanated from Buck, whose patience had been exhausted. "I said, 'Guys, I'm too old to spend nine months doing something I don't want to do, making work I'm not proud of. We should try something different, or else you can do it without me.'"

"He took a stand and said, 'We're going to do it differently,'" says McCaughey. "And Michael and Mike were agreeable to it."

"It was a very important moment for us," stated Michael Stipe. "We decided to do something that was really raw, immediate, unrehearsed – basically, gut and instinctual. And we chose the most obvious thing, which is to write really fast songs and record them in a really fast way."

All this meant hiring a producer who could not only capture something "immediate" and "instinctual" and do it "in a really fast way", but who could ensure it still met the sonic demands of an R.E.M. record. That person needed to be able to call the shots if need be, and yet R.E.M. were not necessarily the type to take orders. The call went out to Garret 'Jacknife' Lee.

414

Twenty-seven

By coincidence, Lee had grown up alongside Pat McCarthy in Dublin; at the age of 12, they'd formed a band together, playing covers of The Cure and The Cars. When McCarthy later landed a summer job at the famed Windmill Lane studios and the group fell apart, Lee was openly jealous. But then he stumbled into music production himself, partly through his role as guitarist in the punk group Compulsion (whose debut album *Comforter* made the UK charts in 1994), but more so, once that band broke up, via his solo immersion in the world of electronic dance music at the point that it was booming both commercially and creatively. Making his name as a club DJ, playing "eclectic dance music throughout the ages", he claimed the name Jacknife from the Radiohead song 'Airbag' when releasing his first album in 1999. His knowledge of modern production techniques and his affinity for guitar rock, his instinct for what worked on the dance floor balanced by his decisive nature in the studio, and especially, his ability to talk down his own importance despite the fact that he had his own ongoing career as a musician (he would release further solo albums in 2001 and 2007), all served to make him a natural go-to person in the studio. Over the first decade of the 2000s he found himself producing two massively successful albums for Snow Patrol, with global sales of almost ten million copies between them. He had also handled albums by Aqualung, Bloc Party and The Editors, a who's who of happening, anthemic, populist and mostly credible new British/Irish bands. There was also the small matter of his contributions to U2's 2004 album *How To Dismantle An Atomic Bomb*. All told, it was hardly surprising that he should be recommended to R.E.M. both by those he had worked with (Bono and the Edge), and those he had not (Chris Martin). As early as September 2006, when R.E.M. reunited with Bill Berry for a week, the group was mentioning Lee as a possible contender, but it wasn't until the following January that they invited him to meet with them. Peter Buck was playing with Robyn Hitchcock as part of the Venus 3 in Oxford; if Lee, living in London by now, could get there for a pre-show dinner, Mike Mills and Michael Stipe would fly over with Bertis Downs to join them.

Lee had been an early fan of R.E.M., partly thanks to his sister raving about their first Dublin show in 1984, and also from seeing them himself at the Hammersmith Odeon five years later, though he had fallen away after *Automatic For The People* because of his own burgeoning career. Confident in his production abilities and sure of his reputation, it wasn't until he set off for the three-hour journey to Oxford on January 7, 2007, that he loaded himself up with R.E.M.'s last few albums to acquaint himself with the records produced by his childhood friend. He was, to put it mildly, underwhelmed.

At the dinner table, he was confronted by what he admitted was a "daunting" line-up: Buck, Mills and Stipe, Bertis Downs, and Oxford's own international rock anti-superstar, Thom Yorke, "all grilling me about what I wanted and how I would record an R.E.M. record." This was a difficult topic given that Lee had backed into record production and as a result, didn't have "any method of recording at all . . . it depends on the project." Finally, Stipe asked Lee what *he* wanted from an R.E.M. record. "I want it to be visceral and thrilling," he said, and with that, he appeared to have passed a test. Jacknife attended the Robyn Hitchcock gig after dinner, where Mills and Stipe joined Buck, McCaughey and Rieflin (and Hitchcock) at various points to perform 'Electrolite', the unreleased 'I'm Gonna DJ' and a cover of Eighties English indie hit, 'Listening To The Higsons'. Watching the band have this much fun, Lee immediately warmed to the prospect of working with them; whatever spark had gone out of their records had certainly not vanished from the stage.

At the end of January, Lee was invited over to Athens, where the group was recording demos at its West Clayton Street studios with mutual friend Dave Barbe. Lee made some suggestions for the song 'On The Fly', went out for a couple of dinners – and was confirmed for the job. By the time Pat McCarthy was thanked by Michael Stipe at the Rock And Roll Hall of Fame Induction Ceremony, Jacknife Lee had superseded him as R.E.M.'s next producer. (Understandably, Lee renewed contact with McCarthy along the way, trusting that there were no hard feelings. There were not, he was assured in return.)

As he got to know the three band members – and their musical and business partners – Lee developed a quick understanding of what had gone awry of late. "People talk about how a producer is great if the record sounds good, but sometimes, that's the last thing on the list of a producer's job," he says. More important is to "get people in the room and talking to each other", for which, in the case of R.E.M. in recent years, "Pat McCarthy had one of the hardest jobs any producer could." As far as Lee could understand it, R.E.M. had stopped functioning as a unit and started operating as individuals. "When bands start working separately things go a little weird in the studio. When someone comes back in and changes something back to the way it was, then the battle is about trying to keep track of what the . . . original idea was. And not having the newest thing you've recorded be the loudest thing." Lee's conclusion? "The fact that they actually finished [*Around The Sun*] is amazing."

Lee's solution to R.E.M.'s past problems lay, partly, in his own view of the recording studio. "I don't like any of them," he says. "The furniture in them is too dominant and the atmosphere isn't conducive to talking to people. I like the surprise that you get from being somewhere else." This wasn't an argument he could immediately win with a group that was well versed with the comforts of the modern recording studio (even at a time when so many of them were going out of business due to falling budgets and increased computer capacities), but when the group recommended returning to Vancouver, Lee at least insisted that they find a new location there. "I'm already on my back foot when I'm going into a situation with a band because they all know each other and they don't know me," he says. "I didn't want to go into a studio that they knew and I didn't." Together they settled on the Armoury.

Lee was fortunate in his initial workings with R.E.M. in that the band had ironed out many of their internal problems before appointing him. They came to the three-week session at the Armoury loaded with songs that, lyrics and overdubs aside, were largely formulated. But Lee came with his own methods to ensure that past mistakes were not repeated. "My process of working is, we talk about the song and then once we finish it, all the equipment gets stripped down and then we talk about the new song and put it all back up again." This was anathema to the Seattle band members who, with all their independently financed side projects, were used to "going in, getting a sound on the instruments and then recording as many songs as you possibly can because it's a budgetary thing", as McCaughey puts it. But as McCaughey and Rieflin came in early each day to help experiment with and set up the appropriate sounds, they quickly came to see that Lee's method not only ensured the producer's desire for "a new sound for every song", as Lee saw it, but that the focus remained on just that one song at a time.

Lee sensed Buck's occasional frustration at waiting around while the producer set up the sounds, but there was unanimity over the recording itself. On the last several albums, the musicians in the group would pick up different instruments according to who had written the song and what instrument that person might desire to play. Now, the newly reconfigured five-piece band played to more conventional, defined roles. "About half to two-thirds of those songs it's Peter's guitar on the right, mine on the left, and bass and drums," says McCaughey. "Peter was very specific. He was doing these very interesting chord voicings or arpeggios and he didn't want me to get in the way of those – and I didn't want to get in the way of those – so he'd ask me to play single note lines. So a lot on those records I'm playing crazy sounding fuzzed out almost-melodies or single note lines that complement what's going on."

Just about all these backing tracks went down on first, second or third take – and as the band tore through the material they had soundchecked on the road back in 2005, their formerly instinctive understanding of each other renewed itself in the positive environment. The song 'Accelerate', for example, which would ultimately become the title track for the album, "was pretty much written and recorded at the same time," says Jacknife Lee. "That was the first time the band ever played it and we recorded it – and that was the take." By the time they left Vancouver, they had eight or nine songs close to instrumental completion already. And all of them were loud.

"The record we had in Vancouver was full on," says Lee. "It was for the most part pretty punk rock. Peter's sound is really dense. There's no delicacy with Peter; even when he's playing acoustic guitar he's trying to kill it! So the sound is just fucking huge. I used to walk out into the live room and it would just be deafening. And violent. These were grown men, that were filled with . . . there was rage there. And they sounded really pissed off."

This was true even – or especially – with the slow songs, such as that which became 'Houston', one of the subsequent album's most powerful numbers and one of its more interesting evolutionary tales. The 6/8 ballad initially came from Peter Buck, who took Stipe's request to write short songs quite literally. (Stipe had discovered a South American musician who wrote only one-minute songs and thought it would be interesting to emulate the idea.) "I had a clock, and I looked at the minute hand, and after a minute and a half it was done." The riff was quickly built on by Mike Mills, who heard Buck and McCaughey playing it on guitars in the studio, "and started playing what came to mind. I felt the darkness of the song, and I wanted a really angry keyboard sound." He played heavy chords on "a nasty Farfisa" through "a big old rat pedal", after which McCaughey came up with the idea of playing "a bass through a really nasty fuzz pedal doubled with a bowed upright bass, also through some nasty fuzz." The result was what Mills called "a big ugly scary sound", and proved Buck's intuition that, "the more cinematic something is, the more it will catch Michael's ear." Stipe then set about trying to put lyrics to the 90-second arrangement from the perspective of a Hurricane Katrina victim at the mercy of the Administration's incompetence: "If the storm doesn't kill me, the Government will," ran the opening line. Only on hearing Stipe sing of Katrina did Mills realise that the backing track "sounds like a hurricane going by". As Buck noted, "It's not always about the forethought." When R.E.M. were firing on all cylinders, creativity such as this came naturally.

For the next studio session – to record overdubs and, especially, vocals – Lee had recommended that the group come to Grouse Lodge in Ireland, where he had successfully worked with both Snow Patrol and The Editors. "It's in the middle of nowhere," he says. "There's not much to do. You can get into your own rhythm, you have your own pub. It's just a fun place." When Bertis Downs came over to approve the location, R.E.M.'s 'advisor', as he was still credited on record sleeves, suggested another idea to go with it. R.E.M.'s career was at stake with this album and it was vital that the group make the extra effort to reaffirm their credibility in advance, to build anticipation and excitement in the process. They were also making an album that screamed to be heard live, even now – and playing the songs on stage could only enhance the results in the studio. Why not, then, pre-empt the Irish residential studio sessions with a week's live 'rehearsal'? Five nights were booked at the Olympia Theatre in Dublin; they sold out instantly and, in their first real foray into web 2.0, R.E.M. put up an remdublin.com site to make the most of the immediate buzz. At almost the exact same time, plans were made to turn the concert footage from their previous visit to Ireland, at the Point Arena on the world tour, into a *R.E.M. Live* CD/DVD package for October release. It would be advertised as R.E.M.'s 'first live album', a claim that fell on deaf ears to those who'd bought the three official concert films over the years along with the countless audio boot-legs. Any doubts were superseded, however, by the importance of re-claiming the *Around The Sun* material, of re-enforcing R.E.M.'s strengths as a live act, and of undoing the visual damage of *Perfect Square* and replacing it with something closer to the frenetic, kinetic audio-visual overload of the XL special effects. The attrac-tion, from the label perspective, of keeping 'product' in the stores at a point that R.E.M. studio albums were coming once every three or four years, probably did no harm either.

The 'Live Rehearsals' residency at the Olympia, from June 30–July 5, proved an emphatic triumph. For archive material, the set list drew extensively from *Chronic Town* and *Reckoning*, with barely a nod to anything beyond *Lifes Rich Pageant*. In the process, the group performed, for the first time since the Eighties, such songs as 'Second Guessing', 'Little America', '1,000,000', 'West of The Fields', 'Harborcoat', 'Kahoutek' and 'Auctioneer'. Soundchecks became trips down memory lane for three of the band – and a quick learning process for McCaughey and Rieflin. But the early material was only ever there to service the new songs, of which the band generally played eleven a night, only one of which was familiar to fans from the last tour ('I'm Gonna DJ', which would see release on *R.E.M. Live* a few months later). "It isn't a side thing doing these shows," Peter Buck told RTE radio's Dave Fanning just before the residency commenced. "This is an integral part of what this record's going to be – us performing these things here in a theatre we all love."

"It was good that Michael agreed to do this," said Mills in the

420

same interview, "because he knew that it would put him on a very definite deadline to have enough songs finished where we don't go out there and say, 'Well, here's two new songs and 20 old ones.' We had to have enough new ones to make this worth doing. I think he enjoyed the self-imposed deadline of this."

Onstage, Stipe called it "an experiment in terror", but after the event he admitted that "The material benefited from it. I took notes on stage each night during songs, going back and changing things." Stipe was, in fact, seen to enjoy himself enormously, joking freely with the crowd in admitting that he had had to look up many of his old lyrics on the Internet – where he did not recognise them. But he also worked hard to fulfil his deadline, completing the lyrics to 'Houston', for example, only shortly before the shows. And he learned to listen, such as when he introduced 'Man-Sized Wreath' with the news that it would *not* be on the new record, to which he was informed by one of his bandmates that "It's a little early to make that call." (It would end up as the second song on *Accelerate*.) Increasingly relaxed, Stipe took to drinking Guinness on stage. Peter Buck was seen sharing champagne after the shows. "It's a thrill watching a great band rediscover its mojo," wrote Keith Cameron in Q.

The sense of camaraderie and commitment carried over to Grouse Lodge for the three-week session through July. Jacknife Lee had fully expected that the group would head off to Dublin at the weekends, or find other rock star excuses to skive. Instead, "they never left." There were localised breaks to drive a tank and shoot guns on the extensive local property, and there were lock-ins at a local pub – until the group eventually set up its own draught Guinness operation within the studio itself. And yet for all that Lee refers to a "serious amount of fun", the producer was determined not to let old habits return. Partly at Peter Buck's behest, when the group broke for dinner at the end of an eight-hour workday, they did not allow themselves back in to record afterwards, which was when most of the infamous 'tinkering' had occurred in the past. The only exception was for Michael Stipe, who often preferred to sing at night.

Lee had learned by now that Stipe preferred not to sing at all until he felt he had the lyrics down right, and that when he did, "Michael will only sing something once or twice. The takes on that will be the first time he's ever heard himself sing those songs." Given that with an album like *Accelerate*, "the music is so loud he can only hear it in his own head", the playback would therefore be the first time he had heard himself sing melody and lyrics. And yet on most occasions, says Lee, "that will be *it*" for the words. Further changes might occur, but they were more likely to be wholesale, weeks or months down the line, than incremental over the course of a single session.

Between the Olympia concerts and the Grouse Lodge sessions, some songs were improved, others rewritten and re-arranged. In particular, a song R.E.M. had been playing live called 'Disguised' – the ending to which they had literally reworked on stage at the Olympia, living up to the 'Live Rehearsals' promise – was figured to need a chorus; rewritten, it would eventually turn into the album's lead single, 'Supernatural Superserious'. A number called 'Sing For The Submarine' took shape, slowly but surely. 'Tomorrow', only briefly teased at the Olympia Theatre, was recorded to powerful effect. 'On The Fly' and 'Staring Down The Barrel Of The Middle Distance', both of which were played each night at the Olympia, were more or less completed. 'Houston' was edited up to all of two minutes in length. "We just felt it was *too* short," says Lee. "We just didn't feel we were getting what we needed to get across, across." An instrumental called 'Kick Out The Traces' took shape, awaiting only vocals. 'I'm Gonna DJ', four years old already, was just about beaten into shape. The result of all this creativity was sufficient excitement for Stipe to record a fresh vocal over the latter part of 'I'm Gonna DJ', with good news for R.E.M.'s number one fan and manager. "Hey Bertis Downs, you know I think we might be touring, hey Bertis Downs, we might just tour next year."

The group had asked to finish the album in Athens, perhaps figuring that this would complete the return to their roots. Jacknife Lee again held out against a conventional studio. There was talk of renting a house, but after driving around looking for suitable venues, the producer and the group instead settled on the Steney-Stovall Chapel, where R.E.M. had been filmed for the *Athens, Ga – Inside/Out* movie back in 1985. There was, of course, a considerable difference between playing a short, live acoustic set on camera as a rising band, and recording overdubs and vocals for a major label album, but where there was a will there was a way: R.E.M. set up on stage, Lee set up on the floor, Dewitt Burton and his wife hung up a bundle of rugs to help dampen the sound, the recording equipment was brought in, and from late September into early October the record was, eventually, completed.

This was the point in proceedings at which Jacknife Lee saw how things could spiral out of control, as he learned to deal with the perfectionist tendencies of Mills and Stipe. "Mike would get annoyed if we hadn't got the bass line right, or the harmonies. He spends a long time on his harmonies." As for Stipe, there was a desire on Lee's part to support the singer's tendency to await his striking muse. "Michael does a lot of visual art and it does require a different thought process. You really have to just sit with it until it makes sense." At the same time Lee had been hired to make a short, fast record in a short, fast amount of time. "I used to say to him, 'Don't be so hard on yourself.' He would say, 'I have to sing, and I have to believe every single word.' Even if it makes no sense to anyone else, every single thing needs to make sense as to why it's there." An ideal case in point would be the title track, 'Accelerate': knocked out in a single take in Vancouver by the band, Stipe "was in there for months", writing the lyrics, says Lee.

To prevent the band from falling back into their self-confessed worst habits of studio tinkering, if there was nothing to do but wait for Stipe to sing, Lee would send the band members home. Giving direction, he figured, was "what they pay me for". Lee's decisiveness was generally fine with Buck who, again figuring that the album was complete, and this time for sure in far better shape, once more headed home to Seattle. That left Lee to galvanise Mills and Stipe into similarly letting go. "It's inevitable. You're ending something that you're enjoying, and it's a big part of a band's life to . . . stop and then go to the next stage, which is gruelling, which is the touring thing, where your life isn't your own for two years. So some people want to extend the recording."

The album was next taken to London, for mixing at The Hospital, as recommended by Radiohead. At that stage, finished mixes of 'Staring Down The Barrel Of The Middle Distance' and 'On The Fly' were sacrificed. With *Around The Sun*, there had been the belated understanding that the album would have been better for including a couple of faster songs. With *Accelerate*, there was a contrary debate about how many slow songs to include – and how long the album need run overall. 'Staring Down The Barrel Of The Middle Distance' was a damn fine song, but perhaps just a little too steady; the newly re-energised R.E.M. was willing to keep the album short rather than pad it out for the sake of it. 'On The Fly' proved more contentious. Lee considered that it had "the same kind of vibe as *Around The Sun*". To his mind, then, including it "on *Accelerate* would have changed the album title". It therefore surprised him when, of all people, Buck proved its biggest proponent. "Peter really fought for that song and I fought against it." Lee won. *Accelerate* would have less songs than any R.E.M. album since *Out Of Time*; at under 35 minutes, it would also be their shortest.

"Our focus is back," crowed Stipe only weeks later. "And it's razor sharp." There was ample evidence of this throughout 2007, though perhaps nothing quite so assured as their performance for a web channel entitled 'Take Away Show'. Typically an opportunity for a young(er) band to play unplugged, out of doors, Stipe, who had already recruited the director Vincent Moon to film the concerts at the Olympia, sensed that it would provide an ideal platform for R.E.M. to re-affirm their own such capabilities. On September 21, in the midst of the Athens sessions, Moon shot the group performing new songs in the grounds of the Steney-Stovall chapel, at Michael Stipe's guest house, under a trestle bridge lit only by the headlights of his car, and even inside a silo on Stipe's grounds. All of it was magnificent – but none more so than 'Living Well Is The Best Revenge'. In the studio, the song was almost vitriolic. In a station wagon driving around Athens, it proved transcendent. As Moon filmed from the front passenger seat, Bill Rieflin hammered out the rhythm on the steering wheel while driving, Mills in the row behind sought to angle the neck of his acoustic bass away from Stipe alongside him, while Buck and McCaughey lay on the floor of the station wagon's storage space, their backs to their bandmates with acoustics in hand. Over the course of four minutes of a single take, the viewer could see these five musicians become aware of creating something magical even as they joked with each other mid-performance; on the last chorus-go-round, Stipe removed his glasses to give himself over to the intensity of his vocal, while Mills held the harmony and simultaneously played a rapid fire melody at the top of his bass. As they drew to a conclusion, they appeared stunned by their own performance and broke into equal parts applause and laughter: they still had it, whatever "it" might be. Unable to stop on such a high, they carried on driving and performed an impromptu version of 'Born To Be Wild' that wouldn't make it onto the blogosphere. At that moment, all the stress and strain of the last few years, the pressure of a creative comeback, meant nothing: this was back to being a band of musical brothers, heading down the highway.

★   ★   ★

The act of making an energetic record proved contagious for R.E.M., who quickly demonstrated themselves equally enthused to promote it. "Part of me feels like it's 1985 and we're a brand-new band again," Mike Mills told *Rolling Stone* as they embarked on the publicity trail.

January 1 saw the launch of a NinetyNights website that unveiled a new 30–60 second video clip every day up until *Accelerate*'s April 1 release date. Once 'Supernatural Superserious' was announced as the lead single, and Vincent Moon hired to direct the promo video, the trio reprised the success of the Take Away video concept and ventured onto New York's Rivington Street where, guitars in hand, they wandered into boutique wine shops, sex toy stores and trendy bistros alike (this was not your father's Lower East Side) seeking permission to play – and be filmed in the process. Moon then launched a supernaturalsuperserious.com site that brought the multiple clips onto one single screen; fans were encouraged to edit their own video and upload it to YouTube. The group announced a world tour – not quite as exhaustive as that of 2004–5, but major all the same – and simultaneously engaged in an activity that might previously have seemed beneath them: attending Austin for the annual South By South West convention and playing a gig for the indie cognoscenti. (It was, however, reflective of their approach to the new album that they attended and played at the Interactive end of the convention, not the musical merry-go-round; they were additionally filmed by PBS playing for Austin City Limits.)

They travelled to Europe for promo, where in London they

played both the Royal Albert Hall *and* the Apple Store. Back in New York, they achieved a personal career ambition when they guested on Comedy Central's late-night spoof news show 'The Colbert Report', and they got up at dawn to play the CBS *Today* show's outdoor plaza in Manhattan, where they actually looked to be enjoying themselves doing so. Indeed, it was evidence of how much fun they were having as a band again that Michael Stipe even put up a YouTube video in which he turned the table on his own years in the closet and "confirmed", in a mock public announcement, that his bandmates had come out as "heterosexual". "I can say on their behalf that they are relieved to finally acknowledge their real selves publicly," he said with a straight face that nonetheless cracked up at the end of the minute-long clip.

The online barrage reached blitz-like proportions when a mini-site was launched for the *Accelerate* album itself, and R.E.M. embraced for the first time the concept of live streaming an album in advance of release; by April 1, says Ethan Kaplan, the Murmurs.com founder who had been hired by Warner Brothers in 2005 as a tech guru, R.E.M. had five distinct websites of their own up and running.

Nobody who subsequently heard *Accelerate* was under any illusions: the band had admitted to its last album being a disaster, had stated clearly that it wanted to rediscover its fire, had gone back to its roots with the Dublin shows, had even dressed the new album artwork down in black and white typography and urban imagery for what Stipe freely called a "punk rock aesthetic". Throw in the latest promo video and the various online campaigns and this was indisputably the work of a major rock group attempting to re-affirm its indie rock credentials. The point, then, was not how hard it had tried – but that it succeeded.

Accelerate opened with a jolt: the semi-distorted arpeggio guitar riff of 'Living Well Is The Best Revenge' leading into a drum roll, a power chord and a proudly articulated statement of intent (borrowed from 17th century poet George Herbert) reminiscent of 'Begin The Begin' and other early R.E.M. opening track clarion calls; barely a second's pause and 'Man-Sized Wreath', the holdover from *Around The Sun* that might have been consigned to obscurity but for the Dublin residency, came crashing into being

426

on its heels, concluding after just two and a half minutes of almost unbridled musical fury with Mike Mills' backing vocal extending long beyond the song's final note, as if determined to confirm his intent. 'Supernatural Superserious' was not just big and bold, but had a sing-along chorus and middle eight as had once seemed part and parcel of the R.E.M. experience; along with 'Hollow Man', it was the album's obvious single.

As for the slower songs, they were sensibly sequenced away from each other, and received that much more attention for it. 'Houston' in particular, finally upped to 2:05 with an additional riff edited on the front end, was heralded for its brevity, its bravery and its ultimate compassion. (When refugees were moved from New Orleans to temporary shelter in Houston, former First Lady Barbara Bush observed after visiting that "What I'm hearing, which is sort of scary, is they all want to stay in Texas . . . Everybody is so over-whelmed by the hospitality, and so many of the people in the arenas here, you know, were underprivileged anyway, so this is working very well for them." Rather than respond with something equally patronising, Stipe defended the Lone Star State in the chorus, with lines like, "Galveston sings like that song that I love, its meaning has not been erased.")

Acoustic guitars and grand piano bristled with equal tension throughout the album's other 6/8 arrangement, 'Until The Day Is Done', the first song from *Accelerate* to be 'released', late in 2007, as part of an Anderson Cooper CNN show about climate change. (In case anyone really wondered to which "addled republic" Stipe was referring, the lyric sheet included a quote from Sinclair Lewis's "when fascism comes to America".) On the album's longest cut, 'Sing For The Submarine', Stipe teased listeners with references to "gravity's pull" and "electron blue" while the dark arrangement recalled the more experimental edges of the *Monster/New Adventures* period. Jacknife Lee's triumphs with *Accelerate* were many, but surely the most important was to ensure that even these ballads and/or "prog rock" tracks were loud and energetic, that the album did not let up for a single one of its 35 minutes. Indeed, *Accelerate* ended with a double-shot of pure glam punk, both 'Horse To Water' and 'I'm Gonna DJ' representing R.E.M. at their most emphatically voluminous. 'I'm Gonna DJ', in particular, demonstrated the importance of persisting with a good idea; when Stipe cried "I'm not gonna go 'til I'm good and ready", he appeared to be singing not just about mortality, but about his role in R.E.M. itself. To that end, its closing line held much more true on *Accelerate* than it ever would have done on *Around The Sun*. "Music will provide the light you cannot resist," Stipe roared, repeating those last three words twice more, and then ending the entire album with an affirmative yell. "Yeah!"

Yeah! echoed the listeners in return. *Accelerate* was received with as much warmth as its predecessor had encountered the cold shoulder; almost across the board, it met with four to four-star-plus reviews. The lack of 'perfect' ratings seemed to reflect the reviewers' (understandable) sense that *Accelerate*, as an apology of sorts for *Around The Sun*, was mildly forced, a view summed up by the *Guardian* with the backhanded compliment that, "If bullish self-belief was all that was needed to make an album great, then *Accelerate* would be the best thing REM have ever done." But similar criticisms had been laid at the feet of *Lifes Rich Pageant*, when R.E.M.'s decision to work with Don Gehman and for Stipe to enunciate his words had been viewed as equally careerist; now, 22 years later, it was being viewed as R.E.M.'s golden hour, and comparisons to *Accelerate* were therefore welcomed. "They haven't redlined so engagingly since 1986's *Lifes Rich Pageant*," said *Spin* in one of the most effusive reviews, noting that " 'These Days' lives on in spirit here." "This collection of songs is a welcome throwback to the politically engaged and musically brash R.E.M. of the *'Lifes Rich Pageant'/'Document'* era of '86/'87," said *NME*. And at AllMusic Guide, founder Stephen Thomas Erlewine bounced back from his disappointment with *Around The Sun* to fairly observe that "the eerie, ramshackle grace of 'Swan Swan H' . . . [from *Lifes Rich Pageant*] echoes through both 'Houston' and 'Until The Day Is Done'," pronouncing that "reverential self-reference is the whole idea of this project."

Even where comparisons were not drawn with late eighties R.E.M., the conclusions were much the same. "Redeemed, revived, irresistible," concluded *Q*. "A decade-long period of internal artistic crisis has been resolved, beautifully, even triumphantly," confirmed *Mojo*. "One of the best records R.E.M. have ever made," said *Rolling Stone*, and if some fans still felt otherwise, they might at least have agreed with the magazine's statement that, "the best thing about *Accelerate* is that R.E.M. sound whole again, no longer three-legged but complete in their bond and purpose."

Reaction from fans suggested that they trusted not just the critics, but the band's self-confidence and therefore their own purchasing instincts. *Accelerate* entered the charts at number one in the UK, Ireland, Denmark, Canada and those small bastions of R.E.M. fandom, Switzerland and Norway. Its biggest achievement came in America, where *Accelerate* crashed in at number two, R.E.M.'s highest chart entry since *New Adventures In Hi-Fi*; equally important was the opening week's sales of 115,000, double that of *Around The Sun*. If this only put them back to where they had been with *Reveal*, it bears necessary observation that album sales had collapsed in the States by almost 50% over the previous seven years; platinum certifications were fast becoming a thing of the past, and not just for R.E.M.

The decline in album sales was not quite so pronounced in the UK (as yet); the shift in the role music played in its listeners' lives was more strongly articulated in the singles charts, which had transformed in meaning now that the word 'single', once a treasured 7″ vinyl artefact, was shorthand for 'digital download'. In a pop music scene that celebrated the youthful stars of TV 'talent' shows and a constant turnover in largely anonymous hi-energy-R&B/hip-hop/pop, R.E.M. suddenly looked like a bunch of ageing uncles gate-crashing a teenage party. Though they took some comfort from the fact that 'Supernatural Superserious' graced the American top 100, *Accelerate* would mark the first R.E.M. album not to chart a UK top 50 single since, ironically, *Lifes Rich Pageant,* despite best efforts with heavily animated videos for 'Hollow Man' and 'Man-Sized Wreath', each of which portrayed the lyrics as part of the art, and a more sombre, mostly black and white semi-performance piece for 'Until The Day Is Done', the first R.E.M. single to be available as a download only.

None of this impacted on R.E.M.'s draw as a concert act, and the six-month world tour from May–November 2008 was celebrated for affirming, onstage, the same back-to-basics approach that had proven so successful in the studio. The coherent new five-piece line-up was central to this. "It felt really really comfortable and fun to go play," says Scott McCaughey. "It probably was the first time since they toured back in the Eighties with Bill (Berry) that it felt like a really cool little rock'n'roll combo again. We were more of a lean, mean machine. We didn't have six trucks, we had three; we always came up with a cool backdrop but it wasn't quite as big an endeavour as it had been." (Actually, Blue Leach was hired to undertake only a slightly smaller live-video mix operation than he had done in 2005, though the colourful stage props were absent, bringing more attention to the musicians on stage.) It's like, basically it's two guitars, bass and drums, we've got some lights, a sound guy, a couple of guitar techs, let's go!"

The month-long tour of American arenas typically commenced with 'Living Well Is The Best Revenge', but Peter Buck, in his long-standing role as set-list coordinator, frequently mixed it up with the songs that had so influenced the new album, such as 'Pretty Persuasion', 'These Days' and 'Finest Worksong'. A harrowing version of 'Let Me In' saw the group clustered around Peter Buck on keyboards, the three other playing members each on acoustics. And the introduction of 'Ignoreland' for the first time ever served as part acknowledgment that for all R.E.M.'s endeavours, here they were in a Presidential election year once more, and with George W. Bush still in the White House after eight years, none too certain that the country would choose to change course. (As R.E.M. criss-crossed the States, Democratic candidates Barack Obama and Hillary Clinton continued to battle it out through the last of the Primaries, leading many leftists to worry that unnecessary negative energy was being expended on each other that should instead have been focused on Senator John McCain, who had clinched the Republican nomination months earlier.)

Ticket sales in the States were bolstered by a pair of strong opening acts in The National and Modest Mouse (whose most recent album had in fact *topped* the American charts), and it was only a matter of time before the latter band's guitarist, Johnny Marr, formerly of The Smiths, was lured into sharing the stage with Peter Buck and R.E.M. As noted elsewhere in this book, mutual admiration between R.E.M. and The Smiths back in the Eighties had been complicated by accusations of similarities, R.E.M. frustrated on their arrival in Europe in 1983 to find themselves compared to a band they had predated by a couple of years. But Buck and Marr, each a walking musical encyclopedia and multi-act workaholic, were birds of a feather, and their equally similar approach to the guitar was confirmed when Marr joined Buck, each playing a Rickenbacker, for 'Fall On Me' at the end of each night and, further into the tour, 'Man On The Moon' too.*

The tour of Europe through the summer represented a slightly smaller version of that undertaken three years earlier: there were the familiar festival headline appearances (from Werchter in Belgium to T In The Park in Scotland), there was another visit to the former Eastern Europe (Hungary, Czech Republic, Latvia), and there were the now almost requisite outdoor sports ground shows in Britain, including the Twickenham rugby ground in London and the Old Trafford cricket ground in Manchester. There were additional forays into Greece and Turkey, and there was also the matter of Peter Buck's signature Rickenbacker – the same black 330 he had used since 1982 – being stolen, post-show, from the stage in Helsinki, Finland. (It was returned, anonymously, ten days later, after what seemed at times like an Interpol manhunt.) After a couple more shows in North America (where R.E.M., breaking with tradition, played both the Sasquatch and Voodoo Experience outdoor festivals), the world tour concluded with a foray to South America, including concerts in Colombia, Venezuela, Brazil and Argentina. The group were in Santiago, Chile, on the night of

---

* There was a subtext at work here for those who were looking for it. The Smiths had fulfilled the role in Britain in the Eighties that R.E.M. enjoyed in the States, and when they broke up in 1987 (in no small part due to lack of manager – or, rather, the failure of Smiths vocalist Morrissey to trust in one), they were also selling almost 500,000 albums in America, not far behind R.E.M. Had they been able to weather the internal storms, one could posit, they might well have reaped similar rewards. And if it was true that by breaking up after four albums, The Smiths never experienced a commercial decline or a "creative torpor", it could not have been lost on Johnny Marr that R.E.M. had built the catalogue – and the legacy – that could well have been his. The fact that R.E.M.'s stratospheric Nineties popularity had never prevented Peter Buck from playing with all manner of side projects might only have furthered the question: What if?

November 4, 2008, halfway through their encore, when Bertis Downs walked on stage with a laptop to announce that, shortly after the polls had closed, Barack Obama had been officially projected to become the next President of the United States of America.

R.E.M. had supported Obama since his eventual nomination, just as they had championed the Democratic candidate throughout their career; it so happened that this time the American people, after eight years of Bush's hostile governing, dubious foreign wars, and a sudden, frightening economic collapse, were very much with them; as such, there had not been the same *visceral* need for a Vote For Change tour. Nonetheless, that night in Santiago, Stipe changed into an Obama T-shirt and invited those in the audience wearing their own to come onstage and join a rendition of 'I Believe'. Back in the States, people were dancing in the streets. R.E.M. did so in their own way.

The world tour, all 31 countries of it, wound up in Mexico City on November 18. Being R.E.M., they posted a video of the six-song, 35-minute encore on their website the next day; being R.E.M., it showed not the stage, but the backdrop video screen as edited in real time by Blue Leach. It was a generous gesture either way, for who knew when, or indeed if, R.E.M. might ever play live again.

A week later, a deluxe, excellently remastered edition of *Murmur*, highlighting all manner of sonic detail that had never made the original digital transfer, was released, complete with bonus live CD from 1983 and copious first-person memories for sleeve notes. It was now 25 years since *Murmur* had initially established R.E.M. as the great American hope. With similar deluxe editions set for the rest of the albums on their silver anniversary, R.E.M.'s career was set to take on a second life all of its own. And as they successfully measured *Accelerate* against *Murmur*, the question nonetheless had to be asked: could the revitalised R.E.M. maintain similar momentum as their Eighties selves?

Twenty-eight

R.E.M.'s stature in modern music was further celebrated on March 11, 2009, with a Tribute Concert in New York. There had been similar such events over the years, of course, including the one in 2006 in Athens where the trio had reunited with Bill Berry, but nothing on the level of this, at Carnegie Hall. With Calexico taking the reins as house band, the benefit concert (for children's music education charities) featured a veritable who's who of R.E.M.'s Eighties independent peers (the dB's, Feelies, Throwing Muses), a healthy smattering of acclaimed newer acts (Kimya Dawson, Keren Ann, Guster), a couple of their Athens compatriots (Apples In Stereo, Vic Chesnutt); it was closed out by their leading light, Patti Smith. Each act got to perform just the one song, and they ran the range of R.E.M.'s catalogue, from 'Sitting Still' (Bob Mould) to 'Supernatural Superserious' (Marshall Crenshaw). After Patti Smith sang 'New Test Leper', Peter Buck, Mike Mills and Michael Stipe came out to join her for a finale of 'E-Bow The Letter'. This was to be the last time that the three remaining founding members of R.E.M. performed together in public.

Did they know as much at the time? It was certainly on their minds. Eighteen months later, after the break-up, Michael Stipe confessed that the discussion had started "On our last tour, 2008. During that we were kind of going, well, where could we go from here? We could tell we were on an upswing. It was important to us that we didn't whimper out with our tails between our legs. We wanted to feel we were at the peak of our powers, and the tour felt like that." It had become apparent to audiences that as Michael Stipe got older, he got better as a frontman; in hindsight that was because he knew he had a finite time to prove as much. "Once I reached my forties, I thought to myself that if I'm going to play live now, I need to really mean this. I can't go out and be a little bit, for one moment slovenly in my choices as a performer."

Mike Mills confirmed that, "We were discussing various options on the 2008 tour and I think each of us individually came to the conclusion that probably the best thing to do would be to stop. And once we started broaching that subject with each other we agreed that that was the direction to go."

And yet for all this talk between the band members, there was never any question but that R.E.M. would make another album; all interviews, blog posts, and press statements in the wake of the 2008 world tour assured people as much. By R.E.M.'s recent standards, they were relatively quick about getting back into it as well. Come May of 2009, and Buck, Mills, McCaughey, Rieflin and Jacknife Lee gathered at the Jackpot! Recording Studio in Portland (where McCaughey now lived, as did Buck's girlfriend, the guitarist going through a messy divorce with his second wife, Stephanie) to record over a dozen instrumentals. Several of the louder ideas laid down that week would turn into songs for the next album ('All The Best', 'That Someone Is You' and, in more aggressive form than as finally released, 'It Happened Today') although, when interviewed by Pitchfork Media during the Portland demos, Buck announced that "If it were me making all the decisions, I'd say the record would be a lot broader than the last one."

Jacknife Lee felt that there had been consensus on this even before making the previous album. *Accelerate* "had an agenda behind it," he says, one that he defined as "Let's puff our chests out and stretch our limbs a bit and stand up and jump about." (The group also frequently used the word 'agenda' when describing *Accelerate*.) He recalls telling Bertis Downs that, "Once we get past that, we've made a point, now we can just concentrate on making a great record." *Accelerate was* a great record of course, and for the first time in at least seven years, an R.E.M. album showed up on a number of annual American year-end polls. But as the group approached what they suspected would be their swansong – a decision that, for all the commonality within the trio, had yet to be finalised, let alone discussed with anyone else – there was no doubt that the group wanted to make an equally excellent, but musically more varied, album.

Allocating the time to record it, as a band, with Stipe, was easier considered than done, however, given that the members remained constantly in motion. Michael Stipe continued to engage his multiple personalities – the activist and celebrity who co-hosted one of President Obama's Inauguration parties and showed up on late-night talk shows was also a reinvigorated visual artist. "About five years ago I sat bolt upright in bed and said to myself, 'I want to make sculpture,'" he told the *Guardian* after the final album was completed. "I don't know where it came from, and I'm not even sure what sculpture is any more, but it just hit me like a truck." Stipe's medium was to replicate items of personal relevance in bronze, and in the summer of 2008, as his rock group toured the planet, he presented a show of five such items (a camera, a cassette tape, etc.) at Manhattan's Rogan Gallery under the title 'Relics'. In August 2009, his life-size sculpture of an American buffalo would be installed in the window of Athens' new Hotel Indigo, his first exhibited piece in his college hometown, where he had initially signed up as an art student almost 30 years beforehand.

For his part, Buck (along with McCaughey and Rieflin) had a new album by Robyn Hitchcock and the Venus 3 to promote, and their travels not only took them through Europe as usual, but to opening slots with Portland's prominent new stars The Decemberists that concluded at New York's Radio City Music Hall, where Buck joined the headliners for a tour-ending encore of 'Begin The Begin' and accepted an invitation to play on their next album. Buck and McCaughey also got to tour yet *another* of their acts, The Baseball Project, whose album, released in the midst of all the attention afforded *Accelerate*, was the realisation of a long-term dream between McCaughey and (former Dream Syndicate front man) Steve Wynn, to write and record songs about America's pastime. (Though heartfelt, they were appropriately irreverent, as the title 'Ted Fucking Williams' no doubt clarifies.) The tour in September, with Linda Pitmon on drums, turned into a two-hour-plus bonanza that rotated The Minus 5 into The Baseball Project and then the Steve Wynn IV. Buck would take to the merchandising table in the interval, knowing that the presence of a bona fide rock star – and his willingness to sign newly purchased CDs – could often play its part in helping double the night's overall take.

While waiting for the group to arrange their calendars, Lee was hired to revisit the Dublin Olympia tapes and compile a double CD; Vincent Moon likewise was asked to compile his films from across the residency into a single reel. The live package was released as both a CD and a CD/DVD package in October under the name *R.E.M. Live At The Olympia* – though if the CD cover was to be taken at face value, that title continued as *In Dublin 39 Songs*. By any standards – even those of R.E.M. on a mission to reacquire their magic – that represented a phenomenal turnover of material on a five-night run. As well as revealing all but two of the *Accelerate* songs in suitably "raw, immediate" form, to quote Stipe's initial intent for the material, and apart from providing suitably energetic revisitations of so much *Chronic Town* and *Reckoning* material, the *Live At The Olympia* CD offered the added bonus of the previously unreleased 'On The Fly' and 'Staring Down The Barrel Of The Middle Distance', each sounding phenomenally complete already for songs that were ultimately considered unworthy of inclusion on *Accelerate*. Further to the choice and number of songs, and the fact that, to use the necessary terminology, they *rocked*, the recordings captured the group in almost candid, light-hearted mood, and the comfortable environment of the small theatre provided for more intimate video footage too. It was as far removed as possible from *Perfect Square* while still depicting the same band, and a further return to basics from the *previous* Dublin concert to have been released on CD/DVD, 2007's *R.E.M. Live*. Unfortunately, in a living instance of 'the boy who cried wolf' the public, having been force-fed official R.E.M. live releases on a tourly basis of late, didn't buy it – certainly not in the numbers that they should have. A $100, 4LP, 2CD, 1DVD package appeared to pale in importance next to the inexpensive deluxe double-CD remastered edition of *Reckoning* released earlier in the year. *Live At The Olympia* remains R.E.M.'s most under-rated, under-sold official release – and for new fans looking for a way into the band's live appeal, the essential purchase.

★ ★ ★

R.E.M. eventually reconvened to record their fifteenth album, in November. Part of the delay had been down to a struggle to find the right (non) studio. Stipe liked to be somewhere warm for his vocal cords. "So we started looking in the Southern Hemisphere," says Lee, but they came up short. "Started looking in France and couldn't find anything." Eventually the group decided to hone in on New Orleans, the scene of many a momentous gig, some important recording sessions and, given the horrors of Hurricane Katrina, a good place to bring their business. A studio aptly called the Music Shed – essentially a big warehouse – was booked, Jacknife Lee brought in the same engineers (Sam Bell and Tom McFall) as had helped make *Accelerate* a success, and in a three-week spate of activity, the group recorded much as they had in Vancouver last time around, laying down a large chunk of the album in first, second or third takes. All of them loud. "It could have been *Accelerate* Part 2," says McCaughey, "because we had a real brace of 'two guitars, bass and drums' songs."

As such, there was a concerted effort to move away from this constriction. "The last thing any of us wanted to do was *Accelerate* Part 2, and so we tried to, I guess, expand on that," stressed Stipe as the album reached completion, to which Buck noted that, "The record was meant to be a very inclusive, wide record, so there's all kinds of stuff on there: fast, slow, loud, quiet, a lot of really emotional things." That emotional bent was evident on 'Oh My Heart', which Buck was to note as a rare case of a song being influenced by its recording location, "Just because I've spent so much time in New Orleans and it's got that vibe to it." The pace of initial recording proved sufficiently rapid that New Orleans' Bonerama horns were brought in to add subtle colour to its introduction. The horns were also used on 'Discoverer', the guitar riff for which Buck wrote one night after leaving the studio and which was quickly recorded the following day. The energy and enjoyment factor was such that Michael Stipe allowed fans a relatively rare insight into the process, taking smart-phone video around the studio and uploading it to YouTube for the fun of it.

Given this satisfying speed, it was frustrating for certain parties that it was to be almost five months before the group reconvened. (Jacknife Lee did travel to Athens in March to record vocals for the song 'Every Day Is Yours To Win' at Michael Stipe's house.) Part of the delay was a result of searching, again, for a suitable foreign (non) studio, this time as far as Italy; eventually, the group circled back to New Orleans, but only if they could find a bigger room to record in. The Music Shed, aided by local grants, converted another part of the warehouse largely to R.E.M.'s specs, and the sessions resumed in April.

The down time had not exactly been wasted. When Gary Lightbody of Snow Patrol, Jacknife Lee's other major client, sought to record a "pure country music" album (though his influences were in fact modern *alt-c*ountry acts like Calexico and Wilco), Lee suggested he recruit Peter Buck as partner. At the start of January 2010, the pair entered the studio in Portland, with Jacknife Lee, Scott McCaughey and many others, on an eight-day recording blitz that resulted in a complete album, *The Place We Ran From* ("a twisted love letter to the States," as Lightbody put it) featuring guest vocals from singer M Ward and actress Zooey Deschanel and a host of minor-league stars. Even by the standards of R.E.M.'s bullish guitarist, this was a rapid recording session, and Lee's ability to effectively out-Buck Peter Buck helped bring the two closer together. (Lee notes that after completing *Accelerate,* he was "friends with all the band, but less so with Peter before we started the Tired Pony record.") *The Place We Ran From* was considered sufficiently successful that a nucleus of Tired Pony, including the producer, agreed to tour it in July, which would serve to keep R.E.M.'s recording on task when the two projects clashed.

But in the meantime, there was the return to New Orleans. Peter Buck who, like Michael Stipe, had visited the city in the wake of Katrina and been horrified to find "a ghost town", now saw that it had "really come back. It still has the same vibe." Part of that vibe was its reputation as a party town and R.E.M., while never going too far over the top, were always a party band. There were some long nights, and yet they were productive – such as the soiree in Mike Mills' suite after an evening with Michael Stipe on the town where the former settled onto the piano and hammered out what would become 'Walk It Back' alongside a group of carousing friends. It was recorded in one take the next day, warts and all, to which Stipe would apply some simply stated lyrics: "You, you can't turn away/You've asked me to stay/But something needs to change." For 'Oh My Heart', Stipe picked up where he had left off in 'Houston', his protagonist now back in New Orleans. "The storm didn't kill me, the government changed," he noticed with rare repetition of a previous lyric and a proud pronouncement of Obama's election. 'That Someone Is You', one of the album's most entertaining numbers, included a pop-culture reference to indie icons New Order and Young Marble Giants.

As for the track that would become the album's opening cut, the anthemic 'Discoverer', it "wrote itself for me", Stipe said, with evident delight. "I didn't have to work real hard on it, and I always love those songs because they just come from some more unconscious place." That may not have been coincidental to the fact that, "It's somewhat autobiographic which is also for me as a writer very unusual. It's unique to us and it's unique to me, in terms of what I write about." More so than 'Leaving New York', 'Discoverer' was a love letter to his adopted home city, and as he explained in giving an interview from Manhattan on the record's release, "It's about a moment that occurred on Houston Street, when I was stumbling down the street having been at a party, a vodka in one hand and an espresso in the other, and just being so inspired by the energy of the city and the people. It's a moment-of-discovery song, about discovering oneself and suddenly feeling this huge sense of possibility. New York can do that to you." Indeed.

The song that would follow 'Discoverer' on the album, 'All The Best', seemed to follow on both musically (brash and bold) and lyrically (optimistic and confident). Except that this one was a love letter to the fans, and in that sense the most important song on the album: "Let's sing and rhyme, let's give it one more time, let's show the kids how to do it, fine, fine, fine."

For Jacknife Lee, who had already been given hints by Bertis Downs and who had picked up on individual and collective vibes ("We never really spoke about it, though there were a few moments individually where we touched on it"), and who debated and dissected the lyrics with Stipe more so than anyone else, these words were bold as daylight: 'All The Best', he says, "is about the end of the band."

Stipe would not deny this: "That whole record was a whole big goodbye," he said afterwards, staggered that the fans had not picked up on such blatant clues.

But if so, the fans were not the only ones. "I just thought we were carrying off the high we were on from *Accelerate* and the fun we were having being a band and just making another record," says Scott McCaughey, who was excluded from the break-up conversations, despite his long tenure with the band and his incredibly close friendship with Peter Buck. "I knew it would be the last record in the (Warner Brothers) contract but to me that didn't mean anything necessarily."

It was common knowledge that R.E.M.'s contract was up after the new album, their three consecutive five-album deals representing a longer run of unbroken contracts than perhaps any band had honoured, ever. R.E.M. would have no trouble securing a new record deal: they were still one of the biggest bands on the planet (*Accelerate* had gone to number one in nine countries and top ten in countless more), arguably the most consistent, and were in the midst of a creative upswing. But they would never again be able to secure a deal even remotely like the one they'd (re-)signed with Warner Brothers at the peak of their global popularity, a deal – regardless of whether or not it was worth $60,000,000, or whether it was the biggest of all time – that had demonstrated excessive faith in R.E.M.'s continued popularity, even *before* the industry collapsed. All around R.E.M., superstar acts were suffering from declining record sales; some had taken to abandoning major labels and/or giving away their albums for whatever the fans wanted to pay (Radiohead, Nine Inch Nails); others stepped down to independent labels and potentially larger slices of what was most certainly now a smaller pie. And some stayed within the major label fray, recognising that there were distribution and marketing benefits that the independents could not match. It was a confusing and disconcerting time, and R.E.M. could be excused for not fancying the massive reduction in both financial advances and commercial expectations that any new contract would bring.

Money, of course, had never been their reason for making music, and the fact that they were thriving creatively had to weigh heavily on any decision to call it a day. But that, of itself, was perhaps all the justification that was needed. If their fifteenth album could come close to their fourteenth in quality, that would mean two back-to-back triumphs and the ability to close the curtain on a high note. Did they really want to push on, beyond that, with a different label and a different set-up, and run the risk of making albums that would, almost inevitably, disappoint all over again, and cause personal disharmony once more? What would they be sticking around for if they went for a sixteenth (and seventeenth, etc.) album: acceptance into the Rock & Roll Hall of Fame? They'd done it all, they'd said it all, and at this point, with the new album, they were starting to repeat it all; the songs they were finalising in New Orleans were beginning to sound very much like a journey through R.E.M.'s catalogue, as if they wanted to make a Greatest Hits out of songs they'd never released from across their thirty years.

★   ★   ★

R.E.M. chose Hansa TonStudio in Berlin for the final session of their final album. Berlin was a favoured city – especially for Michael Stipe, and it was his vocals that would be the main beneficiary of the location – and the studio itself was globally renowned for the David Bowie and Iggy Pop albums of the late Seventies, as well as the source of U2's comeback record, *Achtung Baby*. More recently, Jacknife Lee had produced Snow Patrol's *A Hundred Million Suns* there in 2008, and R.E.M. had stopped in to see him and check out the location when their tour passed through Berlin that summer. Hansa was located in the heart of the city, near Potsdamer Platz by the old Berlin Wall; Grouse Lodge this was not. With only three weeks available before Buck, McCaughey and Lee set off on their Tired Pony tour, R.E.M. nonetheless worked hard to make the most of it. The songs grew more varied, and the lyrics became defined; Stipe took the opportunity to pen another love song to another favoured city – in this case, 'Überlin'. Throughout, his perfectionism did not waver, as evident from his description of the process behind the seemingly stream-of-consciousness 'Alligator_ Aviator_Autopilot_Antimatter'.

"That song was a surprise. I had concern about the chorus; it took me a long time to write. I rewrote it 14 times, and wrote the background part and had all that and rewrote that seven times and discarded it. I did what I do. I finally landed on a chorus that I liked; I recorded it." It was only when the band performed it live in the Hansa studio, to film, that Stipe realised his attention to detail had paid off: "It was really the first time that as a band we'd performed the song, and I sang the chorus, and by the time I got to the third chorus, I realised, 'This is not an okay chorus, this is a *great* chorus.'"

While in Berlin, the band also sent out another (unheeded?) signal that they might be wrapping things up for ever as they took to the bars and concert halls of Berlin and invited their friends to appear on the album. Two of the guest vocalists were Canadian-born gay/bisexual musicians who had found refuge in modern Berlin's artistic embrace. Singer/rapper/musician/performance artist Peaches, famed for her explicit sexual subject matter (e.g. a 2006 album entitled *Impeach My Bush*), proved a natural addition to 'Alligator_Aviator_Autopilot_Antimatter', shout-singing along to the chorus, throwing in a semi-rap dialogue and adding something approximating harmonies. Joel Gibb of indie group Hidden Cameras was recruited to sing backing vocals on 'It Happened Today', written about the death of someone close to the band ("This is not a parable, this is a terrible thing," Stipe warned listeners with the opening line). When Pearl Jam came to Berlin for a concert, Eddie Vedder stopped into Hansa for a social visit, and left with his distinctive holler further filling the enormous phonetic chorus for 'It Happened Today'. Patti Smith played Berlin a week later and, as with Pearl Jam, R.E.M. took the evening off to see her in concert, the various members joining in on various encores. Attempts to get Smith into the studio were stymied by her band's tight touring schedule, but the idea was not completely discounted – there was still a mixing session to follow in Nashville in September, after all.

The album had taken sufficient shape that on the last day of recording at Hansa, the group opted to record one more track. Scott McCaughey recalls Peter Buck saying, 'Let's just go in and do this really fucked up thing.' Jacknife Lee played his newly acquired musical saw, partly to settle a bet with Peter Buck that he wouldn't be able to get a note out of it. McCaughey played lead guitar – "my best Neil Young whatever" – at Buck's request. The jam went down on tape "because we're always recording," says Lee, "but it wasn't like a performance."

"We did it one time and forgot about it." McCaughey, who was not needed for the mix session, might have done so; Lee did not.

It was no small matter that R.E.M. brought in a camera crew during that final week at Hansa. As a group that typically documented everything, it made sense to get additional mileage out of a famous studio location; given that the band had sent out firm signals that there would be no tour for the album, it was necessary to get some live footage. But for those in the know – limited, largely, to the three founding members, Bertis Downs and, having gleaned it over the course of the recording sessions, Jacknife Lee – it would mark something potentially much more significant: a final performance by the band.

A small audience of family and friends was invited into the downstairs hall at Hansa, where they mostly sat on flight cases up against the walls; R.E.M. set up facing each other, more or less in the round, and played their way through as much of the new album as they could, as emphatically as they could. In the process, they delivered vastly more powerful, thoroughly live audio-visual renditions of what would be the album's lead single, 'Mine Smell Like Honey', 'All The Best', and 'Alligator_Aviator_Autopilot_Antimatter'; for 'Oh My Heart', with Scott McCaughey on accordion, they huddled close together, as when they had recorded it, to the point that they were almost breathing on each other. The edits that would be shared with the public revealed a band entirely on top of its game, as powerful and present as it had ever been: Peter Buck still on treasured black Rickenbacker, swaying with the rhythm if no longer jumping around to it, Mike Mills resolutely focused on those melodic bass lines and distinctive vocals, Michael Stipe's professorial beard, horn-rimmed glasses and work-day suit failing to disguise his complete emotional commitment, and McCaughey and Rieflin serving notice that for the past three years, R.E.M. had been very much a band once again. Throughout, the boom of the vast hall lent itself to a particularly resonant live sound. To all outwards intents and purposes, this was a group very much looking forward.

It was the performance of 'Discoverer' that gave it away. The official film showed Michael Stipe's complete giving of himself to his delivery – "It was what it was! Let's all get on with it, now!" –

before removing his glasses, always a signal of immersion in the moment, and following that line with the four further cries of the title and then the fifth and final one, drawing out its four syllables into as many measures. "Wow," concluded Mike Mills, and Stipe blinked, grinned and led a round of applause, as the camera edits ducked and dived amongst the various band members. The camera that was fixed on Stipe's face throughout the take, however, would prove that much more revealing of the emotional meaning: Stipe was clearly blinking away tears. "Hooray, we're done," he said quietly, leading the applause (the words were not included on the official video); it would appear evident that he didn't know whether to laugh or cry. Either the man behind the camera presumed that Stipe broke into tears at the end of every performance, else he was damned good at keeping a secret. Either way, R.E.M. had just played their last gig.

★　★　★

Under the circumstances, it should come as no surprise that the final sessions for the final album, in Nashville, would prove tense. "It was heated at times," says Jacknife Lee. "Michael was saying, 'This is an amazing record and we have to get it right' but I knew there was something else going on, that it was 'We have to get it right because it's the last one.' We were all put under pressure." And yet pressure can sometimes bring out the best in people. Earlier in the sessions, Michael Stipe had recorded a spoken word piece reminiscent of 'Low' from *Out Of Time*; it hadn't worked and was lying unused, amidst the jumble of half-finished songs that were the residue of every R.E.M. album. Jacknife Lee now took it and fed it over the arrangement to the jam from the last day in Berlin, given the simple name 'Blue'. "It took a bit of constructing," he says, "but it sounds great." When Patti Smith and guitarist Lenny Kaye flew down to lend their presence for what they might have suspected by now would be a final opportunity, Kaye provided it with some additional tension; he also delivered a wailing, taut, free jazz solo as was his talent on 'Alligator_Aviator . . .'

Stipe had initially envisioned Patti Smith singing some of her beloved doo-wop to 'Every Day Is Yours To Win', but "It didn't sound right," says Lee. The suggestion was made that she use her more familiar voice on 'Blue' instead. It took two days. "She's a heavyweight," says Jacknife Lee. "She has to channel certain things to sing."

But it worked a treat. With her softly wailing intonations about a Cinderella figure, a jam session that had seemed like so much time-filler in Berlin now become an archetypal weird R.E.M. song such as they hadn't perfected since, come to think of it, *New Adventures In Hi-Fi*, back when Patti Smith last appeared on an R.E.M. album. 'Blue' was *so* out of place that it could only make sense closing out the album; yet, as Lee points out, "The final voice on the final record couldn't be Patti Smith, it had to be Michael." And so the idea came about to do something R.E.M. had never done before: reprise the opening song. "It bookends the album but it also bookends the career. 'Discoverer' is about experience, finding new experience, all those feelings. I thought that at the end by singing the same thing it would seem different, it would feel different because the experience would impart something to the reprise." Stipe and Mills went back in for another vocal take over the existing guitar riffs, imbued with the almost certain knowledge that they were putting a full stop on R.E.M.'s album career. "It took half a day to do," says Lee, "but I think once we did it, it all made perfect sense and seemed to solidify the record."

'Blue' provided the album with its title track – per Patti Smith's suggestion, who looked at Stipe's lyric sheet and pronounced his final words, 'Collapse Into Now', as an obvious choice. Given the full line – "20th Century collapse into now" – it did indeed make sense. "In my head, it's like I'm addressing a nine-year-old and I'm saying, 'I come from a faraway place called the 20th century,'" Stipe told *Interview*. "And these are the values and these are the mistakes we've made and these are the triumphs. These are the things that we held in the highest esteem. These are the things to learn from."

As the team wrestled with final choices of final mixes, one song remained problematic: 'Me, Marlon Brando, Marlon Brando And I'. The twisted ballad had been put to tape back in New Orleans, where "Michael sang it the first day but almost whispered the whole song," says Lee. "He got really attached to it but I could never get it to sound any good." The lyric was oblique in the old-fashioned Michael Stipe manner, disguising a reference to the Neil Young song 'Pocahontas' in which that singer had imagined himself with Marlon Brando around a campfire; Stipe's own lyric was effectively an update, "me going to Neil Young for advice", as he told the *Guardian*. It nearly didn't make it. On the final day in Nashville, Lee turned to Stipe and said, "I still can't get this song sounding any good." Stipe casually volunteered to sing it one more time. He went back in the vocal booth and nailed the delivery. "Had he said that maybe a year before I would have been very happy," says Lee, ecstatic nonetheless to have perfected a troublesome song.

That quest for perfection was now threatening to override what was already an extraordinarily emotive process. The album was done, but "some of them wanted it to go on for a long time, because it was the end," says Lee. "Not just the end of the record, but the end of the band. So there was a reluctance to actually finish the record. I'm sure Michael would have had us there for another week, just listening."

That was the last thing Peter Buck wanted. Not much given to over-sentimentality, he wasn't about to allow *Collapse Into Now* to collapse into itself just because it represented R.E.M.'s final long-playing statement. "Peter's attitude was, 'We are over, it's sad, I've got to go,'" recalls Lee. "And other people were saying, 'We want to linger for a while.' I didn't want the record to get mixed up in whatever feelings or conflicts people were having with themselves in terms of what this meant."

It was finally decided: *Collapse Into Now* was complete. The night before he flew home to the Pacific North-West, Peter Buck called the group out to watch the sun set. "It was all very poetic and nice," says Lee, "and we all knew that was the end of it." The week that *Collapse Into Now* was released, Peter Buck set off on tour with The Baseball Project.

★   ★   ★

The very week that R.E.M. finished the album, a shake-up at Warner Brothers saw Tom Whalley let go as chairman. He had been at the label almost a decade, and though he had presided over R.E.M.'s worst and worst-selling record, he had never lost faith;

he'd shepherded the platinum *In Time* compilation, had backed the group through the return to form and commercial prominence with *Accelerate,* had encouraged (perhaps over-encouraged) a continued profile with the live albums. He had been a *fan*, and in the ever-changing world of ever-shrinking major labels, that was rare indeed. As his job was split between three Warner Brothers veterans, so two other important champions of R.E.M., publicist Brian Bumbery and tech manager Ethan Kaplan, also left the company. The group was to release its last album for the label in something of a managerial void.*

It may have been to ensure time for replacement figures to get behind their desks and hopefully behind the band that the release date was held until March 8. In the meantime, the group got on with its own self-promotion, most notably in the form of Michael Stipe commissioning videos for every song on the album. Most were a far cry from the hi-tech masterpieces that had been his stock in trade; this was an art project for Stipe and friends as much as a statement of indie marketing. The video for 'Mine Smell Like Honey' focused on Stipe being pushed up the Hansa staircase by several men in their underwear; 'Discoverer', directed by Stipe himself with sister Lynda, was pure graphic light; handed the reins to 'All The Best', Athens' Jim Hibbert filmed precisely according to type, depicting enough young naked men that his latest exercise in 're-photography' came with a parental warning 'sticker'. 'Überlin' was gifted with two videos – one, put out in advance, that featured the lyrics as part of a subway map, the other shot with young actor Aaron Johnson parading through the run-down suburban streets of London. The best video by far was 'It Happened Today', which not only brought some emotive cinematography to the story of personal loss, but was re-edited to feature a lengthy breakdown in the midst of the song, removing the instruments and reducing the voices until just Eddie Vedder's distinct moan was left holding the song from petering into silence.

They were eminently creative pieces, and they were but a part of

---

* Whalley's contract was reputedly worth $30,000,000 over those ten years. This helps put into perspective R.E.M.'s supposed $60,000,000 in recoupable advances for a five-album deal split between the whole band.

the overall attempt to replicate the kind of grass-roots buzz that had so aided *Accelerate*, but as the R.E.M. office unleashed one online video followed by another free download, a four-song online sampler along with an open-source remix competition, it seemed as if they were diluting the album from its own artistic statement. In the old days, an album was trailed by a single, but then listened to as a complete body of work. With *Collapse Into Now*, it was hard enough to ascertain the single to begin with. In Britain and America, it was 'Mine Smell Like Honey'. Internationally, whatever that meant, it was 'Überlin'. Both were fine songs in their own right; they had choruses and hooks, and an energy that had been lacking from the McCarthy era. But neither was necessarily the most commercial song on *Collapse Into Now*, let alone the best; they were strange choices. Regardless, most fans would have heard – and seen, and perhaps even remixed – most of the songs before they ever got a chance to hear the album in its sequenced entirety. It was perhaps no surprise then, that when they did, it felt less like a coherent body of work than a collection of fine but disparate songs, some of which were immediately reminiscent of previous fine but disparate songs.

This was hardly accidental. As Peter Buck said on release, "Emotionally and musically it covers pretty much everything we've done in the past." Or, as Rob Sheffield put it in a four-star *Rolling Stone* review, "*Collapse Into Now* touches on all their favourite tricks: punk raves, stately ballads, piano, accordion and the most mandolin they've put in one place since 'Losing My Religion'."

Other reviews were equally positive and equally likely to raise comparisons, as each new R.E.M. song appeared to set off a nostalgic reminder of an old R.E.M. song. "*Collapse* sounds like a familiar friend," said *Spin*; "*Collapse* shuffles through all of R.E.M.'s past lives," noted *Paste*; "Feeling comfortable in their own skin," observed the *Guardian*, kindly; "Most of this record's musical temperament seems reheated or purchased," said the *New York Times*, less so. In a more humorous echo of the same theme, hipster web site *CokeMachineGlow* noted that "If there's any band that's completely earned the right to gracefully knock themselves off, it's R.E.M. It only took them fourteen years." Perhaps the most eloquent of the many similar (mostly positive) reviews was that by the

Village Voice, which stated that "R.E.M. have figured out how to be R.E.M. again – how to affect the signature balance of folky and punky that's inspired bands far less worshipful than Pearl Jam or the Decemberists." Peter Buck had indeed found the necessary time to play on The Decemberists' new album, *The King Is Dead*. It did not go unnoticed that the arrangement on lead single 'Down By The Water' matched R.E.M.'s 'The One I Love' so perfectly that the two could be played side by side. Nor did it go un-noticed that *The King Is Dead* went to number one in America; as with previous chart-toppers Modest Mouse and The Shins, R.E.M. now had serious peer rivalry for the role of pre-eminent American left-field rock band.

Collapse Into Now did not fare as well as the recent albums by these other acts, although its number five American chart placement was respectable given the vagaries of the last 14 years. But a similar number five peak in the UK was baffling. Every R.E.M. album since *Out Of Time* had gone to number one or number two in the UK; what had they done to deserve this sudden abandonment in the course of just three years? A number one in Germany spoke to that country's relative loyalty but the message was nonetheless as plain as day: *Collapse Into Now* had not connected with ageing R.E.M. fans the way *Accelerate* had done, and with total lack of singles success, and no accompanying tour, nor was it winning new fans.

The disconnect was not a product of the individual songs, all of which improved on repeated listens; nor was it a product of production, which was as big and bold as *Accelerate*. And there was nothing specifically lacking from the group's performance – although there were many who felt that Michael Stipe had had finer hours. The fact was that *Collapse Into Now* sounded too much like what it was: an attempt to cover all R.E.M.'s musical ground in one massive go, one final time. Somehow, one cannot help but now conclude, R.E.M.'s prior knowledge of their demise seeped into the musical grooves; there was something within it that distanced the final record from some of the fans, even as, at that point, those fans could not quite put their finger on it.

As far as Michael Stipe was concerned, he had all but advertised the impending split. "I'm shocked no one noticed," he said just afterwards, in an amusing "job exit" interview with *The Quietus*. "No-one going: 'Wait! This band have never put themselves on the cover of album before.' And I'm waving goodbye on it! My Patti Smith wave. I thought it was the most obvious thing on earth." But then coming from someone who had once been falsely rumoured as dying of AIDS, perhaps he should have expected that the one time he actually *invited* the press and the public to speculate on something, they failed to take the hint.

The media proved oddly oblivious. The opening sentence of an interview with Mike Mills in *Music & Musicians* actually took the most blatant line from 'All The Best' – "Let's sing and rhyme, let's give it one more time" – and called it a "loud-and-clear statement for a band in the midst of an artistic renaissance." It then had the gall to ask Mills if "fans read things into R.E.M.'s songs that you didn't intend," and, as a follow-up question "Did you ever consider splitting?" The lack of present tense afforded Mills a relatively easy out.

The hired band members, meanwhile, proved equally unaware. Scott McCaughey had not been party to the Nashville sessions almost a year earlier, which had enabled him to be enormously pleased by the outcome afforded 'Blue,' and to be touched – but nothing more – by the subsequent reprise of 'Discoverer'. "I thought it was just like putting a bow on it!" In the summer of 2011, he heard that R.E.M. were compiling another Greatest Hits, the first to draw from both the I.R.S. *and* the Warner Brothers catalogue. As with *In Time*, there was a demand (from the label, no doubt) and an apparent desire (on the band's part) to add a couple of new songs. Unfortunately, the one week that Jacknife Lee, Michael Stipe and Mike Mills were all available to record in Athens (the same week that *Lifes Rich Pageant* saw its 25th Anniversary Deluxe Edition double CD release, garnering five-star nostalgic reviews far beyond the praise it had received back in 1986), Peter Buck and Scott McCaughey were on holiday in Vanuatu in the South Seas. The final R.E.M. session was not, in fact, an R.E.M. session.

Nonetheless, three songs were ultimately recorded for the compilation, entitled *Part Lies, Part Heart, Part Truth, Part Garbage 1982–2011* after a descriptor of the band that Buck had used back in the Eighties. Each of them already existed in some form or another. 'A Month Of Saturdays' was drawn from a fun, left-over instrumental from the Dublin sessions for *Accelerate* that Stipe was finally able to find lyrics for; it sounded like an R.E.M. B-side. 'We All Go Back To Where We Belong' was far more profound. Written by Mike Mills in his hotel room in New Orleans, and recorded by the band for *Collapse Into Now*, it had lacked for lyrics, even though Michael Stipe had worked feverishly on it when Lee came to Athens in the spring of 2010 to record vocals. When they reunited at John Keane's studio for the final supposed band session, Stipe finally caught the muse. Unquestionably a love song ("I can taste the ocean on your skin"), its title nonetheless spoke directly to R.E.M.'s demise. And now that there was melody and words to go with the arrangement, "We chopped it up," says Lee. "Lost a chorus, turned a verse into a chorus, classic old school bad behaviour from R.E.M. Endless tinkering. And we eventually got it to be the way it is now, which I think is a perfect ending."

Later in July 2011, Lee flew up to Seattle to work with Buck and McCaughey, the intent being that everyone should get to contribute to the recordings. Sadly, Buck was suffering from a debilitating back injury that, for the first time in his entire life, necessitated the cancellation of (Baseball Project) shows. "He couldn't play or walk," says Lee. "It was very sad, he was in severe pain."

To ensure that Buck could contribute to his song 'Hallelujah', says McCaughey, "We used acoustic guitar from a demo we did in my basement and I had to bring it in and fit it to the track." It was a frustrating end to Buck's 30-plus years of constant forward momentum with R.E.M., but the effort was worth it, the song eventually building from its 6/8 acoustic lilt – reminiscent in style if not tempo of 'Walk It Back' – to a grand orchestral chorus, a baroque breakdown, a fiery guitar interlude and spiritual guttural vocals (similar to 'It Happened Today') the likes of which R.E.M. excelled at. "It's unusual," says Lee, who worked hard to stitch together the various disparate parts, "in that it takes folk rock and adds, not electronic elements, but odd processing of audio signals in a new way. It doesn't sound like an electronic record but there's a lot of things in it."

The compilation was lined up for November release, and for those who were looking that far ahead, must have seemed as if it was bordering on the desperate: how many retrospectives did R.E.M. need to put out each year to remind the public of their existence? The answer came on Wednesday, September 21. After letting those closest to them in on their decision with a series of phone calls and meetings and vows to secrecy, R.E.M. released the following statement through their website:

> "To our Fans and Friends: As R.E.M., and as lifelong friends and co-conspirators, we have decided to call it a day as a band. We walk away with a great sense of gratitude, of finality, and of astonishment at all we have accomplished. To anyone who ever felt touched by our music, our deepest thanks for listening." R.E.M.

A few hours later, having let the initial message sink in, the statement was updated with comments from each member of the band. "We have always been a band in the truest sense of the word," said Mike Mills in part. "Brothers who truly love, and respect, each other. We feel kind of like pioneers in this – there's no disharmony here, no falling-outs, no lawyers squaring-off. We've made this decision together, amicably and with each other's best interests at heart. The time just feels right."

"Mike, Michael, Bill, Bertis, and I walk away as great friends," wrote Peter Buck. "I know I will be seeing them in the future, just as I know I will be seeing everyone who has followed us and supported us through the years. Even if it's only in the vinyl aisle of your local record store, or standing at the back of the club: watching a group of 19-year-olds trying to change the world."

And Michael Stipe said it best, even if he claimed to be quoting someone else. "A wise man once said, 'The skill in attending a party is knowing when it's time to leave.' We built something extraordinary together. We did this thing. And now we're going to walk away from it."

Endgame

Few people get to write their own obituaries. Fewer still get to read them. But in breaking up the way that they did – as a band, of friends – R.E.M. got to fashion the terms by which they would be remembered. And that had been very much their purpose since day one. Asked by Norwegian television just after the break-up, "What have you achieved?" Michael Stipe was almost embarrassingly articulate as he avoided all mention of hit records, award-winning videos, stadium concerts and celebrity status.

"As people," he said instead, "we managed to do something and to not ever feel like we were compromised by external forces, to not feel like we capitulated to an idea of what a pop band should be, or what a rock band should be, to not give in to the industry or the market – to do car commercials or liquor commercials or whatever." (It was often lost within the assumption of R.E.M.'s self-righteousness that this was one of the very last acts not to sell [out] its music.) "We made decisions ourselves, and we owned those decisions. We had triumphs and we owned those; we had mistakes and we owned those. And so, not only being in the middle of it but also looking back now, I feel that we managed to somehow create something that I can be very proud of, not only at the highest but at the very low points, and say: 'I owned that. We made that choice ourselves.'"

Music aside, it was what their fans had always loved about them.

★   ★   ★

After the initial (and anticipated, no doubt) reaction from the haters – 'You mean to say that R.E.M. hadn't split up years ago?' – and an almost delayed response from the life-long fans, especially the older ones who were forced to weigh up whether R.E.M.'s continued existence, or indeed their break-up, was something they should necessarily get worked up about, the tributes started to pour in. R.E.M. had provided the teenage, college-era and 20-something soundtrack to many a now middle-aged American writer, and one by one, they flexed their literary muscles to say as much; the existence of the publish-it-now, edit-it-later blogosphere ensured, likewise, that no fan was denied their chance to share a trip down nostalgia avenue. These tributes exist in their hundreds, and they make for evocative and frequently emotional reading; there may even be a separate book of collected personal essays. In Europe, meanwhile, R.E.M. had provided a different kind of soundtrack, one that spanned two or three generations, often at the same time, and what was surely the most constantly lauded group of modern times continued to receive all due praise as Mills and Stipe got back on the international promo mill and braved the peak-time UK TV, press and radio circuit one final time.

"The passion is still there," said Mike Mills, to a Dutch journalist who had tried comparing their three-way relationship to a tired marriage. "We're not quitting because we're bored, or we can't make great music any more. We just made two of my favourite R.E.M. records. But the fact is, you take your opportunities when you see them. And this was the time to walk away for reasons really that you don't need to say. It's just time to go. It feels right."

And to relentless questions about Peter Buck's absence from the promo mill, Mills and Stipe were at pains to point out that it was because, being Peter, he was busy doing what he wanted to be doing: playing gigs. The night that *Part Lies, Part Heart, Part Truth, Part Garbage, 1982–2011* was released, November 15, 2011, Buck was on stage at a club in Philadelphia, performing as a member of both The Minus 5 and John Wesley Harding's backing band. The night before, Mike Mills, Bill Berry and Bertis Downs all attended the album's pre-release party (an Athens R.E.M. tradition) at the 40 Watt Club, where the group auctioned off a signed Rickenbacker amongst many other items. And the night after the album's release, Michael Stipe went on *Late Night With Jimmy Fallon* in New York and talked about the break-up alongside Martin Short, Kermit the Frog and Miss Piggy. We all go back to where we belong.

★   ★   ★

Michael Stipe furthered his artistic credentials by co-directing two videos for R.E.M.'s last single as a (non-)functioning band, alongside Dominic DeJoseph. One focused a black and white movie camera on young female actress Kirsten Dunst for the length of the song, the other on ageing male beat poet John Giorno. The two faces represented deeply contrasting images of the human condition, but each subject had the power of presence to hold the viewer's attention for the full three and a half minutes. In doing so, they freed the song from a literal translation, and yet evoked some sense of its lyrical intent. It was a breathtakingly simple concept, and it worked beautifully. After three decades of dealing with the promo pop video, Michael Stipe appeared to be enjoying the process more than ever. 'We All Go Back To Where We Belong' did not chart, however, anywhere. The 40-song double CD retrospective sold but respectfully. "It's for a teenager out there who only knows R.E.M. as that band who do that song that plays in the elevator, or the grocery store, or the deli, or the cab, or for being that band with the bald guy in it," said Stipe. "This is for them." In time, presumably.

★ ★ ★

Everyone has a story to tell about R.E.M. and for the author it is no different. I had the pleasure of seeing all three of R.E.M.'s first shows in Britain in 1983. I say all three because as well as attending the two official gigs at Dingwall's and the Marquee in London, I was working for the television show *The Tube* at the time, in Newcastle, where the group made their official European debut, performing three songs entirely live to camera and almost single-handedly, instantaneously, resetting the British nation's understanding of what constituted the American new wave. The thing I remember about the shows in London is the sweat dripping off the walls and the length of their sets; British bands simply didn't play over an hour in clubs. The thing I remember about their appearance on *The Tube*, in Newcastle, is Bill Berry saying hello to me as he walked down the corridor: British bands didn't do that either, being usually too wrapped up in their own self-importance. Berry's politeness was not, I was soon to discover, that of the southern hick who didn't know better from British aloofness. It was the mark of the southern gentleman, a quality that R.E.M. carried with them at all times.

Twenty-five years later, I invited myself, my wife and our younger son, all of three years old, to see R.E.M. at Jones Beach on Long Island, on the *Accelerate* tour. (Our older son had been dragged along to a similar shed show many years earlier, where Michael Stipe had sat down and played with him on the grass after the show.) We were supplied with backstage passes, which proved extremely useful when the skies opened, the thunderclouds roared, and Modest Mouse's opening set was cut short as lightning hit one of the lighting trusses, almost taking Johnny Marr with it. Over the ensuing 90 minutes, we huddled in the rather ramshackle backstage area like everyone else with credentials to do so; there was no 'green room', no café, no bar. For most of that time, it wasn't certain that R.E.M. would take to the stage and many fans out front headed home, disappointed, perhaps, that their idols chose such venues that were privy to such risks. At one point, following my three-year old around the outdoor backstage area, I got too close to the lead singer's dressing room. The door opened, and a worried looking Stipe came out to get an update on the weather for himself. He looked straight at me. We wouldn't have seen each other for years. I've never made any claims to his friendship. He had very important things on his mind. "Hello, Tony," he said. It was exactly the same politeness I'd seen on display from Bill Berry at his first European gig. Nothing, really, had changed. Except, along the way, everything.

There is so much to say about the music, and hopefully I have said it all, within these pages. I honestly can't contemplate these 30 years of my life without R.E.M. providing it with a soundtrack for at least a large part of it. Indeed, I could head off on various tangents about my own preferred records, songs, concerts and videos, but for the fact that, per the best of bands, every day brings a different first listening choice according to mood, and every album, every song, seems to have both its fierce proponents and fiercer *opponents*, even amongst R.E.M.'s most dedicated of fans. But there *is* something more to say about R.E.M.'s way of doing business, and it is hardly unconnected to everything else that goes above. R.E.M. always treated people differently. Even at the giddiest of their commercial heights, they maintained a civility in their behaviour that was almost unbecoming from a rock band – although, paradoxically, this never seemed to stop them enjoying themselves. And that sense of fun, too, played into their appeal as much as did the timeless quality of so many of their songs. R.E.M. were not so much the group you always wanted to be a member of – after all, some people don't dream of being a rock star – but they *were* the group you always wanted to be around. They emanated a goodness, a grace, a joy, a sincerity, and at the same time still maintained some sort of punk rock *attitude*, and together, those qualities really made it look like they were having the greatest time in the world, and that maybe you could, too – if only you'd been fortunate enough to have been born one of them.

R.E.M.'s acts of decency are many, and many of them are well known. This is a band that supported all manner of social causes, that wore its politics on its sleeves, that campaigned for Presidential candidates and performed fund-raisers for local schools alike. It was the smaller acts that truly became them. What other band sent out limited edition, lovingly designed Christmas records to their fan club members for 24 years straight? What other group sent out calendars as a matter of course? What other band typically beat its fans to the punch when it came to sharing live tapes or, in later years, video footage? What other group sent out thank you notes to people who should be thanking *them*? Ensured of its video directors and record producers that every member of the crew be properly paid? Bought gifts for people who worked for them for but a short period of time? What other band, the day after that horrendously rain-soaked evening at Jones Beach, would call up the writer who had just freeloaded his way into the event, apologise for the weather and the shortened show, and request that he come back and see them at Madison Square Garden the next week as their guest (again)?

Two events from the summer of 2012 may help close out the story. In July, I stopped by the Full Moon Resort in the Catskills hamlet of Big Indian, where Peter Buck was participating in Todd Rundgren's annual summer camp. A week or so earlier, Peter had, for the first time in our decades-long acquaintance, not so much refused as punted my request to be interviewed in an update for this book. "I'm not really sure," he'd written. "I feel like the rem Peter Buck is gone, and I'm not sure the new guy wants to have anything to do with show biz." At the Full Moon, while Todd Rundgren led campers through a running commentary of his risotto preparation, we had lunch at one of the picnic tables, inevitably joined by campers, many of whom were of course bowled over by Buck's proximity. Buck reaffirmed his feelings regarding talking about R.E.M., that for now, it was "dead", but that he might change his mind about revisiting the group's history somewhere down the line. For the time being, he was enthused about his forthcoming solo record. Not another of what now feels like several hundred collaborations, but his *own* record, soon to be released under his own name. (Though at that point he was still wrestling with the alternate moniker of Richard M. Nixon.)

It wasn't a solo album by the usual measure of the famous guitarist; his singing voice would make sure of that. So too, would the lack of apparent title or artist once he got around to releasing it the way he wanted to: on vinyl, as a 12″ analogue album, even if it meant hunting down a custom-made lacquering machine that didn't require digital conversion. The record was made in the manner to which he had become accustomed in almost every act except R.E.M. − with friends, in one go, generally on first take, over the course of a mere five days in this case. It was particularly pleasing to him that Mike Mills had come up to Portland to participate; allow that Bill Rieflin and Scott McCaughey were on most songs too, and you had a couple of tracks that were, in effect, R.E.M. minus Michael Stipe. Of course, you would never have known as much by listening to them, and therein lies part of R.E.M.'s magic − the way that three, formerly four, individuals would meet on common ground, each prepared to push just hard enough, each prepared to give way when it mattered. Buck, Mills and Stipe had had dinner together recently; their friendship was inviolable, but only Peter Buck had continued making music without taking a break. Mike Mills had awarded himself time off to travel and see family and friends. Stipe had discovered that just announcing the break-up proved 'liberating' and felt under no pressure to make any decisions about future musical activities. There is − given the life-long camaraderie and in-built support structure, allowing for the fact that the R.E.M. website continues its daily updates as if the band were still an ongoing entity – a distinct possibility that all three will show up on the same record again soon enough. There remains a vow that it won't be as R.E.M.

★   ★   ★

And then, on a Saturday night in October, in the village of Rosendale, just south of the Catskills, a local venue put on a tribute night to R.E.M. It was but one of many over the years, some of which have been referenced in the last few chapters. And there had been tribute albums along the way – and quite a splendid re-interpretation of *Automatic For The People* put together by the Stereogum site back in 2007, to celebrate its fifteenth anniversary. Plus, all manner of major acts had covered R.E.M., and some of the group's songs had become part of the public lexicon. After the Dunblane massacre in 1996, when a gunman shot dead 16 Scottish primary age schoolchildren along with their teacher, the song that Radio 1 returned with after the national moment of silence was 'Everybody Hurts'. After the attacks of 9/11, the song that was most frequently set to home-made videos of the aftermath, the song that became a peer-to-peer mash-up with news clips, was 'Everybody Hurts'. On that final promo-go-round in November 2011, Mills and Stipe were shown a clip from Norwegian national television that commemorated the victims of their own terrorist massacre that July: two of the nation's most popular singers singing, to full orchestra, and in perfect English, 'Everybody Hurts'. "What an incredible honour for us as songwriters to have a song that touches people so deeply as that song," said Stipe.

Nobody performed 'Everybody Hurts' that night at Market Market in Rosendale. Nobody performed an R.E.M. song that dated beyond 1992, either, unfortunate confirmation that R.E.M.'s period of genuine influence on an American generation had ended after a decade. But over the course of a couple of hours, act after act – solo, duo, baroque quintet, and four-square rock group of my local dad friends blasting their way through the anthems of their college days – demonstrated the depth of R.E.M.'s musical appeal. It's always said that the test of a great song is whether, regardless of its original arrangement, it can be played with just an acoustic guitar, and late in the evening, a male and female couple, too young to have experienced R.E.M.'s early years, shuffled onto what passed as a stage. His name was Dylan Glenn-Johanson, he sang and he played an acoustic guitar; her name was Geneva (just Geneva), and she sang, like an angel. Over the next four minutes, they took that most maligned of R.E.M. songs, 'Shiny Happy People', and reconstructed it, bending both melody and riff along the way, into the most delicate of folk ballads. By the time they were done, it bore no resemblance to the alt-rock bubblegum duet between Michael Stipe and Kate Pierson; instead, it had turned into something quite deep and mysterious, something truly inspiring. The room fell silent in the process; you could have heard a beer being poured in the pauses between Dylan's purposefully tentative guitar picking and Geneva's new take on melody, had anyone been rude enough to have ordered one.

It's a suitably small, possibly minor, arguably inconsequential place to end: a quiet Saturday night at a café-bar in a small town in Little America. But it makes sense, to me at least, and not least for the line in 'Shiny Happy People' that speaks to R.E.M.'s legacy: "Put it in the ground where the flowers grow." When I left Market Market in Rosendale that evening, it was with the feeling of immense joy for having attended. R.E.M. had pulled up their roots a year earlier already, but the flowers were blooming. As such, this story has a happy ending. And those are all too rare.

Appendices

ALBUMS DISCOGRAPHY

Previous editions of this biography (and other R.E.M. books too) have attempted to catalogue R.E.M.'s single releases, but as the list grows ever longer, and formats vary so widely according to country, the task becomes painfully like pushing an elephant up the stairs. Besides, all R.E.M. singles have been released on R.E.M. albums; original B-sides and rarities were assembled on a couple of compilations; more recent B-sides lean towards live material with only the occasional unreleased track or cover. An albums discography such as that which follows thereby includes the vast majority of R.E.M. music. Side projects and collaborations are far too numerous to mention here (though they have been frequently referred to in the text); likewise, cover versions for tribute albums and contributions to soundtracks and benefits are omitted from the following list but generally referred to in the text.

Those songs listed in brackets on the first five studio albums plus *Dead Letter Office* were added to 'Expanded Version' CDs, released by I.R.S. Records in Holland in 1992 and 1993. They are all either outtakes, alternative versions or live recordings.

MURMUR
Radio Free Europe/ Pilgrimage/ Laughing/ Talk About The Passion/ Moral Kiosk/ Perfect Circle/ Catapult/ Sitting Still/ 9-9/ Shaking Through/ We Walk/ West Of The Fields (There She Goes Again/ 9-9/ Gardening At Night/ Catapult)

IRS SP70604 April 1983 (US)
IRS SP70604 August 1983 (UK)

461

R.E.M.

RECKONING
Harborcoat/ 7 Chinese Brothers/ So. Central Rain/ Pretty Persuasion/ Time After Time (Annelise)/ Second Guessing/ Letter Never Sent/ Camera/ (Don't Go Back To) Rockville/ Little America (Windout/ Pretty Persuasion/ White Tornado/ Tighten Up/ Moon River)

IRS SP70044 April 1984 (US)
IRS 1RSA7045 April 1984 (UK)

FABLES OF THE RECONSTRUCTION
Feeling Gravitys Pull/ Maps and Legends/ Driver 8/ Life And How To Live It/ Old Man Kensey/ Can't Get There From Here/ Green Grow The Rushes/ Kohoutek/ Auctioneer (Another Engine)/ Good Advices/ Wendell Gee (Crazy/ Burning Hell/ Bandwagon/ Driver 8/ Maps And Legends)

IRS IRS-5592 June 1985 (US)
IRS MIRF 1003 July 1985 (UK)

LIFES RICH PAGEANT
Begin The Begin/ These Days/ Fall On Me/ Cuyahoga/ Hyena/ Underneath The Bunker/ The Flowers Of Guatemala/ I Believe/ What If We Give It Away?/ Just A Touch/ Swan Swan H/ Superman (Tired Of Singing Trouble/ Rotary Ten/ Toys In The Attic/ Just A Touch/ Dream (All I Have To Do)/ Swan Swan H)

IRS IRS-5783 July 1986 (US)
IRS MIRG 1014 July 1986 (UK)

DOCUMENT
Finest Worksong/ Welcome To The Occupation/ Exhuming McCarthy/ Disturbance At The Heron House/ It's The End Of The World As We Know It (And I Feel Fine)/ The One I Love/ Fireplace/ Lightnin' Hopkins/ King Of Birds/ Oddfellows Local 151 (Finest Worksong/ Last Date/ The One I Love/ Time After Time Etc/ Disturbance At The Heron House/ Finest Worksong)

IRS IRS-42059 September 1987 (US)
IRS MIRG 1025 September 1987 (UK)

GREEN
Pop Song 89/ Get Up/ You Are The Everything/ Stand/ World Leader Pretend/ The Wrong Child/ Orange Crush/ Turn You Inside-Out/ Hairshirt/ I Remember California/ (Untitled)

Warner Brothers WX2349–25795–1 November 1988 (US)
Warner Brothers WX234 November 1988 (UK)

OUT OF TIME
Radio Song/ Losing My Religion/ Low/ Near Wild Heaven/ Endgame/ Shiny Happy People/ Belong/ Half A World Away/ Texarkana/ Country Feedback/ Me In Honey

Warner Brothers 9–26496–2 March 1991 (US)
Warner Brothers 7599–26496–2 March 1991 (UK)

AUTOMATIC FOR THE PEOPLE
Drive/ Try Not To Breathe/ The Sidewinder Sleeps Tonite/ Everybody Hurts/ New Orleans Instrumental No. 1/ Sweetness Follows/ Monty Got A Raw Deal/ Ignoreland/ Man On The Moon/ Star Me Kitten/ Nightswimming/ Find The River

Warner Brothers 9 45055–2 October 1992 (US)
Warner Brothers 9362–45055–2 October 1992 (UK)

MONSTER
What's The Frequency, Kenneth?/ Crush With Eyeliner/ King Of Comedy/ I Don't Sleep, I Dream/ Star 69/ Strange Currencies/ Tongue/ Bang And Blame/ I Took Your Name/ Let Me In/ Circus Envy/ You

Warner Brothers 9 45740-1 September 1994 (US & UK)
Warner Brothers 9362-46740-2 September 1994 (UK)

NEW ADVENURES IN HI-FI
How The West Was Won And Where It Got Us/ The Wake-Up Bomb/ New Test Leper/ Undertow/ E-Bow The Letter/ Leave/ Departure/ Bittersweet Me/ Be Mine/ Binky The Doormat/ Zither/ So Fast, So Numb/ Low Desert/ Electrolite

Warner Brothers 9 46320-1 September 1996 (US)
Warner Brothers 9362-46320-2 September 1996 (UK)

R.E.M.

UP
Airportman/ Lotus/ Hope/ At My Most Beautiful/ The Apologist/
Sad Professor/ You're In the Air/ Walk Unafraid/ Why Not Smile/
Daysleeper/ Diminished/ [I'm Not Over You]/ Parakeet/ Falls To
Climb

Warner Brothers 9 47112-2 October 1998 (US)
Warner Brothers 9362-47112-2 October 1998 (US)

REVEAL
The Lifting/ I've Been High/ All The Way To Reno (You're Gonna Be
A Star)/ She Just Wants To Be/ Disappear/ Saturn Return/ Beat A
Drum/ Imitation Of Life/ Summer Turns To High/ Chorus And The
Ring/ I'll Take The Rain/ Beachball

Warner Brothers 9 47946-2 May 2001 (US)
Warner Brothers 9362-47946-2 May 2001 (UK)

AROUND THE SUN
Leaving New York/ Electron Blue/ The Outsiders/ Make It All Okay/
Final Straw/ I Wanted To Be Wrong/ Wanderlust/ Boy In The Well/
Aftermath/ High Speed Train/ The Worst Joke Ever/ The Ascent Of
Man/ Around The Sun

Warner Bros 48894-2 (US)
Warner Bros 9362-48911-2 (UK)

ACCELERATE
Hollow Man/ Houston/ Accelerate/ Until The Day Is Done/ Mr
Richards/ Sing For The Submarine/ Horse To Water/ I'm Gonna DJ
Bonus tracks: Redhead Walking/ Airliner/ Horse To Water/ Living
Well Is The Best Revenge/ Until The Day Is Done/ Supernatural
Superstitious

Warner Bros 418620-2 (US)
Warner Bros 9362-49874-1 (UK)

COLLAPSE INTO NOW
Discoverer/ All The Best/ Überlin/ Oh My Heart/ It Happened Today/
Every Day Is Yours To Win/ Mine Smell Like Honey/ Walk It Back/
Alligator_Aviator_Autopilot_Antimatter/ That Someone Is You/ Me,
Marlon Brando, Marlon Brando and I/ Blue

Warner Bros 525611-2 (US)
Warner Bros 9362-49626-8 UK)

COMPILATION ALBUMS

DEAD LETTER OFFICE (with CHRONIC TOWN)
Crazy/ There She Goes Again/ Burning Down/ Voice Of Harold/
Burning Hell/ White Tornado/ Toys In The Attic/ Windout/ Ages Of
You/ Pale Blue Eyes/ Rotary Ten/ Bandwagon/ Femme Fatale/
Walter's Theme/ King Of The Road/ Wolves, Lower/ Gardening At
Night/ Carnival Of Sorts (Box Cars)/ 1,000,000/ Stumble (Gardening
At Night/ All The Right Friends)

IRS SP70054 April 1987 (US)
IRS SP70064 April 1987 (UK)

EPONYMOUS
Radio Free Europe/ Gardening At Night/ Talk About The Passion/ So.
Central Rain/ (Don't Go Back To) Rockville/ Can't Get There From
Here/ Driver 8/ Romance/ Fall On Me/ The One I Love/ Finest
Worksong/ It's The End Of The World As We Know It (And I Feel
Fine)

IRS IRS-6262 October 1988 (US)
IRS MIRG 1038 October 1988 (UK)

THE BEST OF R.E.M.
Carnival Of Sorts/ Radio Free Europe/ Perfect Circle/ Talk About The
Passion/ So. Central Rain/ (Don't Go Back To) Rockville/ Pretty
Persuasion/ Green Grow The Rushes/ Can't Get There From Here/
Driver 8/ Fall On Me/ I Believe/ Cuyahoga/ The One I Love/ Finest
Worksong/ It's The End Of The World As We Know It (And I Feel Fine)

IRS DMIRH1 August 1991 (UK)
Not Released In The USA

MAN ON THE MOON
R.E.M. scored the soundtrack to the movie. Besides several short
instrumentals written, the band performs on three songs: Man On The
Moon/ The Great Beyond/ This Friendly World

Warner Brothers/ Jersey 9-47483-2 February 2000 (US)

IN TIME
Man On The Moon/ The Great Beyond/ Bad Day/ What's The
Frequency Kenneth/ All The Way To Reno (You're Gonna Be A Star)/
Losing My Religion/ E Bow The Letter/ Orange Crush/ Imitation Of
Life/ Daysleeper/ Animal/ The Sidewinder Sleeps Tonight/ Stand/
Electrolyte/ All The Right Friends/ Everybody Hurts/ At My Most
Beautiful/ Nightswimming

Warner Bros 48381-2 (US)
Warner Bros 9362-48550-2 (UK)

AND I FEEL FINE . . . THE BEST OF THE I.R.S. YEARS
1982–1987 (COLLECTORS' EDITION)
Begin The Begin/ Radio Free Europe/ Pretty Persuasion/Talk About
The Passion/ (Don't Go Back To) Rockville/ Sitting Still/ Gardening At
Night/ 7 Chinese Brothers/ So. Central Rain/ Driver 8/ Can't Get
There From Here/ Finest Worksong/ Feeling Gravity's Pull/ I Believe/
Life And How To Live It/ Cuyahoga/ The One I Love/ Fall On Me/
Perfect Circle/ It's The End Of The World As We Know It (And I Feel
Fine)
Bonus disc: Pilgrimage/ These Days/ Gardening At Night (Demo)/
Radio Free Europe (Hibtone)/ Sitting Still/ Life And How To Live It
(Live)/ Ages Of You (Live)/ We Walk (Live)/ 1,000,000 (Live)/
Finest Worksong (Live)/ Finest Worksong (Other Mix)/ Hyena
(Demo)/ Theme From Two Steps Onward (Demo)/ Superman/ All
The Right Friends (Outtake)/ Mystery To Me (Demo)/ Just A Touch
(Live In Studio)/ Bad Day (Outtake)/ King Of Birds/ Swan Swan H
(Acoustic Version)/ Disturbance At The Heron House/ Time After
Time (AnnElise)

Capitol Records 09463-74444-2-9 (US)
Capitol Records 09463-69942-2-2 (UK)

PART LIES PART HEART PART TRUTH PART GARBAGE
1982–2011
Radio Free Europe/ Talk About The Passion/ Sitting Still/ So. Central
Rain/ (Don't Go Back To) Rockville/ Driver 8/ Life And How To Live
It/ Begin The Begin/ Fall On Me/ Finest Worksong/ It's The End Of
The World As We Know It (And I Feel Fine)/ The One I Love/ Stand/
Pop Song 89/ Get Up/ Orange Crush/ Losing My Religion/ Country
Feedback/ Shiny Happy People/ The Sidewinder Sleeps Tonite/

Everybody Hurts/ Man On The Moon/ Nightswimming/ What's The
Frequency Kenneth/ New Test Leper/ Electrolyte/ At My Most
Beautiful/ The Great Beyond/ Imitation Of Life/ Bad Day/ Leaving
New York/ Living Well Is The Best Revenge/ Supernatural
Superstitious/ Überlin/ Oh My Heart/
Alligator_Aviator_Autopilot_Antimitter/ A Month Of Saturdays/ We
All Go Back To Where We Belong/ Hallelujah

Warner Bros 529088-2 (US)
Warner Bros 9362-49536-4 (UK)

LIVE ALBUMS

R.E.M. LIVE
I Took Your Name/ So Fast, So Numb/ Boy In The Well/ Cuyahoga/
Everybody Hurts/ Electron Blue/ Bad Day/ The Ascent Of Man/ The
Great Beyond/ Leaving New York/ Orange Crush/ I Wanted To Be
Wrong/ Final Straw/ Imitation Of Life/ The One I Love/ Walk
Unafraid/ Losing My Religion/ What's The Frequency, Kenneth?/
Drive/ (Don't Go Back To) Rockville/ I'm Gonna DJ/ Man On The
Moon

Warner Bros 292668-2 (US)
Warner Bros 9362-49925-3 (UK)

LIVE AT THE OLYMPIA IN DUBLIN 39 SONGS
Living Well Is The Best Revenge/ Second Guessing/ Letter Never Sent/
Staring Down The Barrel Of The Middle Distance/ Disturbance At The
Heron House/ Mr Richards/ Houston/ New Test Leper/ Cuyahoga/
Electrolyte/ Man-Sized Wreath/So. Central Rain/ On The Fly/ Maps
And Legends/ Sitting Still/ Driver 8/ Horse To Water/ I'm Gonna DJ/
Circus Envy/ These Days/ Drive/ Feeling Gravitys Pull/ Until The Day
Is Done/ Accelerate/ Auctioneer/ Little America/ 1,000,000/
Disguised/ The Worst Joke Ever/ Welcome To The Occupation/
Carnival Of Sorts [Box Cars]/ Harborcoat/ Wolves, Lower/ I've Been
High/ Kohoutek/ West Of The Fields/ Pretty Persuasion/ Romance/
Gardening At Night

Warner Bros 9362-49733-0 (UK)
Warner Bros 520872-2 (US)

VIDEOGRAPHY

Brief clips from every single R.E.M. promotional video are available at the group's official web site, www.remhq.com. Several documentaries and concert films (most notably, *Rough Cut*, *This Way Up* and *A Stirling Performance*) have yet to be released commercially. The failure to compile the post-*Monster* promo videos is a mystery. Bootleg tapes abound of the group's many television appearances as well as dozens of concerts. The following list, then, is merely that of the official long-form video releases, all referred to in detail within the text of this book. Those marked with an ★ are available on DVD as well as VHS, and were released together as *The R.E.M. Collection* on DVD in 2001.

R.E.M. Succumbs, 1987
Tourfilm, 1990★
Pop Screen, 1990
This Film Is On, 1991★
Parallel, 1995★
Roadmovie, 1996
Parallel, 2000
In View, The Best Of R.E.M.1988–2003, 2003
Perfect Square, 2004
When The Light Is Mine – The Best Of The I.R.S. Years 1982–1987
Video Collection, 2006
R.E.M. Live, 2007
This Is Not A Show, 2009
R.E.M. Live From Austin, Tex, 2009

Index

Index

Index

Index

Index

Index

Index

Index

TONY FLETCHER has been immersed in music for 25 years, as a print and television journalist, a DJ, and a record company consultant. The publisher and editor of *Jamming!* Magazine in his teens, he is the author of the best selling *Dear Boy: The Life Of Keith Moon*, and the official biography of Echo & The Bunnymen. He witnessed all three of R.E.M.'s début British shows in 1983, and has followed the band closely ever since, interviewing and writing about them many times. The original edition of *Remarks: The Story of R.E.M.* – the first biography of the band – was published in six languages. Born in Yorkshire and raised in London, Fletcher has lived in New York City since 1988. His web site is *www.ijamming.net*.